Finance

D1494048

Frank Wood and Joe Townsley

481616

WARRE'S FATHER

WARRE CLAYDEN
444907

N2CU CoCA

Pitman

5

PITMAN PUBLISHING LIMITED
128 Long Acre, London WC2E 9AN

A Longman Group Company

©Frank Wood, 1986

First published in Great Britain 1986

British Library Cataloguing in Publication Data

Wood, Frank
  Finance.
  1. Finance—Great Britain
  I. Title II. Townsley, Joe
  332'.0941   HG186.G7

ISBN 0 273 02587 2

Printed in Great Britain by
Richard Clay (The Chaucer Press) Ltd,
Bungay, Suffolk

Contents

23408

Preface

The unit 'Finance' is common to all BTEC National Certificates and Diplomas in Business and Finance, Distribution Studies and Public Administration. It has to be covered in the first year of these courses. This book has been produced specifically to cover the unit.

Chapters 1 to 29 have been based on the book 'Business Accounting' written by Frank Wood, and also published by Pitman. This part of the book has been adapted in a suitable fashion to fit the BTEC unit. The remainder of the book has either been written specifically for this unit, or else it has been based on other books written by Frank Wood and Joe Townsley.

It is hoped that lecturers will fully integrate this unit with the other units in the course. Finance is all-pervasive throughout all spheres of business activity. It should therefore be possible to co-operate with lecturers on the other units to produce interesting assignments which are relevant in the eyes of their students.

Frank Wood
Joe Townsley
Cheshire · Spring 1986

Introduction

Most of the readers of this book will be studying the unit 'Finance' in a BTEC National Awards course. What you are about to study includes both personal finance, the finance of businesses in the private sector from small shops to large concerns such as Marks and Spencer or of Imperial Chemical Industries (ICI), and also the finance of publicly owned organisations such as the National Coal Board or of your own local council.

In the first instance we will start by looking at the finance of business in the private sector, for it is from here that most of the basic ideas and methods of finance have begun and spread to other areas. Then we will have a look at finance in the public sector and then, finally, personal finance. Leaving the finances of the reader until the end may seem unusual, but in fact you will be applying some of the techniques you will have learned from business situations, and therefore it is more logical to deal with the items in this order.

The underlying financial information system of all types of organisations is called 'Accounting'. Decisions about finance are based in whole or in part upon the information which comes out of this system. This means that 'Accounting' is going to be the subject of the first part of this book. Before we start to examine this subject in any great detail we will first examine what it is, how it has developed, and also consider who will use the information.

What is accounting?

Accounting is concerned to give people information of an economic type about businesses or organisations. Economic information basically means that it is information capable of being measured in money terms. For example the amount a business spent last year on wages is economic information. Telling people that all the employees were very happy is not economic information because there is no precise way of measuring happiness in money units.

Because information of a non economic sort is often very useful, accounting reports are frequently issued with supplements containing more general material. This helps to overcome the limitation of accounting being expressed in purely economic data.

The information included in accounting statements is of two sorts. Firstly there is information about the resources used. For most organisations the resources cover a very wide range of items. On the one hand there will be things with a very long life such as land and buildings and at the other extreme small items like elastic bands and ball point pens. It would be possible to list thousands of individual items that a large business includes in its resources. Accounting will also list the obligations an organisation incurs in obtaining its resources. For example if someone lends £5,000 cash to a business accounting is concerned to record both the new cash resource and quite separately the obligation to repay the lender.

The second type of information in accounting statements is concerned with the organisation's performance. This is basically a measurement of the changes that have taken place between two points in time. For accounting measurement one year is the normal time span. For commercial and industrial organisations the changes are expressed in a statement which shows whether the business has made a profit or loss. The profit or loss figure is a very important measure of success. Virtually everybody who has anything to do with a firm will want to know how profitable it is. Investors, employees and government are all concerned with this accounting index of performance.

Accounting is still useful for organisations which do not operate for profit. Organisations of this type such as the National Health Service still need to measure their resources and to assess performance over time.

ACCOUNTING COMMUNICATES INFORMATION OF AN ECONOMIC NATURE WITH PARTICULAR REFERENCE TO THE RESOURCES AND THE PERFORMANCE OF AN ORGANISATION.

How has accounting developed?

Accounting methods have changed over many hundreds of years to reflect the nature of the organisations being accounted for. A small farmer in the reign of Elizabeth I would have little need for accounts as he could probably remember all his resources because he lived amongst them. He could also assess his performance from year to year by inspection of his herd and crops and with reference to his memory. It is also likely that he could neither read, write, nor calculate with numbers. The steward who managed the estates of a large landowner was in a different position. The landowner would expect the steward to be able to account to him both for all the resources of the estate and the performance in managing resources over time. This type of situation demands a proper method of accounting because the estates could be large and the transactions many. Also the landlord might be absent over long periods. Proper accounts were essential then as now to provide a check on honest management. Stewardship is just as important for the manager of a large modern corporation who acts on behalf of absent owners.

Who is Accounting information for?

Traditionally we are accustomed to preserving information about our personal wealth and income as private rather than public knowledge. There is nothing to stop us telling anybody what we like about our own affairs but nothing in the UK requires private individuals to make public disclosure of their wealth or income. This is not true however in our dealings with the government. They are entitled to ask us for information they require about all out wealth and income in order to tax us. Many small businesses prepare accounts largely for the benefit of the tax authorities.

The position of limited companies and their shareholders has already been mentioned. The accounts of limited companies are required by law and are basically prepared for the shareholders in their capacity as owners but with specific provisions to safeguard the creditors of the business. However as time has passed more and more people have become involved in the need to obtain accounting information. Limited Companies have become the most popular form of organisation in commerce and industry. Some companies are very small family concerns; others have become huge organisations operating internationally. Increasingly there ahs been recognition that there may be greater need for special disclosure particularly from the very large firms, who wield considerable economic power and employ important resources both of labour and capital.

In addition to stewardship information therefore there is a general movement toward disclosure of information specifically for employees, government and the public at large. The sort of Accounting which is aimed at providing information to people outside management is called Financial Accounting.

So far all the emphasis has been given to describing accounts which a company is required by law to produce for those outside who do not have managements' access to inside information. In a large and complex modern business it poses quite a problem simply to provide management with enough of the right information to manage the business properly. As we said earlier a small farmer can probably remember most of what he needs to manage the operations of his farm. Very soon however if the business grows this becomes impossible and proper records need to be kept so that proper decisions can be taken. This type of accounting which is for use inside the business is called Management Accounting.

ACCOUNTING WHICH IS FOR THOSE OUTSIDE THE BUSINESS IS CALLED FINANCIAL ACCOUNTING. ACCOUNTING WHICH IS PREPARED TO HELP MANAGERS RUN THEIR BUSINESS EFFICIENTLY IS CALLED MANAGEMENT ACCOUNTING.

The other situation which gave rise to a need for proper accounts was trading ventures where more than one man was sharing in the profits or losses of the business. Indeed the basic framework of modern accounting started in fifteenth century Italy. The merchants of Venice and the other Italian states would charter a vessel between them which they would send to the East to buy spices and other scarce commodities. The risks of such ventures were high but the rewards were correspondingly great. Human nature then as now tends to be suspicious of fraud where large amounts of money are involved. Therefore a system of accounting which fairly recorded and reported the economic results of the business had to be devised. The system of recorded events known as 'Double entry' has stood the test of time for five hundred years although the ways in which it is applied have changed a great deal.

The Industrial Revolution and the changes it led to in the organisation of society gave rise to the next major development in accounting. It was the need to collect large amounts of capital to build large units such as railways in the 1830's which led to the development of the modern concept of the limited liability company. The main feature of this type of organisation is that many people can invest an amount of money in a company by buying 'shares'. Although some shareholders may be managers of the firm particularly in small firms, the majority will not, especially in large companies. Whilst a senior manager has access to whatever information is available, a shareholder does not. The reason for this is that it is considered likely to be harmful to a business if detailed information on its affairs were available to its competitors. If shareholders could obtain any information they wanted, then competitors would only have to buy a few shares to obtain what information they needed. The conflict of interest here is vital for accounting. On the one hand the owner of shares must have enough information to ensure that the management carry out their function honestly and efficiently; on the other hand the company will need to preserve some confidential information.

The company law enactments which have been passed by Parliament throughout a century or more have reflected changes in society's attitudes and the experience gained with time. Accounting requirements for companies have grown substantially both in quantity and in sophistication.

ACCOUNTING DEVELOPED AS A RECORD OF STEWARDSHIP FOR EXAMPLE WHERE AN OWNER EMPLOYED SOMEONE ELSE TO MANAGE HIS PROPERTY. WHERE A NUMBER OF PEOPLE COMBINE TOGETHER IN A BUSINESS VENTURE THE NEED FOR ACCOUNTING INFORMATION IS ESPECIALLY IMPORTANT. THIS NEED IS OF GREAT IMPORTANCE FOR MODERN COMPANIES.

1 The Accounting Equation and the Balance Sheet

The Accounting Equation

The whole of financial accounting in the private sector is based on the accounting equation. This can be stated to be that for a firm to operate it needs resources, and that these resources have had to be supplied to the firm by someone. The resources possessed by the firm are known as Assets, and obviously some of these resources will have been supplied by the owner of the business. The total amount supplied by him is known as Capital. If in fact he was the only one who had supplied the assets then the following equation would hold true:

Assets = Capital

On the other hand, some of the assets will normally have been provided by someone other than the owner. The indebtedness of the firm for these resources is known as Liabilities. The equation can now be expressed as:

Assets = Capital + Liabilities

It can be seen that the two sides of the equation will have the same totals. This is because we are dealing with the same thing from two different points of view. It is:

Resources: What they are = Resources: Who supplied them
(Assets)   (Capital + Liabilities)

It is a fact that the totals of each side will always equal one another, and that this will always be true no matter how many transactions are entered into. The actual assets, capital and liabilities may change, but the equality of assets with that of the total of capital and liabilities will always hold true.

Assets consist of property of all kinds, such as buildings, machinery, stocks of goods and motor vehicles, also benefits such as debts owing by customers and the amount of money in the bank account.

Liabilities consist of money owing for goods supplied to the firm, and for expenses, also for loans made to the firm.

Capital is often called the owner's equity or net worth.

The Balance Sheet and the Effects of Business Transactions

The accounting equation is expressed in a financial position statement called the Balance Sheet. It is not the first accounting record to be made, but it is a convenient place to start to consider accounting.

The Introduction of Capital

On 1 May 19-7 B. Blake started in business and deposited £5,000 into a bank account opened specially for the business. The balance sheet would appear:

B. Blake
Balance Sheet as at 1 May 19-7

Assets	£		£
Cash at bank	5,000	Capital	5,000
	5,000		5,000

The Purchase of an Asset by Cheque

On 3 May 19-7 Blake buys a building for £3,000. The effect of this transaction is that the cash at bank is decreased and a new asset, buildings, appears.

B. Blake
Balance Sheet as at 3 May 19-7

Assets	£		£
Buildings	3,000	Capital	5,000
Cash at bank	2,000		
	5,000		5,000

The Purchase of an Asset and the Incurring of a Liability

On 6 May 19-7 Blake buys some goods for £500 from D. Smith, and agrees to pay for them some time within the next two weeks. The effect of this is that a new asset, stock of goods, is acquired, and a liability for the goods is created. A person to whom money is owed for goods is known in accounting language as a creditor.

B. Blake
Balance Sheet as at 6 May 19-7

Assets	£	Capital and Liabilities	£
Buildings	3,000	Capital	5,000
Stock of goods	500	Creditor	500
Cash at bank	2,000		
	5,500		5,500

Sale of an Asset on Credit

On 10 May 19-7 goods which had cost £100 were sold to J. Brown for
the same amount, the money to be paid later. The effect is a reduction
in the stock of goods and the creation of a new asset. A person who
owes the firm money is known in accounting language as a debtor.
The balance sheet now appears as:

B. Blake
Balance Sheet as at 10 May 19-7

Assets	£	Capital and Liabilities	£
Buildings	3,000	Capital	5,000
Stock of goods	400	Creditor	500
Debtor	100		
Cash at bank	2,000		
	5,500		5,500

Sale of an Asset for Immediate Payment

On 13 May 19-7 goods which had cost £50 were sold to D. Daley for
the same amount, Daley paying for them immediately by cheque.
Here one asset, stock of goods, is reduced, while another asset, bank,
is increased. The balance sheet now appears:

B. Blake
Balance Sheet as at 13 May 19-7

Assets	£	Capital and Liabilities	£
Buildings	3,000	Capital	5,000
Stock of goods	350	Creditor	500
Debtor	100		
Cash at bank	2,050		
	5,500		5,500

The Payment of a Liability

On 15 May 19-7 Blake pays a cheque for £200 to D. Smith in part
payment of the amount owing. The asset of bank is therefore reduced,
and the liability of the creditor is also reduced. The balance sheet now
appears:

B. Blake
Balance Sheet as at 15 May 19-7

Assets	£	Capital and Liabilities	£
Buildings	3,000	Capital	5,000
Stock of goods	350	Creditor	300
Debtor	100		
Cash at bank	1,850		
	5,300		5,300

Collection of an Asset

J. Brown, who owed Blake £100, makes a part payment of £75 by cheque on 31 May 19-7. The effect is to reduce one asset, debtor, and to increase another asset, bank. This results in a balance sheet as follows:

B. Blake
Balance Sheet as at 31 May 19-7

Assets	£	Capital and Liabilities	£
Buildings	3,000	Capital	5,000
Stock of goods	350	Creditor	300
Debtor	25		
Cash at bank	1,925		
	5,300		5,300

It can be seen that every transaction has affected two items. Sometimes it has changed two assets by reducing one and increasing the other. Other times it has reacted differently. A summary of the effect of transactions upon assets, liabilities and capital is shown below.

Example of Transaction

1.	Buy goods on credit.	Increase Asset (Stock of Goods)	Increase Liability (Creditors)
2.	Buy goods by cheque.	Increase Asset (Stock of Goods)	Decrease Asset (Bank)
3.	Pay creditor by cheque.	Decrease Asset (Bank)	Decrease Liability (Creditors)
4.	Owner pays more capital into the bank.	Increase Asset (Bank)	Increase Capital
5.	Owner takes money out of the business bank for his own use.	Decrease Asset (Bank)	Decrease Capital
6.	Owner pays creditor from private money outside the firm.	Decrease Liability (Creditors)	Increase Capital

Note: Generally, the figures used for exhibits and for exercises have been kept down to relatively small amounts. This has been done deliberately to make the work of the user of this book that much easier. Constantly handling large figures does not add anything to the study of the principles of accounting, instead it simply wastes a lot of the student's time, and he/she will probably make far more errors if larger figures are used.

It could lead to the authors being accused of not being 'realistic' with the figures given, but we believe that it is far more important to make learning easier for the student.

Assignment Exercises

Note: **Assignments with the letter A shown after the assignment number do NOT have answers shown at the back of the book. Answers to the others are shown on pages 392 onwards.**

1.1 You are to complete the gaps in the following table:

	Assets	Liabilities	Capital
	£	£	£
(a)	12,500	1,800	?
(b)	28,000	4,900	?
(c)	16,800	?	12,500
(d)	19,600	?	16,450
(e)	?	6,300	19,200
(f)	?	11,650	39,750

1.2A You are to complete the gaps in the following table:

	Assets	Liabilities	Capital
	£	£	£
(a)	55,000	16,900	?
(b)	?	17,200	34,400
(c)	36,100	?	28,500
(d)	119,500	15,400	?
(e)	88,000	?	62,000
(f)	?	49,000	110,000

1.3 Distinguish from the following list the items that are liabilities from those that are assets:
(a) Office machinery *a*
(b) Loan from C. Shirley *L*
(c) Fixtures and fittings
(d) Motor vehicles *a*
(e) We owe for goods *L*
(f) Bank balance. *a*

1.4A Classify the following items into liabilities and assets:
Motor vehicles
Premises
Creditors for goods
Stock of goods
Debtors
Owing to bank
Cash in hand
Loan from D. Jones
Machinery.

1.5 A. Smart sets up a new business. Before he actually sells anything he has bought Motor Vehicles £2,000, Premises £5,000, Stock of goods £1,000. He did not pay in full for his stock of goods and still owes £400 in respect of them. He had borrowed £3,000 from D. Bevan. After the events just described, and before trading starts, he has £100 cash in hand and £700 cash at bank. You are required to calculate the amount of his capital.

1.6A T. Charles starts a business. Before he actually starts to sell anything he has bought, Fixtures £2,000, Motor Vehicles £5,000 and a stock of goods £3,500. Although he has paid in full for the fixtures and the motor vehicle, he still owes £1,400 for some of the goods. J. Preston had lent him £3,000. Charles, after the above, has £2,800 in the business bank account and £100 cash in hand. You are required to calculate his capital.

1.7 Draw up A. Foster's balance sheet from the following as at 31 December 19-4:

	£
Capital	23,750
Debtors	4,950
Motor vehicles	5,700
Creditors	2,450
Fixtures	5,500
Stock of goods	8,800
Cash at bank	1,250

1.8A Draw up Kelly's balance sheet as at 30 June 19-2 from the following items:

	£
Capital	13,000
Office machinery	9,000
Creditors	900
Stock of goods	1,550
Debtors	275
Cash at bank	5,075
Loan from C. Smith	2,000

1.9 Complete the columns to show the effects of the following transactions:

Effect upon
Assets   Liabilities   Capital

(*a*)   We pay a creditor £70 in cash
(*b*)   Bought fixtures £200 paying by cheque
(*c*)   Bought goods on credit £275
(*d*)   The proprietor introduces another £500 cash into the firm
(*e*)   J. Walker lends the firm £200 in cash
(*f*)   A debtor pays us £50 by cheque
(*g*)   We return goods costing £60 to a supplier whose bill we had not paid
(*h*)   Bought additional shop premises paying £5,000 by cheque.

1.10A Complete the columns to show the effects of the following transactions:

Effect upon
Assets   Liabilities   Capital

(*a*)   Bought a motor van on credit £500
(*b*)   Repaid by cash a loan owed to P. Smith £1,000
(*c*)   Bought goods for £150 paying by cheque
(*d*)   The owner puts a further £5,000 cash into the business
(*e*)   A debtor returns to us £80 goods. We agree to make an allowance for them.
(*f*)   Bought goods on credit £220
(*g*)   The owner takes out £100 cash for his personal use
(*h*)   We pay a creditor £190 by cheque.

2 The Double Entry System for Assets and Liabilities

It has been seen that each transaction affects two items. To show the full effect of each transaction, accounting must therefore show its effect on each of the two items, be they assets, capital or liabilities. From this need arose the double entry system where to show this twofold effect each transaction is entered twice, once to show the effect upon one item, and a second entry to show the effect upon the other item.

It may be thought that drawing up a new balance sheet after each transaction would provide all the information required. However, a balance sheet does not give enough information about the business. It does not, for instance, tell who the debtors are and how much each one of them owes the firm, nor who the creditors are and the details of money owing to each of them. Also, the task of drawing up a new balance sheet after each transaction becomes an impossibility when there are many hundreds of transactions each day, as this would mean drawing up hundreds of balance sheets daily. Because of the work involved, balance sheets are in fact only drawn up periodically, at least annually, but sometimes half-yearly, quarterly, or monthly.

The double entry system has an account (meaning details of transactions in that item) for every asset, every liability and for capital. Thus there will be a Shop Premises Account (for transactions in shop premises), a Motor Vans Accounts (for transactions in Motor Vans), and so on for every asset, liability and for capital.

Each account should be shown on a separate page. The double entry system divides each page into two halves. The left-hand side of each page is called the debit side, while the right-hand side is called the credit side. The title of each account is written across the top of the account at the centre.

It must not be thought that the words 'debit' and 'credit' in book-keeping mean the same as the words 'debit' or 'credit' in normal language usage. Anyone who does will become very confused.

This is a page of an accounts book:

Title of account written here

Left-hand side of the page.   Right-hand side of the page.
This is the 'debit' side.   This is the 'credit' side.

If you have to make an entry of £10 on the debit side of the account, the instructions could say 'debit the account with £10' or 'the account needs debiting with £10'.

In Chapter 1 transactions were to increase or decrease assets, liabilities or capital. Double entry rules for accounts are:

Accounts	To record	Entry in the account
Assets	an increase	Debit
	a decrease	Credit
Liabilities	an increase	Credit
	a decrease	Debit
Capital	an increase	Credit
	a decrease	Debit

Once again look at the accounting equation:

	Assets	= Liabilities	and	Capital
To increase each item	Debit	Credit		Credit
To decrease each item	Credit	Debit		Debit

The double-entry rules for liabilities and capital are the same, but they are exactly the opposite as those for assets. This is because assets are on the opposite side of the equation and therefore follow opposite rules.

Looking at the accounts the rules will appear as:

Any asset account		Any liability Account		Capital account	
Increases	Decreases	Decreases	Increases	Decreases	Increases
+	−	−	+	−	+

There is not enough space in this book to put each account on a separate page, so we will have to list the accounts under each other. In a real firm at least one full page would be taken for each account.

The entry of a few transactions can now be attempted:
1. The proprietor starts the firm with £1,000 in cash on 1 August 19-6.

Effect	*Action*
(a) Increases the asset of cash in the firm	Debit the cash account
(b) Increases the capital	Credit the capital account

These are entered:

Cash

19-6	£		
Aug 1	1,000		

Capital

		19-6	£
		Aug 1	1,000

The date of the transaction has already been entered. Now there remains the description which is to be entered alongside the amount. This is completed by a cross reference to the title of the other account in which double entry is completed. The double entry to the item in the cash account is completed by an entry in the capital account, therefore the word 'Capital' will appear in the cash account. Similarly, the double entry to the item in the capital account is completed by an entry in the cash account, therefore the word 'Cash' will appear in the capital account.

The finally completed accounts are therefore:

Cash

19-6	£		
Aug 1 Capital	1,000		

Capital

		19-6	£
		Aug 1 Cash	1,000

2. A motor van is bought for £275 cash on 2 August 19-6.

Effect	*Action*
(*a*) Decreases the asset of cash	Credit the cash account
(*b*) Increases the asset of motor van	Debit the motor van account

Cash

	19-6		£
	Aug 2 Motor van		275

Motor Van

19-6	£
Aug 2 Cash	275

3. Fixtures bought on credit from Shop Fitters £115 on 3 August 19-6.

Effect	*Action*
(*a*) Increase in the asset of fixtures	Debit fixtures account
(*b*) Increase in the liability of the firm to Shop Fitters	Credit Shop Fitters account

Fixtures

19-6	£
Aug 3 Shop Fitters	115

Shop Fitters

	19-6		£
	Aug 3 Fixtures		115

4. Paid the amount owing in cash to Shop Fitters on 17 August 19-6.

Effect	*Action*
(*a*) Decrease in the asset of cash	Credit the cash account
(*b*) Decrease in the liability of the firm to Shop Fitters	Debit Shop Fitters account

Cash

	19-6		£
	Aug 17 Shop Fitters		115

Shop Fitters

19-6	£
Aug 17 Cash	115

Transactions to date

Taking the transactions numbered 1 to 4 above, the records will now appear:

Cash

19-6	£	19-6	£
Aug 1 Capital	1,000	Aug 2 Motor van	275
		" 17 Shop Fitters	115

Motor Van

19-6	£
Aug 2 Cash	275

Shop Fitters

19-6	£	19-6	£
Aug 17 Cash	115	Aug 3 Fixtures	115

Fixtures

19-6	£
Aug 3 Shop Fitters	115

Capital

		19-6	£
		Aug 1 Cash	1,000

A Further Worked Example

Now you have actually made some entries in accounts you are to go carefully through the following example. Make certain you can understand every entry.

		Transactions	Effect	Action
19-4				
May	1	Started an engineering business putting £1,000 into a business bank account.	Increases asset of bank.	Debit bank account.
			Increases capital of proprietor.	Credit capital account.
,,	3	Bought works machinery on credit from Unique Machines £275.	Increases asset of machinery.	Debit machinery account.
			Increases liability to Unique Machines.	Credit Unique Machines account.
,,	4	Withdrew £200 cash from the bank and placed it in the cash till.	Decreases asset of bank.	Credit bank account.
			Increases asset of cash.	Debit cash account.
,,	7	Bought motor van paying in cash £180.	Decreases asset of cash.	Credit cash account.
			Increases asset of motor van.	Debit motor van account.
,,	10	Sold some of machinery for £15 on credit to B. Barnes.	Decreases asset of machinery.	Credit machinery account.
			Increases asset of money owing from B. Barnes.	Debit B. Barnes account.
,,	21	Returned some of machinery value £27 to Unique Machines.	Decreases asset of machinery.	Credit machinery account.
			Decreases liability to Unique Machines.	Debit Unique Machines.
,,	28	B. Barnes pays the firm the amount owing, £15, by cheque.	Increases asset of bank.	Debit bank account.
			Decreases asset of money owing by B. Barnes.	Credit B. Barnes account.
,,	30	Bought another motor van paying by cheque £420.	Decreases asset of bank.	Credit bank account.
			Increases asset of motor vans.	Debit motor van account.
,,	31	Paid the amount of £248 to Unique Machines by cheque.	Decreases asset of bank.	Credit bank account.
			Decreases liability to Unique Machines.	Debit Unique Machines.

In account form this is shown:

Bank

	£		£
May 1 Capital	1,000	May 4 Cash	200
,, 28 B. Barnes	15	,, 30 Motor van	420
		,, 31 Unique Machines	248

Cash

	£		£
May 4 Bank	200	May 7 Motor van	180

Capital

			£
		May 1 Bank	1,000

Machinery

	£		£
May 3 Unique Machines	275	May 10 B. Barnes	15
		,, 21 Unique Machines	27

Motor Van

	£		
May 7 Cash	180		
,, 30 Bank	420		

Unique Machines

	£		£
May 21 Machinery	27	May 3 Machinery	275
,, 31 Bank	248		

B. Barnes

	£		£
May 10 Machinery	15	May 28 Bank	15

Assignment Exercises

Note: **Assignments with the letter A shown after the question number do NOT have answers shown at the back of the book. Answers to the others are shown on pages 392 onwards.**

2.1 Complete the following table showing which accounts are to be credited and which to be debited:

	Account to be debited	Account to be credited
(a) Bought motor van for cash		
(b) Bought office machinery on credit from J. Grant & Son		
(c) Introduced capital in cash		
(d) A debtor, J. Beach, pays us by cheque		
(e) Paid a creditor, A. Barrett, in cash.		

2.2A Complete the following table:

	Account to be debited	Account to be credited
(a) Bought office machinery on credit from D. Isaacs Ltd		
(b) The proprietor paid a creditor, C. Jones, from his private monies outside the firm		
(c) A debtor, N. Fox, paid us in cash		
(d) Repaid part of loan from P. Exeter by cheque		
(e) Returned some of office machinery to D. Isaacs Ltd		
(f) A debtor, N. Lyn, pays us by cheque		
(g) Bought motor van by cash.		

2.3 Write up the asset and liability and capital accounts to record the following transactions in the records of G. Powell.

19-3

July	1	Started business with £2,500 in the bank
,,	2	Bought office furniture by cheque £150
,,	3	Bought machinery £750 on credit from Planers Ltd
,,	5	Bought a motor van paying by cheque £600
,,	8	Sold some of the office furniture − not suitable for the firm − for £60 on credit to J. Walker & Sons
,,	15	Paid the amount owing to Planers Ltd £750 by cheque
,,	23	Received the amount due from J. Walker £60 in cash
,,	31	Bought more machinery by cheque £280.

2.4 You are required to open the asset and liability and capital accounts and record the following transactions for June 19-4 in the records of C. Williams.

19-4

June	1	Started business with £2,000 in cash.
,,	2	Paid £1,800 of the opening cash into a bank account for the business
,,	5	Bought office furniture on credit from Betta-Built Ltd. for £120
,,	8	Bought a motor van paying by cheque £950
,,	12	Bought works machinery from Evans & Sons on credit £560
,,	18	Returned faulty office furniture costing £62 to Betta-Built Ltd
,,	25	Sold some of the works machinery for £75 cash
,,	26	Paid amount owing to Betta-Built Ltd £58 by cheque
,,	28	Took £100 out of the bank and put it in the cash till
,,	30	J. Smith lent us £500 – giving us the money by cheque.

2.5A Write up the asset, capital and liability accounts in the books of C. Walsh to record the following transactions:

19-5

June	1	Started business with £5,000 in the bank
,,	2	Bought motor van paying by cheque £1,200
,,	5	Bought office fixtures £400 on credit from Young Ltd
,,	8	Bought motor van on credit from Super Motors £800
,,	12	Took £100 out of the bank and put it into the cash till
,,	15	Bought office fixtures paying by cash £60
,,	19	Paid Super Motors a cheque for £800
,,	21	A loan of £1,000 cash is received from J. Jarvis
,,	25	Paid £800 of the cash in hand into the bank account
,,	30	Bought more office fixtures paying by cheque £300.

2.6A Write up the accounts to record the following transactions:

19-3

March	1	Started business with £1,000 cash
,,	2	Received a loan of £5,000 from M. Chow by cheque, a bank account being opened and the cheque paid into it
,,	3	Bought machinery for cash £60
,,	5	Bought display equipment on credit from Better-View Machines £550
,,	8	Took £300 out of the bank and put it into the cash till
,,	15	Repaid part of Chow's loan by cheque £800
,,	17	Paid amount owing to Better-View Machines £550 by cheque
,,	24	Repaid part of Chow's loan by cash £100
,,	31	Bought additional machinery, this time on credit from D. Smith for £500.

3 The Asset of Stock

Goods are sometimes sold at the same price at which they are bought, but this is not usually the case. Normally they are sold above cost price, the difference being profit; sometimes however they are sold at less than cost price, the difference being loss.

If all sales were at cost price, it would be possible to have a stock account, the goods sold being shown as a decrease of an asset, i.e. on the credit side. The purchase of stock could be shown on the debit side as it would be an increase of an asset. The difference between the two sides would then represent the cost of the goods unsold at that date, if wastages and losses of stock are ignored. However, most sales are not at cost price, and therefore the sales figures include elements of profit or loss. Because of this, the difference between the two sides would not represent the stock of goods. Such a stock account would therefore serve no useful purpose.

The Stock Account is accordingly divided into several accounts, each one showing a movement of stock. These can be said to be:

1. Increases in the stock. This can be due to one of two causes.

(*a*) By the purchase of additional goods.

(*b*) By the return in to the firm of goods previously sold. The reasons for this are numerous. The goods may have been the wrong type, they may have been surplus to requirements, have been faulty and so on.

To distinguish the two aspects of the increase of stocks of goods two accounts are opened. These are:

(i) Purchases Account − in which purchases of goods are entered.

(ii) Returns Inwards Account − in which goods being returned in to the firm are entered. The alternative name for this account is the Sales Returns Account.

2. Decreases in the stock ot goods. This can be due to one of two causes if wastages and losses of stock are ignored.

(*a*) By the sale of goods.

(*b*) Goods previously bought by the firm now being returned out of the firm to the supplier.

To distinguish the two aspects of the decrease of stocks of goods two accounts are opened. These are:

(i) Sales Account—in which sales of goods are entered.

(ii) Returns Outwards Account—in which goods being returned out to a supplier are entered. The alternative name for this is the Purchases Returns Account.

Some illustrations can now be shown.

Purchase of Stock on Credit

1 August. Goods costing £165 are bought on credit from D. Henry.

First, the twofold effect of the transactions must be considered in order that the book-keeping entries can be worked out.

1. The asset of stock is increased. An increase in an asset needs a debit entry in an account. Here the account concerned is a stock account showing the particular movement of stock, in this case it is the 'Purchases' movement so that the account concerned must be the purchases account.

2. An increase in a liability. This is the liability of the firm to D. Henry in respect of the goods bought which have not yet been paid for. An increase in a liability needs a credit entry, so that to enter this aspect of the transaction a credit entry is made in D. Henry's account.

Purchases

	£
Aug 1 D Henry	165

D. Henry

	£
Aug 1 Purchases	165

Purchases of Stock for Cash

2 August. Goods costing £22 are bought, cash being paid for them immediately.

1. The asset of stock is increased, so that a debit entry will be needed. The movement of stock is that of a purchase, so that it is the purchases account which needs debiting.

2. The asset of cash is decreased. To reduce an asset a credit entry is called for, and the asset is that of cash so that the cash account needs crediting.

Cash

	£
Aug 2 Purchases	22

Purchases

	£
Aug 2 Cash	22

Sales of Stock on Credit

3 August. Sold goods on credit for £250 to J. Lee.
1.   The asset of stock is decreased. For this a credit entry to reduce an asset is needed. The movement of stock is that of a 'Sale' so the account credited is the sales account.
2.   An asset account is increased. This is the account showing that J. Lee is a debtor for the goods. The increase in the asset of debtors requires a debit and the debtor is J. Lee, so that the account concerned is that of J. Lee.

Sales

		£
	Aug 3 J. Lee	250

J. Lee

	£
Aug 3 Sales	250

Sales of Stock for Cash

4 August. Goods are sold for £55, cash being received immediately upon sale.
1.   The asset of cash is increased. This needs a debit in the cash account to show this.
2.   The asset of stock is reduced. The reduction of an asset requires a credit and the movement of stock is represented by 'Sales'. Thus the entry needed is a credit in the sales account.

Sales

		£
	Aug 4 Cash	55

Cash

	£
Aug 4 Sales	55

Returns Inwards

5 August. Goods which had been previously sold to F. Lowe for £29 are now returned by him.
1.   The asset of stock is increased by the goods returned. Thus a debit representing an increase of an asset is needed, and this time the movement of stock is that of 'Returns Inwards'. The entry therefore required is a debit in the returns inwards account.

2. A decrease in an asset. The debt of F. Lowe to the firm is now reduced, and to record this a credit is needed in F. Lowe's account.

Returns Inwards

	£
Aug 5 F. Lowe	29

F. Lowe

	£
Aug 5 Returns Inwards	29

An alternative name for a Returns Inwards Account would be a Sales Returns Account.

Returns Outwards

6 August. Goods previously bought for £96 are returned by the firm to K. Howe.

1. The asset of stock is decreased by the goods sent out. Thus a credit representing a reduction in an asset is needed, and the movement of stock is that of 'Returns Outwards' so that the entry will be a credit in the returns outwards account.

2. The liability of the firm to K. Howe is decreased by the value of the goods returned to him. The decrease in a liability needs a debit, this time in K. Howe's account.

Returns Outwards

	£
Aug 6 K. Howe	96

K. Howe

	£
Aug 6 Returns outwards	96

An alternative name for a Returns Outwards Account would be a Purchases Returns Account.

A Worked Example

May	1	Bought goods on credit £68 from D. Small
,,	2	Bought goods on credit £77 from A. Lyon & Son
,,	5	Sold goods on credit to D. Hughes for £60
,,	6	Sold goods on credit to M. Spencer for £45
,,	10	Returned goods £15 to D. Small
,,	12	Goods bought for cash £100
,,	19	M. Spencer returned £16 goods to us
,,	21	Goods sold for cash £150
,,	22	Paid cash to D. Small £53
,,	30	D. Hughes paid the amount owing by him £60 in cash
,,	31	Bought goods on credit £64 from A. Lyon & Son

Purchases

19-5		£
May 1	D. Small	68
,, 2	A. Lyon & Son	77
,, 12	Cash	100
,, 31	A. Lyon & Son	64

Sales

	19-5		£
	May 5	D. Hughes	60
	,, 6	M. Spencer	45
	,, 21	Cash	150

Returns Outwards

	19-5		£
	May 10	D. Small	15

Returns Inwards

19-5		£
May 19	M. Spencer	16

D. Small

19-5		£	19-5		£
May 10	Returns outwards	15	May 1	Purchases	68
,, 22	Cash	53			

A. Lyon & Son

			19-5		£
			May 2	Purchases	77
			,, 31	Purchases	64

D. Hughes

19-5		£	19-5		£
May 5	Sales	60	May 30	Cash	60

M. Spencer

19-5		£	19-5		£
May 6	Sales	45	May 19	Returns inwards	16

Cash

19-5		£	19-5		£
May 21	Sales	150	May 12	Purchases	100
,, 30	D. Hughes	60	,, 22	D. Small	53

Special Meaning of 'Sales' and 'Purchases'

It must be emphasized that 'Sales' and 'Purchases' have a special meaning in accounting when compared to ordinary language usage.

'Purchases' in accounting means the purchase of those goods which the firm buys with the prime intention of selling. Obviously, sometimes the goods are altered, added to, or used in the manufacture of something else, but it is the element of resale that is important. To a firm that deals in typewriters for instance, typewriters constitute purchases. If something else is bought, such as a motor van, such an item cannot be called purchases, even though in ordinary language it may be said that a motor van has been purchased. The prime intention of buying the motor van is for usage and not for resale.

Similarly, 'Sales' means the sale of those goods in which the firm normally deals and were bought with the prime intention of resale. The word 'Sales' must never be given to the disposal of other items.

Failure to keep to these meanings would result in the different forms of stock account containing something other than goods sold or for resale.

Comparison of Cash and Credit Transactions for Purchases and Sales

The difference between the records needed for cash and credit transactions can now be seen.

The complete set of entries for purchases of goods where they are paid for immediately needs entries:

1. Credit the cash account.
2. Debit the purchases account.

On the other hand the complete set of entries for the purchase of goods on credit can be broken down into two stages. First, the purchase of the goods and second, the payment for them.

The first part is:

1. Debit the purchases account.
2. Credit the supplier's account.

While the second part is:

1. Credit the cash account.
2. Debit the supplier's account.

The difference can now be seen in that with the cash purchase no record is kept of the supplier's account. This is because cash passes immediately and therefore there is no need to keep a check of indebtedness to a supplier. On the other hand, in the credit purchase the records should reveal the identity of the supplier to whom the firm is indebted until payment is made.

A study of cash sales and credit sales will reveal a similar difference.

Cash Sales	*Credit Sales*

Cash Sales
Complete entry:
   Debit cash account
   Credit sales account

Credit Sales
First part:
   Debit customer's account
   Credit sales account
Second part:
   Debit cash account
   Credit customer's account

Assignment Exercises

Note: **Assignments with the letter A shown after the question number do NOT have answers shown at the back of the book. Answers to the other questions are shown on pages 392 onwards.**

3.1 Complete the following table showing which accounts are to be credited and which are to be debited:

	Account to be debited	*Account to be credited*
(a) Goods bought, cash being paid immediately		
(b) Goods bought on credit from E. Flynn		
(c) Goods sold on credit to C. Grant		
(d) A motor van sold for cash		
(e) Goods sold for cash.		

3.2A Complete the following table:

	Account to be debited	*Account to be credited*
(a) Goods bought on credit from T. Morgan		
(b) Goods returned to us by J. Thomas		
(c) Machinery returned to L. Jones Ltd		
(d) Goods bought for cash		
(e) Motor van bought on credit from D. Davies Ltd		
(f) Goods returned by us to I. Prince		
(g) D. Picton paid us his account by cheque		
(h) Goods bought by cheque		
(i) We paid creditor, B. Henry, by cheque		
(j) Goods sold on credit to J. Mullings.		

3.3 You are to enter the following in the accounts needed:

19-6

Aug   1 Started business with £1,000 cash
,,   2 Paid £900 of the opening cash into the bank
,,   4 Bought goods on credit £78 from S. Holmes
,,   5 Bought a motor van by cheque £500
,,   7 Bought goods for cash £55
,, 10 Sold goods on credit £98 to D. Moore
,, 12 Returned goods to S. Holmes £18
,, 19 Sold goods for cash £28
,, 22 Bought fixtures on credit from Kingston Equipment Co £150
,, 24 D. Watson lent us £100 paying us the money by cheque
,, 29 We paid S. Holmes his account by cheque £60
,, 31 We paid Kingston Equipment Co by cheque £150.

3.4 Enter up the following transactions in the records of E. Sangster:

19-7

July   1 Started business with £10,000 in the bank
,,   2 T. Cooper lent us £400 in cash
,,   3 Bought goods on credit from F. Jones £840 and S. Charles £3,600
,,   4 Sold goods for cash £200
,,   6 Took £250 of the cash and paid it into the bank
,,   8 Sold goods on credit to C. Moody £180
,, 10 Sold goods on credit to J. Newman £220
,, 11 Bought goods on credit from F. Jones £370
,, 12 C. Moody returned goods to us £40
,, 14 Sold goods on credit to H. Morgan £190 and J. Peat £320
,, 15 We returned goods to F. Jones £140
,, 17 Bought motor van on credit from Manchester Motors £2,600
,, 18 Bought office furniture on credit from Faster Supplies Ltd £600
,, 19 We returned goods to S. Charles £110
,, 20 Bought goods for cash £220
,, 24 Goods sold for cash £70
,, 25 Paid money owing to F. Jones by cheque £1,070
,, 26 Goods returned to us by H. Morgan £30
,, 27 Returned some of office furniture costing £160 to Faster Supplies Ltd
,, 28 E. Sangster put a further £500 into the business in the form of cash
,, 29 Paid Manchester Motors £2,600 by cheque
,, 31 Bought office furniture for cash £100.

3.5A Enter up the following transactions in the records:

19-5

May 1 Started business with £2,000 in the bank
,, 2 Bought goods on credit from C. Shaw £900
,, 3 Bought goods on credit from F. Hughes £250
,, 5 Sold goods for cash £180
,, 6 We returned goods to C. Shaw £40
,, 8 Bought goods on credit from F. Hughes £190
,, 10 Sold goods on credit to G. Wood £390
,, 12 Sold goods for cash £210
,, 18 Took £300 of the cash and paid it into the bank
,, 21 Bought machinery by cheque £550
,, 22 Sold goods on credit to L. Moore £220
,, 23 G. Wood returned goods to us £140
,, 25 L. Moore returned goods to us £10
,, 28 We returned goods to F. Hughes £30
,, 29 We paid Shaw by cheque £860
,, 31 Bought machinery on credit from D. Lee £270.

3.6A You are to enter the following in the accounts needed:

June 1 Started business with £1,000 cash
,, 2 Paid £800 of the opening cash into a bank account for the firm
,, 3 Bought goods on credit from H. Grant £330
,, 4 Bought goods on credit from D. Clark £140
,, 8 Sold goods on credit to B. Miller £90
,, 8 Bought office furniture on credit from Barrett's Ltd £400
,, 10 Sold goods for cash £120
,, 13 Bought goods for credit from H. Grant £200
,, 14 Bought goods for cash £60
,, 15 Sold goods on credit to H. Sharples £180
,, 16 We returned goods £50 to H. Grant
,, 17 We returned some of the office furniture £30 to Barrett's Ltd
,, 18 Sold goods on credit to B. Miller £400
,, 21 Paid H. Grant's account by cheque £480
,, 23 B. Miller paid us the amount owing in cash £490
,, 24 Sharples returned to us £50 goods
,, 25 Goods sold for cash £150
,, 28 Bought goods for cash £370
,, 30 Bought motor van on credit from J. Kelly £600.

4 The Double Entry System for Expenses and Revenues. The Effect of Profit or Loss on Capital

Up to now this book has been concerned with the accounting need to record changes in assets and liabilities, but this is subject to one exception, the change in the capital caused by the profit earned in the business. By profit is meant the excess of revenues over expenses for a particular period. Revenues consist of the monetary value of goods and services that have been delivered to customers. Expenses consist of the monetary value of the assets used up in obtaining these revenues. Particularly in American accounting language the word 'income' is used instead of 'profit'.

It is possible to see the effect of profit upon capital by means of an example:

On 1 January the assets and liabilities of a firm are:

Assets: Motor van £500, Fixtures £200, Stock £700, Debtors £300, Cash at Bank £200.

Liabilities: Creditors £600.

The capital is therefore found by the formula Assets − Liabilities = Capital.

£500 + £200 + £700 + £300 + £200 − £600 = £1,300.

During January the whole of the £700 stock is sold for £1,100 cash. On the 31 January the assets and liabilities have become:

Assets: Motor van £500, Fixtures £200, Stock −, Debtors £300, Cash at Bank £1,300.

Liabilities: Creditors £600.

Assets − Liabilities = Capital
£500 + £200 ÷ £300 + £1,300 − £600 = £1,700.

Profit therefore affects the capital thus:

Old Capital + Profit = New Capital
£1,300   + £400 =   £1,700

On the other hand a loss would have reduced the capital so that it would become:

Old Capital – Loss = New Capital.

To alter the capital account it will therefore have to be possible to calculate profits and losses. They are, however, calculated only at intervals, usually annually but sometimes more often. This means that accounts will be needed to collect together the expenses and revenues pending the periodical calculation of profits. All the expenses could be charged to an omnibus 'Expenses Account', but obviously it is far more informative if full details of different expenses are shown in Profit and Loss Calculations. The same applies to revenues also. Therefore a separate account is opened for every type of expense and revenue. For instance there may be accounts as follows:

Rent Account	Postages Account
Wages Account	Stationery Account
Salaries Account	Insurance Account
Telephone Account	Motor Expenses Account
Rent Receivable Account	General Expenses Account

It is purely a matter of choice in a firm as to the title of each expense or revenue account. For example, an account for postage stamps could be called 'Postage Stamps Account', 'Postages Account', 'Communication Expenses Account' and so on. Also different firms amalgamate expenses, some having a 'Rent and Telephone Account', others a 'Rent, Telephone and Insurance Account', etc. Infrequent or small items of expense are usually put into a 'Sundry Expenses Account' or a 'General Expenses Account'.

Debit or Credit

It must now be decided as to which side of the records revenues and expenses are to be recorded. Assets involve expenditure by the firm and are shown as debit entries. Expenses also involve expenditure by the firm and are therefore also recorded on the debit side of the books. In fact assets may be seen to be expenditure of money for which something still remains, while expenses involve expenditure of money which has been used up in the running of the business and for which there is no benefit remaining at the date of the balance sheet.

Revenue is the opposite of expenses and therefore appears on the opposite side to expenses, that is revenue accounts appear on the credit side of the books. Revenue also increases profit, which in turn increases capital. Pending the periodical calculation of profit therefore, revenue is collected together in appropriately named accounts, and until it is transferred to the profit calculations it will therefore need to be shown as a credit.

An alternative explanation may also be used for expenses. Every expense results in a decrease in an asset or an increase in a liability, and because of the accounting equation this means that the capital is reduced by each expense. The decrease of capital needs a debit entry and therefore expense accounts contain debit entries for expenses.

Consider too that expenditure of money pays for expenses, which are used up in the short term, or assets, which are used up in the long term, both for the purpose of winning revenue. Both of these are shown on the debit side of the pages, while the revenue which has been won is shown in the credit side of the pages.

Effect of Transactions

A few illustrations will demonstrate the double entry required.

1.   The rent of £20 is paid in cash.
Here the twofold effect is:
(a) The asset of cash is decreased. This means crediting the cash account to show the decrease of the asset.
(b) The total of the expenses of rent is increased. As expense entries are shown as debits, and the expense is rent, so the action required is the debiting of the rent account.
Summary: Credit the cash account with £20.
           Debit the rent account with £20.

2.   Motor expenses are paid by cheque £55.
The twofold effect is:
(a) The asset of money in the bank is decreased. This means crediting the bank account to show the decrease of the asset.
(b) The total of the motor expenses paid is increased. To increase an expenses account needs a debit, so the action required is to debit the motor expenses account.
Summary: Credit the bank account with £55
           Debit the motor expenses account with £55.

3.   £60 cash is received for commission earned by the firm.
(a) The asset of cash is increased. This needs a debit in the cash account to increase the asset.
(b) The revenue of commissions received is increased. Revenue is shown by a credit entry, therefore to increase the revenue account in question the Commissions Received Account is credited.
Summary: Debit the cash account
           Credit the commissions received account

It is now possible to study the effects of some more transactions showing the results in the form of a table:

	Increase	Action	Decrease	Action
June 1 Paid for postage stamps by cash £5	Expense of postages	Debit postages account	Asset of cash	Credit cash account
,, 2 Paid for electricity by cheque £29	Expense of electricity	Debit electricity account	Asset of bank	Credit bank account
,, 3 Received rent in cash £38	Asset of cash	Debit cash account		
	Revenue of rent	Credit rent received account		
,, 4 Paid insurance by cheque £42	Expense of insurance	Debit insurance account	Asset of bank	Credit bank account

The above four examples can now be shown in account form:

Cash

	£		£
June 3 Rent received	38	June 1 Postages	5

Bank

			£
		June 2 Electricity	29
		,, 4 Insurance	42

Electricity

	£
June 2 Bank	29

Insurance

	£
June 4 Bank	42

Postages

	£
June 1 Cash	5

Rent Received

		£
	June 3 Cash	38

It is clear that from time to time the proprietor will want to take cash out of the business for his private use. In fact he will sometimes take goods. This will be dealt with later. However, whether the withdrawals are cash or goods they are known as 'Drawings'. Drawings in fact decrease the claim of the proprietor against the resources of the business, in other words they reduce the amount of capital. According to the way in which the accounting formula is represented by debits and credits the decrease of capital needs a debit entry in the capital account. However, the accounting custom has grown up of debiting a 'Drawings Account' as an interim measure.

An example will demonstrate the twofold effect of cash withdrawals from the business.

Example: 25 August. Proprietor takes £50 cash out of the business for his own use.

Effect	*Action*
1. Capital is decreased by £50	Debit the drawings account £50
2. Cash is decreased by £50	Credit the cash account £50

Cash

		£
	Aug 25 Drawings	50

Drawings

	£
Aug 25 Cash	50

Assignment Exercises

4.1 You are to complete the following table, showing the accounts to be debited and those to be credited:

	Account to be debited	Account to be credited
(a) Paid rates by cheque		
(b) Paid wages by cash		
(c) Rent received by cheque		
(d) Received by cheque refund of insurance previously paid		
(e) Paid general expenses by cash		

4.2A Complete the following table, showing the accounts to be debited and those to be credited:

	Account to be debited	Account to be credited
(a) Paid insurance by cheque		
(b) Paid motor expenses by cash		
(c) Rent received in cash		
(d) Paid rates by cheque		
(e) Received refund of rates by cheque		
(f) Paid for stationery expenses by cash		
(g) Paid wages by cash		
(h) Sold surplus stationery receiving proceeds by cheque		
(i) Received sales commission by cheque		
(j) Bought motor van by cheque.		

4.3 You are to enter the following transactions, completing double-entry in the books for the month of May 19-7:

19-7

May 1   Started business with £2,000 in the bank

,,   2   Purchased goods £175 on credit from M. Mills

,,   3   Bought fixtures and fittings £150 paying by cheque

,,   5   Sold goods for cash £275

,,   6   Bought goods on credit £114 from S. Waites

,, 10   Paid rent by cash £15

,, 12   Bought stationery £27, paying by cash

,, 18   Goods returned to M. Mills £23

,, 21   Let off part of the premises receiving rent by cheque £5

,, 23   Sold goods on credit to U. Henry for £77

,, 24   Bought a motor van paying by cheque £300

,, 30   Paid the month's wages by cash £117

,, 31   The proprietor took cash for himself £44.

4.4 Write up the following transactions in the books of L. Thompson:

19-8

March 1   Started business with cash £1,500

,,   2   Bought goods on credit from A. Hanson £296

,,   3   Paid rent by cash £28

,,   4   Paid £1,000 of the cash of the firm into a bank account

,,   5   Sold goods on credit to E. Linton £54

,,   7   Bought stationery £15 paying by cheque

,, 11   Cash sales £49

,, 14   Goods returned by us to A. Hanson £17

,, 17   Sold goods on credit to S. Morgan £29

,, 20   Paid for repairs to the building by cash £18

,, 22   E. Linton returned goods to us £14

,, 27   Paid Hanson by cheque £279

,, 28   Cash purchases £125

,, 29   Bought a motor van paying by cheque £395

,, 30   Paid motor expenses in cash £15

,, 31   Bought fixtures £120 on credit from A. Webster.

4.5A Enter the following transactions in double entry:

July 1 Started business with £8,000 in the bank
,, 2 Bought stationery by cheque £30
,, 3 Bought goods on credit from I. Walsh £900
,, 4 Sold goods for cash £180
,, 5 Paid insurance by cash £40
,, 7 Bought machinery on credit from H. Morgan £500
,, 8 Paid for machinery expenses by cheque £50
,, 10 Sold goods on credit to D. Small £320
,, 11 Returned goods to I. Walsh £70
,, 14 Paid wages by cash £70
,, 17 Paid rent by cheque £100
,, 20 Received cheque £200 from D. Small
,, 21 Paid H. Morgan by cheque £500
,, 23 Bought stationery on credit from Express Ltd £80
,, 25 Sold goods on credit to N. Thomas £230
,, 28 Received rent £20 in cash for part of premises sub-let
,, 31 Paid Express Ltd by cheque £80.

4.6A Write up the following transactions in the records of D. DaSilva:

Feb 1 Started business with £3,000 in the bank and £500 cash
,, 2 Bought goods on credit: T. Small £250; C. Todd £190; V. Ryan £180
,, 3 Bought goods for cash £230. Feb 4 Paid rent in cash £10
,, 5 Bought stationery paying by cheque £49
,, 6 Sold goods on credit: C. Crooks £140; R. Rogers £100; B. Grant £240
,, 7 Paid wages in cash £80
,, 10 We returned goods to C. Todd £60. Feb 11 Paid rent in cash £10
,, 13 R. Rogers returns goods to us £20
,, 15 Sold goods on credit to: J. Burns £90; J. Smart £130; N. Thorn £170
,, 16 Paid rates by cheque £130. Feb 18 Paid insurance in cash £40
,, 19 Paid rent by cheque £10
,, 20 Bought motor van on credit from C. White £600
,, 21 Paid motor expenses in cash £6. Feb 23 Paid wages in cash £90
,, 24 Received part of amount owing from B. Grant by cheque £200
,, 28 Received refund of rates £10 by cheque
,, 28 Paid by cheque: T. Small £250; C. Todd £130; C. White £600.

5 Balancing off Accounts

What you have been reading about so far is the recording of transactions in the books by means of debit and credit entries. Every so often we will have to look at each account to see what is revealed by the entries.

Probably the most obvious reason for this is to find out how much our customers owe us in respect of goods we have sold to them. In most firms the custom is that this should be done at the end of each month. Let us look at the account of one of our customers, D. Knight, at the end of a month.

D. Knight

19-6		£	19-6		£
Aug 1 Sales		158	Aug 28 Cash		158
,, 15 ,,		206			
,, 30 ,,		118			

You can see that Knight still owed £206 + £118 = £324 at the end of 31 August 19-6. Our firm will thus start its business for the next month on 1 September 19-6 with that amount owing to it. To show that our firm is carrying these outstanding items from one period to the next one, the 'balance' on each account is found. The 'balance' is the accounting term meaning the arithmetical difference between the two sides of an account.

To balance off an account:

(i) First add up the side of the account having the greatest total.
(ii) Second, insert the difference (the balance) on the other side of the account so as to make the totals of each side equal. When doing this, ensure that the two totals are written on a level with each other.
(iii) The balance has now been entered in the period which has finished, it now has to be entered on the other side of the books to ensure that double-entry of the item is carried out. This is done by making the second entry on the next line under the totals. Let us see Knight's account now 'balanced' off:

D. Knight

19-6		£	19-6		£
Aug 1 Sales		158	Aug 28 Cash		158
,, 15 ,,		206	,, 31 Balance carried down		324
,, 30 ,,		118			
		482			482
Sept 1 Balance brought down		324			

We can now look at another account prior to balancing:

H. Henry

19-6	£	19-6	£
Aug 5 Sales	300	Aug 24 Returns Inwards	50
,, 28 Sales	540	,, 29 Bank	250

This time, and we will always do this in future, for it will save us from unnecessary writing, we will abbreviate 'carried down' to 'c/d' and 'brought down' to 'b/d'.

H. Henry

19-6		£	19-6		£
Aug 5 Sales		300	Aug 24 Returns Inwards		50
,, 28 Sales		540	,, 29 Bank		250
			,, 31 Balance	c/d	540
		840			840
Sept 1 Balance	b/d	540			

Notes:

1. The date given to Balance c/d is the last day of the period which is finishing, and Balance b/d is given the opening date of the next period.
2. As the total of the debit side originally exceeded the total of the credit side, the balance is said to be a debit balance. This being a personal account (for a person), the person concerned is said to be debtor – the accounting term for anyone who owes money to the firm. The use of the term debtor for a person whose account has a debit balance can again thus be seen.

If accounts contain only one entry it is unnecessary to enter the total. A double line ruled under the entry will mean that the entry is its own total. For example:

B. Walters

19-6		£	19-6		£
Aug 18 Sales		51	Aug 31 Balance	c/d	51
Sept 1 Balance	b/d	51			

If an account contains only one entry on each side which are equal to one another, totals are again unnecessary. For example:

D. Hylton

19-6	£	19-6	£
Aug 6 Sales	214	Aug 12 Bank	214

Credit Balances

Exactly the same principles will apply when the balances are carried down to the credit side. We can look at two accounts of our suppliers which are to be balanced off.

E. Williams

19-6	£	19-6	£
Aug 21 Bank	100	Aug 2 Purchases	248
		,, 18 ,,	116

K. Patterson

19-6	£	19-6	£
Aug 14 Returns Outwards	20	Aug 8 Purchases	620
,, 28 Bank	600	,, 15 Purchases	200

When balanced these will appear as:

E. Williams

19-6		£	19-6		£
Aug 21 Bank		100	Aug 2 Purchases		248
,, 31 Balance	c/d	264	,, 18 ,,		116
		364			364
			Sept 1 Balance	b/d	264

K. Patterson

19-6			£	19-6			£
Aug 14 Returns Outwards			20	Aug 8 Purchases			620
,, 28 Bank			600	,, 15 Purchases			200
,, 31 Balance	c/d		200				
			820				820
				Sept 1 Balance	b/d		200

Before you read further attempt Exercises 5.1 and 5.2.

Computers and Book-keeping Machinery

Throughout the main part of this book the type of account used shows the left-hand side of the account as the debit side, and the right-hand side is shown as the credit side. However, when most computers or book-keeping equipment is used the style of the ledger account is different. It appears as three columns of figures, being one column for debit entries, another column for credit entries, and the last column for the balance. If you have a current account at a bank your bank statements will normally be shown using this method.

The accounts used in this chapter will now be redrafted to show the ledger accounts drawn up in this way.

D. Knight

	Debit	Credit	Balance (and whether debit or credit)
19-6	£	£	£
Aug 1 Sales	158		158 Dr
,, 15 ,,	206		364 Dr
,, 28 Cash		158	206 Dr
,, 30 Sales	118		324 Dr

H. Henry

	Debit	Credit	Balance
19-6	£	£	£
Aug 5 Sales	300		300 Dr
,, 24 Returns		50	250 Dr
,, 28 Sales	540		790 Dr
,, 29 Bank		250	540 Dr

B. Walters

	Debit	Credit	Balance
19-6	£	£	£
Aug 18 Sales	51		51 Dr

D. Hylton

	Debit	Credit	Balance
19-6	£	£	£
Aug 6 Sales	214		214 Dr
,, 12 Bank		214	0

E. Williams

	Debit	Credit	Balance
19-6	£	£	£
Aug 2 Purchases		248	248 Cr
,, 18 ,,		116	364 Cr
,, 21 Bank	100		264 Cr

K. Patterson

	Debit	Credit	Balance
19-6	£	£	£
Aug 8 Purchases		620	620 Cr
,, 14 Returns	20		600 Cr
,, 15 Purchases		200	800 Cr
,, 28 Bank	600		200 Cr

It will be noticed that the balance is calculated afresh after every entry. This can be done quite simply when using book-keeping machinery or a computer because it is the machine which automatically calculates the new balance. However, when manual methods are in use it is often too laborious to have to calculate a new balance after each entry, and it also means that the greater the number of calculations the greater the possible number of errors. For these reasons it is usual for students to use two-sided accounts. However, it is important to note that there is no difference in principle, the final balances are the same using either method.

Assignment Exercises

5.1 Enter the folling items in the necessary debtors and creditors accounts only, do *not* write up other accounts. Then balance down each personal account at the end of the month. (Keep you answer, it will be used as a basis for question 5.3A).

19-6

May	1	Sales on credit to H. Harvey £690, N. Morgan £153, J. Lindo £420
,,	4	Sales on credit to L. Masters £418, H. Harvey £66
,,	10	Returns inwards from H. Harvey £40, J. Lindo £20
,,	18	N. Morgan paid us by cheque £153
,,	20	J. Lindo paid us £400 by cheque
,,	24	H. Harvey paid us £300 by cash
,,	31	Sales on credit to L. Masters £203.

5.2 Enter the following in the personal accounts only, do *not* write up the other accounts. Balance down each personal account at the end of the month. After completing this state which of the balances represent debtors and those which are creditors. (Keep your answer, it will be used as a basis for question 5.4A).

19-4

Sept	1	Sales on credit to D. Williams £458, J. Moore £235, G. Grant £98
,,	2	Purchases on credit A. White £77, H. Samuels £231, P. Owen £65
,,	8	Sales on credit to J. Moore £444, F. Franklin £249
,,	10	Purchases on credit from H. Samuels £12, O. Oliver £222
,,	12	Returns Inwards from G. Grant £9, J. Moore £26
,,	17	We returned goods to H. Samuels £24, O. Oliver £12
,,	20	We paid A. White by cheque £77
,,	24	D. Williams paid us by cheque £300
,,	26	We paid O. Oliver by cash £210
,,	28	D. Williams paid us by cash £100
,,	30	F. Franklin pays us by cheque £249.

5.3A Redraft each of the accounts given in your answer to 5.1 in three column ledger style accounts.

5.4A Redraft each of the accounts given in your answer to 5.2 in three column ledger style accounts.

5.5A Enter the following, personal accounts only. Bring down balances at end of the month. After completing this state which of the balances represent debtors and those which are creditors. (Keep your answer, it will be used as the basis of question 5.6A).

19-7

May 1 Credit sales B. Flynn £241, R. Kelly £29, J. Long £887, T. Fryer £124

,,   2 Credit purchases from S. Wood £148, T. DuQuesnay £27, R. Johnson £77, G. Henriques £108

,,   8 Credit sales to R. Kelly £74, J. Long £132

,,   9 Credit purchases from T. DuQuesnay £142, G. Henriques £44

,, 10 Goods returned to us by J. Long £17, T. Fryer £44

,, 12 Cash paid to us by T. Fryer £80

,, 15 We returned goods to S. Wood £8, G. Henriques £18

,, 19 We received cheques from J. Long £500, B. Flynn £241

,, 21 We sold goods on credit to B. Flynn £44, R. Kelly £280

,, 28 We paid by cheque the following: S. Wood £140; G. Henriques £50; R. Johnson £60

,, 31 We returned goods to G. Henriques £4.

5.6A Redraft each of the accounts given in your answer to 5.5A in three column style accounts.

6 The Trial Balance

You have already seen that the method of book-keeping in use is that of the double entry method. This means:

1. For each debit entry there is a corresponding credit entry.
2. For every credit entry there is a corresponding debit entry.

All the items recorded in all the accounts on the debit side should equal in *total* all the items recorded on the credit side of the books. To see if the two totals are equal, or in accounting terminology to see if the two sides of the books 'balance', a Trial Balance may be drawn up periodically.

A form of a trial balance could be drawn up by listing all the accounts and adding together all the debit entries, at the same time adding together all the credit entries. Using the worked exercise on pages 24 and 25 such a trial balance would appear as follows, bearing in mind that it could not be drawn up until after all the entries had been made, and will therefore be dated as on 31 May 19-6.

Trial Balance as on 31 May 19 – 6

	Dr	Cr
	£	£
Purchases	309	
Sales		255
Returns outwards		15
Returns inwards	16	
D. Small	68	68
A. Lyon & Son		141
D. Hughes	60	60
M. Spencer	45	16
Cash	210	153
	708	708

However, this is not the normal method of drawing up a trial balance, but it is the easiest to understand in the first instance. Usually, a trial balance is a list of balances only, arranged as to whether they are debit balances or credit balances. If the above trial balance had been drawn up using the conventional balances method it would have appeared as follows:

Trial Balance as on 31 May 19 – 6

	Dr	Cr
	£	£
Purchases	309	
Sales		255
Returns outwards		15
Returns inwards	16	
A. Lyon and Son		141
M. Spencer	29	
Cash	57	
	411	411

Here the two sides also 'balance'. The sums of £68 in D. Small's account, £60 in D. Hughes' account, £16 in M. Spencer's account and £153 in the cash account have however been cancelled out from each side of these accounts by virtue of taking only the balances instead of totals. As equal amounts have been cancelled from each side, £297 in all, the new totals should still equal one another, as in fact they do at £411.

This latter form of trial balance is the easiest to extract when there are more than a few transactions during the period, also the balances are either used later when the profits are being calculated, or else appear in a balance sheet, so that it is not just for ascertaining whether or not errors have been made that trial balances are extracted.

Trial Balances and Errors

It may at first sight appear that the balancing of a trial balance proves that the books are correct. This however is quite wrong. It means that certain types of errors have not been made, but there are several types of errors that will not affect the balancing of a trial balance. Examples of the errors which would be revealed, provided there are no compensating errors which cancel them out, are errors in additions, using one figure for the debit entry and another figure for the credit entry, entering only one aspect of a transaction and so on. We shall consider these in greater detail in later chapters.

Assignment Exercises

6.1 You are to enter up the necessary amounts for the month of May from the following details, and then balance off the accounts and extract a trial balance as at 31 May 19-6:

19-6

May 1 Started firm with capital in cash of £250
,, 2 Bought goods on credit from the following persons: D. Ellis £54; C. Mendez 87; K. Gibson £25; D. Booth £76; L. Lowe £64
,, 4 Sold goods on credit to: C. Bailey £43; B. Hughes £62; H. Spencer £176
,, 6 Paid rent by cash £12
,, 9 Bailey paid us his account by cheque £43
,, 10 H. Spencer paid us £150 by cheque
,, 12 We paid the following by cheque: K. Gibson £25; D. Ellis £54
,, 15 Paid carriage by cash £23
,, 18 Bought goods on credit from C. Mendez £43; D. Booth £110
,, 21 Sold goods on credit to B. Hughes £67
,, 31 Paid rent by cheque £18.

6.2 Enter up the books from the following details for the month of March, and extract a trial balance as at 31 March 19-6:

19-6

March 1 Started business with £800 in the bank
,, 2 Bought goods on credit from the following persons: K. Henriques £76; M. Hyatt £27; T. Braham £56
,, 5 Cash sales £87
,, 6 Paid wages in cash £14
,, 7 Sold goods on credit to: H. Elliott £35; L. Lane £42; J. Carlton £72
,, 9 Bought goods for cash £46
,, 10 Bought goods on credit from: M. Hyatt £57; T. Braham £98
,, 12 Paid wages in cash £14
,, 13 Sold goods on credit to: L. Lane £32; J. Carlton £23
,, 15 Bought shop fixtures on credit from Betta Ltd £50
,, 17 Paid M. Hyatt by cheque £84
,, 18 We returned goods to T. Braham £20
,, 21 Paid Betta Ltd a cheque for £50
,, 24 J. Carlton paid us his account by cheque £95
,, 27 We returned goods to K. Henriques £24
,, 30 J. King lent us £60 by cash
,, 31 Bought a motor van paying by cheque £400.

6.3A Record the following details for the month of November 19-3 and extract a trial balance as at 30 November:

Nov 1 Started with £5,000 in the bank
,, 3 Bought goods on credit from: T. Henriques £160; J. Smith £230; W. Rogers £400; P. Boone £310
,, 5 Cash sales £240
,, 6 Paid rent by cheque £20
,, 7 Paid rates by cheque £190
,, 11 Sold goods on credit to: L. Matthews £48; K. Allen £32; R. Hall £1,170
,, 17 Paid wages by cash £40
,, 18 We returned goods to: T. Henriques £14; P. Boone £20
,, 19 Bought goods on credit from: P. Boone £80; W. Rogers £270; D. Diaz £130
,, 20 Goods were returned to us: K. Alberga £2; L. Matthews £4
,, 21 Bought motor van on credit from U.Z. Motors £500
,, 23 We paid the following by cheque: T. Henriques £146; J. Smith £230; W. Rogers £300
,, 25 Bought another motor van, paying by cheque immediately £700
,, 26 Received a loan of £400 cash from A. Williams
,, 28 Received cheques from: L. Matthews £44; L. Allen £30
,, 30 Proprietor brings a further £300 into the business, by a payment into the business bank account.

6.4A Record the following for the month of January, balance off all the accounts, and then extract a trial balance as at 31 January 19-4:

19-4
Jan 1 Started business with £3,500 cash
,, 2 Put £2,800 of the cash into a bank account
,, 3 Bought goods for cash £150
,, 4 Bought goods on credit from: L. Coke £360; M. Burton £490; T. Hill £110; C. Small £340
,, 5 Bought stationery on credit from: Subaran Ltd £170
,, 6 Sold goods on credit to: S. Walters £90; T. Binns £150; C. Howard £190; P. Peart £160
,, 8 Paid rent by cheque £55
,, 10 Bought fixtures on credit from Matalon Ltd £480
,, 11 Paid salaries in cash £120
,, 14 Returned goods to M. Burton £40; T. Hill £60
,, 15 Bought motor van by cheque £700
,, 16 Received loan from J. Henry by cheque £600
,, 18 Goods returned to us by: S. Walters £20; C. Howard £40
,, 21 Cash sales £90
,, 24 Sold goods on credit to: T. Binns £100; P. Peart £340; J. Smart £115
,, 26 We paid the following by cheque: M. Burton £450; T. Hill £50
,, 29 Received cheques from: J. Smart £115; T. Binns £250
,, 30 Received a further loan from J. Henry by cash £200
,, 30 Received £500 cash from P. Peart.

7 Trading and Profit and Loss Accounts: An Introduction

Probably the main objective of the accounting function is the calculation of the profits earned by a business or the losses incurred by it. The earning of profit is after all usually the main reason why the business was set up in the first place, and the proprietor will want to know for various reasons how much profit has been made. First he will want to know how the actual profits compare with the profits he had hoped to make. He may also want to know his profits for such diverse reasons as: to assist him to plan ahead, to help him to obtain a loan from a bank or from a private individual, to show to a prospective partner or to a person to whom he hopes to sell the business, or maybe he will need to know his profits for income tax purposes.

Chapter 4 was concerned with the grouping of revenue and expenses prior to bringing them together to compute profit. In the case of a trader, meaning by this someone who is mainly concerned with buying and selling, the profits are calculated by drawing up a special account called a Trading and Profit and Loss Account. For a manufacturer it is also useful to prepare Manufacturing Accounts as well, but this will be dealt with in a later chapter.

Undoubtedly one of the most important uses of the trading and profit and loss account is comparing the results obtained with the results expected. Many businesses attach a great deal of importance to their gross profit percentage. This is the amount of Profit made, before deducting expenses, for every £100 of sales. In order that this may easily be deduced from the profit calculations, the account in which profit is computed is split into two sections − one in which the Gross Profit is found, and the next section in which the Net Profit is calculated.

Gross Profit (calculated in the Trading Account)	This is the excess of sales over the cost of goods sold in the period.
Net Profit (calculated in the Profit and Loss Account)	What remains after all other costs used up in the period have been deducted from the gross profit.

The gross profit, found by the use of the Trading Account, is the excess of sales over the cost of goods sold. The net profit, found when the Profit and Loss Account is prepared, consists of the gross profit plus any revenue other than that from sales, such as discounts received or commissions earned, less the total costs used up during the period. Where the cost of goods sold is greater than the sales the result would be a Gross Loss, but this is a relatively rare occurrence. Where the costs used up exceed the gross profit plus other revenue then the result is said to be a Net Loss. By taking the figure of sales less the cost of goods sold, it can be seen that the accounting custom is to calculate a trader's profits only when the goods have been disposed of and not before.

As was seen in Chapter 4, profit increases the capital of the proprietor, profit in this context meaning the net profit. The fact that an interim figure of profit, known as the gross profit is calculated, is due to the two figures of profit being more useful for purposes of comparison with both these profits of previous periods, than by just comparing net profits only. Were it not for this accounting custom it would not be necessary to calculate gross profit at all.

The trial balance of B. Swift, Exhibit 7.1, drawn up as on 31 December 19-5 after the completion of his first year in business can now be looked at.

Exhibit 7.1
B. Swift
Trial Balance as on 31 December 19-5

	Dr	Cr
	£	£
Sales		3,850
Purchases	2,900	
Rent	240	
Lighting expenses	150	
General expenses	60	
Fixtures and fittings	500	
Debtors	680	
Creditors		910
Bank	1,510	
Cash	20	
Drawings	700	
Capital		2,000
	6,760	6,760

The first task is to draw up the trading account using the above information. Immediately there is a problem. Sales less the cost of goods sold is the definition of gross profit, but purchases will only equal cost of goods sold if in fact all the goods purchased had been sold leaving no stock of goods on 31 December 19-5. It would be normal to find that a trader always keeps a stock of goods for resale, as the stock of goods is constantly being replenished. However, there is no record in the books of the value of the stock of unsold goods, and the only way that Swift can find this out is by stock-taking on 31 December 19-5 after the business of that day. By stocktaking is meant that he would make a list of all the unsold goods and then find out their value. The value he would normally place on them would be the cost price of the goods. Assume that this was £300. Then the cost of purchases less the cost of unsold goods would equal the cost of goods sold, ignoring losses by theft or wastage. This figure would then be deducted from the figure of sales to find the gross profit.

Swift could perform this calculation arithmetically:

Sales – Cost of goods sold   = Gross Profit
   (Purchases – unsold stock)
£3,850 – (£2,900 – £300)   = £1,250

This however is not performing the task by using double entry accounts. In double entry the balance of the sales account is transferred to the trading account by debiting the sales account (thus closing it) and crediting the trading account. The balance of the purchases account would then be transferred by crediting the purchases account (thus closing it) and debiting the trading account. Now the accounts connected with stock movements have been closed, and accounts are being drawn up to a point in time, in this case 31 December 19-5. At this point of time Swift has an asset, namely stock (of unsold goods), for which no account exists. This must be rectified by opening a stock account and debiting the amount of the asset to it. Now as already stated, the closing stock needs to be brought into the calculation of the gross profit, and the calculation of the gross profit is effected in the trading account. Therefore the credit for the closing stock should be in the trading account thus completing the double entry.

It is now usual for the trading and profit and loss accounts to be shown under one combined heading, the trading account being the top section and the profit and loss account being the lower section of this combined account.

B. Swift
Trading and Profit and Loss Account for the year ended 31 December 19-5

	£		£
Purchases	2,900	Sales	3,850
Gross profit c/d	1,250	Closing stock	300
	4,150		4,150
		Gross profit b/d	1,250

The balance shown on the trading account is shown as gross profit rather than being described as a balance. When found the gross profit is carried down to the profit and loss section of the account.

The accounts so far used appear as follows:

Sales

19-5	£	19-5	£
Dec 31 Trading	3,850	Dec 31 Balance b/d	3,850

Purchases

19-5	£	19-5	£
Dec 31 Balance b/d	2,900	Dec 31 Trading	2,900

Stock

19-5	£
Dec 31 Trading	300

The entry of the Closing Stock on the credit side of the trading and profit and loss account is in effect a deduction from the purchases on the debit side. In present-day accounting it is usual to find the closing stock actually shown as a deduction from the purchases on the debit side, and the figure then disclosed being described as 'cost of goods sold'. This is illustrated in Exhibit 7.2.

The profit and loss account can now be drawn up. Any revenue accounts, other than sales which have already been dealt with, would be transferred to the credit of the profit and loss account. Typical examples are commissions received and rent received. In the case of B. Swift there are no such revenue accounts.

The costs used up in the year, in other words the expenses of the year, are transferred to the debit of the profit and loss account. It may also be thought, quite rightly so, that as the fixtures and fittings have been used during the year with the subsequent deterioration of the asset, that something should be charged for this use. The methods for doing this are left until Chapter 19.

The revised trading account with the addition of the profit and loss account will now appear as follows:

Exhibit 7.2

B. Swift

Trading and Profit and Loss Account for the year ended 31 December 19-5

	£		£
Purchases	2,900	Sales	3,850
Less Closing stock	300		
Cost of goods sold	2,600		
Gross Profit c/d	1,250		
	3,850		3,850
Rent	240	Gross profit b/d	1,250
Lighting expenses	150		
General expenses	60		
Net profit	800		
	1,250		1,250

The expense accounts closed off will now appear as:

Rent

19-5	£	19-5	£
Dec 31 Balance b/d	240	Dec 31 Profit and Loss	240

Lighting Expenses

19-5	£	19-5	£
Dec 31 Balance b/d	150	Dec 31 Profit and Loss	150

General Expenses

19-5	£	19-5	£
Dec 31 Balance b/d	60	Dec 31 Profit and Loss	60

Net profit increases the capital of the proprietor. The credit entry for the net profit is therefore in the capital account. The trading and profit and loss accounts, and indeed all the revenue and expense accounts can thus be seen to be devices whereby the capital account is saved from being concerned with unnecessary detail. Every sale of a good at a profit increases the capital of the proprietor as does each item of revenue such as rent received. On the other hand each sale of a good at a loss, or each item of expense decreases the capital of the proprietor. Instead of altering the capital afresh after each transaction the respective items of profit and loss and of revenue and expense are collected together using suitably described accounts. Then the whole of the details are brought together in one set of accounts, the trading and profit and loss account and the increase to the capital, i.e. the net profit is determined. Alternatively, the decrease in the capital as represented by the Net Loss is ascertained.

The fact that a separate drawings account has been in use can now also be seen to have been in keeping with the policy of avoiding unnecessary detail in the capital account. There will thus be one figure for drawings which will be the total of the drawings for the whole of the period, and will be transferred to the debit of the capital account..

The capital account, showing these transfers, and the drawings account now closed is as follows:

Capital

19-5	£	19-5	£
Dec 31 Drawings	700	Jan 1 Cash	2,000
,, 31 Balance c/d	2,100	Dec 31 Net Profit from	
		Profit and Loss A/c	800
	2,800		2,800
		19-6	
		Jan 1 Balance b/d	2,100

Drawings

19-5	£	19-5	£
Dec 31 Balance b/d	700	Dec 31 Capital	700

It should be noticed that not all the items in the trial balance have been used in the Trading and Profit and Loss Account. The remaining balances are assets or liabilities or capital, they are not expenses or sales. These will be used up later when a balance sheet is drawn up, for as has been shown in Chapter 1, assets, liabilities and capital are shown in balance sheets.

In Exhibit 7.3, although it is not necessary to redraft the trial balance after the trading and profit and loss accounts have been pre-pared, it will be useful to do so in order to establish which balances still remain in the books. The first thing to notice is that the stock account, not originally in the trial balance, is in the redrafted trial balance, as the item was not created as a balance in the books until the trading account was prepared. These balances will be used by us when we start to look at the balance sheets.

Exhibit 7.3

B. Swift

Trial Balance as on 31 December 19-5

(after Trading and Profit and Loss Accounts completed)

	Dr	Cr
	£	£
Fixtures and fittings	500	
Debtors	680	
Creditors		910
Stock	300	
Bank	1,510	
Cash	20	
Capital		2,100
	3,010	3,010

Assignment Exercises

7.1 From the following trial balance of B. Webb, extracted after one year's trading, prepare a trading and profit and loss account for the year ended 31 December 19-6. A balance sheet is not required.

Trial Balance as at 31 December 19-6

	Dr	Cr
	£	£
Sales		18,462
Purchases	14,629	
Salaries	2,150	
Motor expenses	520	
Rent	670	
Insurance	111	
General expenses	105	
Premises	1,500	
Motor vehicles	1,200	
Debtors	1,950	
Creditors		1,538
Cash at bank	1,654	
Cash in hand	40	
Drawings	895	
Capital		5,424
	25,424	25,424

Stock at 31 December 19-6 was £2,548.

(Keep your answer − it will be used later in question 8.1)

7.2 From the following trial balance of C. Worth after his first year's trading, you are required to draw up a trading and profit and loss account for the year ended 30 June 19-4. A balance sheet is not required.

Trial Balance as at 30 June 19-4

	Dr	Cr
	£	£
Sales		28,794
Purchases	23,803	
Rent	854	
Lighting and Heating expenses	422	
Salaries and wages	3,164	
Insurance	105	
Buildings	50,000	
Fixtures	1,000	
Debtors	3,166	
Sundry expenses	506	
Creditors		1,206
Cash at bank	3,847	
Drawings	2,400	
Motor vans	5,500	
Motor running expenses	1,133	
Capital		65,900
	95,900	95,900

Stock at 30 June 19-4 was £4,166.
(Keep your answer, it will be used later in question 8.2)

7.3A From the following trial balance of F. Chaplin drawn up on conclusion of his first year in business, draw up a trading and profit and loss account for the year ended 31 December 19-8. A balance sheet is not required.

Trial Balance as at 31 December 19-8

	Dr	Cr
	£	£
General expenses	210	
Rent	400	
Motor expenses	735	
Salaries	3,560	
Insurance	392	
Purchases	18,385	
Sales		26,815
Motor vehicle	2,800	
Creditors		5,160
Debtors	4,090	
Premises	20;000	
Cash at bank	1,375	
Cash in hand	25	
Capital		24,347
Drawings	4,350	
	56,322	56,322

Stock at 31 December 19-8 was £4,960.
(Keep your answer, it will be used later in question 8.3A.)

7.4A Extract a trading and profit and loss account for the year ended 30 June 19-4 for F. Kidd. The trial balance as at 30 June 19-4 after his first year of trading, was as follows:

	Dr	Cr
	£	£
Rent	1,560	
Insurance	305	
Lighting and Heating expenses	516	
Motor expenses	1,960	
Salaries and wages	4,850	
Sales		35,600
Purchases	30,970	
Sundry expenses	806	
Motor vans	3,500	
Creditors		3,250
Debtors	6,810	
Fixtures	3,960	
Buildings	28,000	
Cash at bank	1,134	
Drawings	6,278	
Capital		51,799
	90,649	90,649

Stock at 30 June 19-4 was £9,960.
(Keep your answer, it will be used later in question 8.4A.)

8 Balance Sheets

After the trading and profit and loss accounts have been completed, a statement is drawn up in which the remaining balances in the books are arranged according to whether they are asset balances or liability or capital balances. This statement is called a balance sheet, and it may be recalled that Chapter 1 contained examples. The assets are shown on the left-hand side and the liabilities on the right-hand side.

It is very important to know that the balance sheet is not part of the double-entry system. This contrasts with the Trading and Profit and Loss Account which is part of double-entry. The use of the word 'account' indicates that it is part of double-entry.

It was seen in the last chapter that when sales, purchases and the various expenses were taken into the profit calculations an entry was actually made in each account showing that the item had been transferred to the Trading Account or the Profit and Loss Account. The balance sheet however is not part of double-entry, it is simply a list of the balances remaining after the Trading and Profit and Loss Accounts have been prepared. Therefore items are *not* transferred from accounts to the balance sheet, and accordingly entries are *not* made in the various accounts when a balance sheet is drawn up.

In Exhibit 8.1 the trial balance is shown again of B. Swift as on 31 December 19-5 *after* the Trading and Profit and Loss Account had been prepared.

Exhibit 8.1

B. Swift
Trial Balance as at 31 December 19-5
(after Trading and Profit and Loss Accounts completed)

	Dr	Cr
	£	£
Fixtures and fittings	500	
Debtors	680	
Creditors		910
Stock	300	
Bank	1,510	
Cash	20	
Capital		2,100
	3,010	3,010

A balance sheet, Exhibit 8.2, can now be drawn up as at 31 December 19-5. At this point we will not worry whether or not the balance sheet is set out in good style.

Exhibit 8.2

B. Swift
Balance Sheet as at 31 December 19-5

Assets	£	Capital and liabilities	£
Fixtures and fittings	500	Capital	2,100
Stock	300	Creditors	910
Debtors	680		
Bank	1,510		
Cash	20		
	3,010		3,010

Remember, all of the balances per Exhibit 8.1 still remain in the accounts, *no* entries were made in the accounts for the purpose of drawing up the balance sheet. As has been stated already, this is in direct contrast to the trading and profit and loss accounts. The word 'account' means in fact that it is part of the double entry system, so that anything which is not an account is outside the double entry system.

Balance Sheet Layout

You would not expect to go into a first-class store and see the goods for sale all mixed up and not laid out properly. You would expect that the goods would be so displayed so that you could easily find them. Similarly in balance sheets we do not want all the items shown in any order. We would really want them displayed so that desirable information could easily be seen.

For people such as bank managers, accountants and investors who look at a lot of different balance sheets, we would want to keep to a set pattern so as to enable comparison of balance sheets to be made easier. What you are about to look at is a suggested method for displaying items in balance sheets.

Let us look at the assets side first. We are going to show the assets under two headings, Fixed Assets and Current Assets.

Assets are called Fixed Assets when they are of long life, are to be used in the business and were *not* bought with the main purpose of resale. Examples are buildings, machinery, motor vehicles and fixtures and fittings.

On the other hand, assets are called Current Assets when they represent cash or are primarily for conversion into cash or have a short life. An example of a short-lived asset is that of the stock of oil held to power the boilers in a factory, as this will be used up in the near future. Other examples of current assets are cash itself, stocks of goods, debtors and bank balances.

There is a choice of two methods of listing the assets under their respective headings. The first, being the most preferable since it helps standardize the form of sole traders' accounts with those of limited companies, is that the assets are listed starting with the most permanent asset, or to put it another way, the most difficult to turn into cash, progressing to the asset which is least permanent or easiest to turn into cash. The fixed assets will thus appear under that heading followed by the current assets under their heading. The other method, used by banks but fast falling into disuse in most other kinds of organizations, is the complete opposite. In this method it is the least permanent asset that appears first and the most permanent asset which appears last.

Using the first method an illustration may now be seen of the order in which assets are displayed:

Fixed Assets

Land and buildings
Fixtures and fittings
Machinery
Motor vehicles

Current Assets

Stock
Debtors
Bank
Cash

The order with which most students would disagree is that stock has appeared before debtors. On first sight stock would appear to be more easily realizable than debtors. In fact, however, debtors could normally be more quickly turned into cash by factorizing them, i.e. selling the rights to the amounts owing to a finance company for an agreed amount. On the other hand, to dispose of all the stock of a business is often a long and difficult task. Another advantage is that the method follows the order in which full realization of the asset takes place. First, before any sale takes place there must be a stock of goods, which when sold on credit turns into debtors, and when payment is made by the debtors it turns into cash.

The order of the other side of the balance sheet is preferably that of starting with capital, progressing via Long-Term Liabilities such as loans not requiring repayment within the near future, and finishing with Current Liabilities, being liabilities such as debts for goods which will have to be discharged in the near future. This then would be the order in which the claims against the assets would be met. The other method of listing the liabilities is the complete opposite of this, starting with current liabilities and finishing at the bottom with capital. This method conflicts with company accounts and is best avoided if the benefits of standardization are to be attained.

Exhibit 8.3 shows Exhibit 8.2 drawn up in better style. Also read the notes following the exhibit.

Exhibit 8.3

B. Swift
Balance Sheet as at 31 December 19-5

Fixed Assets	£	£	Capital	£	£
Furniture and fittings		500	Cash introduced	2,000	
			Add Net profit		
Current Assets			for the year	800	
Stock	300				
Debtors	680			2,800	
Bank	1,510		Less Drawings	700	
Cash	20				2,100
		2,510	Current Liabilities		
			Creditors		910
		3,010			3,010

Notes to Exhibit 8.3

1. A total for capital and for each class of assets and liabilities should be shown, e.g. the £2,510 total of current assets. For this purpose the individual figures of current assets are inset and the resultant total extended into the end column.

2. It is not necessary to write the word 'account' after each item.

3. The proprietor will obviously be most interested in his capital. To have merely shown the balance of £2,100 would invariably invite his request to show how the final balance of the capital account had been arrived at. To overcome this, accounting custom always shows the full details of the capital account. Compare this with the other items above where only the closing balance is shown.

4. Compare the date on the balance sheet with that on the trading and profit and loss account. You can see from these that the essential natures of these two statements are revealed. A trading and profit and loss account is a period statement, because it covers a specifed period of time, in this case the whole of 19-5. On the other hand a balance sheet is a position statement; it is drawn up at a particular point in time, in this case at the precise end of 19-5.

Assignment Exercises

8.1 Complete question 7.1 by drawing up a balance sheet as at 31 December 19-6.

8.2 Complete question 7.2 by drawing up a balance sheet as at 30 June 19-4.

8.3A Complete question 7.3A by drawing up a balance sheet as at 31 December 19-8.

8.4A Complete question 7.4A by drawing up a balance sheet as at 30 June 19-4.

9 Trading and Profit and Loss Accounts and Balance Sheets: Further Considerations

1. Returns Inwards and Returns Outwards

In Chapter 3 the idea of different accounts for different movements of stock was introduced. There were accordingly sales, purchases, returns inwards and returns outwards accounts. In our first look at the preparation of a Trading Account in Chapter 7, returns inwards and returns outwards were omitted. This was done deliberately so that the first sight of Trading and Profit and Loss Accounts would not be a difficult one.

However, a large number of firms will return goods to their suppliers (returns outwards), and will have goods returned to them by their customers (returns inwards). When the gross profit is calculated these returns will have to come into the calculations. Suppose that in Exhibit 7.1, the trial balance of B. Swift, the balances showing stock movements had instead been as follows:

Trial Balance as at 31 December 19-5

	Dr	Cr
	£	£
Sales		4,000
Purchases	3,120	
Returns inwards	150	
Returns outwards		220

Looking at Exhibit 7.1 it can be seen that originally the example used was of Sales £3,850 and Purchases £2,900. If it had been as now shown instead, the Trading Account can be shown as it would have been for the year, and what gross profit would have been.

Comparing the two instances, they do in fact amount to the same things as far as gross profit is concerned. Sales were £3,850 in the original example. In the new example returns inwards should be deducted to get the correct figure for goods sold to customers and *kept* by them, i.e. £4,000 − £150 = £3,850. Purchases were £2,900; in the new example returns outwards should be deducted to get the correct figure of purchases *kept* by Swift. The gross profit will remain at £1,250 as per Exhibit 7.1.

The trading account will appear as in Exhibit 9.1.

Exhibit 9.1
Trading and Profit and Loss Account for the year ended 31 December 19-5

	£	£		£	£
Purchases	3,120		Sales	4,000	
Less Returns outwards	220	2,900	*Less* Returns inwards	150	3,850
Less Closing stock		300			
Cost of goods sold		2,600			
Gross profit c/d		1,250			
		3,850			3,850

The term used for Sales less Returns Inwards is often called 'Turnover'. In the illustration in Exhibit 9.1 it is £3,850.

2. Carriage

Carriage (cost of transport of goods) into a firm is called Carriage Inwards. Carriage of goods out of a firm to its customers is called Carriage Outwards.

When goods are bought the cost of carriage inwards may either be included as part of the price, or else the firm may have to pay separately for it. Suppose the firm was buying exactly the same goods. One supplier might sell them for £100, and he would deliver the goods and not send you a bill for carriage. Another supplier might sell the goods for £95, but you would have to pay £5 to a haulage firm for carriage inwards, i.e. a total cost of £100.

To keep cost of buying goods being shown on the same basis, carriage inwards is always added to the purchases in the Trading Account.

Carriage outwards to customers is not part of our firm's expenses in buying goods, and is always entered in the profit and loss account.

Suppose that in the illustration shown in this chapter, the goods had been bought for the same total figure of £3,120, but in fact £2,920 was the figure for purchases and £200 for carriage inwards. The trial balance and trading account appear as Exhibit 9.2.

Exhibit 9.2

Trial Balance as at 31 December 19-5

	Dr	Cr
	£	£
Sales		4,000
Purchases	2,920	
Returns inwards	150	
Returns outwards		220
Carriage inwards	200	

Trading and Profit and Loss Account for the year ended 31 December 19-5

	£	£		£	£
Purchases	2,920		Sales	4,000	
Less Returns outwards	220	2,700	*Less* Returns inwards	150	3,850
Carriage inwards		200			
		2,900			
Less Closing stock		300			
Cost of goods sold		2,600			
Gross profit c/d		1,250			
		3,850			3,850
			Gross profit b/d		1,250

It can be seen that Exhibits 7.1, 9.1 and 9.2 have been concerned with the same overall amount of goods bought and sold by the firm, at the same overall prices. Therefore, as shown, in each case the same gross profit of £1,250 is shown.

Before you proceed further you are to attempt Assignment Exercises 9.1 and 9.2A.

B. Swift's Second Year

At the end of his second year of trading, on 31 December 19-6, B. Swift extracts another trial balance.

Exhibit 9.3

B. Swift
Trial Balance as at 31 December 19-6

	Dr	Cr
	£	£
Sales		6,700
Purchases	4,260	
Lighting and Heating expenses	190	
Rent	240	
Wages: shop assistant	520	
General expenses	70	
Carriage outwards	110	
Buildings	2,000	
Fixtures and fittings	750	
Debtors	1,200	
Creditors		900
Bank	120	
Cash	40	
Loan from J. Marsh		1,000
Drawings	900	
Capital		2,100
Stock (at 31 December 19-5)	300	
	10,700	10,700

The stock shown in the trial balance is that brought forward from the previous year on 31 December 19-5; it is therefore the opening stock of 19-6. The closing stock at 31 December 19-6 can only be found by stocktaking. Assume it amounts at cost to be £550.

First of all calculate the cost of goods sold, showing the calculation in a normal arithmetical fashion.

	£
Stock of goods at start of year	300
Add purchases	4,260
Total goods available for sale	4,560
Less what remains at the end of the year:	
i.e. stock of goods at close	550
Therefore cost of goods that have	
been sold	4,010

Now look at a diagram to illustrate this in Exhibit 9.4.

Exhibit 9.4

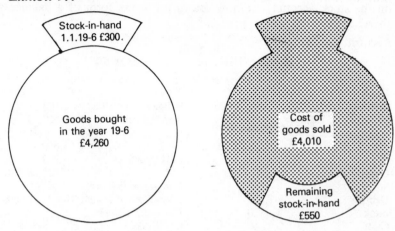

The sales were £6,700, so Sales £6,700 − Cost of Goods Sold £4,010 − Gross Profit £2,690.

Now the trading and profit and loss accounts can be drawn up using double-entry. See Exhibit 9.5.

Exhibit 9.5

B. Swift
Trading and Profit and Loss Account for the year ended 31 December 19-6

	£		£
Opening stock	300	Sales	6,700
Add Purchases	4,260		
	4,560		
Less Closing stock	550		
Cost of goods sold	4,010		
Gross profit c/d	2,690		
	6,700		6,700
Wages	520	Gross profit b/d	2,690
Lighting and Heating expenses	190		
Rent	240		
General expenses	70		
Carriage outwards	110		
Net profit	1,560		
	2,690		2,690

The balances now remaining in the books, including the new balance on the stock account, are now drawn up in the form of a balance sheet. See Exhibit 9.6.

Exhibit 9.6

B. Swift
Balance Sheet as at 31 December 19-6

	£	£		£	£
Fixed Assets			*Capital*		
Buildings		2,000	Balance 1 Jan 19-6	2,100	
Fixtures and fittings		750	Add Net Profit for year	1,560	
		2,750		3,660	
			Less Drawings	900	
Current Assets					2,760
Stock	550		*Long-term liability*		
Debtors	1,200		Loan from J. Marsh		1,000
Bank	120		*Current Liabilities*		
Cash	40		Creditors		900
		1,910			
		4,660			4,660

Stock Account

It is perhaps helpful if the stock account covering both years can now be seen:

Stock

19-5	£	19-6	£
Dec 31 Trading A/c	300	Jan 1 Trading A/c	300
19-6			
Dec 31 Trading A/c	550		

Final Accounts

The term 'Final Accounts' is often used to mean collectively the trading and profit and loss accounts and the balance sheet. The term can be misleading as the balance sheet is not an account.

Other Expenses in the Trading Account

The costs of putting goods into a saleable condition should be charged in the Trading Account. In the case of a trader these are relatively few. An instance could be a trader who sells clocks packed in boxes. If he bought the clocks from one source, and the boxes from another source, both of these items would be charged in the Trading Account as Purchases. In addition, if a man's wages are paid to pack the clocks, then such wages would be charged in the Trading Account. The wages of shop assistants who sold the clocks would be charged in the Profit and Loss Account. The wages of the man packing the clocks would be the only wages in this instance concerned with 'putting the goods into a saleable condition'.

Assignment Exercises

9.1 From the following details draw up the Trading Account of T. Clarke for the year ended 31 December 19-3, which was his first year in business:

	£
Carriage inwards	670
Returns outwards	495
Returns inwards	890
Sales	38,742
Purchases	33,333
Stocks of goods: 31 December 19-3	7,489

9.2A The following details for the year ended 31 March 19-8 are available. Draw up the Trading Account of K. Taylor for that year.

	£
Stocks: 31 March 19-8	18,504
Returns inwards	1,372
Returns outwards	2,896
Purchases	53,397
Carriage inwards	1,122
Sales	54,600

9.3 From the following trial balance of R. Graham draw up a trading and profit and loss account for the year ended 30 September 19-6, and a balance sheet as at that date.

	Dr	Cr
	£	£
Stock 1 October 19-5	2,368	
Carriage outwards	200	
Carriage inwards	310	
Returns inwards	205	
Returns outwards		322
Purchases	11,874	
Sales		18,600
Salaries and wages	3,862	
Rent	304	
Insurance	78	
Motor expenses	664	
Office expenses	216	
Lighting and Heating expenses	166	
General expenses	314	
Premises	5,000	
Motor vehicles	1,800	
Fixtures and fittings	350	
Debtors	3,896	
Creditors		1,731
Cash at bank	482	
Drawings	1,200	
Capital		12,636
	33,289	33,289

Stock at 30 September 19-6 was £2,946.

9.4 The following trial balance was extracted from the books of B. Jackson on 30 April 19-7. From it, and the notes, prepare his trading and profit and loss account for the year ended 30 April 19-7, and a balance sheet as at that date.

	Dr	Cr
	£	£
Sales		18,600
Purchases	11,556	
Stock 1 May 19-6	3,776	
Carriage outwards	326	
Carriage inwards	234	
Returns inwards	440	
Returns outwards		355
Salaries and wages	2,447	
Motor expenses	664	
Rent	576	
Sundry expenses	1,202	
Motor vehicles	2,400	
Fixtures and fittings	600	
Debtors	4,577	
Creditors		3,045
Cash at bank	3,876	
Cash in hand	120	
Drawings	2,050	
Capital		12,844
	34,844	34,844

Stock at 30 April 19-7 was £4,998.

9.5A The following is the trial balance of J. Smailes as at 31 March 19-6. Draw up a set of final accounts for the year ended 31 March 19-6.

	Dr	Cr
	£	£
Stock 1 April 19-5	18,160	
Sales		92,340
Purchases	69,185	
Carriage inwards	420	
Carriage outwards	1,570	
Returns outwards		640
Wages and salaries	10,240	
Rent	3,015	
Communication expenses	624	
Commissions payable	216	
Insurance	405	
Sundry expenses	318	
Buildings	20,000	
Debtors	14,320	
Creditors		8,160
Fixtures	2,850	
Cash at bank	2,970	
Cash in hand	115	
Loan from K. Ball		10,000
Drawings	7,620	
Capital		40,888
	152,028	152,028

Stock at 31 March 19-6 was £22,390.

9.6A L. Stokes drew up the following trial balance as at 30 September 19-8. You are to draft trading and profit and loss accounts for the year to 30 September 19-8 and a balance sheet as at that date.

	Dr £	Cr £
Loan from P. Owens		5,000
Capital		25,955
Drawings	8,420	
Cash at bank	3,115	
Cash in hand	295	
Debtors	12,300	
Creditors		9,370
Stock 30 September 19-7	23,910	
Motor van	4,100	
Office equipment	6,250	
Sales		130,900
Purchases	92,100	
Returns inwards	550	
Carriage inwards	215	
Returns outwards		307
Carriage outwards	309	
Motor expenses	1,630	
Rent	2,970	
Telephone charges	405	
Wages and salaries	12,810	
Insurance	492	
Office expenses	1,377	
Sundry expenses	284	
	171,532	171,532

Stock at 30 September 19-8 was £27,475.

10 Accounting Concepts and Statements of Standard Accounting Practice

The book so far has, in the main, been concerned with the recording of transactions in the books. Much of the rest of the book is about the classifying, summarizing and interpreting of the records that have been made. Before this second stage is reached it would be beneficial for the reader to examine the concepts of accounting, and the Statements of Standard Accounting Practice (from now on this will be abbreviated as SSAP).

The work that you have done in this subject so far has been based on various assumptions. These assumptions have deliberately not been discussed in much detail, they are much easier to understand after basic double entry has been dealt with. These assumptions are known as the 'concepts' of accounting.

The Trading and Profit and Loss Account and Balance Sheets shown in the previous chapter were drawn up so as to be of benefit to the owner of the business. Of course, as is shown later in the book, businesses are often owned by more than just one person and these accounting statements are for the benefit of them all. Now in the case of a sole trader he may well also use copies of the Final Accounts for the purpose of showing them as evidence when he wants to obtain a loan from a bank or from some other person. He may well also show a copy to someone who is interested in buying his business from him, or if he wants to have extended credit for a large amount from a supplier, as proof of his financial stability. In the case of partners and shareholders for businesses owned by more than one person the final accounts will be used for similar purposes.

Now of course if it had always been the custom to draft different kinds of final accounts for different purposes, so that one type was given to a banker, another type to someone wishing to buy the business, etc., then Accounting would be different than it is today. However, as yet it is deemed appropriate to give copies of the same set of final accounts to all the various parties, so that the banker, the prospective buyer of the business, the owner and the other people involved see the same Trading and Profit and Loss Account and Balance Sheet. This is not really an ideal situation as the interests of each party are different and really demand different kinds of information from that possessed by the others. For instance the bank manager would really like to know how much the assets would fetch if the firm ceased trading, so that he could judge in that case what the possibility would be of the bank obtaining repayment of its loan. Other parties would also like to see the information expressed in terms of values which were relevant to them. Yet in fact normally only one sort of final accounts is available for these different parties.

This means that Trading and Profit and Loss Accounts are multi-purpose documents, and to be of any use the various parties have to agree to the way in which they are drawn up. Assume that you are in a class of students and that you are faced with the problem of valuing your assets, which consists of 10 text-books. The first value you decide to assess is that of how much you could sell them for. Your own assessment is £30, but the other members of the class may give figures ranging from (say) £15 to £50. Suppose that you now decide to put a value on their use to you. You may well think that the use of these books will enable you to pass your examinations and so you will get a good job. Another person may well have completely the opposite idea concerning the use of the books to him. The use values placed on the book by individuals will therefore tend to vary widely. Finally you decide to value them by reference to cost. You take out of your pocket the bills for the books which show that you paid a total of £60 for the books. Assuming that the rest of the class do not think that you have altered the bills in any way, then they also can all agree that the value expressed as cost is £60. As this is the only value that you can all agree to then each of you decides to use the idea of showing the value of his asset of books at the cost price.

The use of a measure which gains consensus of opinion, rather than to use one's own measure which might conflict with other people's, is said to be objective. Thus the use of cost for asset valuation is an attempt to be objective. On the other hand the use of your own measure irrespective of whether people agree with it or not is said to be subjective. The desire to provide the same set of accounts for many different parties, and thus to provide a measure that gains their consensus of opinion, means that objectivity is sought for in financial accounting. If you are able to understand this desire for objectivity, then many of the apparent contradictions can be understood because it is often at the heart of the financial accounting methods in use at the present time.

Financial Accounting seeks objectivity, and of course it must have rules which lay down the way in which the activities of the business are recorded. These rules are known as concepts.

Basic Concepts

1. The Cost Concept

The need for this has already been described. It means that assets are normally shown at cost price, and that this is the basis for assessing the future usage of the asset.

2. The Money Measurement Concept

Accounting is only concerned with those facts that can be measured in monetary terms with a fair degree of objectivity. This means that Accounting can never show the whole of the information needed to give you a full picture of the state of the business or how well it is being conducted. Accounting does not record that the firm has a good, or a bad, management team. It does not show that the poor morale prevalent among the staff is about to lead to a serious strike, or that various managers will not co-operate with one another. Nor would it reveal that a rival product is about to take over a larger part of the market occupied at present by the firm's own goods.

This means quite simply that just looking at a set of accounting figures does not tell you all that you would like to know about a business. Some people imagine that Accounting gives you a full picture, but from what has been said they are quite obviously deluding themselves. Others would maintain that really Accounting ought to put monetary values on these other factors as yet ignored in Accounting. Those who object to this state that this would mean a considerable loss of objectivity. Imagine trying to place a value of the future services to be given to the firm by one of its managers. Different people would tend to give different figures, and so, at present, as the final accounts are of a multi-purpose nature, which figures would be acceptable to the many parties who use the accounts? As the answer is that no one set of acceptable figures could be agreed in this case by all parties, then in Accounting as it stands the task is just not undertaken at all. It would seem likely that, eventually the vital factor of placing a value on labour and management, usually known as 'Human Asset' accounting, will play a full part in the construction of balance sheets.

3. The Going Concern Concept

Unless the opposite is known accounting always assumes that the business will continue to operate for an indefinitely long period of time. Only if the business was going to be sold would it be necessary to show how much the assets would fetch. In the accounting records normally this is assumed to be of no interest to the firm. This is obviously connected with the cost concept, as if firms were not assumed to be going concerns the cost concept could not really be used, e.g. if firms were always to be treated as though they were going to be sold immediately after the accounting records were drafted, then the saleable value of the assets would be more relevant than cost.

4. The Business Entity Concept

The transactions recorded in a firm's books are the transactions that affect the firm. The only attempt to show how the transactions affect the owners of a business is limited to showing how their capital in the firm is affected. For instance, a proprietor puts £1,000 more cash into the firm as capital. The books will then show that the firm has £1,000 more cash and that his capital has increased by £1,000. They do not show that he has £1,000 less cash in his private resources. The accounting records are therefore limited to the firm and do not extend to the personal resources of the proprietors.

5. The Realization Concept

In accounting, profit is normally regarded as being earned at the time when the goods or services are passed to the customer and he incurs liability for them, i.e. this is the point at which the profit is treated as being realized. Note that it is not when the order is received, nor the contract signed, neither is it dependent on waiting until the customer pays for the goods or services. It can mean that profit is brought into account in one period, and it is found to have been incorrectly taken as such when the goods are returned in a later period because of some deficiency. Also the services can turn out to be subject to an allowance being given in a later period owing to poor performance. If the allowances or returns can be reasonably estimated an adjustment may be made to the calculated profit in the period when they passed to the customer.

6. The Dual Aspect Concept

This states that there are two aspects of Accounting, one represented by the assets of the business and the other by the claims against them. The concept states that these two aspects are always equal to each other. In other words:

Assets = Liabilities + Capital.

Double entry is the name given to the method of recording the transactions so that the dual aspect concept is upheld.

7. The Accruals Concept

The fact that net profit is said to be the difference between revenues and expenses rather than between cash receipts and expenditures is known as the Accruals Concept. A great deal of attention is therefore paid to this which, when the mechanics needed to bring about the Accruals Concept are being performed, is known as 'matching' expenses against revenues.

This concept is particularly misunderstood by people not well versed in Accounting. To many of them, actual payment of an item in a period is taken as being matched against the revenue of the period when the net profit is calculated. The fact that expenses consist of the assets used up in a particular period in obtaining the revenues of that period, and that cash paid in a period and expenses of a period are usually different as you will see later, comes as a surprise to a great number of them.

Further Over-riding Concepts

The concepts of Accounting already discussed have become accepted in the business world, their assimilation having taken place over many years. These concepts, however, are capable of being interpreted in many ways. What has therefore grown up in Accounting are generally accepted approaches to the application of the earlier concepts. The main ones in these further concepts may be said to be: 1. Materiality, 2. Prudence, 3. Consistency.

1. Materiality

Accounting does not serve a useful purpose if the effort of recording a transaction in a certain way is not worthwhile. Thus, if a box of paperclips was bought it would be used up over a period of time, and this cost is used up every time someone uses a paper-clip. It is possible to record this as an expense every time it happens, but obviously the price of a box of paper-clips is so little that it is not worth recording it in this fashion. The box of paper-clips is not a material item, and therefore would be charged as an expense in the period it was bought, irrespective of the fact that it could last for more than one accounting period. In other words do not waste your time in the elaborate recording of trivial items.

Similarly, the purchase of a cheap metal ashtray would also be charged as an expense in the period it was bought because it is not a material item, even though it may in fact last for twenty years. A motor lorry would however be deemed to be a material item, and so, as will be seen in chapter on depreciation, an attempt is made to charge each period with the cost consumed in each period of its use.

Firms fix all sorts of arbitrary rules to determine what is material and what is not. There is no law that lays down what these should be, the decision as to what is material and what is not is dependent upon judgment. A firm may well decide that all items under £100 should be treated as expenses in the period which they were bought even though they may well be in use in the firm for the following ten years. Another firm, especially a large one, may fix the limit of £1,000. Different limits may be set for different types of items.

It can be seen that the size and the type of firm will affect the decisions as to which items are material. With individuals, an amount of £1,000 may well be more than you, as a student, possess. For a multi-millionaire as to what is a material item and what is not will almost certainly not be comparable. Just as individuals vary then so do firms. Some firms have a great deal of machinery and may well treat all items of machinery costing less than £1,000 as not being material, whereas another firm which makes about the same amount of profits, but has very little machinery, may well treat a £600 machine as being a material item as they have fixed their limit at £250.

2. Prudence

Very often an accountant has to make a choice as to which figure he will take for a given item. The prudence concept means that normally he will take the figure which will understate rather than overstate the profit. Alternatively, this could be expressed as choosing the figure which will cause the capital of the firm to be shown at a lower amount rather than at a higher one. This could also be said to be to make sure that all losses are recorded in the books, but that profits should not be anticipated by recording them prematurely.

It was probably this concept that led to accountants being portrayed as being rather miserable by nature; they were used to favouring looking on the black side of things and ignoring the bright side. However, the concept has been considerable changes in the last few decades, and there has been a shift along the scale away from the gloomy view and more towards the desire to paint a brighter picture when it is warranted.

3. Consistency

The concepts already listed are so broad that in fact there are many different ways in which items may be recorded in the accounts. Each firm should, within these limits, select the methods which give the most equitable picture of the activities of the business. However, this cannot be done if one method is used in one year and another method in the next year and so on. Constantly changing the methods would lead to a distortion of the profits calculated from the accounting records. Therefore the concept of consistency comes into play. This concept is that when a firm has once fixed a method of the accounting treatment of an item it will enter all similar items that follow in exactly the same way.

However, it does not bind the firm to following the method until the firm closes down. A firm can change the method used, but such a change is not affected without the deepest consideration. When such a change occurs and the profits calculated in that year are affected by a material amount, then either in the profit and loss account itself or in one of the reports accompanying it, the effect of the change should be stated.

Stock Valuation and Accounting Concepts

Stock valuation provides a good example of the combined use of several concepts. The first concept to be used is the cost concept, so that, as you have been told already, stock is normally valued at its cost price to us. However, there is always a chance that some or all of our stock may have to be sold for less than its cost price. In this case the prudence concept is brought into play. Here we would value that part of the stock, not at its cost price, but at its 'net realisable value'. This term means the sale price expected less selling expenses. We can thus see one concept, in this case cost, being overridden by another one, 'prudence'.

Of course there are limitations when using concepts. How do we know for certain that the stock is going to be sold at all? The answer is that we simply do not know, all we can do is to use our concepts on what we think is going to happen. An owner of a shop selling a certain kind of foodstuff may find overnight that he has to destroy all of his stock without compensation, because some forms of highly poisonous substances have been found in the foodstuffs and several customers have lost their lives. Almost certainly he would never have imagined such a probability when he last valued his stock, which has proved to be worth, not its cost price, but absolutely nothing at all.

Even where such an unusual thing is not present, it is very often the case that you do not know for certain for how much you can sell your stock. You may not be far wrong from the truth as seen eventually, but you will often be wrong. We all guess all of the time. You may think that you *will* be at the college at 9 a.m. tomorrow morning, but you are guessing. Your bus may not turn up, you may be held up for a long time by traffic lights, you may oversleep, you may be ill, your house may set on fire and so on. Similarly we have to guess at future events when valuing stock.

The concept of materiality will also come into play. Imagine that we have about a ton of a particular kind of powder matter which is very cheap to buy, and it would be very troublesome and expensive to weigh it exactly. In such a case we might possibly estimate the weight of the stuff simply by looking at it rather than weighing it carefully. In this case an exact calculation is not worthwhile, therefore we will not attempt to be so precise.

It is almost certain as well that the going concern concept will be used. There can be a great deal of difference between the selling price of our stock if the business is carried on as a going concern rather than one which stops trading, and then has to sell its stock off quickly.

We will also have to use the concept of consistency when valuing stock. We cannot normally value stock using one method at the end of one year and then change it to another at the end of the next year.

Finally, there is a limitation to anyone's understanding of the value of stock in that the cost concept may be interpreted in different ways, as 'cost' can have several meanings. This is not the place to discuss this aspect in detail, but students who take Accounting in the second year will examine the meanings of the Last In, First Out method (LIFO), the First In, First Out method (FIFO), and the Average Cost methods (AVCO).

The Assumption of the Stability of Currency

One does not have to be very old to remember that a few years ago many goods could be bought with less money than today. If one listens to one's parents or grandparents then many stories will be heard of how little this item or the other could be bought for *x* years ago. The currencies of the countries of the world are not stable in terms of what each unit of currency can buy over the years.

Accounting, however, uses the cost concept, this stating that the asset is normally shown at its cost price. This means that accounting statements will be distorted because assets will be bought at different points in time at the price then ruling, and the figures totalled up to show the value of the assets in cost terms. As an instance, suppose that you had bought a building 20 years ago for £20,000. You now decide to buy an identical additional building, but the price has now risen to £40,000. You buy it, and the buildings account now shows buildings at a figure of £60,000. One building is measured cost-wise in terms of the currency of 20 years ago, whilst the other is taken at today's currency value. The figure of a total of £60,000 is historically correct, but, other than that, the total figure cannot be said to be particularly valid for any other use.

This means that to make a correct assessment of accounting statements one must bear in mind the distorting effects of changing price levels upon the accounting entries as recorded. There are techniques of adjusting accounts so as to try and eliminate these distortions, but these are outside the scope of this book.

Statements of Standard Accounting Practice (SSAP's)

Despite the use of the concepts there will still be differences of opinion between accountants when profits are being calculated. In the late 1960's a number of cases led to a general outcry against the lack of uniformity in Accounting. One concerned the takeover of AEI (Associated Electrical Industries) by GEC (General Electric Company). AEI had resisted the takeover, and had produced a profit forecast, in the tenth month of their financial year, that profit before tax for the year would be £10 million. After the takeover, the accounts for AEI for that year showed a loss of £4½ million. Of this difference of £14½ million, £5 million was said to be matters of fact, whilst the remaining £9½ million was attributed to adjustments which remain matters substantially of judgement arising from variations in accounting policies.

To reduce the possibility of such large variations in reported profits, the accountancy bodies have responded by issuing SSAP's, these are Statements of Standard Accounting Practice. 23 SSAP's have been issued to the date of writing this impression of the book. Accountants and auditors are expected to comply with the SSAP's, if they are not complied with then the audit report should give the reasons why the SSAP has been ignored.

The advent of the SSAP's does not mean that the two identical businesses already described will show exactly the same profits year by year. They have, however, considerably reduced the possibilities of very large variations in such profit reporting.

In this book the SSAP's will only be mentioned when it is essential.

11 The Division of the Ledger

While the firm is very small indeed, all the double-entry accounts could be kept in one book, which we would call the ledger. As the firm grows it would be found impossible just to use one book, as the larger number of pages needed for a lot of transactions would mean that the book would be too big to handle (but see effect of computers – later in this chapter).

This problem could be solved in several ways. One method would be to have more than one ledger, but the accounts contained in each ledger would be chosen simply by chance. There would be no set method for deciding which account should go into which ledger. This would not be very efficient, as it would be difficult to remember which accounts were in each ledger.

Another method would be to divide the ledger up into different books and each book would be for a specific purpose or function. The functions could be:

(a) One book just for customers' personal accounts. We could call this the Sales Ledger.
(b) Another book just for suppliers' personal accounts. We could call this the Purchases Ledger or Bought Ledger.
(c) A book concerned with the receiving and paying out of money both by cash and cheque. This would be a Cash Book.
(d) The remaining accounts would be contained in a Ledger which we could call a General Ledger, an alternative name being a Nominal Ledger.

These ledgers all contain accounts and are part of double entry.

If more than one person becomes involved in book-keeping, the fact that the ledger has been divided into different books would make their job easier. The book-keeping to be done could be split between the people concerned, each book-keeper having charge of one or more books.

The General Ledger would be used quite a lot, because it would contain the sales account, purchases accounts, returns inwards and returns outwards accounts, as well as all the other accounts for assets, expenses, income, etc.

When the General Ledger becomes overloaded, we could deal with this problem by taking a lot of the detailed work out of it. Most entries in it would have been credit sales, credit purchases and returns inwards and returns outwards. We can therefore start four new books, for credit transactions only. One book will be for credit sales (the Sales Journal), one for credit purchases (the Purchases Journal) and one each for Returns Inwards (Returns Inwards Journal) and Returns Outwards (Returns Outwards Journal).

When a credit sale is made it will be entered in the customer's personal account in the Sales Ledger exactly the same as before. However, instead of entering the sale in the sales account in the General Ledger, we would enter it in the Sales Journal. At regular intervals, usually once a month, the total of the Sales Journal would be transferred to the credit of the Sales Account in the General Ledger.

What this means is that even if there were 1,000 credit sales in the month, only one entry, the total of the Sales Journal, would need entering in the General Ledger. This saves the General Ledger from being overloaded with detail.

Similarly credit purchases are entered in the suppliers' account and listed in a Purchases Journal. The total is then entered, at regular intervals, in the debit side of the Purchases Account.

Returns Inwards are entered in the customer's personal accounts, and are listed in the Returns Inwards Journal. The total is then transferred to the debit of the Returns Inwards Account.

Returns Outwards are entered in the suppliers' personal accounts, and are listed in the Returns Outwards Journal. The total is then transferred to the credit of the Returns Outwards Account.
This can be summarized:

Sales Ledger Purchases Ledger Cash Book General Ledger	All contain accounts and are therefore part of the double-entry system
Sales Journal Purchases Journal Returns Inwards Journal Returns Outwards Journal	Mere listing devices to save the accounts in the General Ledger from unnecessary detail.

These will be described in full detail in the following chapters.

Computers and Accounting

In chapter 32 the effect of computers on accounting is examined. At this point it might be thought that the author had never heard of computers, as the text has been discussing 'books' of various sorts, and it is well-known that computers do not use bound books.

In fact the term 'book' or 'journal' is simply a convenient way of describing what is in effect a 'collection point' for a particular type of information. The principles of accounting can therefore be more easily discussed if the author keeps to standard terms. The principles remain exactly the same no matter whether manual, computerised or other mechanical methods are in use.

Classifications of Accounts

Some people describe all accounts either as Personal Accounts or as Impersonal Accounts. Personal accounts are those of debtors and creditors. Impersonal accounts are then divided up further into Real accounts and Nominal accounts. Real accounts refer to accounts in which property is recorded, such as building, machinery, or stock. Nominal accounts are those which are concerned with revenue and expenses.

The Accountant as a Communicator

Quite often the impression is given that all that the accountant does is to produce figures, arranged in various ways. Naturally, such forms of computation do take up quite a lot of the accountant's time, but what then takes up the rest of his time is exactly how he communicates these figures to other people.

First of all, he can obviously arrange the figures in such a way as to present the information in as meaningful a way as possible. Suppose for instance that the figures he has produced are to be given to several people all of whom are very knowledgeable about accounting. He could, in such an instance, present the figures in a normal accounting way, knowing full well that the recipients of the information will understand it.

On the other hand, the accounting figures may well be needed by people who have absolutely no knowledge at all of accounting. In such a case a normal accounting statement would be no use to them at all, they would not understand it. In this case he might set out the figures in a completely different way to try to make it easy for them to grasp. For instance, instead of preparing a normal Trading and Profit and Loss Account he might show it as follows:

		£
In the year ended 31 December 19-6 you sold goods for		50,000
Now how much had those goods cost you to buy?		
At the start of the year you had stock costing	6,000	
+ You bought some more goods in the year costing	28,000	
So altogether you had goods available to sell of	34,000	
− At the end of the year you had stock of goods unsold of	3,000	
So the goods you had sold in the year had cost you	31,000	
Let us deduct this from what you had sold the goods for		31,000
This means that you had made a profit on buying and selling goods, before any other expenses had been paid, amounting to (We call this sort of profit the Gross Profit)		19,000
But you suffered other expenses such as wages, rent, lighting and so on, and during the year the amount of those expenses, not including anything taken for yourself, amounted to		9,000
So, for this year your sales value exceeded all the costs involved in running the business, so that the sales could be made, by (We call this sort of profit the Net Profit)		£10,000

If an accountant cannot arrange the figures to make them meaningful to the recipient then he is failing in his task. His job is not just to produce figures for himself to look at, his job is to communicate these results to other people.

Very often the accountant will have to talk to people to explain the figures, or send a letter or write a report concerning them. He will also have to talk or write to people to find out exactly what sort of accounting information is needed by them or explain to them what sort of information he could provide. This means that if accounting examinations consist simply of computational type questions then they will not test the ability of the candidate to communicate in any other way than by writing down accounting figures. In recent years more attention has been paid by examining boards to these aspects of an accountant's work.

12 The Banking System

Banks operate two main types of account, a current account and a deposit or savings account.

1 Current Accounts

These are the accounts used for the regular banking and withdrawal of money. With this type of account a cheque book will be given by the bank to the customer for him to make payments to people to whom he owes money. He will also be given a paying-in book for him to pay money into the account.

2 Deposit Accounts

This kind of account is one which will be concerned normally with putting money into the bank and not withdrawing it for some time. The usual object of having a deposit account is that interest is given on the balance held in the account, whilst interest is not usually given on balances in current accounts.

The remainder of this chapter will be concerned with current accounts.

Cheques

When the bank has agreed to let you open a current account it will ask you for a specimen signature. This enables them to ensure that your cheques are in fact signed by you, and have not been forged. You will then be issued with a cheque book.

We can then use the cheques to make payments out of the account. Normally we must ensure that we have banked more in the account than the amount paid out. If we wish to pay out more money than we have banked, we will have to see the bank manager. We will then discuss the reasons for this with him, and if he agrees he will give his permission for us to 'overdraw' our account. This is known as a 'bank overdraft'.

The person filling in the cheque and using it for payment, is known as the *drawer*.

The person to whom the cheque is paid is known as the *payee*.

We can now look at Exhibit 12.1, which is a blank cheque form before it is filled in.

Exhibit 12.1

On the face of the cheque are various sets of numbers. These are:

914234   Every cheque printed for the Cheshire Bank will be given a different number, so that individual items can be traced.

09-07-99   Each branch of each bank in the United Kingdom has a different number given to it. Thus this branch has a 'code' number 09-07-99.

058899   Each account with the bank is given a different number. This particular number is kept only for the account of J. Woodstock at the Stockport branch.

When we will in the cheque we copy the details on the counterfoil which we then detach and keep for our records.

We can now look at the completion of a cheque. Let us assume that we are paying seventy-two pounds and eighty-five pence to K. Marsh on 22 May 19-5. Exhibit 12.2 shows the completed cheque.

Exhibit 12.2

In Exhibit 12.2:

The drawer is: J. Woodstock

The payee is: K. Marsh

    The two parallel lines across the face of the cheque are drawn as a safeguard. If we had not done this the cheque would have been an 'uncrossed cheque'. If someone had stolen a signed uncrossed cheque he could have gone to the Stockport branch of the Cheshire Bank and obtained cash in exchange for the cheque. When the cheque is crossed it means it *must* be paid into a bank account, National Giro bank or Savings Bank.

    Cheques can be further safeguarded by using specific crossings, i.e. writing a form of instruction within the crossing on the cheques as shown in Exhibit 12.3.

Exhibit 12.3

These are specific instructions to the banks about the use of the cheque. The use of 'Account Payee only' means the cheques should be paid only into the account of the payee named. If cheques are lost or stolen the drawer must advise his bank immediately and confirm by letter. These cheques will be 'stopped', i.e. payment will not be made on these cheques, provided you act swiftly. The safest crossing is that of 'A/c Payee only, Not Negotiable'. If the cheque is lost or stolen it will be of no use to the thief or finder. This is because it is impossible for this cheque to be paid into any bank account other than that of the named payee.

Paying-in Slips

When we want to pay money into our current accounts, either cash or cheques, or both, we use a paying-in slip. One of these is shown as Exhibit 12.4.

J. Woodstock has banked the following items:

Four	£5 notes
Three	£1 coins
One	50p coin
Other silver	30p
Bronze coins	12p

Cheques received from:		Code numbers:
E. Kane & Son	£184.15	02-58-76
J. Gale	£ 65.44	05-77-85

Exhibit 12.4

Face of paying in-slip

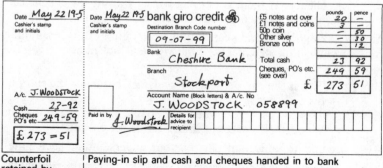

Counterfoil retained by Woodstock

Paying-in slip and cash and cheques handed in to bank

Reverse side of paying-in slip

Details of Cheques, PO's etc					
for cheques please specify **Drawers Name** and	**Bank Code Number** as shown in top right corner				
E. KANE & SON	02-58-76	184	15	184	16
J. GALE	05-77-85	65	44	65	44
In view of the risk of loss in course of clearing, customers are advised to keep an independent record of the drawers of cheques.	Total carried over £	249	59	249	59

Reverse of counterfoil

Cheque Clearings

We will now look at how cheques paid from one person's bank account pass into another person's bank account.

Let us look at the progress of the cheque in Exhibit 12.2. We will assume that the Post Office is being very efficient and delivering all letters the following day after being posted.

19-5

May 22   Woodstock, in Stockport, sends the cheque to K. Marsh, who lives in Leeds. Woodstock enters the payment in his cash book.

May 23   Cheque received by Marsh. He banks it the same day in his bank account at Barclays Bank in Leeds. Marsh shows the cheque in his cash book as being received and banked on 23 May.

May 24   Barclays in London receive it. They exchange it with the Head Office of the Cheshire Bank in London.
The Cheshire bank send the cheque to their Stockport branch.

May 25   The Stockport branch of the Cheshire bank examine the cheque. If there is nothing wrong with it, the cheque can now be debited by the bank to J. Woodstock's account.

Anyone taking the second year option Accounting will be examining bank reconciliation statements. What we have looked at —

19-5

May 22   This is the day on which Woodstock has made the entry in his cash book.

May 25   This is the day when the bank makes an entry in Woodstock's account in respect of the cheque.

— will become an important part of your understanding such statements.

13 Two Column Cash Books

The cash book is merely the cash account and the bank account brought together in one book. Previously we would have shown these two accounts on two separate pages of the ledger. Now it is more convenient to place the account columns together so that the recording of all money received and of all money paid out on a particular date can be found on the same page. The cash book is ruled so that the debit column of the cash account is placed alongside the debit column of the bank account, and the credit columns of the cash and the bank accounts are also placed alongside each other.

We can now look at a cash account and a bank account in Exhibit 13.1 as they would have been if they had been kept separately, and then in Exhibit 13.2 as they would be shown if the transactions had instead been kept in a cash book.

The bank column contains details of the payments made by cheques and of the money received and paid into the bank account. The bank which is handling the firm's money will of course have a copy of the account in its own books. The bank will periodically send a copy of the account in the bank's books to the firm, this copy usually being known as the Bank Statement. When the firm receives the bank statement it will check it against the bank column in its own cash book to ensure that there are no discrepancies.

Exhibit 13.1

Cash

19-5		£	19-5		£
Aug	1 Balance b/d	33	Aug	8 Rent	20
,,	5 G. Bernard	25	,,	12 M. Prince	19
,,	15 B. Hussey	37	,,	28 Wages	25
,,	30 H. Howe	18	,,	31 Balance c/d	49
		113			113
Sept 1	Balance b/d	49			

Bank

19-5		£	19-5		£
Aug 1 Balance b/d		949	Aug 7 Rates		105
,, 3 I. Powell Ltd		295	,, 12 D. Squire Ltd		95
,, 16 G. Potter		408	,, 26 N. Foster		268
,, 30 B. Smith		20	,, 31 Balance c/d		1,204
		1,672			1,672
Sept 1 Balance b/d		1,204			

Exhibit 13.2

Cash Book

19-5	Cash £	Bank £	19-5	Cash £	Bank £
Aug 1 Balances b/d	33	949	Aug 7 Rates		105
,, 3 I. Powell Ltd		295	,, 8 Rent	20	
,, 5 G. Bernard	25		,, 12 M. Prince	19	
,, 15 B. Hussey	37		,, ,, D. Squire Ltd		95
,, 16 G. Potter		408	,, 26 N. Foster		268
,, 30 B. Smith		20	,, 28 Wages	25	
,, ,, H. Howe	18		,, 31 Balance c/d	49	1,204
	113	1,672		113	1,672
Sept 1 Balances b/d	49	1,204			

Cash Paid into the Bank

In Exhibit 13.2, the payments into the bank have consisted of cheques received by the firm which have been banked immediately. There is, however, the case to be considered of cash being paid into the bank.

Now let us look at the position when a customer pays his account in cash, and later a part of this cash is paid into the bank. The receipt of the cash is debited to the cash column on the date received, the credit entry being in the customer's personal account. The cash banked has the following effect needing action as shown:

Effect	*Action*
1. Asset of cash is decreased	Credit the asset account, i.e. the cash account which is represented by the cash column in the cash book.
2. Asset of bank is increased	Debit the asset account, i.e. the bank account which is represented by the bank column in the cash book.

A cash receipt of £100 from J. Davies on 1 August 19-5, later followed by the banking on 3 August of £80 of this amount would appear in the cash book as follows:

	Cash	Bank		Cash	Bank
19-5	£	£	19-5	£	£
Aug 1 J. Davies	100		Aug 3 Bank	80	
,, 3 Cash		80			

The details column shows entries against each item stating the name of the account in which the completion of double entry had taken place. Against the cash payment of £80 appears the word 'bank', meaning that the debit £80 is to be found in the bank column, and the opposite applies.

Where the whole of the cash received is banked immediately the receipt can be treated in exactly the same manner as a cheque received, i.e. it can be entered directed in the bank column.

Sometimes, when the firm requires cash for future payments and it has not got a sufficient amount of cash in hand for the purpose, it may withdraw cash from the bank. This is done by making out a cheque to pay itself a certain amount of cash. The proprietor, or an authorized person, visits the bank where he is given cash in exchange for the cheque. This is sometimes known as 'cashing' a cheque for business use.

The twofold effect and the action required may be summarized:

Effect	Action
1. Asset of bank is decreased.	Credit the asset account, i.e. the bank column in the cash book.
2. Asset of cash is increased.	Debit the asset account, i.e. the cash column in the cash book.

A withdrawal of £75 cash on 1 June 19-5 from the bank would appear in the cash book thus:

	Cash	Bank		Cash	Bank
19-5	£	£	19-5	£	£
June 1 Bank	75		June 1 Cash		75

Where an item does not need entering in another book as double entry has already taken place within the cash book, then this item is known as a 'contra' being the Latin word for against. Thus cash paid into the bank and cash withdrawn from the bank are both contra items. As there is a debit item and a credit item for the same amount double entry has already been completed, so that no account exists elsewhere for contra items in the cash book.

The Use of Folio Columns

As you have already seen, the details column in an account contains the name of the other account in which double entry has been completed. Anyone looking through the books for any purpose would therefore be helped to find where the other half of the double entry was situated. However, with the growth in the number of books in use the mere mention of the name of the other account would not be sufficient to give quick reference to the other account. An extra aid is therefore needed and this is brought about by the use of a 'folio' column. In each account and in each book in use an extra column is added, this always being shown on the immediate left of the money columns. In this column the name of the other book, in abbreviated form, and the number of the page in the other book where double entry is completed is stated against each and every entry in the books.

Thus an entry of receipt of cash from C. Koote whose account was on page 45 of the sales ledger, and the cash recorded on page 37 of the cash book, would use the folio column thus:

In the cash book. In the folio column alongside the entry of the amount would appear SL 45.

In the sales ledger. In the folio column alongside the entry of the amount would appear CB 37.

By this means full cross reference would be given. Each of the contra items, being shown on the same page of the cash book, would use the letter 'C' in the folio column.

The folio column is only filled in when double entry for the item has been completed. The act of using one book as a means for entering the items to the other account so as to complete double entry is known as 'posting' the items. Where the folio column has not been filled it will be seen at a glance that double entry has not been completed, thus the error made when only one-half of the double-entry is completed is made less often and can often be detected easily.

A Worked Example

The following transactions are written up in the form of a cash book. The folio columns are also filled in as though double entry had been completed to the other ledgers.

19-5			£
Sept	1	Balances brought forward from last month:	
		Cash	20
		Bank	940
,,	2	Received cheque from M. Black	115
,,	4	Cash sales	82
,,	6	Paid rent by cash	35
,,	7	Banked £50 of the cash held by the firm	50
,,	15	Cash sales paid direct into the bank	40
,,	23	Paid cheque to M. Brown	277
,,	29	Withdrew cash from bank	120
,,	30	Paid wages in cash	118

Cash Book

		Folio	Cash	Bank				Folio	Cash	Bank
19-5			£	£	19-5				£	£
Sept	1 Balances	b/d	20	940	Sept	6	Rent	GL65	35	
,,	2 M. Black	SL98		115	,,	7	Bank	C	50	
,,	4 Sales	GL87	82		,,	23	M. Brown	PL23		277
,,	7 Cash	C		50	,,	29	Cash	C		120
,,	15 Sales	GL87		40	,,	30	Wages	GL39	118	
,,	29 C		120		,,	30	Balances	c/d	19	748
			222	1,145					222	1,145
Oct	1 Balances	b/d	19	748						

Assignment Exercises

13.1 Write up a two-column cash book from the following details, and balance off as at the end of the month:

19-5

May 1 Started business with capital in cash £100
,, 2 Paid rent by cash £10
,, 3 F. Lake lent us £500, paying by cheque
,, 4 We paid B. McKenzie by cheque £65
,, 5 Cash sales £98
,, 7 N. Miller paid us by cheque £62
,, 9 We paid B. Burton in cash £22
,, 11 Cash sales paid direct into the bank £53
,, 15 G. Moores paid us in cash £65
,, 16 We took £50 out of the cash till and paid it into the bank account
,, 19 We repaid F. Lake £100 by cheque
,, 22 Cash sales paid direct into the bank £66
,, 26 Paid motor expenses by cheque £12
,, 30 Withdrew £100 cash from the bank for business use
,, 31 Paid wages in cash £97.

13.2 Write up a two-column cash book from the following details, and balance off as at the end of the month:

19-6

Mar 1 Balances brought down from last month:
　　　Cash in hand £56: Cash in bank £2,356
,, 2 Paid rates by cheque £156
,, 3 Paid for postage stamps in cash £5
,, 5 Cash sales £74
,, 7 Cash paid into bank £60
,, 8 We paid T. Lee by cheque £75: We paid C. Brooks in cash £2
,, 12 J. Moores pays us £150, £50 being in cash and £100 by cheque
,, 17 Cash drawings by proprietor £20
,, 20 P. Jones pays us by cheque £79
,, 22 Withdrew £200 from the bank for business use
,, 24 Bought a new motor van for £195 cash
,, 28 Paid rent by cheque £40
,, 31 Cash sales paid direct into the bank £105.

13.3A A two-column cash book is to be written up from the following, carrying the balances down to the following month:

19-4

Jan	1	Started business with £4,000 in the bank
,,	2	Paid for fixtures by cheque £660
,,	4	Cash sales £225: Paid rent by cash £140
,,	6	T. Thomas paid us by cheque £188
,,	8	Cash sales paid direct into the bank £308
,,	10	J. King paid us in cash £300
,,	12	Paid wages in cash £275
,,	14	J. Walters lent us £500 paying by cheque
,,	15	Withdrew £200 from the bank for business use
,,	20	Bought stationery paying by cash £60
,,	22	We paid J. French by cheque £166
,,	28	Cash Drawings £100
,,	30	J. Scott paid us by cheque £277
,,	31	Cash Sales £66.

13.4A Write up a two-column cash book from the following:

19-6

Nov	1	Balance brought forward from last month: Cash £105; Bank £2,164
,,	2	Cash Sales £605
,,	3	Took £500 out of the cash till and paid it into the bank
,,	4	J. Matthews paid us by cheque £217
,,	5	We paid for postage stamps in cash £60
,,	6	Bought office equipment by cheque £189
,,	7	We paid J. Lucas by cheque £50
,,	9	Received rates refund by cheque £72
,,	11	Withdrew £250 from the bank for business use
,,	12	Paid wages in cash £239
,,	14	Paid motor expenses by cheque £57
,,	16	L. Levy lent us £200 in cash
,,	20	R. Norman paid us by cheque £112
,,	28	We paid general expenses in cash £22
,,	30	Paid insurance by cheque £74.

14 Cash Discounts and the Three Column Cash Book

Cash Discounts

To encourage customers to pay their accounts promptly a firm may offer to accept a lesser sum in full settlement providing payment is made within a specified period of time. The amount of the reduction of the sum to be paid is known as a cash discount. The term 'cash discount' thus refers to the allowance given for speedy payment, it is still called cash discount, even if the account is paid by cheque.

The rate of cash discount is usually quoted as a percentage, and full details of the percentage allowed and the period within which payment is to be made are quoted on all sales documents by the selling company. A typical period during which discount may be allowed is one month from the date of the original transaction.

A firm will meet with cash discounts in two different ways. First, it may allow cash discounts to firms to whom it sells goods, and second it may receive cash discounts from firms from whom it buys goods. To be able to distinguish easily between the two, the first kind are known as Discounts Allowed, the second kind are known as Discounts Received.

We can now see the effect of discounts by looking at two examples.

Example 1

W. Clarke owed us £100. He pays on 2 September 19-5 by cash within the time limit laid down, and the firm allows him 5 per cent cash discount. Thus he will pay £100 − £5 = £95 in full settlement of his account.

Effect	*Action*
1. Of cash:	
Cash is increased by £95.	Debit cash account, i.e. enter £95 in debit column of cash book.
Asset of debtors is decreased by £95.	Credit W. Clarke £95.

Effect	Action

2. Of discounts:
Asset of debtors is decreased by £5. (After the cash was paid the balance still appeared of £5. As the account is deemed to be settled this asset must now be cancelled.) | Credit W. Clarke £5.

Expenses of discounts allowed increased by £5. | Debit discounts allowed account £5.

Example 2

The firm owed W. Small £400. It pays him on 3 September 19-5 by cheque within the time limit laid down by him and he allows 2½ per cent cash discount. Thus the firm will pay £400 − £10 = £390 in full settlement of the account.

Effect	Action

1. Of cheque:
Asset of bank is reduced by £390. | Credit bank, i.e. enter in credit bank column, £390.
Liability of creditors is reduced by £390. | Debit W. Small's account £390.

2. Of discounts:
Liability of creditors is reduced by £10. (After the cheque was paid the balance of £10 remained. As the account is deemed to be settled the liability must now be cancelled.) | Debit W. Small's account £10.

Revenue of discounts received increased by £10. | Credit discounts received account £10.

The accounts in the firm's books would appear:

Cash Book (Page 32)

		Cash	Bank			Cash	Bank
		£	£			£	£
19-5				19-5			
Sept 2 W. Clarke	SL12	95		Sept 3 W. Small	PL75		390

Discounts Received (General Ledger page 18)

		£
19-5		
Sept 2 W. Small	PL75	10

Discounts Allowed (General Ledger page 17)

19-5		£
Sept 2 W. Clarke SL12		5

W. Clarke (Sales Ledger page 12)

19-5		£	19-5		£
Sept 1 Balance b/d		100	Sept 2 Cash	CB32	95
			,, 2 Discount	GL17	5
		100			100

W. Small (Purchases Ledger page 75)

19-5		£	19-5	£
Sept 3 Bank	CB32	390	Sept 1 Balance b/d	400
,, 3 Discount	GL18	10		
		400		400

It is the accounting custom merely to enter the word 'Discount' in the personal account, not stating whether it is a discount received or a discount allowed. This is obviously to save time as the full description against each discount would be unnecessary. After all, the sales ledger accounts will only contain discounts allowed, and the purchases ledger accounts will only contain discounts received.

The discounts allowed account and the discounts received account are contained in the general ledger along with all the other revenue and expense accounts. It has already been stated that every effort should be made to avoid constant reference to the general ledger. In the case of discounts this is achieved quite simply by adding an extra column on each side of the cash book in which the amounts of discounts are entered. Discounts received are entered in the discounts column on the credit side of the cash book, and discounts allowed in the discounts column on the debit side of the cash book.

The cash book, if completed for the two examples so far dealt with, would appear:

Cash Book

	Discount	Cash	Bank		Discount	Cash	Bank
19-5	£	£	£	19-5	£	£	£
Sept 2 W. Clarke SL12	5	95		Sept 3 W. Small PL75	10		390

There is no alteration to the method of showing discounts in the personal accounts.

The discounts columns in the cash book are not however part of the double entry system. They are merely lists of discounts. Half of the double entry has already been made in the personal accounts.

What is now required is the entry in the discounts accounts. The way that is done in this case is by transferring the total of the discounts received column to the credit of a discounts received account, and the total of the discounts allowed account is transferred to the debit of a discounts allowed account.

This at first sight appears to be incorrect. How can a debit total be transferred to the debit of an account? Here one must look at the entries for discounts in the personal accounts. Discounts allowed have been entered on the credit sides of the individual personal accounts. The entry of the total in the expense account of discount allowed must therefore be on the debit side to preserve double entry balancing. The opposite sides apply to discounts received.

The following is a worked example of a three-column cash book for the whole of a month, showing the ultimate transfer of the totals of the discount columns to the discount accounts.

		£
19-5		
May 1	Balances brought down from April:	
	Cash Balance	29
	Bank Balance	654
	Debtors accounts:	
	B. King	120
	N. Campbell	280
	D. Shand	40
	Creditors accounts:	
	U. Barrow	60
	A. Allen	440
	R. Long	100
,, 2	B. King pays us by cheque, having deducted 2½ per cent cash discount £3	117
,, 8	We pay R. Long his account by cheque, deducting 5 per cent cash discount £5	95
,, 11	We withdrew £100 cash from the bank for business use	100
,, 16	N. Campbell pays us his account by cheque, deducting 2½ per cent discount £7	273
,, 25	We paid wages in cash	92
,, 28	D. Shand pays us in cash after having deducted 2½ per cent cash discount	38
,, 29	We pay U. Barrow by cheque less 5 per cent cash discount £3	57
,, 30	We pay A. Allen by cheque less 2½ per cent cash discount £11	429

Cash Book — Page 64

	Folio	Discount	Cash	Bank		Folio	Discount	Cash	Bank
		£	£	£			£	£	£
19-5					19-5				
May 1					May 8				
Balances	b/d		29	654	R. Long	PL58	5		95
May 2					May 11				
B. King	SL13	3		117	Cash	C			100
May 11					May 25				
Bank	C		100		Wages	GL77		92	
May 16					May 29				
N. Campbell	SL84	7		273	U. Barrow	PL15	3		57
May 28					May 30				
D. Shand	SL91	2	38		A. Allen	PL98	11		429
					May 31				
					Balances	c/d		75	363
		12	167	1,044			19	167	1,044
Jun 1 Balances	b/d		75	363					

Sales Ledger

B. King

19-5			£	19-5				£
May	1 Balance b/d		120	May	2 Bank		CB 64	117
				,,	2 Discount		CB 64	3
			120					120

N. Campbell

19-5			£	19-5				£
May	1 Balance b/d		280	May	16 Bank		CB 64	273
				,,	16 Discount		CB 64	7
			280					280

D. Shand

19-5			£	19-5				£
May	1 Balance b/d		40	May	28 Cash		CB 64	38
				,,	28 Discount		CB 64	2
			40					40

Purchases Ledger

U. Barrow

19-5			£	19-5			£
May	29 Bank	CB 64	57	May	1 Balance b/d		60
,,	29 Discount	CB 64	3				
			60				60

R. Long

19-5			£	19-5			£
May	8 Bank	CB 64	95	May	1 Balance b/d		100
,,	8 Discount	CB 64	5				
			100				100

A. Allen

19-5			£	19-5			£
May	30 Bank	CB 64	429	May	1 Balance b/d		440
,,	30 Discount	CB 64	11				
			440				440

General Ledger

Wages   Page 77

19-5		£
May 25 Cash	CB 64	92

Discounts Received   Page 88

	19-5		£
	May 31 Total for the month	CB 64	19

Discounts Allowed

19-5		£
May 31 Total for the month	CB 64	12

As you can check, the discounts received entered in all of the purchases ledger accounts are £3 + £5 + £11 = £19 on the debit side; the total entered in the discounts received account on the credit side amounts also to £19. Thus double-entry principles are upheld. A check on the discounts allowed will reveal a debit of £12 in the discounts allowed account and a total of £3 + £7 + £2 = £12 on the credit side of the accounts in the sales ledger.

Bank Overdrafts

A firm may borrow money from a bank by means of a bank overdraft. This means that the firm is allowed to pay more out of the bank account, by paying out cheques, for a total amount greater than that which it has placed in the account.

Up to this point the bank balances have all represented money at the bank, thus they have all been assets, i.e. debit balances. When the account is overdrawn the firm owes money to the bank, the account is a liability and the balance becomes a credit one.

Taking the cash book last illustrated, suppose that the amount payable to A. Allen was £1,429 instead of £429. Thus the amount placed in the account, £1,044, is exceeded by the amount withdrawn. The Cash book would appear as follows:

Cash Book

	Discount	Cash	Bank		Discount	Cash	Bank
19-5	£	£	£	19-5	£	£	£
May 1 Balances b/d		29	654	May 8 R. Long	5		95
,, 2 B. King	3		117	,, 11 Cash			100
,, 11 Bank		100		,, 25 Wages		92	
,, 16 N. Campbell	7		273	,, 29 U. Barrow	3		57
,, 28 D. Shand	2	38		,, 30 A. Allen	11		1,429
,, 31 Balance c/d			637	,, 31 Balance c/d		75	
	12	167	1,681		19	167	1,681
Jun 1 Balance b/d			75	Jun 1 Balance b/d			637

On a balance sheet a bank overdraft will be shown as an item included under the heading Current Liabilities.

Assignment Exercises

14.1 Enter up a three column cash book from the details following. Balance off at the end of the month, and show the relevant discount accounts as they would appear in the general ledger.

19-7

May	1	Started business with £6,000 in the bank
,,	1	Bought fixtures paying by cheque £950
,,	2	Bought goods paying by cheque £1,240
,,	3	Cash Sales £407
,,	4	Paid rent in cash £200
,,	5	N. Morgan paid us his account of £220 by a cheque for £210, we allowed him £10 discount
,,	7	Paid S. Thompson & Co £80 owing to them by means of a cheque £76, they allowed us £4 discount
,,	9	We received a cheque for £380 from S. Cooper, discount having been allowed £20
,,	12	Paid rates by cheque £410
,,	14	L. Curtis pays us a cheque for £115
,,	16	Paid M. Monroe his account of £120 by cash £114, having deducted £6 cash discount
,,	20	P. Exeter pays us a cheque for £78, having deducted £2 cash discount
,,	31	Cash Sales paid direct into the bank £88.

14.2 A three column cash book is to be written up from the following details, balanced off and the relevant discount accounts in the general ledger shown.

19-5

Mar	1	Balances brought forward: Cash £230; Bank £4,756
,,	2	The following paid their accounts by cheque, in each case deducting 5 per cent cash discounts; Accounts: R. Burton £140; E. Taylor £220; R. Harris £300
,,	4	Paid rent by cheque £120
,,	6	J. Cotton lent us £1,000 paying by cheque
,,	8	We paid the following accounts by cheque in each case deducting a 2½ per cent cash discount; N. Black £360; P. Towers £480; C. Rowse £800.
,,	10	Paid motor expenses in cash £44
,,	12	H. Hankins pays his account of £77 by cheque £74, deducting £3 cash discount
,,	15	Paid wages in cash £160
,,	18	The following paid their accounts by cheque, in each case deducting 5 per cent cash discount: Accounts: C. Winston £260; R. Wilson & Son £340; H. Winter £460
,,	21	Cash withdrawn from the bank £350 for business use
,,	24	Cash Drawings £120
,,	25	Paid T. Briers his account of £140, by cash £133, having deducted £7 cash discount
,,	29	Bought fixtures paying by cheque £650
,,	31	Received commission by cheque £88.

14.3A Enter the following in a three column cash book. Balance off the cash book at the end of the month and show the discount accounts in the general ledger.

19-8

June 1 Balances brought forward: Cash £97; Bank £2,186.

,, 2 The following paid us by cheque in each case deducting a 5 per cent cash discount: R. Harris £1,000; C. White £280; P. Peers £180; O. Hardy £600

,, 3 Cash Sales paid direct into the bank £134

,, 5 Paid rent by cash £88

,, 6 We paid the following accounts by cheque, in each case deducting 2½ per cent cash discount J. Charlton £400; H. Sobers £640; D. Shallcross £200

,, 8 Withdrew cash from the bank for business use £250

,, 10 Cash Sales £206

,, 12 D. Deeds paid us their account of £89 by cheque less £2 cash discount

,, 14 Paid wages by cash £250

,, 16 We paid the following accounts by cheque: L. Lucas £117 less cash discount £6; D. Fisher £206 less cash discount £8

,, 20 Bought fixtures by cheque £8,000

,, 24 Bought motor lorry paying by cheque £7,166

,, 29 Received £169 cheque from D. Steel

,, 30 Cash Sales £116

,, 30 Bought stationery paying by cash £60.

14.4A You are to write up a three column cash book for M. Pinero from the details which follow. Then balance off at the end of the month and show the discount accounts in the general ledger.

19-6

May 1 Balances brought forward:
　　　　Cash in hand £58
　　　　Bank overdraft £1,470

,, 2 M. Pinero pays further Capital into the bank £1,000

,, 3 Bought office fixtures by cheque £780

,, 4 Cash Sales £220

,, 5 Banked cash £200

,, 6 We paid the following by cheque, in each case deducting 2½ per cent cash discount: B. Barnes £80; T. Horton £240; T. Jacklin £400

,, 8 Cash Sales £500

,, 12 Paid motor expenses in cash £77

,, 15 Cash withdrawn from the bank £400

,, 16 Cash Drawings £120

,, 18 The following firms paid us their accounts by cheque, in each case deducting a 5 per cent discount: L. Graham £80; B. Crenshaw £140; H. Green £220

,, 20 Salaries paid in cash £210

,, 22 T. Weiskopf paid us his account in cash £204

,, 26 Paid insurance by cheque £150

,, 28 We banked all the cash in our possession except for £20 in the cash till

,, 31 Bought motor van, paying by cheque £4,920.

15 The Sales Journal

You have read in Chapter 11 that the recording of transactions has been divided up into the various functions of the business. Mention has been made on page 80 of the fact that, in order to keep the general ledger free from unnecessary detail, separate journals are kept for credit transactions concerning sales and purchases. The Sales Journal can now be examined in detail.

There will be many businesses, such as a lot of retail shops, where all the sales will be cash sales. On the other hand, in many businesses a considerable proportion of sales will be made on credit rather than for immediate cash. In fact, the sales of some businesses will consist entirely of credit sales. For each credit sale the selling firm will send a document to the buyer showing full details of the goods sold and the prices of the goods. This document is known as an Invoice, and to the seller it is known as a Sales Invoice. The seller will keep one or more copies of each sales invoice for his own use. Exhibit 15.1 is an example of an invoice.

Exhibit 15.1

Your Purchase Order 10/A/980		J. Blake 7 Over Warehouse Leicester LE1 2AP 1 September 19-5
INVOICE No. 16554		
To: D. Prendergast 45 Charles Street Manchester M1 5ZN		
	Per unit	Total
	£	£
21 cases McBrand Pears	20	420
5 cartons Kay's Flour	4	20
6 cases Joy's Vinegar	20	120
		560
Terms: 1¼% cash discount if paid within one month		

You must not think that all invoices will look exactly like the one chosen as Exhibit 15.1. Each business will have its own design. All invoices will be numbered, and they will contain the names and addresses both of the supplier and of the customer. In this case the supplier is J. Blake and the customer is D. Prendergast.

As soon as the sales invoices for the goods being sent have been made out, whether they are typed, hand-written, or produced by a computer, they are then despatched to the customer. The firm will keep copies of all these sales invoices. These copies will have been automatically produced at the same time as the original, usually by using some form of carbon paper or special copying paper.

It is from the copy sales invoices that the seller enters up his sales journal. This book is merely a list, in date order, of each sales invoice, showing the date, the name of the the firm to whom the goods have been sold, the number of the invoice for reference purposes, and the net amount of the invoice. There is no need to show in the sales journal a description of the goods sold, as this information can be found by referring to the copy of the sales invoice which will have been filed after recording it in the sales journal. The practice of copying all the details of the goods sold in the sales journal finished many years ago.

We can now look at Exhibit 15.2, which is a sales journal, starting with the record of the sales invoice already shown in Exhibit 15.1. 15.1.

Exhibit 15.2

		Sales Journal		
		Invoice No.	*Folio*	Page 26
19-5				£
Sept	1 D. Prendergast	16554	SL 12	560
,,	8 T. Cockburn	16555	SL 39	1,640
,,	28 C. Carter	16556	SL 125	220
,,	30 D. Stevens & Co	16557	SL 249	1,100
	Transferred to Sales Account		GL 44	3,520

The entry of these credit sales in the customers' accounts in the sales ledger keeps to the same principles of personal accounts as described in earlier chapters. Apart from the fact that the customers' accounts are now contained in a separate book known as the sales ledger, and that the reference numbers in the folio columns will be different, each individual personal account is the same as previous. The act of using the sales journal entries as the basis for entering up the customers' accounts is known as 'posting' the sales journal.

Sales Ledger

D. Prendergast   Page 12

| 19-5 | | | £ |
| Sept 1 Sales | SJ 26 | | 560 |

T. Cockburn   Page 39

| 19-5 | | | £ |
| Sept 8 Sales | SJ 26 | | 1,640 |

C. Carter   Page 125

| 19-5 | | | £ |
| Sept 28 Sales | SJ 26 | | 220 |

D. Stevens & Co   Page 249

| 19-5 | | | £ |
| Sept 30 Sales | SJ 26 | | 1,100 |

You can see that the customers' personal accounts have been debited with a total of £3,520 for these sales. However, as yet no credit entry has been made for these items. The sales journal is simply a list, it is not an account and is therefore not a part of the double-entry system. We must complete double-entry however, and this is done by taking the total of the sales journal for the period and entering it on the credit side of the sales account in the general ledger.

General Ledger

Sales   Page 44

		19-5		£
		Sept 30 Credit Sales for		
		the month SJ 26		3,520

If you now compare this with entries that would have been made when all the accounts were kept in one ledger, the overall picture should become clearer. The eventual answer is the same, personal accounts would have been debited with credit sales amounting in total to £3,520 and the sales account would have been credited with sales amounting in total to £3,520. The differences are now that first the personal accounts are contained in a separate sales ledger, and second, the individual items of credit sales have been listed in the sales journal, merely the total being credited to the sales account. The different books in use also mean a change in the reference numbers in the folio columns.

Alternative names for the Sales Journal are Sales Book and Sales Day Book.

Before you proceed further you are to attempt Assignment Exercise 15.1.

Trade Discounts

Suppose you are the proprietor of a business. You are selling to three different kinds of customers:

(a) Traders who buy a lot of goods from you.
(b) Traders who buy only a few items from you.
(c) Direct to the general public.

The traders themselves have to sell the goods to the general public in their own areas. They have to make a profit to help finance their businesses, so they will want to pay you less than retail price.

The traders (a) who buy in large quantities will not want to pay as much as traders (b) who buy in small quantities. You want to attract such large customers, and so you are happy to sell to traders (a) at a lower price.

All of this means that your selling prices are at three levels: (a) to traders buying large quantities, (b) to traders buying small quantities, and (c) to the general public.

To save your staff from dealing with three different price lists, (a), (b) and (c), all goods are shown at the same price. However, a reduction (discount), called a *trade discount,* is given to traders (a) and (b).

Example

You are selling a make of food mixing machine. The basic price is £200. Traders (a) are given 25 per cent trade discount, traders (b) 20 per cent, the general public get no trade discount. The prices paid by each type of customer would be:

	Trader (a) £	Trader (b) £	General Public (c) £
Basic Price	200	200	200
Less Trade discount	(25%) 50	(20%) 40	nil
Price to be paid by customer	150	160	200

Exhibit 15.3 is an invoice for goods sold to D. Prendergast. It is for the same items as were shown in Exhibit 15.1, but this time the seller is R. Grant and he uses trade discounts to get to the price paid by his customers.

Exhibit 15.3

Your Purchase Order 11/A/G80		R. Grant Higher Side Preston PR1 2NL 2 September 19-5
INVOICE No. 30756		
To: D. Prendergast 45 Charles Street Manchester M1 5ZN		
	Per unit	Total
	£	£
21 cases McBrand Pears	25	525
5 cartons Kays' Flour	5	25
6 cases Joys' Vinegar	25	150
		700
Less 20% Trade discount		140
		560

By comparing Exhibits 15.1 and 15.3 you can see that the prices paid by D. Prendergast were the same. It is simply the method of calculating the price that is different.

As Trade Discount is simply a way of calculating sales prices, no entry for trade discount should be made in the double entry records nor in the Sales Journal. The record of this item in R. Grant's Sales Journal and Prendergast's personal account will appear:

Sales Journal

		Invoice No.	Folio	Page 87
19-5				£
Sept 2 D. Prendergast		30756	SL 32	560

Sales Ledger (page 32)

		D. Prendergast	
19-5		£	
Sept 2 Sales	SJ87	560	

This is in complete contrast to *Cash Discounts* which are shown in the double-entry accounts.

There are in fact several other reasons for using Trade Discounts to the one described in this chapter. However, the calculation of the Trade Discount and its display on the invoice will remain the same as that described in this book.

Assignment Exercises

15.1 You are to enter up the sales journal from the following details. Post the items to the relevant accounts in the sales ledger and then show the transfer to the sales account in the general ledger.

19-6

Mar	1	Credit sales to J. Gordon	£187
,,	3	Credit sales to G. Abrahams	£166
,,	6	Credit sales to V. White	£12
,,	10	Credit sales to J. Gordon	£55
,,	17	Credit sales to F. Williams	£289
,,	19	Credit sales to U. Richards	£66
,,	27	Credit sales to V. Wood	£28
,,	31	Credit sales to L. Simes	£78

15.2 F. Benjamin of 10 Lower Street, Plymouth, is selling the following items, the recommended retail prices as shown: white tape £10 per roll, green baize at £4 per metre, blue cotton at £6 per sheet, black silk at £20 per dress length. He makes the following sales:

19-7

May 1 To F. Gray, 3 Keswick Road, Portsmouth: 3 rolls white tape, 5 sheets blue cotton, 1 dress length black silk. Less 25 per cent trade discount.

,, 4 To A. Gray, 1. Shilton Road, Preston: 6 rolls white tape, 30 metres green baize. Less 33⅓ per cent trade discount.

,, 8 To E. Hines, 1 High Road, Malton: 1 dress length black silk. No trade discount.

,, 20 To M. Allen, 1 Knott Road, Southport: 10 rolls white tape, 6 sheets blue cotton, 3 dress lengths black silk, 11 metres green baize. Less 25 per cent trade discount.

,, 31 To B. Cooper, 1 Tops Lane, Andrews: 12 rolls white tape, 14 sheets blue cotton, 9 metres green baize. Less 33⅓ per cent trade discount.

You are to (a) draw up a sales invoice for each of the above sales, (b) enter them up in the Sales Journal, post to the personal accounts, (c) transfer the total to the Sales Account in the General Ledger.

15.3A J. Fisher, White House, Bolton, is selling the following items, the retail prices as shown: plastic tubing at £1 per metre, polythene sheeting at £2 per length, vinyl padding at £5 per box, foam rubber at £3 per sheet. He makes the following sales:

19-5

June 1 To A. Portsmouth, 5 Rockley Road, Worthing: 22 metres plastic tubing, 6 sheets foam rubber, 4 boxes vinyl padding. Less 25 per cent trade discount.

,, 5 To B. Butler, 1 Wembley Road, Colwyn Bay: 50 lengths polythene sheeting, 8 boxes vinyl padding, 20 sheets foam rubber. Less 20 per cent trade discount.

,, 11 To A. Gate, 1 Bristol Road, Hastings: 4 metres plastic tubing, 33 lengths of polythene sheeting, 30 sheets foam rubber. Less 25 per cent trade discount.

,, 21 To L. Mackeson, 5 Maine Road, Bath: 29 metres plastic tubing. No trade discount is given.

,, 30 To M. Alison, Daley Road, Box Hill: 32 metres plastic tubing, 24 lengths polythene sheeting, 20 boxes vinyl padding. Less 33⅓ per cent trade discount.

Required:
(*a*) Draw up a sales invoice for each of the above sales, (*b*) then enter up in the Sales Journal and post to the personal accounts, (*c*) transfer the total to the Sales Account in the general ledger.

16 The Purchases Journal

When a firm buys goods on credit it will receive an invoice from the seller for those goods. In the last chapter, Exhibit 15.1, J. Blake sold goods to D. Prendergast and sent an invoice with those goods.

To the seller, J. Blake, that invoice is a sales invoice. To the buyer, D. Prendergast, that same invoice is regarded as a purchases invoice. This often confuses students. What we have to do to identify whether or not an invoice is a sales invoice or a purchases invoice is to think about it from the point of view as to which firm's books we are entering up. If the firm is the buyer of the goods then the invoice is a purchases invoice.

The net amount of the invoice, i.e. after deduction of trade discount, is listed in the purchases journal and the items are then posted to the credit of the personal accounts in the purchases ledger. The invoice is then filed away for future reference. At the end of the period the total of the purchases journal is transferred to the debit of the purchases account in the general ledger. An example of a purchase journal and the posting of the entries to the purchases ledger and the total to the purchases account is now shown:

		Purchases Journal *Invoice No.*	*Folio*	Page 49
19-5				£
Sept	2 R. Simpson	9/101	PL 16	670
,,	8 B. Hamilton	9/102	PL 29	1,380
,,	19 C. Brown	9/103	PL 55	120
,,	30 K. Gabriel	9/104	PL 89	510
	Transferred to Purchases Account		GL63	2,680

Purchases Ledger
R. Simpson
Page 16

			£
	19-5		
	Sept 2 Purchases	PJ 49	670

B. Hamilton
Page 29

			£
	19-5		
	Sept 8 Purchases	PJ 49	1,380

C. Brown
Page 55

			£
	19-5		
	Sept 19 Purchases	PJ 49	120

K. Gabriel
Page 89

			£
	19-5		
	Sept 30 Purchases	PJ 49	510

General Ledger
Purchases
Page 63

19-5			£
Sept 30 Credit			
purchases			
for the			
month	PJ 49	2,680	

The Purchases Journal is often known also as the Purchases Book or as the Purchases Day Book.

Assignment Exercises

16.1 B. Mann has the following purchases for the month of May 19-4:

19-4

May 1 From K. King: 4 radios at £30 each, 3 music centres at £160 each. Less 25 per cent trade discount.

,, 3 From A. Bell: 2 washing machines at £200 each, 5 vacuum cleaners at £60 each, 2 dish dryers at £150 each. Less 20 per cent trade discount.

,, 15 From J. Kelly: 1 music centre at £300 each, 2 washing machines at £250 each. Less 25 per cent trade discount.

,, 20 From B. Powell: 6 radios at £70 each, less 33⅓ per cent trade discount.

,, 30 From B. Lewis: 4 dish dryers at £200 each, less 20 per cent trade discount.

Required:

(a) Enter up the Purchases Journal for the month.

(b) Post the transactions to the suppliers' accounts.

(c) Transfer the total to the Purchases Account.

16.2A A. Rowland has the following purchases for the month of June 19-9:

19-9

June 2 From C. Lee: 2 sets golf clubs at £250 each. 5 footballs at £20 each. Less 25 per cent trade discount.

,, 11 From M. Elliott: 6 cricket bats at £20 each, 6 ice skates at £30 each, 4 rugby balls at £25 each. Less 25 per cent trade discount.

,, 18 From B. Wood: 6 sets golf trophies at £100 each, 4 sets golf clubs at £300. Less 33⅓ per cent trade discount.

,, 25 From B. Parkinson: 5 cricket bats at £40 each. Less 25 per cent trade discount.

,, 30 From N. Francis: 8 goal posts at £70 each. Less 25 per cent trade discount.

Required:
(a) Enter up the Purchases Journal for the month.
(b) Post the items to the suppliers' accounts.
(c) Transfer the total to the Purchases Account.

16.3 C. Phillips, a sole trader, has the following purchases and sales for March 19-5:

19-5

Mar 1 Bought from Smith Stores: silk £40, cotton £80, all less 25 per cent trade discount

,, 8 Sold to A. Grantley: linen goods £28, woollen items £44. No trade discount

,, 15 Sold to A. Henry: silk £36, linen £144, cotton goods £120. All less 20 per cent trade discount

,, 23 Bought from C. Kelly: cotton £88, linen £52. All less 25 per cent trade discount

,, 24 Sold to D. Sangster: linen goods £42, cotton £48. Less 10 per cent trade discount

,, 31 Bought from J. Hamilton: linen goods £270 less 33⅓ per cent trade discount.

Required:
(a) Prepare the Purchases and Sales Journals of C. Phillips from the above.
(b) Post the items to the personal accounts.
(c) Post the totals of the journals to the Sales and Purchases Accounts.

16.4A A. Henriques has the following purchases and sales for May 19-6:

19-6

May 1 Sold to M. Marshall: brass goods £24, bronze items £36. Less 25 per cent trade discount

,, 7 Sold to R. Richards: tin goods £70, lead items £230. Less 33⅓ per cent trade discount

,, 9 Bought from C. Clarke: tin goods £400 less 40 per cent trade discount

,, 16 Bought from A. Charles: copper goods £320 less 50 per cent trade discount

,, 23 Sold to T. Young: tin goods £50, brass items £70, lead figures £80. All less 20 per cent trade discount

,, 31 Bought from M. Nelson: brass figures £100 less 50 per cent trade discount.

Required:

(a) Write up Sales and Purchases Journals.
(b) Post the items to the personal accounts.
(c) Post the totals of the journals to the Sales and Purchases Accounts.

17 The Returns Journals

The Returns Inwards Journal

Sometimes we will agree to customers returning goods to us. It may be that they had been sent goods of the wrong colour, the wrong type etc., or simply that the customer had found that he had bought more than he needed. At other times goods will have been supplied and there will be something wrong with them. The customer may agree to keep the goods if an allowance is given so as to reduce their price.

In each of these cases a document known as a 'credit note' will be sent to the customer, showing the amount of the allowance given by us in respect of the returns or of the faulty goods. The term 'credit note' takes its name from the fact that the customer's account will be credited with the amount of the allowance, so as to show the reduction in the amount owing by him.

Exhibit 17.1

<table>
<tr><td></td><td colspan="2">R. Grant,
Higher Side,
Preston PR1 2NL
8 September 19-5</td></tr>
<tr><td>To: D. Prendergast
45 Charles Street,
Manchester M1 5ZN
CREDIT NOTE No. 9/37</td><td>Per Unit</td><td>Total</td></tr>
<tr><td></td><td>£</td><td>£</td></tr>
<tr><td>2 cases McBrand Pears
Less 20% Trade Discount</td><td>25</td><td>50
10
—
40
=</td></tr>
</table>

Very often credit notes are printed in red so that they are easily distinguishable from invoices.

Imagine that the firm of D. Prendergast to whom goods were sold on 1 September 19-5 as per Exhibit 15.3 returned some of the goods on 8 September 19-5. The credit note might appear as shown in Exhibit 17.1.

The credit notes are listed in a Returns Inwards Journal which is then used to post the items to the credit of the personal accounts in the sales ledger. To complete the double entry the total of the returns inwards book for the period is transferred to the debit of the Returns Inwards Account in the general ledger.

An example of a returns inwards book showing the items posted to the sales ledger and the general ledger is now shown:

Returns Inwards Journal

	Note No.	Folio	Page 10
19-5			£
Sept 8 D. Prendergast	9/37	SL 12	40
,, 17 A. Brewster	9/38	SL 58	120
,, 19 C. Vickers	9/39	SL 99	290
,, 29 M. Nelson	9/40	SL 112	160
Transferred to Returns Inwards Account		GL 114	610

Sales Ledger
D. Prendergast   Page 12

			£
19-5			
Sept 8 Returns			
	Inwards	RI 10	40

A. Brewster   Page 58

			£
19-5			
Sept 17 Returns			
	Inwards	RI 10	120

C. Vickers   Page 99

			£
19-5			
Sept 19 Returns			
	Inwards	RI 10	290

M. Nelson   Page 112

			£
19-5			
Sept 29 Returns			
	Inwards	RI 10	160

General Ledger
Returns Inwards

19-5			£
Sept 30 Returns for the month	RI 10		610

Alternative names in use for the returns inwards journal are Returns Inwards Book or Sales Returns Book, the latter name arising from the fact that it is the sales which are returned at a later date.

The Returns Outwards Journal

The exact opposite to returns inwards is when goods are returned to a supplier. A document called a 'debit note' is sent to the supplier stating the amount of allowance to which the firm returning the goods is entitled. The debit note could also cover allowances due because the goods bought were deficient in some way. The term 'debit note' stems from the fact that as the liability to the supplier is accordingly reduced his personal account must be debited to record this. The debit note is the evidence that this has been done.

The debit notes are listed in a Returns Outwards Journal and the items then posted to the debit of the personal accounts in the purchases ledger. To complete double-entry the total of the returns outwards, journal for the period is transferred to the credit of the Returns Outwards Account in the general ledger. An example of a returns outwards journal followed by the subsequent postings to the purchases ledger and the general ledger is now shown:

Returns Outwards Journal

	Note No.	Folio	Page 7
19-5			£
Sept 11 B. Hamilton	9/34	PL 29	180
,, 16 B. Rose	9/35	PL 46	100
,, 28 C. Blake	9/36	PL 55	30
,, 30 S. Saunders	9/37	PL 87	360
Transferred to Returns Outwards Account		GL 116	670

Purchases Ledger
B. Hamilton Page 29

19-5			£
Sept 11 Returns Outwards	RO 7		180

B. Rose			Page 46

19-5		£	
Sept 16 Returns			
Outwards	RO 7	100	

	C. Blake		Page 55

19-5		£	
Sept 28 Returns			
Outwards	RO 7	30	

	S. Saunders		Page 87

19-5		£	
Sept 30 Returns			
Outwards	RO 7	360	

General Ledger
Returns Outwards   Page 116

19-5		£
Sept 30 Returns for		
the month	RO 7	670

Alternative names in use for the returns outwards journal are Returns Outwards Book or Purchases Returns Book, the latter name arising from the fact that it consists of the purchases which are returned to the supplier at a later date.

Internal Check

When sales invoices are being made out they should be scrutinized very carefully. A system is usually set up so that each stage of the preparation of the invoice is checked by someone other than the person whose job it is to send out the invoice. If this was not done then it would be possible for someone inside a firm to send out an invoice, as an instance, at a price less than the true price. Any difference could then be split between that person and the outside firm. If an invoice should have been sent to Ivor Twister & Co for £2,000, but the invoice clerk made it out deliberately for £200, then, if there was no cross-check, the difference of £1,800 could be split between the invoice clerk and Ivor Twister & Co.

Similarly outside firms could send invoices for goods which were never received by the firm. This might be in collaboration with an employee within the firm, but there are firms sending false invoices which rely on the firms receiving them being inefficient and paying for items never received. There have been firms sending invoices for such items as advertisements which have never been published. The cashier of the firm receiving the invoice, if the firm is an inefficient one, might possibly think that someone in the firm had authorized the advertisements and would pay the bill.

Besides these there are of course genuine errors, and these should also be detected. A system is therefore set up whereby the invoices have to be subject to scrutiny, at each stage, by someone other than the person who sends out the invoices or is responsible for paying them. Incoming invoices will be stamped with a rubber stamp, with spaces for each stage of the check. For instance, one person will have authority to certify that the goods were properly ordered, another that the goods were delivered in good order, another that the prices are correct, that the calculations are correct, and so on. Naturally in a small firm, simply because the office staff might be quite small, this cross-check may be in the hands of only one person other than the person who will pay it. A similar sort of check will be made in respect of sales invoices being sent out.

Statements

At the end of each month a statement should be sent to each debtor who owes money on the last day of the month. The statement is really a copy of the account for the last month, showing the amount owing at the start of the month, then the totals of each of the sales invoices sent to him in that month, the credit notes sent to him in the month for the goods returned, the cash and cheques received from the debtor, and finally the amount owing at the end of the month.

The debtor will use this to see if the account in his accounting records agree with his account in our records. Put simply, if in our books he is shown as owing £798 then, depending on items in transit between us, his books should show us as a creditor for £798. The statement also acts as a reminder to the debtor that he owes us money and will show the date by which he should make payment.

Credit Control

Any organisation which sells goods on credit should ensure that a tight control is kept on the amount owing from individual debtors. Failure to do so could mean that the amount of debtors increases past the point which the organisation can afford to finance, also there is a much higher possibility of bad debts occurring if close control is not kept.

For each debtor a credit limit should be set. This will depend partly on the past record of dealings with the debtor, whether or not the relationship has been a good one with the debtor always paying his account on time or not. The size of the debtor firm and the nature of its financial backing will also help determine what would be a safe credit limit to set. For instance, you might set a credit limit of only £250 for a fairly new and untried customer, but this could be as much as (say) £20,000 for a large well-known international firm with large financial resources. In the business world most business men are optimistic by nature, and they usually feel that they can manage to pay off debts much easier than is the case. Therefore it is a wise policy to err on the side of caution. On the other hand this should be tempered down by the fact that if you are too cautious you will probably not do much business, so a sensible middle course is the answer.

Therefore the debtor should know the length of the term of credit, i.e. how many days or weeks or months he has in which to pay the bill. He should also know that you will not supply goods to him if the amount that he owes you exceeds a stated amount.

Factoring

One of the problems that face many businesses is the time taken by debtors to pay their accounts. Few businesses have so much cash available to them that they do not mind how long the debtor takes to pay. It is a rather surprising fact that a lot of businesses which become bankrupt do so, not because the business is not making profits, but instead because the business has run out of cash funds. Once that happens, the confidence factor in business evaporates, and the business then finds that very few people will supply it with goods, and it also cannot pay its employees. Bankruptcy then happens fairly quickly in many cases.

In the case of debtors, the cash problem may be alleviated by using the services of a financial intermediary called a 'factor':

Factoring is a financial service designed to improve the cash flow of healthy, growing companies, enabling them to make better use of management time and the money tied up in trade credit to customers.

In essence, factors provide their clients with three closely integrated services covering sales accounting and collection, credit management which can include protection against bad debts, and the availability of finance against sales invoices.

Factors assume total responsibility for these functions, including assessing the creditworthiness of customers, the maintenance of a sales ledger, the dispatch of statements and the collection of money owed.

Factors provide clients with a predictable cash flow by paying them against sales factored either as each individual invoice is settled or on an agreed future date which represents the average time taken by the clients' customers to pay.

In addition, a factor will, if required, make payments against its clients' sales invoices: up to 80 per cent being available immediately with the balance paid when the customers pay the factor or after an agreed period.

In the case of non-recourse factoring, the factor gives 100 per cent protection against bad debts on all approved sales.

The benefits of factoring include savings in administration costs and management time, the elimination of bad debts, a guaranteed cash flow and the availability of funds which would otherwise be financing debtors. Factoring, therefore, provides a logical way for companies to develop, with their cash position always under contyrol and the availability of finance linked to actual sales performance.

Assignment Exercises

17.1 You are to enter up the purchases journal and the returns outwards journal from the following details, then to post the items to the relevant accounts in the purchases ledger and to show the transfers to the general ledger at the end of the month.

19-7

May 1 Credit purchase from H. Lloyd £119
  ,, 4 Credit purchases from the following: D. Scott £98; A. Simpson £114; A. Williams £25; S. Wood £56
  ,, 7 Goods returned by us to the following: H. Lloyd £16; D. Scott £14
  ,, 10 Credit purchase from A. Simpson £59
  ,, 18 Credit purchases from the following: M. White £89; J. Wong £67; H. Miller £196; H. Lewis £119
  ,, 25 Goods returned by us to the following: J. Wong £5; A. Simpson £11
  ,, 31 Credit purchases from: A. Williams £56; C. Cooper £98.

17.2A Enter up the sales journal and the returns inwards journal from the following details. Then post to the customer's accounts and show the transfers to the general ledger.

19-4

June 1 Credit sales to: A. Simes £188; P. Tulloch £60; J. Flynn £77; B. Lopez £88
  ,, 6 Credit sales to: M. Howells £114; S. Thompson £118; J. Flynn £66
  ,, 10 Goods returned to us by: A. Simes £12; B. Lopez £17
  ,, 20 Credit sales to M. Barrow £970
  ,, 24 Goods returned to us by S. Thompson £5
  ,, 30 Credit sales to M. Parkin £91.

17.3 You are to enter up the sales, purchases and the returns inwards and returns outwards journals from the following details, then to post the items to the relevant accounts in the sales and purchase ledgers. The total of the journals are then to be transferred to the accounts in the general ledger.

19-6

May 1 Credit sales: T. Thompson £56; L. Rodriguez £148; K. Barton £145
  ,, 3 Credit purchases: P. Potter £144; H. Harris £25; B. Spencer £76
  ,, 7 Credit sales: K. Kelly £89; N. Mendes £78; N. Lee £257
  ,, 9 Credit purchases: B. Perkins £24; H. Harris £58; H. Miles £123
  ,, 11 Goods returned by us to: P. Potter £12; B. Spencer £22
  ,, 14 Goods returned to us by: T. Thompson £5; K. Barton £11; K. Kelly £14
  ,, 17 Credit purchases: H. Harris £54; B. Perkins £65; L. Nixon £75
  ,, 20 Goods returned by us to B. Spencer £14
  ,, 24 Credit sales: K. Mohammed £57; K. Kelly £65; O. Green £112
  ,, 28 Goods returned to us by N. Mendes £24
  ,, 31 Credit sales: N. Lee £55.

17.4A You are to enter the following items in the books, post to personal accounts, and show transfers to the general ledger:

19-5

July 1   Credit purchases from: K. Hill £380; M. Norman £500; N. Senior £106

,, 3   Credit sales to: E. Rigby £510; E. Phillips £246; F. Thompson £356

,, 5   Credit purchases from: R. Morton £200; J. Cook £180; D. Edwards £410; C. Davies £66

,, 8   Credit sales to: A. Green £307; H. George £250; J. Ferguson £185

,, 12   Returns outwards to: M. Norman £30; N. Senior £16

,, 14   Returns inwards from: E. Phillips £18; F. Thompson £22

,, 20   Credit sales to: E. Phillips £188; F. Powell £310; E. Lee £420

,, 24   Credit purchases from: C. Ferguson £550; K. Ennevor £900

,, 31   Returns inwards from E. Phillips £27; E. Rigby £30

,, 31   Returns outwards to: J. Cook £13; C. Davies £11.

18 Value Added Tax

Value Added Tax, which will be shown hereafter in its abbreviated form as VAT, is charged in the United Kingdom on both the supply of goods and of services by persons and firms who are taxable. Some goods and services are not liable to VAT. Examples of this are food and postal charges. The rates at which VAT is levied have changed from time to time. Some goods have also attracted a different rate of VAT from the normal rate. Instances of this in the past have been motor-cars and electrical goods which have varied from the rates levied on most other goods. In this book the examples shown will all be at a VAT rate of 10 per cent. This does not mean that this is the rate applicable at the time when you are reading this book. It is, however, an easy figure to work out in an examination room, and most examining bodies have set questions assuming that the VAT rate was 10 per cent.

The Government department which deals with VAT in the United Kingdom is the Customs and Excise department.

Taxable Firms

Imagine that firm A takes raw materials that it has grown and processes them and then wants to sell them. If VAT did not exist it would sell them for £100, but VAT of 10 per cent must be added, so it sells them to firm B for £100 + VAT £10 = £110. Firm A must now pay the figure of £10 VAT to the tax authorities. Firm B having bought for £110 alters the product slightly and then resells to firm C for £140 + 10 per cent VAT £14 = £154. Firm B now give the tax authorities a cheque for the amount added less the amount it had paid to firm A for VAT £10, so that the cheque payable to the tax authorities by firm B is £4. Firm C is a retailer who then sells the goods for £200 to which he must add VAT 10 per cent £20 = £220 selling price to the customer. Firm C then remits £20 − £14 = £6 to the tax authorities.

It can be seen that the full amount of VAT tax has fallen on the ultimate customer who bought the goods from the retail shop, and that he suffered a tax of £20. The machinery of collection was however geared to the value added at each stage of the progress of the goods from manufacture to retailing, i.e. Firm A handed over £10, Firm B £4 and Firm C £6, making £20 in all.

Exempted Firms

If a firm is exempted then this means that it does not have to add the VAT tax on to the price at which it sells its products or services. On the other hand it will not get a refund of the amount it has paid itself on the goods and services which it has bought and on which it has paid VAT tax. Thus such a firm may buy goods for £100 + VAT tax £10 = £110. When it sells them it may sell at £130, there being no need to add VAT tax at all. It will not however get a refund of the £10 VAT tax it had itself paid on those goods.

Instances of firms being exempted are insurance companies, which do not charge VAT on the amount of insurance premiums payable by its customers, and banks, which do not add VAT on to their bank charges. Small firms with a turnover of less than a certain amount (the limit is changed upwards from time to time and so is not given here) do not have to register for VAT if they don't want to, and they would not therefore charge VAT on their goods and services. On the other hand many of these small firms could register if they wished, but they would then have to keep full VAT records in addition to charging out VAT. It is simply an attempt by the U.K. Government to avoid crippling very small businesses with unnecessary record-keeping that gives most small businesses this right to opt out of charging VAT.

Zero Rated Firms

These do not add VAT tax to the final selling price of their products or services. They do however obtain a refund of all VAT tax paid by them on goods and services. This means that if one of the firms buys goods for £200 + VAT tax £20 = £220, and later sells them for £300 it will not have to add VAT on to the selling price of £300. It will however be able to claim a refund of the £20 VAT tax paid when the goods were purchased. It is this latter element that distinguishes it from an exempted firm. A zero rated firm is therefore in a better position than an exempted firm. Illustrations of these firms are food, publishing and the new construction of buildings.

Partly Exempt Traders

Some traders will find that they are selling some goods which are exempt and some which are zero rated and others which are standard rated. These traders will have to apportion their turnover accordingly, and follow the rules already described for each separate part of their turnover.

Accounting for VAT

It can be seen that, except for firms that are exempted from VAT, firms do not suffer VAT as one expense. They either get a refund of whatever VAT they have paid, in the case of zero-rated business, or else additionally collect VAT from their customers and merely therefore act as tax collectors in the case of taxable firms. Only the exempted firms actually suffer VAT as they pay it and are not allowed a refund and cannot specifically pass it on to their customers. The following discussion will therefore be split between those two sorts of firms who do not suffer VAT expense, compared with the exempted firms who do suffer VAT.

Firms Which Can Recover VAT Paid

1. Taxable Firms

Value Added Tax and Sales Invoices A taxable firm will have to add VAT to the value of the Sales invoices. It must be pointed out that this is based on the amount of the invoice *after* any trade discount has been deducted.

Exhibit 18.1 is an invoice drawn up from the following details:

On 2 March 19-2, W. Frank & Co, Hayburn Road, Stockport, sold the following goods to R. Bainbridge Ltd, 267 Star Road, Colchester: Bainbridge's order No was A/4/559, for the following items:

    200 Rolls T56 Black Tape at £6 per 10 rolls
    600 Sheets R64 Polythene at £10 per 100 sheets
    7,000 Blank Perspex B49 Markers at £20 per 1,000

All of these goods are subject to VAT at the rate of 10 per cent. A trade discount of 25 per cent is given by Frank & Co. The sales invoice is numbered 8851.

Exhibit 18.1

W. Frank & Co,
Hayburn Road,
Stockport SK2 5DB

INVOICE No. 8851   Date: 2 March 19-2

To: R. Bainbridge Ltd   Your order no. A/4/559
    267 Star Road
    Colchester CO1 1BT

	£
200 Rolls T56 Black Tape @ £6 per 10 rolls	120
600 Sheets R64 Polythene @ £10 per 100 sheets	60
7,000 Blank Perspex B49 Markers @ £20 per 1,000	140
	320
Less Trade Discount 25%	80
	240
Add VAT 10%	24
	264

Where a cash discount is offered for speedy payment, VAT is calculated on an amount represented by the value of the invoice less such a discount. Even if the cash discount is lost because of late payments, the VAT will not change.

The Sales Book will normally have an extra column for the VAT content of the Sales Invoices. This is needed to facilitate accounting for VAT. The entry of several sales invoices in the Sales Book and in the ledger accounts can now be examined:

W. Frank & Co sold the following goods during the month of March 19-2:

	Total of Invoice, after trade discount deducted but before VAT added	VAT 10%
19-2	£	£
March 2 R. Bainbridge Ltd (see Exhibit 18.1)	240	24
,, 10 S. Lange & Son	300	30
,, 17 K. Bishop	160	16
,, 31 R. Andrews & Associates	100	10

Sales Book				Page 58
	Invoice No.	Folio	Net	VAT
19-2			£	£
March 2 R. Bainbridge Ltd	8851	SL 77	240	24
,, 10 S. Lange & Son	8852	SL 119	300	30
,, 17 K. Bishop	8853	SL 185	160	16
,, 31 R. Andrews & Associates	8854	SL 221	100	10
Transferred to General Ledger			GL 76 800	GL 90 80

The Sales Book having been written up, the first task is then to enter the invoices in the individual customer's accounts in the Sales Ledger. The customer's accounts are simply charged with the full amounts of the invoices including VAT. For instance, K. Bishop will owe £176 which he will have to pay to W. Frank & Co. He does not remit the VAT £16 to the Customs and Excise, instead he is going to pay the £16 to W. Frank & Co. who will thereafter ensure that the £16 is included in the total cheque payable to the Customs and Excise.

126

Sales Ledger
R. Bainbridge Ltd   Page 77

19-2			£
March 2 Sales	SB 58		264

S. Lang & Son   Page 119

19-2			£
March 10 Sales	SB 58		330

K. Bishop   Page 185

19-2			£
March 17 Sales	SB 58		176

R. Andrews & Associates   Page 221

19-2			£
March 31 Sales	SB 58		110

In total therefore the personal accounts have been debited with £880, this being the total of the amounts which the customers will have to pay. The actual sales of the firm are not £880, the amount which is actually sales is £800, the other £80 being simply the VAT that W. Frank & Co are collecting on behalf of the Government. The credit transfer to the Sales Account in the General Ledger is restricted to the Sales content, i.e. £800. The other £80, being VAT, is transferred to a VAT account.

General Ledger
Sales   Page 76

	19-2		£
	March 31 Credit Sales for the month	SB 58	800

Value Added Tax   Page 90

	19-2		£
	March 31 Sales Book: VAT content	SB 58	80

Value Added Tax and Purchases In the case of a taxable firm, the firm will have to add VAT to its sales invoices, but it will also be able to claim a refund of the VAT which it pays on its purchases. What will happen is that the total of the amount of VAT paid on Purchases will be deducted from the total of the VAT collected by the additions to the Sales Invoices. Normally the VAT on Sales will be greater than that on Purchases, and therefore periodically the net difference will be paid to the Customs and Excise. It can happen sometimes that more VAT has been suffered on Purchases than has been charged on Sales, and in this case it would be the Customs and Excise which would refund the difference to the firm. These payments or receipts via the Customs and Excise will be either monthly or quarterly depending on the arrangement which the particular firm has made.

The recording of Purchases in the Purchases Book and Purchases Ledger is similar to that of Sales, naturally with items being shown in a reverse fashion. These can now be illustrated by continuing the month of March 19-2 in the books of the firm already considered, W. Frank & Co, this time for Purchases.

W. Frank & Co made the following purchases during the month of March 19-2:

		Total of Invoice, after trade discount deducted but before VAT added	VAT 10%
19-2		£	£
March 1	E. Lyal Ltd (see Exhibit 18.2)	180	18
,, 11	P. Portsmouth & Co	120	12
,, 24	J. Davidson	40	4
,, 29	B. Cofie & Son Ltd	70	7

Before looking at the recording of these in the Purchases Records, compare the first entry for E. Lyal Ltd with Exhibit 18.2, to ensure that the correct amounts have been shown.

Exhibit 18.2

E. Lyal Ltd
College Avenue
St Albans
Hertfordshire ST2 4JA

INVOICE No. K453/A

Date: 1/3/19-2
Your order No. BB/667

To: W. Frank & Co   Terms: Strictly net 30 days
    Hayburn Road
    Stockport

	£
50 metres of BYC plastic 1 metre wide × £3 per metre	150
1,200 metal tags 500 mm × 10p each	120
	270
Less Trade Discount at 33⅓%	90
	180
Add VAT 10%	18
	198

It can be seen that the purchases invoice from E. Lyal Ltd differs slightly in its layout to that of W. Frank & Co per Exhibit 18.3. This is to illustrate that in fact each firm designs its own invoices, and there will be wide variations. The basic information shown will be similar, but they may have such information displayed in quite different ways.

| | *Purchases Book* | | | Page 38 |
	Folio		*Net*	*VAT*
19-2			£	£
March 1 E. Lyal Ltd	PL 15		180	18
,, 11 P. Portsmouth & Co	PL 70		120	12
,, 24 J. Davidson	PL 114		40	4
,, 29 B. Cofie & Son Ltd	PL 166		70	7
Transferred to General Ledger		GL 54	410	GL 90 41

These are entered in the Purchases Ledger. Once again there is no need for the VAT to be shown as separate amounts in the accounts of the suppliers.

Purchases Ledger

E. Lyal Ltd   Page 15

			£
19-2			
March 1 Purchases	PB 38		198

P. Portsmouth & Co.   Page 70

			£
19-2			
March 11 Purchases	PB 38		132

J. Davidson   Page 114

			£
19-2			
March 24 Purchases	PB 38		44

B. Cofie & Son Ltd   Page 166

19-2	£		
March 29 Purchases	PB 38		77

The personal accounts have accordingly been credited with a total of £451, this being the total of the amounts which Frank & Co will have to pay to them. The actual purchases are not however, £451; the correct amount is £410 and the other £41 is the VAT which the various firms are collecting for the Customs & Excise, and which amount is reclaimable from the Customs and Excise by Frank & Co. The debit transfer to the Purchases Account is therefore restricted to the figure of £410, for this is the true amount that the goods are costing the firm. The other £41 is transferred to the debit of the VAT account. It will be noticed that in this account there is already a credit of £80 in respect of VAT on Sales for the month.

General Ledger

Purchases   Page 54

19-2		£
March 31 Credit Purchases for the month		410

Value Added Tax   Page 90

19-2	£	19-2	£
March 31 Purchase Book: VAT content PB 38	41	March 31 Sales Book: VAT content SB 58	80
,, 31 Balance c/d	39		
	80		80
		April 1 Balance b/d	39

Assuming that a Trading and Profit and Loss Account was being drawn up for the month, the Trading Account would be debited with £410 as a transfer from the Purchases Account, whilst the £800 in the Sales Account would be transferred to the credit side of the Trading Account. The Value Added Tax would simply appear as a creditor of £39 in the Balance Sheet as at 31 March 19-2.

2.   Zero Rated Firms

It has been already stated that these firms do not have to add VAT on to their sales invoices, as their rate of VAT is zero or nil. On the other hand any VAT that they pay on Purchases can be reclaimed from the Customs and Excise. Such firms, which include publishers, are therefore in a rather fortunate position. There will accordingly be no need at all to enter VAT in the Sales Book as VAT simply does not apply to Sales in such a firm. The Purchases Book and the Purchases Ledger will appear exactly as has been seen in the case of W. Frank & Co. The VAT account will only have debits in it, representing the VAT on Purchases. This balance will be shown on the Balance Sheet as a debtor until it is settled by the Customs and Excise.

Firms Which Cannot Recover VAT Paid

These firms do not have to add VAT on to the value of their Sales Invoices. On the other hand they do not get a refund of VAT paid on Purchases. All that happens in this type of firm is that there is no Value Added Tax Account, the VAT paid is simply included as part of the cost of goods. If therefore a firm receives an invoice from a supplier for Purchases of £80, with VAT added of £8, then £88 will have to be paid for these goods and the firm will not receive a refund from the Customs and Excise. In the Purchases Book the item of

Purchases will be shown as £88, and the supplier's account will be credited with £88. As VAT is not added to Sales Invoices then there cannot be any entries for VAT in the Sales Book.

Perhaps a comparison of two firms with identical Purchases from the same supplier, one a zero rated firm, and one a firm which cannot recover VAT paid, would not come amiss here. On the assumption that for each firm the only item of Purchases for the month was that of goods £120 plus VAT £12 from D. Oswald Ltd, the entries for the month of May 19-4 would be as follows:

(a) Firm which cannot recover VAT:

Purchases Book

	£
19-4	
May 16 D. Oswald Ltd.	132

Purchases Ledger
D. Oswald Ltd

	£
19-4	
May 16 D. Oswald Ltd.	132

General Ledger
Purchases

19-4	£	19-4	£
May 31 Credit Purchases for the month	132	May 31 Transfer to Trading Account	132

Trading Account for the month ended 31 May 19-4 (extract)

	£
Purchases	132

(b) Firm which can recover VAT (e.g. zero rated firm):

Purchases Book

	Net	VAT
	£	£
19-4		
May 16 D. Oswald Ltd	120	12

Purchases Ledger
D. Oswald Ltd

	£
19-4	
May 16 Purchases	132

General Ledger
Purchases

19-4		£	19-4		£
May	31 Credit Purchases for the month	120	May	31 Transfer to Trading Account	120

Value Added Tax

19-4		£
May	31 Purchases Book	12

Trading Account for the month ended 31 May 19-4 (extract)

	£
Purchases	120

Balance Sheet as at 31 May 19-4 (extract)

	£
Debtor	12

VAT included in Gross Amount

You will often know only the gross amount of an item, this figure will in fact be made up of the net amount plus VAT. To find the amount of VAT which has been added to the net amount, a formula capable of being used with any rate of VAT can be used. It is:

$$\frac{\% \text{ rate of VAT}}{100 + \% \text{ Rate of VAT}} \times \text{Gross Amount} = \text{VAT in £}$$

Suppose that the gross amount of sales was £1,650 and the rate of VAT was 10%. Find the amount of VAT and the net amount before VAT was added.

Using the formula:—

$$\frac{10}{100 + 10} \times £1,650 = \frac{10}{110} \times £1,650 = £150.$$

Therefore the net amount was £1,500, which with VAT £150 added, becomes £1,650 gross.

VAT on Items Other Than Sales and Purchases

Value Added Tax is not just paid on purchases, it is also payable on many items of expense and on the purchase of fixed assets. In fact it would not be possible for this to be otherwise, as an item which is a Purchase for one firm would be a Fixed Asset in another. The firm which sells goods on which VAT is added does not concern itself whether or not the firm buying it is doing so for resale, or whether it is for use. The VAT will therefore be added to all of its Sales Invoices. The treatment of VAT in the accounts of the firm buying the item will depend on whether or not that firm can reclaim VAT paid or not. The general rule is that if the VAT can be reclaimed then the item should be shown net, i.e. VAT should be excluded from the expense or fixed asset account. When VAT cannot be reclaimed then VAT should be included in the expense or fixed asset account as part of the cost of the item. For example, two businesses buying similar items, would treat the following items as shown:

	Firm which can reclaim VAT	Firm which cannot reclaim VAT
Buys Machinery £200 + VAT £20	Debit Machinery £200 Debit VAT Account £20	Debit Machinery £220
Buys Stationery £150 + VAT £15	Debit Stationery £150 Debit VAT Account £15	Debit Stationery £165

VAT Owing

VAT owing by or to the firm can be included with debtors or creditors, as the case may be. There is no need to show the amount(s) owing as separate items.

Assignment Exercises

18.1 On 1 May 19-7, D. Wilson Ltd, 1 Hawk Green Road, Stockport, sold the following goods on credit to G. Christie & Son, The Golf Shop, Hole-in-One Lane, Marple, Cheshire:
Order No. A/496
3 sets of 'Boy Michael' golf clubs at £270 per set.
150 Watson golf balls at £8 per 10 balls.
4 Faldo golf bags at £30 per bag.
Trade discount is given at the rate of 33⅓%.
All goods are subject to VAT at 10%.
(i)   Prepare the Sales Invoice to be sent to G. Christie & Son. The invoice number will be 10586.
(ii) Show the entries in the Personal Ledgers of D. Wilson Ltd and G. Christie & Son.

18.2 The following sales have been made by S. Thompson Ltd during the month of June 19-5. All the figures are shown net after deducting trade discount, but before adding VAT at the rate of 10 per cent.

19-5
August	1 to M. Sinclair & Co	£150
,,	8 to M. Brown & Associates	£260
,,	19 to A. Axton Ltd	£80
,,	31 to T. Christie	£30

You are required to enter up the Sales Book, Sales Ledger and General Ledger in respect of the above items for the month.

18.3 The following sales and purchases were made by R. Colman Ltd during the month of May 19-6.

	Net	VAT added
19-6	£	£
May 1 Sold goods on credit to B. Davies & Co	150	15
,, 4 Sold goods on credit to C. Grant Ltd	220	22
,, 10 Bought goods on credit from:		
G. Cooper & Son	400	40
J. Wayne Ltd	190	19
,, 14 Bought goods on credit from B. Lugosi	50	5
,, 16 Sold goods on credit to C. Grant Ltd	140	14
,, 23 Bought goods on credit from S. Hayward	60	6
,, 31 Sold goods on credit to B. Karloff	80	8

Enter up the Sales and Purchases Books, Sales and Purchases Ledgers and the General Ledger for the month of May 19-6. Carry the balance down on the VAT account.

18.4A On 1 March 19-6, C. Black, Curzon Road, Stockport, sold the following goods on credit to J. Booth, 89 Andrew Lane, Stockport. Order No. 1697.

20,000 Coils Sealing Tape @ £4.46 per 1,000 coils
40,000 Sheets Bank A5   @ £4.50 per 1,000 sheets
24,000 Sheets Bank A4   @ £4.20 per 1,000 sheets
    All goods are subject to VAT at 10%.
(a) Prepare the Sales Invoice to be sent to J. Booth.
(b) Show the entries in the Personal Ledgers of J. Booth, and C. Black.

18.5A The credit sales and purchases for the month of December 19-3 in respect of C. Dennis & Son Ltd were:

	Net, after trade discount	VAT 10%
19-3	£	£
December 1 Sales to M. Morris	140	14
,, 4 Sales to G. Ford Ltd	290	29
,, 5 Purchases from P. Hillman & Son	70	7
,, 8 Purchases from J. Lancia	110	11
,, 14 Sales to R. Volvo Ltd	180	18
,, 18 Purchases from T. Leyland & Co	160	16
,, 28 Sales to G. Ford Ltd	100	10
,, 30 Purchases from J. Lancia	90	9

Write up all of the relevant books and ledger accounts for the month.

19 Depreciation of Fixed Assets: Nature and Calculations

Fixed Assets have already been stated to be those assets of material value that are of long-life, are held to be used in the business, and are not primarily for resale or for conversion into cash.

Usually, with the exception of land, fixed assets have a limited number of years of useful life. Motor vans, machines, buildings and fixtures, for instance, do not last for ever. Even land itself may have all or part of its usefulness exhausted after a few years. Some types of land used for quarries, mines, or land of another sort of wasting nature would be examples. When a fixed asset is bought, then later put out of use by the firm, that part of the cost that is not recovered on disposal is called depreciation.

It is obvious that the only time that depreciation can be calculated accurately is when the fixed asset is disposed of, and the difference between the cost to its owner and the amount received on disposal is then ascertained. If a motor van was bought for £1,000 and sold five years later for £20, then the amount of depreciation is £1,000 − £20 = £980.

Depreciation is thus the part of the cost of the fixed asset consumed during its period of use by the firm. Therefore, it has been a cost for services consumed in the same way as costs for such items as wages, rent, lighting etc. Depreciation is, therefore, an expense and will need charging to the profit and loss account before ascertaining net profit or loss. Provision for depreciation suffered will therefore have to be made in the books in order that the net profits may be profits remaining after charging all the expenses of the period.

In fact SSAP 12 defines depreciation as 'the measure of the wearing out, consumption or other loss of *value* of a fixed asset whether arising from use, effluxion of time or obsolescence through technology and market changes.' This definition refers to loss of *value* rather than cost. This has been done deliberately so that it also covers depreciation in any form of inflation accounting system, such systems are outside the coverage of this book.

Causes of Depreciation

These may be divided into the main classes of physical deterioration, economic factors, the time factor, and depletion.

Physical deterioration is caused mainly from wear and tear when the asset is in use, but also from erosion, rust, rot, and decay from being exposed to wind, rain, sun and other elements of nature.

Economic factors may be said to be those that cause the asset to be put out of use even though it is in good physical condition. These are largely obsolescence and inadequacy.

Obsolescence means the process of becoming obsolete or out of date. An example of this were the steam locomotives, some of them in good physical condition, which were rendered obsolete by the introduction of diesel and electric locomotives. The steam locomotives were put out of use by British Rail when they still had many more miles of potential use, because the newer locomotives were more efficient and economical to run.

Inadequacy refers to the termination of the use of an asset because of the growth and changes in the size of a firm. For instance, a small ferryboat that is operated by a firm at a seaside resort is entirely inadequate when the resort becomes more popular. It is found that it would be more efficient and economical to operate a larger ferry-boat, and so the smaller boat is put out of use by the firm.

Both obsolescence and inadequacy do not necessarily mean that the asset is scrapped. It is merely put out of use by the firm. Another firm will often buy it. For example, many of the aeroplanes put out of use by large airlines are bought by smaller firms.

The time factor is obviously associated with all the causes mentioned already. However, there are fixed assets to which the time factor is connected in another way. These are assets with a fixed period of legal life such as leases, patents and copyrights. For instance a lease can be entered into for any period, while a patent's legal life is sixteen years, but there are certain grounds on which this can be extended. Provision for the consumption of these assets is called amortisation rather than depreciation.

Other assets are of a wasting character, perhaps due to the extraction of raw materials from them. These materials are then either used by the firm to make something else, or are sold in their raw state to other firms. Natural resources such as mines, quarries and oil wells come under this heading. To provide for the consumption of an asset of a wasting character is called provision for depletion.

Land and Buildings

Prior to SSAP 12, which applied to periods starting on or after 1st January 1978, freehold and long leasehold properties were very rarely subject to a charge for depreciation. It was contended that, as property values tended to rise instead of fall, it was inappropriate to charge depreciation.

However, SSAP 12, requires that depreciation be written off over the property's useful life, with the exception that freehold *land* will not *normally* require a provision for depreciation. This is because land does not *normally* depreciate. Buildings do however eventually fall into disrepair or become obsolete, and must be subject to a charge for depreciation each year. When a revaluation of property takes place the depreciation charge must be on the revalued figure.

An exception to all this are 'Investment Properties'. These are properties owned not for use, but simply for investment. In this case investment properties will be shown in the balance sheet at their open market value.

Appreciation

At this stage of the chapter the reader may well begin to ask himself about the assets that increase (appreciate) in value. The answer to this is that normal accounting procedure would be to ignore any such appreciation, as to bring appreciation into account would be to contravene both the cost concept and the prudence concept as discussed in Chapter 10. Nevertheless, in certain circumstances appreciation is taken into account in partnership and limited company accounts, but this is left until partnerships and limited companies are considered.

Provisions for Depreciation as Allocation of Cost

Depreciation in total over the life of an asset can be calculated quite simply as cost less amount receivable when the asset is put out of use by the firm. If the item is bought and sold within the one accounting period then the depreciation for that period is charged as a revenue expense in arriving at that period's Net Profit. The difficulties start when the asset is used for more than one accounting period, and an attempt has to be made to charge each period with the depreciation for that period.

Even though depreciation provisions are now regarded as allocating cost to each accounting period (except for accounting for inflation), it does not follow that there is any 'true' method of performing even this task. All that can be said is that the cost should be allocated over the life of the asset in such a way as to charge it as equitably as possible to the periods in which the asset is used. The difficulties involved are considerable and some of them are now listed.

1. Apart from a few assets, such as a lease, how accurately can a firm assess an assets useful life? Even a lease may be put out of use if the premises leased have become inadequate.

2. How does one measure use? A car owned by a firm for two years may have been driven one year by a very careful driver and another year by a reckless driver. The standard of driving will affect the motor car and also the amount of cash receivable on its disposal. How should such a firm apportion the car's depreciation costs?

3. There are other expenses besides depreciation such as repairs and maintenance of the fixed asset. As both of these affect the rate and amount of depreciation should they not also affect the depreciation provision calculations?

4. How can a firm possibly know the amount receivable in x years time when the asset is put out of use?

These are only some of the difficulties. Therefore, the methods of calculating provisions for depreciation are mainly accounting customs.

The Main Methods of Calculating Provisions for Depreciation

The two main methods in use are the Straight Line Method and the Reducing Balance Method. In fact it has now become regarded that though other methods may be more applicable in certain cases, the straight line method is the one that is generally most suitable.

1. Straight Line Method

This allows an equal amount to be charged as depreciation for each year of expected use of the asset.

The basic formula is:

$$\frac{\text{Cost} - \text{Estimated Residual Value}}{\text{Number of years of expected use}} = \text{Depreciation provision per annum.}$$

The reason for this method being called the straight line method is that if the charge for depreciation was plotted annually on a graph and the points joined together, then the graph would reveal a straight line.

For example, a machine costs £10,000, it has an expected life of four years, and has an estimated residual value of £256. The depreciation provision per annum will be

$$\frac{£10,000 - £256}{4} = £2,436.$$

In practice, the residual value is often ignored where it would be a relatively small amount.

2. Reducing Balancing Method

To calculate the depreciation provision annually, a fixed percentage is applied to the balance of costs not yet allocated as an expense at the end of the previous accounting period. The balance of unallocated costs will therefore decrease each year, and as a fixed percentage is being used the depreciation provision will therefore be less with each passing year. Theoretically, the balance of unallocated costs at the end of the expected life should equal the estimated residual value.

The basic formula used to find the requisite percentage to apply with this method is:

$$r = 1 - \sqrt[n]{\frac{s}{c}}$$

where n = the number of years

s = the net residual value (this must be a significant amount or the answers will be absurd, since the depreciation rate would amount to nearly one)

c = the cost of the asset

r = the rate of depreciation to be applied.

Using, as an example, the figures used for the machine for which depreciation provisions were calculated on the straight line method, the calculations would appear as:

$$r = 1 - \sqrt[4]{\frac{£256}{£10,000}} = 1 - \frac{4}{10} = 0.6 \text{ or } 60 \text{ per cent}$$

The depreciation calculation applied to each of the four years of use would be:

	£
Cost	10,000
Year 1. Depreciation provision 60 per cent of £10,000	6,000
Cost not yet apportioned, end of year 1.	4,000
Year 2. Depreciation provision 60 per cent of £4,000	2,400
Cost not yet apportioned, end of year 2.	1,600
Year 3. Depreciation provision 60 per cent of £1,600	960
Cost not yet apportioned, end of year 3.	640
Year 4. Depreciation provision 60 per cent of £640	384
Cost not yet apportioned, end of year 4.	256

In this case the percentage to be applied worked out conveniently to a round figure. However, the answer will often come out to several places of decimals. In this case it would be usual to take the nearest whole figure as a percentage to be applied.

The percentage to be applied, assuming a significant amount for residual value, is usually between two to three times greater for the reducing balance method than for the straight line method.

The advocates of this method usually argue that it helps to even out the total charged as expenses for the use of the asset each year. They state that provisions for depreciation are not the only costs charged, there are the running costs in addition and that the repairs and maintenance element of running costs usually increase with age. Therefore, to equate total usage costs for each year of use the depreciation provisions should fall as the repairs and maintenance element increases. However, as can be seen from the figures of the example already given, the repairs and maintenance element would have to be comparatively large to bring about an equal total charge for each year of use.

To summarise, the people who favour this method say that:

In the early years		*In the later years*
A higher charge for depreciation	will tend to be fairly equal to	A lower charge for depreciation
+		+
A lower charge for repairs and upkeep		A higher charge for repairs and upkeep

Exhibit 19.1 gives a comparison of the calculations using the two methods, if the same cost is given for the two methods.

Exhibit 19.1

A firm has just bought a machine for £8,000. It will be kept in use for 4 years, when it will be disposed of for an estimated amount of £500. They ask for a comparison of the amounts charged as depreciation using both methods.

For the straight line method a figure of (£8,000 − £500) ÷ 4 = £7,500 ÷ 4 = £1,875 per annum is to be used. For the reducing balance method a percentage figure of 50 per cent will be used.

	Method 1 Straight Line		Method 2 Reducing Balance
	£		£
Cost	8,000		8,000
Depreciation: Year 1	1,875	(50% of £8,000)	4,000
	6,125		4,000
Depreciation: Year 2	1,875	(50% of £4,000)	2,000
	4,250		2,000
Depreciation: Year 3	1,875	(50% of £2,000)	1,000
	2,375		1,000
Depreciation: Year 4	1,875	(50% of £1,000)	500
Disposal value	500		500

This illustrates the fact that using the reducing balance method has a much higher charge for depreciation in the early years, and lower charges in the later years.

Another name for the Reducing Balance Method is the 'Diminishing Balance Method'.

Depreciation Provisions and Assets Bought or Sold

There are two main methods of calculating depreciation provisions for assets bought or sold during an accounting period.

1. To ignore the dates during the year that the assets were bought or sold, merely calculating a full period's depreciation on the assets in use at the end of the period. Thus, assets sold during the accounting period will have had no provision for depreciation made for that last period irrespective of how many months they were in use. Conversely, assets bought during the period will have a full period of depreciation provision calculated even though they may not have been owned throughout the whole of the period.

2. Provision for depreciation made on the basis of one month's ownership, one month's provision for depreciation. Fractions of months are usually ignored. This is obviously a more scientific method than that already described.

For examination purposes, where the date on which assets are bought and sold are shown then method No. 2 is the method expected by the examiner. If no such dates are given then obviously method No. 1 will have to be used.

Provisions for Depreciation: The Effect of Concepts

Similar to the description of the application of various concepts to stock valuation, as described at the end of Chapter 10, some of the concepts used with depreciation can be listed.

1. Depreciation is based on the cost of an asset, therefore this uses the cost concept.

2. It will be assumed normally that the business is a going concern.

3. The accruals concept is used, as you are matching up that period's expenses against the revenues of the period.

4. Materiality may come into it, as some items which could be regarded as fixed assets may be treated as revenue expenditure because they are not material items.

5. Prudence will also affect the provisions, as the estimate of the life of the fixed asset will veer towards an underestimation of the years of use rather than an overestimate. Similarly prudence will also tend to underestimate any future disposal value.

6. Consistency will be used, as we would not normally swing from the use of, say, the straight line method to the reducing balance method, and then change again often over the years.

The limitations of depreciation provisions have been described several times in the last two chapters, so they will not be examined again here.

Assignment Exercises

19.1 A machine costs £12,500. It will be kept for 4 years, and then sold for an estimated figure of £5,120. Show the calculations of the figures for depreciation for each of the four years using (*a*) the straight-line method, (*b*) the reducing balance method, for this method using a depreciation rate of 20 per cent.

19.2 A motor vehicle costs £6,400. It will be kept for 5 years, and then sold for scrap £200. Calculate the depreciation for each year using (*a*) the reducing balance method, using a depreciation rate of 50 per cent, (*b*) the straight line method.

19.3A A machine costs £5,120. It will be kept for 5 years, and then sold at an estimated figure of £1,215. Show the calculations of the figures for depreciation each year using (*a*) the straight line method, (*b*) the reducing balance method using a depreciation rate of 25 per cent.

19.4A A tractor is bought for £6,000. It will be used for 3 years, and then sold back to the supplier for £3,072. Show the depreciation calculations for each year using (*a*) the reducing balance method with a rate of 20 per cent, (*b*) the straight line method.

19.5 A company, which makes up its accounts annually to 31 December, provides for depreciation of its machinery at the rate of 10 per cent per annum on the diminishing balance system.

On 31 December 19-6, the machinery consisted of three items purchased as under:

		£
On 1 January 19-4 Machine A		Cost 3,000
On 1 April 19-5 Machine B		Cost 2,000
On 1 July 19-6 Machine C		Cost 1,000

Required: Your calculations showing the depreciation provision for the year 19-6.

20 Double Entry Records for Depreciation

Looking back quite a few years, the charge for depreciation always used to be shown in the fixed asset accounts themselves. This method is now falling into disuse but as a fair number of small firms still use it this will be illustrated and called the 'old method'.

The method now normally used is where the fixed assets accounts are always kept for showing the assets at cost price. The depreciation is shown accumulating in a separate 'provision for depreciation' account.

An illustration can now be looked at, using the same information, but showing the records using both methods.

In a business with financial years ended 31 December a machine is bought for £2,000 on 1 January 19-5. It is to be depreciated at the rate of 20 per cent using the reducing balance method. The records for the first three years are now shown:

1. The Old Method

Here the double-entry for each year's depreciation charge is:

Debit the depreciation account
Credit the asset account

and then, this is transferred to the profit and loss account, by the following:

Debit the profit and loss account
Credit the depreciation account

Machinery

19-5	£	19-5	£
Jan 1 Cash	2,000	Dec 31 Depreciation	400
		,, ,, Balance c/d	1,600
	2,000		2,000
19-6		19-6	
Jan 1 Balance b/d	1,600	Dec 31 Depreciation	320
		,, ,, Balance c/d	1,280
	1,600		1,600
19-7		19-7	
Jan 1 Balance b/d	1,280	Dec 31 Depreciation	256
		,, ,, Balance c/d	1,024
	1,280		1,280
19-8			
Jan 1 Balance b/d	1,024		

Depreciation

19-5	£	19-5	£
Dec 31 Machinery	400	Dec 31 Profit and Loss	400
19-6		19-6	
Dec 31 Machinery	320	Dec 31 Profit and Loss	320
19-7		19-7	
Dec 31 Machinery	256	Dec 31 Profit and Loss	256

Profit and Loss Account for the year ended 31 December

19-5 Depreciation	400
19-6 Depreciation	320
19-7 Depreciation	256

Usually shown on the balance sheet as follows:

Balance Sheets

	£	£
As at 31 December 19-5		
Machinery at cost	2,000	
Less Depreciation for the year	400	
		1,600
As at 31 December 19-6		
Machinery as at 1 January 19-6	1,600	
Less Depreciation for the year	320	
		1,280
As at 31 December 19-7		
Machinery as at 1 January 19-7	1,280	
Less Depreciation for the year	256	
		1,024

2. The Modern Method

Here, no entry is made in the asset account for depreciation. Instead, the depreciation is shown accumulating in a separate account.

The double entry is:

Debit the profit and loss account
Credit the provision for depreciation account

Machinery

19-5	£
Jan 1 Cash	2,000

Provision for Depreciation – Machinery

19-5	£	19-5	£
Dec 31 Balance c/d	400	Dec 31 Profit and Loss	400
19-6		19-6	
Dec 31 Balance c/d	720	Jan 1 Balance b/d	400
		Dec 31 Profit and Loss	320
	720		720
19-7		19-7	
Dec 31 Balance c/d	976	Jan 1 Balance b/d	720
		Dec 31 Profit and Loss	256
	976		976
		19-8	
		Jan 1 Balance b/d	976

Profit and Loss Account for the year ended 31 December

19-5 Depreciation	400
19-6 Depreciation	320
19-7 Depreciation	256

Now the balance on the Machinery Account is shown on the balance sheet at the end of each year less the balance on the Provision for Depreciation Account.

Balance Sheets

	£	£
As at 31 December 19-5		
Machinery at cost	2,000	
Less Depreciation to date	400	
		1,600
As at 31 December 19-6		
Machinery at cost	2,000	
Less Depreciation to date	720	
		1,280
As at 31 December 19-7		
Machinery at cost	2,000	
Less Depreciation to date	976	
		1,024

The modern method is much more revealing as far as the balance sheet is concerned. By comparing the depreciation to date with the cost of the asset, a good indication as to the relative age of the asset can be obtained. In the second and third balance sheets using the old method no such indication is available. For instance an item in a balance sheet as follows:

Motor Car as at 1 January 19-5	500	
Less Depreciation for the year	100	
		400

might turn out to be using the new method as either of the following:

Motor Car at cost	6,000	
Less Depreciation to date	5,600	
		400
Motor Car at cost	600	
Less Depreciation to date	200	
		400

The modern method is therefore more revealing and is far preferable from the viewpoint of more meaningful accounting reports.

The Sale of An Asset

When we charge depreciation on a fixed asset we are having to make guesses. We cannot be absolutely certain how long we will keep the asset in use, nor can we be certain at the date of purchase how much the asset will be sold for when we dispose of it. To get our guesses absolutely correct would be quite rare. This means that when we dispose of an asset, the cash received for it is usually different from our original guess.

This can be shown by looking back at the illustration already shown in this chapter. At the end of 19-7 the value of the machinery on the balance sheet is shown as £1,024. Using both the old and new methods of depreciation in the recording accounts, we can now see the entries needed if (a) the machinery was sold on 2 January 19-8 for £1,070 and then (b) if instead it had been sold for £950.

1. Old Method

(a) Asset sold at a profit
Book-keeping entries needed –

For cheque received:	Dr Bank
	Cr Machinery Account
For profit on sale:	Dr Machinery Account
	Cr Profit and Loss Account

Machinery

19-8	£	19-8	£
Jan 1 Balance b/d	1,024	Jan 2 Bank	1,070
Dec 31 Profit and Loss	46		
	1,070		1,070

Cash Book (bank columns)

19-8	£
Jan 2 Bank	1,070

Profit and Loss Account for the year ended 31 December 19-8

	£
Profit on sale of machinery	46

(b) Asset sold at a loss
Book-keeping entries needed –

For cheque received:	Dr Bank
	Cr Machinery Account
For loss on sale:	Dr Profit and Loss Account
	Cr Machinery Account

Machinery

19-8		£	19-8		£
Jan 1	Balance b/d	1,024	Jan 2	Bank	950
			Dec 31	Profit and Loss	74
		1,024			1,024

Cash Book (bank columns)

19-8		£
Jan 2	Bank	950

Profit and Loss Account for the year ended 31 December 19-8

	£
Loss on sale of machinery	74

2. Modern Method

(A) Transfer the cost price of the asset sold to an Assets Disposal Account (in this case a Machinery Disposals Account).

Dr Machinery Disposals Account
Cr Machinery Account

(B) Transfer the depreciation already charged to the Assets Disposal Account.

Dr Provision for Depreciation – Machinery
Cr Machinery Disposals Account

(C) For remittance received on disposal.

Dr Cash Book
Cr Machinery Disposals Account

(D) Transfer balance (difference) on Machinery Disposals Account to the Profit and Loss Account.

If the difference is on the debit side of the disposal account, it is a profit on sale.

Debit Machinery Disposals Account
Credit Profit and Loss Account

If the difference is on the credit side of the disposal account, it is a loss on sale.

Debit Profit and Loss Account
Cr Machinery Disposals Account

(a) Asset sold at a profit

Machinery

19-5		£	19-8			£
Jan 1 Cash		2,000	Jan 2 Machinery Disposals	(A)		2,000

Provision for Depreciation: Machinery

19-8		£	19-8		£
Jan 2 Machinery Disposals	(B)	976	Jan 1 Balance b/d		976

Machinery Disposals

19-8			£	19-8			£
Jan 2 Machinery	(A)		2,000	Jan 2 Cash	(C)		1,070
Dec 31 Profit and Loss	(D)		46	Jan 2 Provision for Depreciation	(B)		976
			2,046				2,046

Profit and Loss Account for the year ended 31 December 19-8

		£
Profit on sale of machinery	(D)	46

(b) Asset sold at a loss

Machinery

19-5	£	19-8		£
Jan 1 Cash	2,000	Jan 2 Machinery Disposals	(A)	2,000

Provision for Depreciation: Machinery

19-8		£	19-8	£
Jan 2 Machinery Disposals	(B)	976	Jan 1 Balance b/d	976

Machinery Disposals

19-8			£	19-8			£
Jan 2 Machinery	(A)		2,000	Jan 2 Cash	(C)		950
				Jan 2 Provision for Depreciation	(B)		976
				Dec 31 Profit and Loss	(D)		74
			2,000				2,000

Profit and Loss Account for the year ended 31 December 19-8

		£
Loss on sale of machinery	(D)	74

Modern Method: Further Examples

So far the examples shown have been deliberately kept simple. Only one item of an asset has been shown in each case. Exhibits 20.1 and 20.2 give examples of more complicated cases.

Exhibit 20.1

A machine is bought on 1 January 19-5 for £1,000 and another one on 1 October 19-6 for £1,200. The first machine is sold on 30 June 19-7 for £720. The firm's financial year ends on 31 December. The machinery is to be depreciated at ten per cent, using the straight line method and based on assets in existence at the end of each year ignoring items sold during the year.

Machinery

	£			£
19-5				
Jan 1 Cash	1,000			
19-6			19-6	
Oct 1 Cash	1,200		Dec 31 Balance c/d	2,200
	2,200			2,200
19-7			19-7	
Jan 1 Balance b/d	2,200		Jun 30 Disposals	1,000
			Dec 31 Balance c/d	1,200
	2,200			2,200
19-8				
Jan 1 Balance b/d	1,200			

Provision for Depreciation – Machinery

	£		£
		19-5	
		Dec 31 Profit and Loss	100
19-6		19-6	
Dec 31 Balance c/d	320	Dec 31 Profit and Loss	220
	320		320

19-7		£	19-7	£
Jun 30 Disposals			Jan 1 Balance b/d	320
	(2 years × 10 per cent		Dec 31 Profit and Loss	120
	× £1,000)	200		
Dec 31 Balance c/d		240		
		440		440
			19-8	
			Jan 1 Balance b/d	240

Disposals of Machinery

19-7			19-7	
Jun 30 Machinery		1,000	Jun 30 Cash	720
			Jun 30 Provision for	
			Depreciation	200
			Dec 31 Profit and Loss	80
		1,000		1,000

Profit and Loss Account for the year ended 31 December

19-5 Provision for		
Depreciation		100
19-6 Provision for		
Depreciation		220
19-7 Provision for		
Depreciation		120
Loss on machinery sold		80

Balance Sheet (Extracts) as at 31 December

	£	£
19-5 Machinery		
at cost	1,000	
Less		
Depreciation		
to date	100	900
19-6 Machinery		
at cost	2,200	
Less		
Depreciation		
to date	320	1,880
19-7 Machinery		
at cost	1,200	
Less		
Depreciation		
to date	240	960

Another example can now be given. This is somewhat more complicated owing first to a greater number of items, and secondly because the depreciation provisions are calculated on a proportionate basis, i.e. one month's depreciation for every one month's ownership.

Exhibit 20.2

A business with its financial year end being 31 December buys two motor vans, No. 1 for £800 and No. 2 for £500, both on 1 January 19-1. It also buys another motor van, No. 3, on 1 July 19-3 for £900 and another, No. 4, on 1 October 19-3 for £720. The first two motor vans are sold, No. 1 for £229 on 30 September 19-4, and the other No. 2, was sold for scrap £5 on 30 June 19-5.

Depreciation is on the straight line basis, 20 per cent per annum, ignoring scrap value in this particular case when calculating depreciation per annum. Show the extracts from the assets account, provision for depreciation account, disposal account, profit and loss account for the years ended 31 December 19-1, 19-2, 19-3, 19-4, and 19-5, and the balance sheets as at those dates.

Motor Vans

19-1		£			£
Jan	1 Cash	1,300			
19-3					
July	1 Cash	900	19-3		
Oct	1 Cash	720	Dec 31 Balance c/d		2,920
		2,920			2,920
19-4			19-4		
Jan	1 Balance b/d	2,920	Sept 30 Disposals		800
			Dec 31 Balance c/d		2,120
		2,920			2,920
19-5			19-5		
Jan	1 Balance b/d	2,120	June 30 Disposals		500
			Dec 31 Balance c/d		1,620
		2,120			2,120
19-6					
Jan	1 Balance b/d	1,620			

Provision for Depreciation — Motor Vans

	£		£
		19-1	
		Dec 31 Profit and Loss	260
19-2		**19-2**	
Dec 31 Balance c/d	520	Dec 31 Profit and Loss	260
	520		520
19-3		**19-3**	
		Jan 1 Balance b/d	520
Dec 31 Balance c/d	906	Dec 31 Profit and Loss	386
	906		906
19-4		**19-4**	
Sept 30 Disposals	600	Jan 1 Balance b/d	906
Dec 31 Balance c/d	850	Dec 31 Profit and Loss	544
	1,450		1,450
19-5		**19-5**	
June 30 Disposals	450	Jan 1 Balance b/d	850
Dec 31 Balance c/d	774	Dec 31 Profit and Loss	374
	1,224		1,224
		19-6	
		Jan 1 Balance b/d	774

Workings — Depreciation Provisions

		£	£
19-1	20% of £1,300		260
19-2	20% of £1,300		260
19-3	20% of £1,300 × 12 months	260	
	20% of £900 × 6 months	90	
	20% of £720 × 3 months	36	386
19-4	20% of £2,120 × 12 months	424	
	20% of £800 × 9 months	120	544
19-5	20% of £1,620 × 12 months	324	
	20% of £500 × 6 months	50	374

Workings — Transfers of Depreciation Provisions to Disposal Accounts

Van 1 Bought Jan 1 19-1 Cost £800
  Sold Sept 30 19-4
  Period of ownership 3¾ years
  Depreciation provisions 3¾ × 20% × £800 = £600
Van 2 Bought Jan 1 19-1 Cost £500
  Sold June 30 19-5
  Period of ownership 4½ years
  Depreciation provisions 4½ × 20% × £500 = £450

Disposals of Motor Vans

19-4	£	19-4	£
Sept 30 Motor Van	800	Sept 30 Provision for	
Dec 31 Profit and Loss	29	Depreciation	600
		,, ,, Cash	229
	829		829
19-5		19-5	
June 30 Motor Van	500	June 30 Provision for	
		Depreciation	450
		,, ,, Cash	5
		Dec 31 Profit and Loss	45
	500		500

Profit and Loss Account for the year ended 31 December (extracts)

	£		
19-1 Provision for			
Depreciation	260		
19-2 Provision for			
Depreciation	260		
19-3 Provision for			
Depreciation	386		
19-4 Provision for		19-4 Profit on motor van sold	29
Depreciation	544		
19-5 Provision for			
Depreciation	374		
Loss on motor van sold	45		

Balance Sheets (Extracts) as at 31 December

	£	£
19-1 Motor Vans at cost	1,300	
Less Depreciation to date	260	1,040
19-2 Motor Vans at cost	1,300	
Less Depreciation to date	520	780
19-3 Motor Vans at cost	2,920	
Less Depreciation to date	906	2,014
19-4 Motor Vans at cost	2,120	
Less Depreciation to date	850	1,270
19-5 Motor Vans at cost	1,620	
Less Depreciation to date	774	846

Depreciation Provisions and the Replacement of Assets

The purpose of making provision for depreciation is to ensure that the cost of an asset is charged as an expense in an equitable fashion over its useful life in the firm. Parts of the cost are allocated to different years until the whole of the asset's cost has been expensed. This does not mean that depreciation provisions of the type described already provide funds with which to replace the asset when it is put out of use. Such provisions might affect the owner's actions so that funds were available to pay for the replacement of the asset, but this is not necessarily true in all cases.

Imagine a case when a machine is bought for £1,000 and it is expected to last for 5 years, at the end of which time it will be put out of use and will not fetch any money from its being scrapped. If the machine has provisions for depreciation calculated on the straight line basis then £200 per year will be charged as an expense for 5 years. This means that the recorded net profit will be decreased £200 for each of the 5 years because of the depreciation provisions. Now the owner may well, as a consequence, because his profits are £200 less also reduce his drawings by £200 per annum. If the action of charging £200 each year for depreciation also does reduce his annual drawings by £200, then that amount will increase his bank balance (or reduce his bank overdraft), so that at the end of 5 years he may have the cash available to buy a new machine for £1,000 to replace the one that has been put out of use. In fact this is not necessarily true at all, the owner may still take the same amount of drawings for each of the 5 years whether or not a provision for depreciation is charged. In this case nothing has been deliberately held back to provide the cash with which to buy the replacement machine.

There is nothing by law that say that if your recorded profits are £x then the drawings must not exceed £y. For instance a man may make £5,000 profit for his first year in business whilst his drawings were £1,000 in that year, whilst in the second year his profit might be £2,000 and his drawings are £4,000. In the long run an owner may go out of business if his drawings are too high, but in the short term his drawings may well bear no relationship to profits whatsoever. This means that the amounts charged for depreciation provisions thus affecting the profits recorded may not affect the drawings at all in the short term.

Assignment Exercises

20.1 A company starts in business on 1 January 19-1. You are to write up the motor vans account and the provision for depreciation account for the year ended 31 December 19-1 from the information given below. Depreciation is at the rate of 20 per cent per annum, using the basis of 1 month's ownership needs one month's depreciation.

19-1 Bought two motor vans for £1,200 each on 1 January
      Bought one motor van for £1,400 on 1 July

20.2 A company starts in business on 1 January 19-3, the financial year end being 31 December. You are to show:

(*a*) The machinery account
(*b*) The provision for depreciation account
(*c*) The balance sheet extracts

for each of the years 19-3, 19-4, 19-5, 19-6.

The machinery bought was:

19-3	1 January	1 machine costing £800
19-4	1 July	2 machines costing £500 each
	1 October	1 machine costing £600
19-6	1 April	1 machine costing £200

Depreciation is at the rate of 10 per cent per annum, using the straight line method, machines being depreciated for each proportion of a year.

20.3 A company depreciates its plant at the rate of 20 per cent per annum, straight line method, for each month of ownership. From the following details draw up the Plant Account and the provision for depreciation account for each of the years 19-4, 19-5, 19-6 and 19-7.

19-4 Bought plant costing £900 on 1 January
       Bought plant costing £600 on 1 October
19-6 Bought plant costing £550 on 1 July
19-7 Sold plant which had been bought on 1 January 19-4 for £900 for the sum of £275 on 30 September 19-7.

You are also required to draw up the plant disposal account and the extracts from the balance sheet as at the end of each year.

20.4A K. Smart started in business on 1 January 19-2. Write up the machinery account and the provision for depreciation account for the years ended 31 December 19-2 and 19-3 from the following information. Depreciation is at the rate of 10 per cent, using the straightline basis and where 1 month's ownership equals 1 month's depreciation provision, and eventual scrap value is to be ignored.

19-2	January 1	Bought machine for £2,000
19-3	January 1	Bought two machines for £1,500 each
	July 1	Bought machine for £1,800

20.5A Young & Co. has bought the following fixed assets:

19-1	1 January	Bought fixtures £500; Machinery £2,000
	1 June	Bought machinery £2,500
19-2	1 March	Bought fixtures £600
	1 November	Bought machinery £3,000; fixtures £700

Machinery is to be depreciated at the rate of 20 per cent, fixtures 10 per cent, both using the reducing balance method. It is to be based on assets in existence at the end of the year, irrespective of the date when the asset was bought during the year.

The financial year end of the business is 31 December. Show for the above two years:

(i)   The machinery account.
(ii)   The fixtures account.
(iii) The provision for depreciation accounts.
(iv)   Balance sheet extracts.

21 Bad Debts and Provisions for Bad Debts

With many businesses a large proportion, if not all, of the sales are on a credit basis. The business is therefore taking the risk that some of the customers may never pay for the goods sold to them on credit. This is a normal business risk, and therefore bad debts as they are called are a normal business expense, and must be charged as such when calculating the profit or loss for the period.

When a debt is found to be bad, the asset as shown by the debtor's account is worthless, and must accordingly be eliminated as an asset account. This is done by crediting the debtor's account to cancel the asset and increasing the expenses account of bad debts by debiting it there. Sometimes the debtor will have paid part of the debt, leaving the remainder to be written off as a bad debt. The total of the bad debts account is later transferred to the profit and loss account.

An example of debts being written off as bad can now be shown:

Exhibit 21.1

C. Bloom

19-5		£	19-5		£
Jan 8	Sales	50	Dec 31	Bad Debts	50

R. Shaw

19-5		£	19-5		£
Feb 16	Sales	240	Aug 17	Cash	200
			Dec 31	Bad Debts	40
		240			240

Bad Debts

19-5		£	19-5		£
Dec 31 C. Bloom		50	Dec 31 Profit and Loss		90
,, ,, R. Shaw		40			
		—			—
		90			90
		==			==

Profit and Loss Account for the year ended 31 December 19-5

	£
Bad Debts	90

Provision for Bad Debts

The ideal situation from the accounting point of view of measuring net income, i.e. calculating net profit, is for the expenses of the period to be matched against the revenue of that period which the expenses have helped to create. Where an expense such as bad debt is matched in the same period with the revenue from the sale, then all is in order for the purposes of net profit calculation. However, it is very often the case that it is not until a period later than that in which the sale took place is it realized that the debt is a bad debt.

Therefore, to try to bring into the period in which the sale was made a charge for the bad debts resulting from such sales, the accountant brings in the concept of an estimated expense. Such an item of expense for an expense that had taken place, but which cannot be calculated with substantial accuracy is known as a Provision. The item of estimated expense for bad debts is therefore known as a Provision for Bad Debts.

Thus, in addition to writing off debts that are irrecoverable i.e. bad, it is necessary as a matter of business prudence, to charge the Profit and Loss Account with the amount of the provision for any debt the recovery of which is in doubt.

The estimate is arrived at on the basis of experience, a knowledge of the customers and of the state of the country's economy at that point in time with its likely effect on customers' debt paying capacity. Sometimes the schedules of debtors are scrutinized and a list of the doubtful debts made. Other firms work on an overall percentage basis to cover possible doubtful debts. Sometimes a provision is based on specified debtors. Another method is that of preparing an ageing schedule and taking different percentages for debts owing for different lengths of time. This is somewhat more scientific than the overall percentage basis, as in most trades and industries the longer a debt is owed the more chance there is of it turning out to be a bad debt. The schedule might appear as in Exhibit 21.2.

Exhibit 21.2

Ageing Schedule for Doubtful Debts

Period debt owing	Amount	Estimated percentage doubtful	Provision for bad debts
	£		£
Less than one month	5,000	1	50
1 month to 2 months	3,000	3	90
2 months to 3 months	800	4	32
3 months to 1 year	200	5	10
Over 1 year	160	20	32
	9,160		214

There are in fact two different methods of recording the provisions for doubtful debts. An adjustment may be made in the Bad Debts Account, or alternatively a completely separate account can be opened catering for the bad debts provision only. The net amount shown as bad debt expenses will be the same using the two methods, also the balance sheet will look exactly the same whichever method is used. The two methods are best illustrated in Exhibit 21.3.

It should be pointed out that, in practice, the more likely method will be that shown in Method A where the adjustment is shown in the Bad Debts Account. Examiners have however very often tended to choose a style having a completely separate account for the provision, this is shown as Method B. Either way is perfectly correct, and if the reader finds that he/she has difficulty with one method, but finds the other method simpler to follow, then obviously the simpler method will be the choice for that person.

(It should be noted that provisions for bad debts are frequently called provisions for doubtful debts).

Exhibit 21.3

A business starts on 1 January 19-2 and its financial year end is 31 December annually. A table of the debtors, the bad debts written off and the estimated doubtful debts at the end of each year is now given.

Year to 31 December	Debtors at end of year (after bad debts written off)	Bad Debts written off during year	Debts thought at end of year to be doubtful to collect
	£	£	£
19-2	6,000	423	120
19-3	7,000	510	140
19-4	8,000	604	155
19-5	6,400	610	130

Method A – using a Bad Debts Account only with adjustments being used for provisions for bad debts.

Profit and Loss Account for the year ended 31 December (extracts)

	£		£
19-2 Bad Debts	543		
19-3 Bad Debts	530		
19-4 Bad Debts	619		
19-5 Bad Debts	585		

Bad Debts

19-2		£	19-2		£
Dec 31 Sundries		423			
,, ,, Provision c/d		120	Dec 31 Profit and Loss		543
		543			543
19-3			19-3		
Dec 31 Sundries		510	Jan 1 Provision b/d		120
,, ,, Provision c/d		140	Dec 31 Profit and Loss		530
		650			650
19-4			19-4		
Dec 31 Sundries		604	Jan 1 Provision b/d		140
,, ,, Provision c/d		155	Dec 31 Profit and Loss		619
		759			759
19-5			19-5		
Dec 31 Sundries		610	Jan 1 Provision b/d		155
,, ,, Provision c/d		130	Dec 31 Profit and Loss		585
		740			740
			19-6		
			Jan 1 Provision for Doubtful debts b/d		130

Balance Sheets as at 31 December (extracts)

	£	£
19-2 Debtors	6,000	
Less Provision for Bad Debts	120	
		5,880
19-3 Debtors	7,000	
Less Provision for Bad Debts	140	
		6,860
19-4 Debtors	8,000	
Less Provision for Bad Debts	155	
		7,845
19-5 Debtors	6,400	
Less Provision for Bad Debts	130	
		6,270

Method B – using a separate Bad Debts Account and a provision for Bad Debts Account.

The Bad Debts Account is charged with the debts found to be bad during the accounting period, while the provision for Bad Debts Account shows the provision as at the end of each period. Once the provision account is created it stays open until the end of the next accounting period, and all that it then requires is the amount needed to increase it or reduce it to the newly estimated figure. In the balance sheet at the end of each period the provision for bad debts is shown as a deduction from debtors, so that the net amount is the expected amount of collectable debts.

Profit and Loss Accounts for the year ended 31 December (extracts)

	£		£
19-2 Bad Debts	423		
Provision for Bad Debts	120		
19-3 Bad Debts	510		
Increase in provision for Bad Debts	20		
19-4 Bad Debts	604		
Increase in provision for Bad Debts	15		
19-5 Bad Debts	610	19-5 Reduction in provision for Bad Debts	25

Provision for Bad Debts

	£	19-2	£
		Dec 31 Profit and Loss	120
19-3		19-3	
Dec 31 Balance c/d	140	Dec 31 Profit and Loss	20
	140		140
		19-4	
19-4		Jan 1 Balance b/d	140
Dec 31 Balance c/d	155	Dec 31 Profit and Loss	15
	155		155
19-5	£	19-5	£
Dec 31 Profit and Loss	25	Jan 1 Balance b/d	155
,, ,, Balance c/d	130		
	155		155
		19-6	
		Jan 1 Balance b/d	130

Bad Debts

19-2	£	19-2	£
Dec 31 Sundries	423	Dec 31 Profit and Loss	423
19-3		19-3	
Dec 31 Sundries	510	Dec 31 Profit and Loss	510
19-4		19-4	
Dec 31 Sundries	604	Dec 31 Profit and Loss	604
19-5		19-5	
Dec 31 Sundries	610	Dec 31 Profit and Loss	610

The balance sheet for Method B will be exactly the same as the balance sheet in Method A.

Comparing the amounts charged as expense to the Profit and loss Account it can be seen that:

	Method A	*Method B*
19-2	543	423 + 120 = total 543
19-3	530	510 + 20 = total 530
19-4	619	604 + 15 = total 619
19-5	585	610 − 25 = net 585

At first sight it might appear that the provisions were far short of reality. For instance at the end of the first year the provision was £120 yet bad debts in the second year amounted to £510. This, however, is not a fair comparison if the amount of debtors at each year end equalled in amount approximately three months of sales, this being the average time in which debtors pay their accounts. In this case the provision is related to three months of sales, while the bad debts written off are those relating to twelve months of sales.

Assignment Exercises

21.1 In a new business during the year ended 31 December 19-4 the following debts are found to be bad, and are written off on the dates shown:

30 April	H. Gordon	£100
31 August	D. Bellamy Ltd	£64
31 October	J. Alderton	£12

On 31 December 19-4 the schedule of remaining debtors, amounting in total to £6,850, is examined, and it is decided to make a provision, for doubtful debts of £220.

You are required to show:
(i) The bad debts account, with the provision to be a part of it.
(ii) The charge to the Profit and Loss Account.
(iii) The relevant extracts from the Balance Sheet as at 31 December 19-4.
(*also see question 21.4A*)

21.2 A business started trading on 1 January 19-6. During the two years ended 31 December 19-6 and 19-7 the following debts were written off to bad debts account on the dates stated:

31 August 19-6	W. Best	£85
30 September 19-6	S. Avon	£140
28 February 19-7	L. J. Friend	£180
31 August 19-7	N. Kelly	£60
30 November 19-7	A. Oliver	£250

On 31 December 19-6 there had been a total of debtors remaining of £40,500. It was decided to make a provision for doubtful debts of £550.

On 31 December 19-7 there had been a total of debtors remaining of £47,300. It was decided to make a provision for doubtful debts of £600.

You are required to show:
(i) The Bad Debts Account for each of the two years, with the provisions included in this account.
(ii) The charges to the Profit and Loss Account for each of the two years.
(iii) The relevant extracts from the balance sheets as at 31 December 19-6 and 19-7.
(*also see question 21.4A*)

21.3A A business, which started trading on 1 January 19-5, adjusted its bad debt provisions at the end of each year on a percentage basis, but each year the percentage rate is adjusted in accordance with the current 'economic climate'. The following details are available for the three years ended 31 December 19-5, 19-6 and 19-7.

Bad Debts written off year to 31 December		Debtors at 31 December	Per cent provision for Doubtful Debts
	£	£	
19-5	656	22,000	5
19-6	1,805	40,000	7
19-7	3,847	60,000	6

Using the method shown as Method A in Chapter 21, you are required to show the following:

(i) Bad Debts Accounts for each of the three years, showing provisions carried forward.

(ii) Balance Sheet extracts as at 31 December 19-5, 19-6 and 19-7.

(*also see question 21.4A*)

21.4A For students sitting examinations where separate Provision for Bad Debt account questions are asked, attempt questions 21.1, 21.2 and 21.3A using Method B as stated in Chapter 21.

22 Other Adjustments for Final Accounts: Accruals, Prepayments etc.

The trading and profit and loss accounts looked at so far have taken the sales for a period and all the expenses for that period have been deducted, the result being a net profit (or a net loss).

Up to this part of the book it has always been assumed that the expenses belonged exactly to the period of the trading and profit and loss account. If the trading and profit and loss account for the year ended 31 December 19-5 was being drawn up, then the rent paid as shown in the trial balance was exactly for 19-5. There was no rent owing at the beginning of 19-5 nor any owing at the end of 19-5, nor had any rent been paid in advance.

However, where on the other hand the costs used up and the amount paid are not equal to one another, then an adjustment will be required in respect of the overpayment or underpayment of the costs used up during the period.

In all of the following examples the trading and profit and loss accounts being drawn up are for the year ended 31 December 19-5.

Accrued Expenses

Consider the case of rent being charged at the rate of £1,000 per year. It is payable at the end of each quarter of the year for the three months' tenancy that has just expired. It can be assumed that the tenancy commenced on 1 January 19-5. The rent was paid for 19-5 on 31 March, 2 July and 4 October and on 5 January 19-6.

During the year ended 31 December 19-5 the rent account will appear:

Rent

19-5		£
Mar 31	Cash	250
Jul 2	,,	250
Oct 4	,,	250

The rent paid 5 January 19-6 will appear in the books of the year 19-6 as part of the double-entry.

The costs used up during 19-5 are obviously £1,000, as that is the year's rent, and this is the amount needed to be transferred to the profit and loss account. But if £1,000 was put on the credit side of the rent account (the debit being in the profit and loss account) the account would not balance. There would be £1,000 on the credit side of the account and only £750 on the debit side. To make the account balance the £250 rent owing for 19-5, but paid in 19-6, must be carried down to 19-6 as a credit balance because it is a liability on 31 December 19-5. Instead of Rent Owing it could be called Rent Accrued or just simply as an accrual. The completed account can now be shown.

Rent

19-5	£	19-5	£
Mar 31 Cash	250	Dec 31 Profit and Loss A/c	1,000
Jul 2 ,,	250		
Oct 4 ,,	250		
Dec 31 Owing c/d	250		
	1,000		1,000
		19-6	
		Jan 1 Owing b/d	250

Expenses Prepaid

Insurance premiums have been paid as follows:

Feb 28 19-5 £210 for period of three months to 31 March 19-5.
Aug 31 19-5 £420 for period of six months to 30 September 19-5.
Nov 18 £420 for period of six months to 31 March 19-6.

The insurance account will be shown in the books:

Insurance

19-5	£
Feb 28 Cash	210
Aug 31 ,,	420
Nov 18 ,,	420

Now the last payment of £420 is not just for 19-5, it can be split as to £210 for the three months to 31 December 19-5 and £210 for the three months ended 31 March 19-6. For a period of 12 months the cost of insurance is £840 and this is therefore the figure needing to be transferred to the profit and loss account. The amount needed to balance the account will therefore be £210 and at 31 December 19-5 this is a benefit paid for but not used up; it is an asset and needs carrying forward as such to 19-6, i.e. as a debit balance.

The account can now be completed.

Insurance

19-5		£	19-5		£
Feb 28 Cash		210	Dec 31 Profit and Loss A/c		840
Aug 31 ,,		420	,, ,, Prepaid c/d		210
Nov 18 ,,		420			
		1,050			1,050
19-6					
Jan 1 Prepaid b/d		210			

Prepayment will also happen when items other than purchases are bought for use in the business, and they are not fully used up in the period.

For instance, packing materials are normally not entirely used up during the period in which they are bought, there being a stock of packing materials in hand at the end of the period. This stock is therefore a form of prepayment and needs carrying down to the following period in which it will be used.

This can be seen in the following example:

Year ended 31 December 19-5
Packing materials bought in the year £2,200
Stock of packing materials in hand as at 31 December 19-5 £400

Looking at the example, it can be seen that in 19-5 the packing materials used up will have been £2,200 − £400 = £1,800 and there will still be a stock of £400 packing materials at 31 December 19-5 to be carried forward to 19-6. The £400 stock of packing materials will accordingly be carried forward as an asset balance (debit balance) to 19-6.

Packing Materials

19-5		£	19-5		£
Dec 31 Cash		2,200	Dec 31 Profit and Loss A/c		1,800
			,, ,, Stock c/d		400
		2,200			2,200
19-6					
Jan 1 Stock b/d		400			

The stock of packing materials is not added to the stock of unsold goods in hand in the balance sheet, but is added to the other prepayments of expenses.

Outstanding Revenue other than Sales

Sales revenue outstanding is already shown in the books as debit balances on the customers' personal accounts, i.e. debtors. It is the other kinds of revenue such as rent receivable, commissions receivable, etc. which need to be considered. Such revenue to be brought into the profit and loss account is that which has been earned during the period. Should all the revenue earned actually be received during the period, then revenue received and revenue earned will be the same amount and no adjustment would be needed in the revenue account. Where the revenue has been earned, but the full amount has not been received, the revenue due to the business must be brought into the accounts; the amount receivable is after all the revenue used when calculating profit.

Example

The warehouse is larger than is needed. Part of it is rented to another firm for £800 per annum. For the year ended 31 December 19-5 the following cheques were received.

19-5
Apr 4   For three months to 31 March 19-5   £200
Jul   6   For three months to 30 June 19-5   £200
Oct 9   For three months to 30 September 19-5   £200

The £200 for the three months to 31 December 19-5 was received 7 January 19-6.

The account for 19-5 appeared:

Rent Receivable

			£
19-5			
Apr	4	Bank	200
Jul	6	Bank	200
Oct	9	Bank	200

Any rent paid by the firm would be charged as a debit to the profit and loss account. Any rent received, being the opposite, is accordingly eventually transferred to the credit of the profit and loss account. The amount to be transferred for 19-5 is that earned for the twelve months. i.e. £800. The rent received account is completed by carrying down the balance owing as a debit balance to 19-6. The £200 owing is, after all, an asset on 31 December 19-5.

The Rent Receivable Account can now be completed:

Rent Receivable

19-5		£	19-5		£
Dec 31 Profit and Loss		800	Apr 4 Bank		200
			Jul 6 Bank		200
			Oct 9 Bank		200
			Dec 31 Accrued c/d		200
		800			800
19-6					
Jan 1 Accrued b/d		200			

Expenses and Revenue Account Balances and the Balance Sheet

In all the cases listed dealing with adjustments in the final accounts, there will still be a balance on each account after the preparation of the trading and profit and loss accounts. All such balances remaining should appear in the balance sheet. The only question left is to where and how they shall be shown.

The amounts owing for expenses are usually added together and shown as one figure. These could be called Expense Creditors, Expenses Owing, or Accrued Expenses. The item would appear under current liabilities as they are expenses which have to be discharged in the near future.

The items prepaid are also added together and called Prepayments, Prepaid Expenses, or Payments in Advance. Often they are added to the debtors in the balance sheet, otherwise they are shown next under the debtors.

Amounts owing for rents receivable or other revenue owing are usually added to debtors.

The balance sheet in respect of the accounts so far seen in this chapter would appear:

Balance Sheets as at 31 December 19-5

Current Assets	£	Current Liabilities	£
Stock		Trade creditors	
Debtors	200	Accrued Expenses	250
Prepayments	610		
Bank			
Cash			

Goods for Own Use

A trader will often take items out of his business stocks for his own use, without paying for them. There is certainly nothing wrong about this, but an entry should be made to record the event. This is effected by:

> Credit Purchases Account
> Debit Drawings Account

Adjustments may also be needed for other private items. For instance, if a trader's private insurance had been incorrectly charged to the Insurance Account, then the correction would be:

> Credit Insurance Account
> Debit Drawings Account

Final Accounts for Non-Traders

If the final accounts are for someone who is not trading in goods as such, for instance accountants, insurance agents, lawyers and the like, there will be no need for a Trading Account. All of the revenue and expense items will be shown in a Profit and Loss Account, disclosing a net profit (or net loss). Balance Sheets for such providers of services (i.e. not goods) will be the same as for traders.

Vertical Form of Accounts

Throughout this book to this point the two-sided presentation of Trading and Profit and Loss Accounts and Balance Sheets is used. For many reasons this is easier to use from a teaching point of view. However, in practice you would not necessarily have to show the final accounts drawn up in that fashion. It would be completely up to the owner(s) of a business to decide on the method of presentation. What really matters is whether or not the presentation still results in the correct answer being shown.

Final accounts are more normally shown in a vertical fashion. This is also referred to as narrative style, or columnar presentation. When this is done the chance is usually taken of displaying 'working capital' as a separate figure. 'Working Capital' is the term for the excess of the current assets over the current liabilities of a business.

The translation of a Trading and Profit and Loss Account from a horizontal format to a vertical format can be shown by means of a diagram Exhibit 22.1

Exhibit 22.1

Horizontal form:

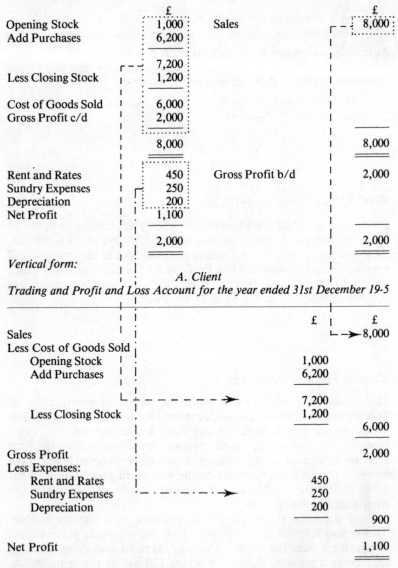

A. Client
Trading and Profit and Account for the year ended 31 December 19-5

	£		£
Opening Stock	1,000	Sales	8,000
Add Purchases	6,200		
	7,200		
Less Closing Stock	1,200		
Cost of Goods Sold	6,000		
Gross Profit c/d	2,000		
	8,000		8,000
Rent and Rates	450	Gross Profit b/d	2,000
Sundry Expenses	250		
Depreciation	200		
Net Profit	1,100		
	2,000		2,000

Vertical form:

A. Client
Trading and Profit and Loss Account for the year ended 31st December 19-5

	£	£
Sales		8,000
Less Cost of Goods Sold		
Opening Stock	1,000	
Add Purchases	6,200	
	7,200	
Less Closing Stock	1,200	
		6,000
Gross Profit		2,000
Less Expenses:		
Rent and Rates	450	
Sundry Expenses	250	
Depreciation	200	
		900
Net Profit		1,100

If there had been any revenue such as commissions or rent received, then this would have followed the figure of gross profit as an addition.

Exhibit 22.2 shows the translation of a balance sheet from the horizontal form to a vertical form.

Exhibit 22.2

Horizontal form:

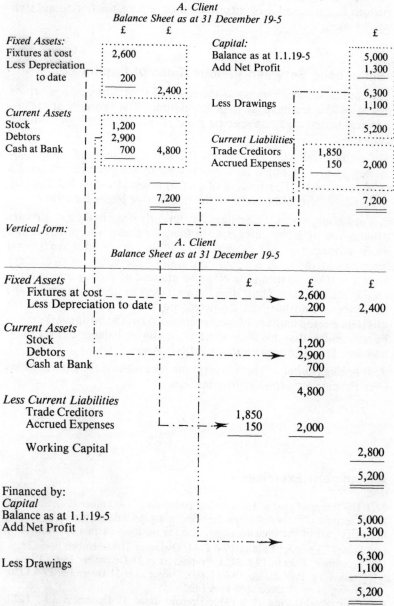

A. Client
Balance Sheet as at 31 December 19-5

	£	£			£
Fixed Assets:			**Capital:**		
Fixtures at cost	2,600		Balance as at 1.1.19-5		5,000
Less Depreciation to date	200		Add Net Profit		1,300
		2,400			6,300
			Less Drawings		1,100
Current Assets					5,200
Stock	1,200				
Debtors	2,900		**Current Liabilities**		
Cash at Bank	700	4,800	Trade Creditors	1,850	
			Accrued Expenses	150	2,000
		7,200			7,200

Vertical form:

A. Client
Balance Sheet as at 31 December 19-5

	£	£	£
Fixed Assets			
Fixtures at cost		2,600	
Less Depreciation to date		200	2,400
Current Assets			
Stock		1,200	
Debtors		2,900	
Cash at Bank		700	
		4,800	
Less Current Liabilities			
Trade Creditors	1,850		
Accrued Expenses	150	2,000	
Working Capital			2,800
			5,200
Financed by:			
Capital			
Balance as at 1.1.19-5			5,000
Add Net Profit			1,300
			6,300
Less Drawings			1,100
			5,200

You should note that there is not just one way of presenting final accounts in a vertical fashion, but the ones shown are in a good style.

From this point most of the final accounts are shown in vertical style, as it accords with normal practice in business and would be looked on with favour by examiners. However, on occasion, because of display reasons in fitting a lot of information on a page the horizontal style will be used.

Distinctions Between Various Kinds of Capital

The capital account represents the claim of the proprietor against the assets of the business at a point in time. The word 'Capital' is, however, often used in a specific sense. The main meanings are listed below:

1. Capital invested. This means the actual amount of money, or money's worth, brought into the business by the proprietor from his outside interests. The amount of capital invested is not disturbed by the amount of profits made by the business or losses incurred.

2. Capital employed. Candidates at an early stage in their studies are often asked to define this term. In fact, for those who progress to a more advanced stage, it will be seen that it could have several meanings as the term is often used quite loosely. At an elementary level it is taken to mean the effective amount of money that is being used in the business. Thus, if all the assets were added together and the liabilities of the business deducted the answer would be that the difference is the amount of money employed in the business. You will by now realize that this is the same as the closing balance of the capital account. It is also sometimes called Net Assets.

3. Working capital. This is a term for the excess of the current assets over the current liabilities of a business.

Assignment Exercises

22.1 The financial year of H. Saunders ended on 31 December 19-6. Show the ledger accounts for the following items including the balance transferred to the necessary part of the final accounts, also the balances carried down to 19-7:

(a) Motor Expenses: Paid in 19-6 £744; Owing at 31 December 19-6 £28.

(b) Insurance: Paid in 19-6 £420; Prepaid as at 31 December 19-6 £35.

(c) Stationery: Paid during 19-6 £1,800; Owing as at 31 December 19-5 £250; Owing as at 31 December 19-6 £490.

(d) Rent: Paid during 19-6 £950; Prepaid as at 31 December 19-5 £220; Prepaid as at 31 December 19-6 £290.

(e) Saunders sub-lets part of the premises. Receives £550 during the year ended 31 December 19-6. Tenant owed Saunders £180 on 31 December 19-5 and £210 on 31 December 19-6.

22.2A J. Owen's year ended on 30 June 19-4. Write up the ledger accounts, showing the transfers to the final accounts and the balances carried down to the next year for the following:

(a) Stationery: Paid for the year to 30 June 19-4 £855; Stocks of stationery at 30 June 19-3 £290; at 30 June 19-4 £345.

(b) General expenses: Paid for the year to 30 June 19-4 £590; Owing at 30 June 19-3 £64; Owing at 30 June 19-4 £90.

(c) Rent and Rates (combined account): Paid in the year to 30 June 19-4 £3,890; Rent owing at 30 June 19-3 £160; Rent paid in advance at 30 June 19-4 £250; Rates owing 30 June 19-3 £205; Rates owing 30 June 19-4 £360.

(d) Motor Expenses: paid in the year to 30 June 19-4 £4,750; Owing as at 30 June 19-3 £180; Owing as at 30 June 19-4 £375.

(e) Owen earns commission from the sales of one item. Received for the year to 30 June 19-4 £850; Owing at 30 June 19-3 £80; Owing at 30 June 19-4 £145.

22.3 On 1 January 19-6 B. Allison started business as a wholesale confectioner. The following were among the balances extracted from his books at 31 December 19-6.

From the following information you are required to prepare the Trading and Profit and Loss Accounts for the year ended 31 December 19-6 using vertical style accounts

	£
Purchases	11,377
Sales	13,475
Returns Inwards	242
Returns Outwards	268
Carriage on Purchases	47
Motor Van Expenses	155
Wages of Driver	652
Office Expenses	104
Bad Debts	79
Insurances	26
Electricity	30
Interest on Loan	21
Discounts Allowed	337
Discounts Received	210
Rent and Rates	365
Rent of Premises Sublet	104

You are given the following additional information:

(i) Stock in hand at 31 December 19-6 was valued at £898.

(ii) A motor van which costs £660 is to be depreciated by 15% on cost.

(iii) Provide £105 for Bad and Doubtful Debts.

(iv) A half year's interest £21 was due on the loan.

(v) A demand notice for rates for the half year ending 31 March 19-7, £56 had been received but no payment made.

(vi) Insurance £6 was prepaid.

(vii) £12 was owing in respect of repairs to the motor van.

22.4A From the following Trial Balance of J. Oliphant, store owner, prepare a Trading Account and Profit and Loss Account, using the vertical style, taking into consideration the adjustments shown below:

Trial Balance as at 31 December 19-7

	Dr £	Cr £
Sales		80,000
Purchases	70,000	
Sales Returns	1,000	
Purchases Returns		1,240
Opening Stock at 1 January 19-7	20,000	
Provision for Bad Debt		160
Wages and salaries	7,200	
Telephone	200	
Store fittings at cost	8,000	
Van at cost	6,000	
Debtors and creditors	1,960	1,400
Bad Debts	40	
Capital		35,800
Bank balance	600	
Drawings	3,600	
	118,600	118,600

Adustments:
(i)   Closing stock at 31 December 19-7 £24,000.
(ii) Accrued wages £450.
(iii) Telephone prepaid £20.
(iv) The Provision for Bad Debts to be increased to 10 per cent of Debtors.
(v) Depreciate store fittings at 10 per cent per annum, and van at 20 per cent per annum, on cost.
A Balance Sheet is not required.

22.5 The following Trial Balance was extracted from the books of A. Scholes at the close of business on 28 February 19-7.

	Dr £	Cr £
Purchases and sales	11,280	19,740
Cash at bank	1,140	
Cash in hand	210	
Capital Account 1 March 19-6		9,900
Drawings	2,850	
Office furniture	1,440	
Rent	1,020	
Wages and salaries	2,580	
Discounts	690	360
Debtors and creditors	4,920	2,490
Stock 1 March 19-6	2,970	
Provision for Bad and Doubtful Debts 1 March 19-6		270
Delivery van	2,400	
Van running costs	450	
Bad Debts written off	810	
	32,760	32,760

Notes:
(*a*) Stock 28 February 19-7 £3,510.
(*b*) Wages and salaries accrued at 28 February 19-7 £90.
(*c*) Rent prepaid at 28 February 19-7 £140.
(*d*) Van running costs owing at 28 February 19-7 £60.
(*e*) Increase the provision for Bad and Doubtful Debts by £60.
(*f*) Provide the depreciation as follows: Office furniture £180. Delivery van £480.

Required:
Draw up the Trading and Profit and Loss Accounts for the year ending 28 February 19-7 together with a Balance Sheet as on 28 February 19-7, using vertical formats throughout.

22.6A A. Jakes is a retail trader. From the following information prepare a Trading and Profit and Loss Account for the year ended 31 December 19-4 and a Balance Sheet on that date, using vertical style of accounts.

Trial Balance – 31 December 19-4

	£	£
Capital 1 January 19-4		32,000
Land and buildings at cost	30,000	
Motor vehicles (at cost)	6,000	
Drawings	7,050	
Stock	4,500	
Bank overdraft		480
Sales		71,300
Purchases	55,500	
Motor expenses	1,550	
Sundry expenses	530	
Wages	7,800	
Debtors	4,100	
Creditors		6,050
Telephone and Insurance	800	
Provision for depreciation:		
Motor vehicles		3,000
Land and Buildings		5,000
	117,830	117,830

The following items should be taken into consideration:
(a) Stock at 31 December 19-4 £9,100.
(b) A provision for doubtful debts of 5 per cent on the debtors at 31 December 19-4 is to be created.
(c) Depreciation is to be provided on motor vehicles at 20 per cent on cost, and buildings at £1,000 per annum.
(d) Insurance prepaid at 31 December 19-4 £60.
(e) Motor expenses bill for December £130 is owing at 31 December 19-4.
(f) Sundry expenses includes £75 for a private telephone bill of A. Jakes.
(g) A cheque for £1,250 was paid to a creditor on 31 December 19-4 but had not been entered in the books at the time of extracting the trial balance.
(h) Wages owing £350.

23 Capital and Revenue Expenditure

When fixed assets are bought, or when a firm spends money to add to the value of an existing fixed asset, such expenditure is called 'Capital Expenditure'. This should include the costs of acquiring the fixed assets and bringing them into the firm; this would include legal costs on buying buildings, carriage inwards on machinery bought and so on.

When there is expenditure which is not concerned with adding to the value of fixed assets, but represents the costs of running the business on a day-to-day basis, then this expenditure is known as 'Revenue Expenditure'.

This means that buying a motor van, which will be used in the business for the next few years, is Capital Expenditure. Paying for the petrol to run the motor van, such petrol to be used within a relatively short time, is Revenue Expenditure. Buying a machine is Capital Expenditure. Repairing the machine when it breaks down is not adding to the original value of the machine, and is therefore Revenue Expenditure. If, on the other hand, £900 was spent on the machine, £300 of which was to repair the machine and the other £600 was to make improvements to the machine in some way – for instance, to fit an extra attachment to it – then £300 would be Revenue Expenditure, whilst the £600 would be Capital Expenditure, as it represents an improvement.

It can be seen that Revenue Expenditure is that chargeable to the Trading or Profit and Loss Account, whilst Capital Expenditure will result in increased figures for Fixed Assets in the balance sheet.

The importance of ensuring that Capital Expenditure is not charged as Revenue Expenditure, and vice-versa, cannot be stressed often enough. Two cases can now be looked at where the different forms of expenditure have got mixed up.

Revenue Expenditure Overstated
Exhibit 23.1

The following trial balance of F. Rankin has been extracted as on 31 December 19-8. In fact, two of the figures shown in it are incorrect.

Included in purchases is £1,500 for the purchase of building materials which were for an addition to the premises. In error they have been charged to purchases, i.e. they have been charged as revenue expenditure instead of as capital expenditure. First will be shown the Trading and Profit and Loss Account for the year, and the Balance Sheet as at the year ended (*a*) as they were drawn up incorrectly, and (*b*) drawn up correctly, showing the £1,500 buildings materials as adding to the value of Premises.

Trial Balance as at 31 December 19-8

	Dr £	Cr £
General expenses	490	
Motor expenses	1,247	
Salaries	3,560	
Purchases	14,305	
Sales		26,815
Stock 1 January 19-8	4,080	
Motor vehicle	2,800	
Creditors		5,160
Debtors	4,090	
Premises	20,000	
Cash at bank	1,400	
Capital		24,347
Drawings	4,350	
	56,322	56,322

Stock at 31 December 19-8 was £4,960.

F. Rankin
Trading and Profit and Loss Account for the year ended 31 December 19-8

	(*a*) Incorrect £	£	(*b*) Corrected £	£
Sales		26,815		26,815
Less Cost of Goods Sold				
Opening Stock	4,080		4,080	
Add Purchases	14,305		12,805*	
	18,385		16,885	
Less Closing Stock	4,960	13,425	4,960	11,925
Gross Profit		13,390		14,890*
Less Expenses				
Salaries	3,560		3,560	
Motor Expenses	1,247		1,247	
General Expenses	490	5,297	490	5,297
Net Profit		8,093		9,593*

Balance Sheet as at 31 December 19-8

	(a) Incorrect £	£	(b) Corrected £	£
Fixed Assets				
Premises		20,000		21,500*
Motor Vehicle		2,800		2,800
		22,800		24,300
Current Assets				
Stock	4,960		4,960	
Debtors	4,090		4,090	
Bank	1,400		1,400	
	10,450		10,450	
Less Current Liabilities				
Creditors	5,160		5,160	
Working Capital		5,290		5,290
		28,090		29,590
Financed by:				
Capital				
Balance as at 1.1.19-8		24,347		24,347
Add Net Profit		8,093		9,593*
		32,440		33,940
Less Drawings		4,350		4,350
		28,090		29,590

The items showing amendments are indicated by asterisks(*).

It can now be seen that, in this particular case, the overstatement of revenue expenditure has resulted in (i) gross profit was understated £1,500, (ii) net profit was understated £1,500, (iii) a fixed asset, Premises, was understated by £1,500.

Capital Expenditure Overstated
Exhibit 23.2

What happens when capital expenditure is overstated? Take the trial balance of F. Rankin, as in Exhibit 23.1, but assume that a different error has been made. Suppose, instead of the error already shown, that one was made which resulted in an overstatement of capital expenditure. Assume that a replacement engine costing £420 has been fitted in the motor vehicle. Instead of charging the cost to Motor Expenses, it had instead been added in to the value of Motor Vehicle to give a total of £2,800. The final accounts can now be looked at (a) before correction, and (b) after correction.

F. Rankin

Trading and Profit and Loss Account for the year ended 31 December 19-8

	(a) Incorrect £	(a) Incorrect £	(b) Corrected £	(b) Corrected £
Sales		26,815		26,815
Less Cost of Goods Sold				
Opening Stock	4,080		4,080	
Add Purchases	14,305		14,305	
	18,385		18,385	
Less Closing Stock	4,960	13,425	4,960	13,425
Gross Profit		13,390		13,390
Less Expenses				
Salaries	3,560		3,560	
Motor Expenses	1,247		1,667*	
General Expenses	490	5,297	490	5,717
Net Profit		8,093		7,673*

Balance Sheet as at 31 December 19-8

	(a) Incorrect £	(a) Incorrect £	(b) Corrected £	(b) Corrected £
Fixed Assets				
Premises		20,000		20,000
Motor Vehicle		2,800		2,380*
		22,800		22,380
Current Assets				
Stock	4,960		4,960	
Debtors	4,090		4,090	
Bank	1,400		1,400	
	10,450		10,450	
Less Current Liabilities				
Creditors	5,160		5,160	
Working Capital		5,290		5,290
		28,090		27,670
Financed by:				
Capital				
Balance as at 1.1.19-8		24,347		24,347
Add Net Profit		8,093		7,673*
		32,440		32,020
Less Drawings		4,350		4,350
		28,090		27,670

The items showing amendment are indicated by asterisks (*).

It can now be seen in this particular case, that overstatement of capital expenditure resulted in (i) overstatement of net profit, (ii) overstatement of value of fixed asset.

Apportioning Expenditure

Sometimes one item of expenditure will need splitting between capital and revenue expenditure. A builder was engaged to tackle some work on your premises, the total bill being for £3,000. If one-third of this was for repair work and two-thirds for improvements, then £1,000 should be charged in the profit and loss account as revenue expenditure, and £2,000 added to the value of premises and shown as such in the balance sheet.

Capital and Revenue Receipts

As seen, 'Capital' items are long term and have an enduring influence on the profit-making capacity of the business. 'Revenue' items are short term and have only a temporary influence on the profit making capacity of the business. The expenditure side of these items has been considered. There will also be a receipts side. 'Capital Receipts' will therefore consist of the sale of 'Capital' items, e.g. the sale of a vehicle used in the business, the sale of premises. 'Revenue Receipts' will be those receipts which cover revenue items received, such as Rent Receivable or Commissions Receivable.

Assignment Exercises

23.1 For the business of J. Charles, wholesale chemist, classify the following between 'Capital' and 'Revenue' expenditure:

(a) Purchase of an extra motor van.
(b) Cost of rebuilding warehouse wall which had fallen down.
(c) Building extension to the warehouse.
(d) Painting extension to warehouse when it is first built.
(e) Repainting extension to warehouse three years later than that done in (d).
(f) Carriage costs on bricks for new warehouse extension.
(g) Carriage costs on purchases.
(h) Carriage costs on sales.
(i) Legal costs of collecting debts.
(j) Legal charges on acquiring new premises for office.
(k) Fire insurance premium.
(l) Costs of erecting new machine.

23.2A For the business of H. Ward, a food merchant, classify the following between 'Capital' and 'Revenue' expenditure:

(*a*) Repairs to meat slicer.
(*b*) New tyre for van.
(*c*) Additional shop counter.
(*d*) Renewing signwriting on shop.
(*e*) Fitting partitions in shop.
(*f*) Roof repairs.
(*g*) Installing thief detection equipment.
(*h*) Wages of shop assistant.
(*i*) Carriage on returns outwards.
(*j*) New cash register.
(*k*) Repairs to office safe.
(*l*) Installing extra toilet.

23.3 Explain clearly the different between capital expenditure and revenue expenditure. State which of the following you would classify as capital expenditure, giving your reasons:

(i)   Cost of building extension to factory.
(ii) Purchase of extra filing cabinets for sales office.
(iii) Cost of repairs to accounting machine.
(iv) Cost of installing reconditioned engine in delivery van.
(v)   Legal fees paid in connection with factory extension.

23.4A The data which follows was extracted from the books of account of H. Kirk, an engineer, on 31 March 19-6, his financial year end.

		£
(*a*)	Purchase of extra milling machine (includes £300 for repair of an old machine)	2,900
(*b*)	Rent	750
(*c*)	Electrical expenses (includes new wiring £600, part of premises improvement)	3,280
(*d*)	Carriage inwards (includes £150 carriage on new cement mixer)	1,260
(*e*)	Purchase of extra drilling machine	4,100

You are required to allocate each or part of the items above to either 'Capital' or 'Revenue' expenditure.

24 The Journal

Previously it has been shown that the work of recording transactions is divided up into its different functions, there being a separate book (or some other sort of collection point for data) for each major function. The books in which entries are made prior to their posting to the ledgers are known as subsidiary books or as books of prime entry. Thus the sales, purchases, returns inwards and returns outwards books are all books of prime entry. The cash book is also regarded as a book of prime entry, although many would regard it as a ledger, for as it has been seen it originated from the cash and bank accounts being detached from the ledger. However, it is the book in which cash and bank entries are first made and from this point of view it may be taken as a book of prime entry.

It is to the firm's advantage if all transactions which do not pass through a book of prime entry are entered in a book called The Journal. The journal is a form of diary for such transactions. It shows:

1. The date.
2. The name of the account(s) to be debited and the amount(s).
3. The name of the account(s) to be credited and the amount(s).
4. A description of the transaction (this is called a 'narrative').

One would also expect to find a reference number for the documents supporting the transaction.

The advantages to be gained from using a journal may be summarized:

1. It eliminates the need for a reliance on the memory of the book-keeper. Some transactions are of a complicated nature, and without the journal the entries may be difficult, if not impossible, to understand. One must also bear in mind that if the book-keeper left the firm the absence of a journal could leave many unexplained items in the books.
2. Errors, irregularities and fraud are more easily effected when entries are made direct into the ledgers without any explanations being given. The journal acts as an explanation of the entries and details the necessary supporting evidence.

3. The risk of omitting the transaction altogether, or of making one entry only is reduced.

Despite these advantages there are many firms which do not have such a book.

Typical Uses of the Journal

Some of the main uses of the journal are listed below. It must not be thought that this list is exhaustive.
1. The purchase and sale of fixed assets on credit.
2. The correction of errors.
3. Opening entries. These are the entries needed to open a new set of books.
4. Other transfers.

The layout of the journal can now be shown:

The Journal

Date	Folio	Dr	Cr

The name of the account to be debited.
   The name of the account to be credited.
The Narrative.

To standardize matters the name of the account to be debited should always be shown first. It also helps with the reading of the journal if the name of the account to be credited is written not directly under the name of the account to be debited, but is inset to the right-hand side.

It must be remembered that the journal is not an integral part of the double entry book-keeping system. It is purely a form of diary, and entering an item in the journal is not the same as recording an item in an account. Once the journal entry is made the necessary entry in the double entry accounts can then be effected.

Examples of the uses of the journal are now given.

1. Purchase and Sale on Credit of Fixed Assets

(a) A machine is bought on credit from Toolmakers Co. for £550 on 1 July.

	Dr	Cr
	£	£
July 1 Machinery	550	
Toolmakers Co.		550
Purchase of milling machine on credit, Capital		
Purchases invoice No. 7/159		

(b) Sale of a Motor Vehicle for £300 on credit to A. Barnes on 2 July.

		Dr	Cr
		£	£
July 2 A. Barnes		300	
Motor vehicles			300
Sales of Motor vehicles per Capital			
Sales Invoice No. 7/43			

2. Correction of Errors

These are dealt with when (and if) you study Accounting in a later year of your course.

3. Opening Entries

J. Brew, after being in business for some years without keeping proper records, now decides to keep a double entry set of books. On 1 July he establishes that his assets and liabilities are as follows:

Assets: Motor Van £840, Fixtures £700, Stock £390, Debtors – B. Young £95, D. Blake £45, Bank £80, Cash £20.

Liabilities: Creditors – M. Quinn £129, C. Walters £41.

The Assets therefore total £840 + £700 + £390 + £95 + £45 + £80 + £20 = £2,170; and the Liabilities total £129 + £41 = £170.

The Capital consists of: Assets – Liabilities, £2,170 – £170 = £2,000

To start the books off on 1 July showing the existing state of the assets and liabilities and capital, these amounts therefore need entering in the relevant asset, liability and capital accounts. The asset accounts will be opened with debit balances and the liability and capital accounts will be opened with credit balances. The journal therefore shows the accounts which are to be debited and those which are to be credited and this is shown in Exhibit 24.1.

Exhibit 24.1   **The Journal**   Page 5

	Fol	Dr	Cr
		£	£
July 1 Motor Van	GL 1	840	
Fixtures	GL 2	700	
Stock	GL 3	390	
Debtors – B. Young	SL 1	95	
D. Blake	SL 2	45	
Bank	CB 1	80	
Cash	CB 1	20	
Creditors – M. Quinn	PL 81		129
C. Walters	PL 2		41
Capital	GL 4		2,000
Assets and liabilities at this date entered to open the books.			
		2,170	2,170

Once these opening balances have been recorded in the books the day-to-day transactions can be entered in the normal manner. The need for opening entries will not occur very often. They will not be needed each year as the balances from last year will have been brought forward. At the elementary level of examinations in book-keeping, questions are often asked which entail opening a set of books and recording the day-by-day entries for the ensuing period.

4. Other Transfers

These can be of many kinds and it is impossible to construct a complete list. However, two examples can be shown.

(*a*)   S. Bennett, a debtor, owed £200 on 1 July. He was unable to pay his account in cash, but offers a motor car in full settlement of the debt. The offer is accepted on 5 July.

The personal account is therefore discharged and needs crediting. On the other hand the firm now has an extra asset, a motor car, therefore the motor car account needs to be debited.

The Journal

	Dr	Cr
	£	£
July 5 Motor Car	200	
S. Bennett		200
Accepted motor car in full settlement of debt per letter dated 5/7/-5		

(*b*) G. Ames is a creditor. On 10 July his business is taken over by A. Iddon to whom the debt now is to be paid.

Here it is just the identity of one creditor being exchanged for another one. The action needed is to cancel the amount owing to G. Ames by debiting his account, and to show it owing to Iddon by opening an account for Iddon and crediting it.

The Journal

	Dr	Cr
	£	£
July 10 G. Ames	150	
A. Iddon		150
Transfer of indebtedness as per letter from Ames ref. A/1335		

Assignment Exercises

24.1 You are to show the journal entries necessary to record the following items:

(i) 19-5 May 1 Bought a motor vehicle on credit from Kingston Garage for £6,790

(ii) 19-5 May 3 A debt of £34 owing from H. Newman was written off as a bad debt

(iii) 19-5 May 8 Office furniture bought by us for £490 was returned to the supplier Unique Offices, as it was unsuitable. Full allowance will be given us

(iv) 19-5 May 12 We are owed £150 by W. Charles. He is declared bankrupt and we receive £39 in full settlement of the debt

(v) 19-5 May 14 We take £45 goods out of the business stock without paying for them

(vi) 19-5 May 28 Some time ago we paid an insurance bill thinking that it was all in respect of the business. We now discover that £76 of the amount paid was in fact insurance of our private house

(vii) 19-5 May 29 Bought machinery £980 on credit from Systems Accelerated.

24.2A Show the journal entries necessary to record the following items:

19-7

Apr 1 Bought fixtures on credit from J. Harper £1,809

,, 4 We take £500 goods out of the business stock without paying for them

,, 9 £28 of the goods taken by us on 4 April is not returned back into stock by us. We do not take any money for the return of the goods

,, 12 K. Lamb owes us £500. He is unable to pay his debt. We agree to take some office equipment from him at the value and so cancel the debt

,, 18 Some of the fixtures bought from J. Harper, £65 worth, are found to be unsuitable and are returned to him for full allowance

,, 24 A debt owing to us by J. Brown of £68 is written off as a bad debt

,, 30 Office equipment bought on credit from Super Offices for £2,190.

25 The Analytical Petty Cash Book and the Imprest System

With the growth of the firm it has been seen that it became necessary to have several books instead of just one ledger. As the firm further increased in size these books also were further sub-divided.

These ideas can be extended to the cash book. It is obvious that in almost any firm there will be a great deal of small cash payments to be made. It would be an advantage if the records of these payments could be kept separate from the main cash book. Where a separate book is kept it is known as a Petty Cash Book.

The advantages of such an action can be summarized:

1. The task of handling and recording the small cash payments could be delegated by the cashier to a junior member of staff who would then be known as the petty cashier. Thus, the cashier, who is a relatively higher paid member of staff, would be saved from routine work easily performed by a junior and lower paid member of staff.

2. If small cash payments were entered into the main cash book these items would then need posting one by one to the ledgers. If travelling expenses were paid to staff on a daily basis this could involve over 250 postings to the Staff Travelling Expenses Account during the year. However, if a form of analytical petty cash book is kept it would only be the periodical totals that need posting to the general ledger. If this was done only 12 monthly entries would be needed in the staff travelling expenses account instead of over 250.

When the petty cashier makes a payment to someone, then that person will have to fill in a voucher showing exactly what the expense was. He may well have to attach bills obtained by him — e.g. bills for petrol — to the petty cash voucher. He would sign the voucher to certify that his expenses had been paid to him by the petty cashier.

The Imprest System

The basic idea of this system is that the cashier gives the petty cashier an adequate amount of cash to meet his needs for the ensuing period. At the end of the period the cashier ascertains the amount spent by the petty cashier, and gives him an amount equal to that spent. The Petty Cash in hand should then be equal to the original amount with which the period was started.

Exhibit 25.1 shows an example of this procedure:

Exhibit 25.1

	£
Period 1 The cashier gives the petty cashier	100
The petty cashier pays out in the period	78
Petty cash now in hand	22
The cashier now reimburses the petty cashier the amount spent	78
Petty cash in hand end of period 1	100
Period 2 The petty cashier pays out in the period	84
Petty cash now in hand	16
The cashier now reimburses the petty cashier the amount spent	84
Petty cash in hand end of period 2	100

Of course, it may sometimes be necessary to increase the fixed sum, often called the cash 'float', to be held at the start of each period. In the above case if it had been desired to increase the 'float' at the end of the second period to £120, then the cashier would have given the petty cashier an extra £20, i.e. £84 + £20 = £104.

Illustration of an Analytical Cash Book

An analytical Petty Cash Book is often used. One of these is shown as Exhibit 25.2.

The receipts column represents the debit side of the petty cash book. On giving £50 to the petty cashier on 1 September, the credit entry is made in the cash book while the debit entry is made in the petty cash book. A similar entry is made on 30 September for the £44 reimbursement.

The entries on the credit side of the petty cash book are first of all made in the totals column, and then are extended into the relevant expense column. At the end of the period, in this case a month, the payments are totalled, it being made sure that the total of the totals column equals the sum of the other payments totals, in this case £44. The expense columns have been headed with the type of expense.

To complete double entry, the total of each expense column is debited to the relevant expense account in the general ledger, the folio number of the page in the general ledger then being shown under each column of the petty cash book.

The end column has been chosen as a ledger column. In this column items paid out of petty cash which need posting to a ledger other than the general ledger are shown. This would happen if a purchases ledger account was settled out of petty cash, or if a refund was made out of the petty cash to a customer who had overpaid his account.

The double-entry for all the items in Exhibit 25.2 appears as Exhibit 25.3

19-4		£
Sept	1 The cashier gives £50 as float to the petty cashier	
	Payments out of petty cash during September:	
,,	2 Petrol	6
,,	3 J. Green – travelling expenses	3
,,	3 Postages	2
,,	4 D. Davies – travelling expenses	2
,,	7 Cleaning expenses	1
,,	9 Petrol	1
,,	12 K. Jones – travelling expenses	3
,,	14 Petrol	3
,,	15 L. Black – travelling expenses	5
,,	16 Cleaning expenses	1
,,	18 Petrol	2
,,	20 Postages	2
,,	22 Cleaning expenses	1
,,	24 G. Wood – travelling expenses	7
,,	27 Settlement of C. Brown's account in the Purchases Ledger	3
,,	29 Postages	2
,,	30 The cashier reimburses the petty cashier the amount spent in the month.	

Exhibit 25.2

Petty Cash Book (page 31)

Receipts	Folio	Date	Details	Voucher No.	Total	Motor Expenses	Staff Travelling Expenses	Postages	Cleaning	Ledger Folio	Ledger Accounts
£					£	£	£	£	£		£
50	CB 19	Sept 1	Cash								
		,, 2	Petrol	1	6	6					
		,, 3	J. Green	2	3		3				
		,, 3	Postages	3	2			2			
		,, 4	D. Davies	4	2		2				
		,, 7	Cleaning	5	1				1		
		,, 9	Petrol	6	1	1					
		,, 12	K. Jones	7	3		3				
		,, 14	Petrol	8	3	3					
		,, 15	L. Black	9	5		5				
		,, 16	Cleaning	10	1				1		
		,, 18	Petrol	11	2	2					
		,, 20	Postages	12	2			2			
		,, 22	Cleaning	13	1				1		
		,, 24	G. Wood	14	7		7				
		,, 27	C. Brown	15	3					PL 18	3
		,, 29	Postages	16	2			2			
					44	12	20	6	3		3
44	CB 22	,, 30	Cash			GL 17	GL 29	GL 44	G 64		3
		,, 30	Balance	c/d	50						
94					94						
50		Oct 1	Balance	b/d							

Exhibit 25.3

Cash Book (Bank Column only)   Page 19

			£
	19-4		
	Sept 1 Petty Cash	PCB 31	50
	,, 30 Petty Cash	PCB 31	44

General Ledger
Motor Expenses   Page 17

19-4			£
Sept 30 Petty Cash	PCB 31		12

Staff Travelling Expenses   Page 29

19-4			£
Sept 30 Petty Cash	PCB 31		20

Postages   Page 44

19-4			£
Sept 30 Petty Cash	PCB 31		6

Cleaning   Page 64

19-4			£
Sept 30 Petty Cash	PCB 31		3

Purchases Ledger
C. Brown   Page 18

19-4			£	19-4		£
Sept 30 Petty Cash	PCB 31		3	Sept 1 Balance b/d		3

In a firm with both a cash book and a petty cash book, the cash book is often known as a bank cash book. This means that *all* cash payments are entered in the petty cash book, and the bank cash book will contain *only* bank columns and discount columns. In this type of firm any cash sales will be paid direct into the bank.

In such a cash book, as in fact could happen in an ordinary cash book, an extra column could be added. In this would be shown the details of the cheques banked, just the total of the banking being shown in the total column.

Example 25.4 shows the receipts side of the Bank Cash Book. The totals of the banings made on the three days were £192, £381 and £1,218. The details column shows what the bankings are made up of.

Exhibit 25.4

Bank Cash Book (Receipts side)

Date	Details	Discount	Items	Total banked
19-6		£	£	£
May 14	G. Archer	5	95	
,, 14	P. Watts	3	57	
,, 14	C. King		40	192
,, 20	K. Dooley	6	114	
,, 20	Cash Sales		55	
,, 20	R. Jones		60	
,, 20	P. Mackie	8	152	381
,, 31	J. Young		19	
,, 31	T. Broome	50	950	
,, 31	Cash Sales		116	
,, 31	H. Tiller	7	133	1,218

Assignment Exercises

25.1 Enter the following transactions in a petty cash book, having analysis columns for motor expenses, postages and stationery, cleaning, sundry expenses, and a ledger column. This is to be kept on the imprest system, the amount spent to be reimbursed on the last day of the month. The opening petty cash float is £100.

19-6		£
May 1	Cleaning	3
,, 3	Speedy Garage – Petrol	2
,, 4	Postage stamps	5
,, 5	Envelopes	1
,, 6	Poison licence	1
,, 8	Unique Garage – Petrol	5
,, 9	Corner Garage – Petrol	6
,, 11	Postage stamps	5
,, 12	F. Lessor – Ledger account	9
,, 13	H. Norris – Ledger account	4
,, 15	Sweeping brush (cleaning)	2
,, 16	Bends Garage – petrol	7
,, 17	K. Kelly – Stationery	6
,, 19	Driving licences	1
,, 21	J. Green – Ledger account	7
,, 25	Cleaning	6
,, 27	Licence for guard dog	1
,, 28	Guard dog – Food	2
,, 31	Corner garage – Petrol	5

25.2A Rule up a petty cash book with analysis columns for office expenses, motor expenses, cleaning expenses, and casual labour. The cash float is £350 and the amount spent is reimbursed on 30 June.

19-7		£
June	1 H. Sangster − casual labour	13
,,	2 Letterheadings	22
,,	2 Unique Motors − motor repairs	30
,,	3 Cleaning Materials	6
,,	6 Envelopes	14
,,	8 Petrol	8
,,	11 J. Higgins − casual labour	15
,,	12 Mrs. Body − cleaner	7
,,	12 Paper clips	2
,,	14 Petrol	11
,,	16 Typewriter repairs	1
,,	19 Petrol	9
,,	21 Motor Taxation	50
,,	22 T. Sweet − casual labour	21
,,	23 Mrs. Body − cleaner	10
,,	24 P. Dennis − casual labour	19
,,	25 Copy paper	7
,,	26 Flat Cars − motor repairs	21
,,	29 Petrol	12
,,	30 J. Young − casual labour	16

26 Receipts and Payments Accounts and Income and Expenditure Accounts

Clubs, associations and other non-profit making organizations do not have trading and profit and loss accounts drawn up for them, as their principal function is not trading or profit making. They are run to further the promotion of an activity or group of activities, such as playing football or engaging in cultural activities. The kind of final accounts prepared by these organizations are either Receipts and Payments Accounts or Income and Expenditure Accounts.

Receipts and payments accounts are merely a summary of the cash book for the period. Exhibit 26.1 is an example.

Exhibit 26.1

The Homers Running Club

Receipts and Payments Account for the year ended 31 December 19-5

Receipts	£	Payments	£
Bank Balance 1.1.19-5	236	Groundsman's wages	728
Subscriptions received for 19-5	1,148	Upkeep of sports stadium	296
		Committee expenses	58
Rent from sub-letting ground	116	Printing and stationery	33
		Bank Balance 31.12.19-5	385
	1,500		1,500

However, when the organization owns assets and has liabilities, the receipts and payments account is an unsatisfactory way of drawing up accounts as it merely shows the cash position. What is required is a balance sheet, and an account showing whether or not the association's capital is being increased. In a commercial firm the latter information would be obtained from a profit and loss account. In a non-profit-making organization it is calculated in an account called the income and expenditure account. In fact the income and expenditure account follows all the basic rules of profit and loss accounts. Thus expenditure consists of those costs consumed during the period and income is the revenue earned in the period. Where income exceeds expenditure the difference is called 'Surplus of Income over Expenditure'. Where expenditure exceeds income the difference is called 'Excess of Expenditure over Income'.

There is, however, one qualification to the fact that normally such an organization would not have a trading or profit and loss account. This is where the organization has carried out an activity deliberately so as to make a profit to help finance the main activities. Running a bar so as to make a profit would be an example of this, or having dances. For this profit-aimed activity a trading or profit and loss account may be drawn up, the profit or loss being transferred to the income and expenditure account.

If the books had been kept on a double entry basis, the income and expenditure account and balance sheet would be prepared in the same manner as the profit and loss account and the balance sheet of a commercial firm, only the titles of the accounts and terms like 'surplus' or 'excess' being different. A specimen set of final accounts for a club can now be shown in Exhibit 26.2.

Exhibit 26.2 The Long Lane Football Club

Bar Trading Account for the year ended 31 December 19-6

	£	£
Sales		5,628
Less Cost of Goods Sold:		
Stock 1.1.19-6	496	
Add Purchases	4,008	
	4,504	
Less Stock 31.12.19-6	558	3,946
Gross Profit		1,682
Less: Bar Expenses	245	
Barman's Wages	624	869
Net Profit to Income & Expenditure Account		813

Income & Expenditure Account for the year ended 31 December 19-6

	£	£	£
Income			
Subscriptions			1,302
Profit from the bar			813
Donations Received			120
			2,235
Less Expenditure			
Wages – Groundsman and Assistant		939	
Repairs to Stands		119	
Ground Upkeep		229	
Secretary's Expenses		138	
Transport Costs		370	
Depreciation			
Stands	200		
Equipment	110	310	2,105
Surplus of Income over Expenditure			130

The Long Lane Football Club
Balance Sheet as at 31 December 19-6

	£	£	£
Fixed Assets			
Land at valuation			4,000
Pavilion at valuation		2,000	
Less Depreciation		200	1,800
Equipment at valuation		550	
Less Depreciation		110	440
Current Assets			6,240
Stock of Bar Supplies		558	
Debtors for Subscriptions		66 -	
Cash at Bank		1,053	
		1,677	
Less Current Liabilities			
Creditors for Bar Supplies	340		
Bar Expenses Owing	36		
Transport Costs Owing	65		
Subscriptions Received in Advance	40	481	
Working Capital			1,196
			7,436
Financed by:			
Accumulated Fund*			
Balance as at 1.1.19-6			7,306
Add Surplus of Income over Expenditure			130
			7,436

*An Accumulated Fund represents what would be capital in a commercial firm.

Life Membership

In some clubs and societies members can make a payment for life membership. This means that by paying a fairly substantial amount now the member can enjoy the facilities of the club for the rest of his life.

Such a receipt should not be treated as Income in the Income and Expenditure Account solely in the year in which the member paid the money. It should be credited to a Life Membership Account, and transfers should be made from that account to the credit of the Income and Expenditure Account of an appropriate amount annually.

Exactly what is meant by an appropriate amount is decided by the committee of the club or society. The usual basis is to establish, on average, how long members will continue to use the benefits of the club. To take an extreme case, if a club was in existence which could not be joined until one achieved the age of 70, then the expected number of years' use of the club on average per member would be relatively few. Another club, such as a golf club, where a fair proportion of the members joined when reasonably young, and where the game is capable of being played by members until and during old age, would expect a much higher average of years of use per member. The simple matter is that the club should decide for itself.

In an examination the candidate has to follow the instructions set for him by the examiner. The credit balance remaining on the account, after the transfer of the agreed amount has been made to the credit of the Income and Expenditure Account, should be shown on the Balance Sheet as a liability. It is, after all, the liability of the club to provide amenities for the member without any further payment by him.

Entrance Fees

In quite a lot of clubs, one has to pay certain fees on application for membership. Such fees are called entrance fees. They are paid quite apart from the usual monthly or quarterly subscription.

Such a receipt should not be treated as Income in the Income and Expenditure Account solely in the year in which the member is admitted. It should be credited to Entrance Fees Account and transfers should be made from that account to the Income and Expenditure Account by an appropriate amount annually, such amounts being decided by the committee of the club or society.

Outstanding Subscriptions and the Prudence Concept

The treatment of subscriptions owing has so far followed the normal procedures as applied to debtors in a commercial firm. However, as most treasurers of associations are fully aware, many members who owe subscriptions leave the association and never pay the amounts owing. This is far more prevalent than with debtors of a commercial firm. It can perhaps be partly explained by the fact that a commercial firm would normally sue for unpaid debts, whereas associations rarely sue for unpaid subscriptions. To bring in an unpaid subscriptions as assets therefore contravenes the prudence concept which tends to understate assets rather than overstate them. With many clubs therefore, unpaid subscriptions are ignored in the income and expenditure account and balance sheet. If they are eventually paid they are then brought in as income in the year of receipt irrespective of the period covered by the subscriptions.

In examinations, the student should bring debtors for subscriptions into account unles he is given instructions to the contrary.

Assignment Exercises

26.1 The following trial balance was extracted from the books of the County Town Sports Club at the close of business on 31 March 19-8:

	Dr £	Cr £
Club premises	4,500	
Sports equipment	1,700	
Bar purchases and sales	3,180	5,090
Bar stocks 1 April 19-7	730	
Balance at bank	930	
Subscriptions received		2,880
Accumulated fund 1 April 19-7		7,430
Salary of secretary	1,200	
Wages of staff	1,760	
Postages and telephone	290	
Office furniture	400	
Rates and insurance	410	
Cash in hand	20	
Sundry expenses	280	
	15,400	15,400

Notes:
(a) All bar purchases and sales were on a cash basis. Bar stocks 31 March 19-8 £820.
(b) No subscriptions have been paid in advance but subscriptions in arrears at 31 March 19-8 amounted to £30.
(c) Rates pre-paid at 31 March 19-8 £20.
(d) Provide for depreciation as follows:
   Sports equipment £200   Office furniture £40

Required:
   Prepare the bar trading account and the income and expenditure account of the Club for the year ended 31 March 19-8 together with a balance sheet as on that date. For this purpose, the wages of staff £1,760 should be shown in the income and expenditure account and not the bar trading account.

26.2A The following trial balance of Haven Golf Club was extracted from the books as on 31 December 19-8:

	Dr £	Cr £
Clubhouse	21,000	
Equipment	6,809	
Profits from raffles		4,980
Subscriptions received		18,760
Wages of bar staff	2,809	
Bar stocks 1 January 19-8	1,764	
Bar purchases and sales	11,658	17,973
Greenkeepers' wages	7,698	
Golf professional's salary	6,000	
General expenses	580	
Cash at bank	1,570	
Accumulated fund at 1 January 19-8		18,175
	59,888	59,888

Notes:
(*a*) Bar purchases and sales were on a cash basis. Bar stocks at 31 December 19-8 were valued at £989.
(*b*) Subscriptions paid in advance by members at 31 December 19-8 amounted to £180.
(*c*) Provide for depreciation of equipment £760.

You are required to:
(i) Draw up the Bar trading account for the year ended 31 December 19-8.
(ii) Draw up the Income and expenditure account for the year ended 31 December 19-8, and a Balance Sheet as at 31 December 19-8.

27 Partnership Accounts: An Introduction

The final accounts so far described have, with the exception of income and expenditure accounts, been concerned with businesses each owned by one person. There must obviously come a time when it is desirable for more than one person to participate in the ownership of the business. It may be due to the fact that the amount of capital required cannot be provided by one person, or else that the experience and ability required to run the business cannot be found in any one person alone. Alternatively, many people just prefer to share the cares of ownership rather than bear all the burden themselves. Very often too there is a family relationship between the owners.

The form of business organization necessary to provide for more than one owner of a business formed with a view of profit is either that of a limited company or of a partnership. This chapter deals with partnerships, the governing act being the Partnership Act 1890. A partnership may be defined as an association of from two to twenty persons (except that there is no maximum limit for firms of accountants, solicitors, Stock Exchange members or other professional bodies which receive the approval of the Board of Trade for this purpose) carrying on business in common with a view of profit. A limited company would have to be formed if it was desired to have more than twenty owners.

With the exception of one special type of partner, known as a limited partner, each partner is liable to the full extent of his personal possessions for the whole of the debts of the partnership firm should the firm be unable to meet them. Barring limited partners, each partner would have to pay his share of any such deficiency. A limited partner is one who is registered under the provisions of the Limited Partnership Act 1907, and whose liability is limited to the amount of capital invested by him; he can lose that but his personal possessions cannot be taken to pay any debts of the firm. A limited partner may not however take part in the management of the partnership business. There must be at least one general partner in a limited partnership.

Persons can enter into partnership with one another without any form of written agreement. It is, however, wiser to have an agreement drawn up by a lawyer, as this will tend to lead to fewer possibilities of misunderstandings and disagreements between partners. Such a partnership deed or articles of partnership can contain as much, or as little, as the partners desire. It does not cover every eventuality. The usual accounting requirements covered can be listed:

1. The capital to be contributed by each partner.

2. The ratio in which profits (or losses) are to be shared.

3. The rate of interest, if any, to be given on capital before the profits are shared.

4. The rate of interest, if any, to be charged on partners' drawings.

5. Salaries to be paid to partners.

Some comments on the above are necessary.

(a) Ratio in Which Profits are to be Shared

It is often thought by students that profits should be shared in the same ratio as that in which capital is contributed. For example, suppose the capitals were Allen £2,000 and Beet £1,000, many people would share the profits in the rato of two-thirds to one-third, even though the work to be done by each partner is similar. A look at the division of the first few years' profits on such a basis would be:

Years	1	2	3	4	5	Total
	£	£	£	£	£	£
Net profits	1,800	2,400	3,000	3,000	3,600	
Shared:						
Allen ⅔	1,200	1,600	2,000	2,000	2,400	9,200
Beet ⅓	600	800	1,000	1,000	1,200	4,600

It can now be seen that Allen would receive £9,200, or £4,600 more than Beet. Equitably the difference between the two shares of profit in this case, as the duties of the partners are the same, should be adequate to compensate Allen for putting extra capital into the firm. It is obvious that £4,600 extra profits is far more than adequate for this purpose.

Consider too the position of capital ratio sharing of profits if one partner put in £99 and the other put in £1 as capital.

To overcome the difficulty of compensating for the investment of extra capital, the concept of interest on capital was devised.

(b) Interest on Capital

If the work to be done by each partner is of equal value but the capital contributed is unequal, it is equitable to grant interest on the partners' capitals. This interest is treated as a deduction prior to the calculation of profits and their distribution according to the profit-sharing ratio.

The rate of interest is a matter for agreement between the partners, but it should theoretically equal the return which they would have received if they had invested the capital elsewhere.

Taking Allen and Beet's firm again, but sharing the profits equally after charging 5 per cent per annum interest on capital, the division of profits would become:

Years	1	2	3	4	5	Total
	£	£	£	£	£	£
Net Profit	1,800	2,400	3,000	3,000	3,600	
Interest on Capitals						
Allen	100	100	100	100	100 =	500
Beet	50	50	50	50	50 =	250
Remainder shared:						
Allen ½	825	1,125	1,425	1,425	1,725 =	6,525
Beet ½	825	1,125	1,425	1,425	1,725 =	6,525

Summary	Allen	Beet
	£	£
Interest on Capital	500	250
Balance of Profits	6,525	6,525
	7,025	6,775

Allen has thus received £250 more than Beet this being adequate return (in the partners' estimation) for having invested an extra £1,000 in the firm for five years.

(c) Interest on Drawings

It is obviously in the best interests of the firm if cash is withdrawn from the firm by the partners in accordance with the two basic principles of: (1), as little as possible, and (2), as late as possible. The more cash that is left in the firm the more expansion can be financed, the greater the economies of having ample cash to take advantage of bargains and of not missing cash discounts because cash is not available and so on.

To deter the partners from taking out cash unnecessarily the concept can be used of charging the partners interest on each withdrawal, calculated from the date of withdrawal to the end of the financial year. The amount charged to them helps to swell the profits divisible between the partners.

The rate of interest should be sufficient to achieve this end without being unduly penal.

(d) Salaries

A partner may have some particular responsibility or extra task that the others have not got. It may in fact be of a temporary nature. To compensate him for this, it is best not to disturb the profit- and loss-sharing ratio. It is better to let him have a salary sufficient to compensate him for the extra tasks performed. This salary is deductible before arriving at the balance of profits to be shared in the profit-sharing ratio. A change in the profit- and loss-sharing ratio to compensate him would have meant bearing a larger share of any loss, hardly a fair means of compensation; or if there was only a small profit the extra amount received by him would be insufficient compensation, while if there was a large profit he may well be more than adequately compensated.

Where No Partnership Agreement Exists

Where no agreement exists, express or implied, Section 24 of the Partnership Act 1890 governs the situation. The accounting contents of this section states:

1. Profits and losses are to be shared equally.
2. There is to be no interest allowed on capital.
3. No interest is to be charged on drawings.
4. Salaries are not allowed.
5. If a partner puts a sum of money into a firm in excess of the capital he has agreed to subscribe, he is entitled to interest at the rate of 5 per cent per annum on such an advance.

This section applies where there is no agreement. There may be an agreement not by a partnership deed but in a letter, or it may be implied by conduct, for instance when a partner signs a balance sheet which shows profits shared in some other ratio than equally.

In some cases of disagreement as to whether agreement existed or not only the courts would be competent to decide.

An Example of the Distribution of Profits

Taylor and Clarke are in partnership sharing profits and losses in the ratio of Taylor 3/5ths, Clarke 2/5ths. They are entitled to 5 per cent per annum interest on capitals, Taylor having £2,000 capital and Clarke £6,000. Clarke is to have a salary of £500. They charge interest on drawings, Taylor being charged £50 and Clarke £100. The net profit, before any distributions to the partners, amounted to £5,000 for the year ended 31 December 19-7.

	£	£	£
Net Profit			5,000
Add Charged for interest on drawings:			
Taylor		50	
Clarke		100	
			150
			5,150
Less Salary: Clarke		500	
Interest on Capital:			
Taylor	100		
Clarke	300		
		400	
			900
			4,250
Balance of profits		£	£
Shared:			
Taylor 3/5ths		2,550	
Clarke 2/5ths		1,700	
			4,250

The £5,000 net profits have therefore been shared:

	Taylor £	Clarke £
Balance of profits	2,550	1,700
Interest on Capital	100	300
Salary	–	500
	2,650	2,500
Less Interest on drawings	50	100
	2,600	2,400

£5,000

For those who are not going on to study Accounting in the second year of their BTEC National course, the contents of this chapter are quite sufficient to give an overall understanding of partnership accounting. Those who will study Accounting in the second year will find further information on partnership accounting in the book *Accounting,* written by the same authors, and published by Pitman Publishing Ltd.

Assignment Exercises

27.1 Stephens, Owen and Jones are partners. They share profits and losses in the ratios of ⅖, ⅖ and ⅕ respectively.

For the year ended 31 December 19-6 their capital accounts remained fixed at the following amounts:

	£
Stephens	6,000
Owen	4,000
Jones	2,000

They have agreed to give each other 10 per cent interest per annum on their capital accounts.

In addition to the above, partnership salaries of £3,000 for Owen and £1,000 for Jones are to be charged.

The net profit of the partnership, before taking any of the above into account was £25,200.

You are required to draw up a statement showing the division of profits of the partnership for the year ended 31 December 19-6.

27.2 Draw up a statement showing division of profits from the following for the year ended 31 December 19-7:

(i) Net Profits £30,350.
(ii) Interest to be charged on capitals: Williams £2,000; Powell £1,500; Howe £900.
(iii) Interest to be charged on drawings: Williams £240; Powell £180; Howe £130.
(iv) Salaries to be credited: Powell £2,000; Howe £3,500.
(v) Profits to be shared: Williams 50%; Powell 30%; Howe 20%.

28 An Introduction to the Final Accounts of Limited Liability Companies

The two main disadvantages of a partnership are that the number of owners cannot normally exceed twenty, and that their liability, barring limited partners, is not limited to the amount invested in the partnership but extends to the individual partners' private possessions. This means that the failure of the business could result in a partner losing both his share of the business assets and also part or all of his private assets as well.

The form of organization to which these two limitations do not apply are known as Limited Liability Companies. There are companies which have unlimited liability, but these are not dealt with in this volume. From this point any reference to a company means a limited liability company. The law governing these companies in the United Kingdom is the Companies Act 1985.

The capital of a limited company is divided into Shares. These can be of any denomination, such as £5 shares or £1 shares. To become a Member of a limited company, alternatively called a Shareholder, a person must buy one of more shares. He may either pay in full for the shares that he takes up, or else the shares may be partly paid for, the balance to be paid as and when the company may arrange. The liability of a member is limited to the shares that he holds, or where a share is only partly paid he is also liable to have to pay the amount owing by him on the shares. Thus, even if a company loses all its assets, a member's private possessions cannot be touched to pay the company's debts, other than in respect of the amount owing on partly paid shares.

Companies thus fulfil the need for the capitalization of a firm where the capital required is greater than that which twenty people can contribute, or where limited liability for all members is desired.

Private and Public Companies

There are two classes of company, the Private Company and the Public Company. In fact, private companies outnumber public companies by a considerable number. In Section 1 of the Companies Act 1985 a public company is defined as one whose memorandum states that the company is a public company, and has registered as such. A public company must normally have an authorised capital of at least £50,000. Minimum membership is two, there is no maximum.

The name of a public company must either end with the words 'public limited company' or the abbreviation 'p.l.c.', or the Welsh equivalent if the recognised office is situated in Wales.

Private companies are usually (but not always) smaller businesses, and may be formed by two or more persons. A private company is defined by the Act as a company which is not a public company. In fact the main difference, other than a private company can have authorised capitals less than £50,000, is that public companies are allowed to offer their shares for subscription by the public at large, whereas 'private companies' cannot do this. Therefore if you were to walk into a bank, or similar public place, and see a prospectus offering anyone the chance to take up shares in a company, then that company would be a 'public' company.

The day-to-day business of a company is not carried on by the shareholders. The possession of a share normally confers voting rights on the holder, who is then able to attend general meetings of the company. At one of these the shareholders will meet and will vote for Directors, these being the people who will be entrusted with the running of the business. At each Annual General Meeting the directors will have to report on their stewardship, and this report is accompanied by a set of Final Accounts for the year.

Share Capital

A shareholder of a limited company obtains his reward in the form of a share of the profits, known as a Dividend. The directors consider the amount of profits and decide on the amount of profits which are placed to reserves. Out of the profits remaining the directors then propose the payment of a certain amount of dividend to be paid. It is important to note that the shareholders cannot propose a higher dividend for themselves than that already proposed by the directors. They can however propose that a lesser dividend should be paid, although this action is very rare indeed. If the directors propose that no dividend be paid then the shareholders are powerless to alter the decision.

The decision by the directors as to the amount proposed as dividends is a very complex one and cannot be fully discussed here. Such points as government directives to reduce dividends, the effect of taxation, the availability of bank balances to pay the dividends, the possibility of take-over bids and so on will all be taken into account.

The dividend is usually expressed as a percentage. Ignoring income tax, a dividend of 10 per cent in Firm A on 500,000 Ordinary Shares of £1 each will amount to £50,000, or a dividend of 6 per cent in Firm B on 200,000 Ordinary Shares of £2 each will amount to £24,000. A shareholder having 100 shares in each firm would receive £10 from Firm A and £12 from Firm B.

There are two main types of share, Preference Shares and Ordinary Shares. A preference share is one whose main characteristics is that it is entitled to a specified percentage rate of dividend before the ordinary shareholders receive anything. On the other hand the ordinary shares would be entitled to the remainder of the profits which have been appropriated for dividends.

For example, if a company had 10,000 5 per cent preference shares of £1 each and 20,000 ordinary shares of £1 each, then the dividends would be payable as in Exhibit 28.1.

Exhibit 28.1

Years	1	2	3	4	5
	£	£	£	£	£
Profits appropriated for Dividends	900	1,300	1,600	3,100	2,000
Preference Dividends (5%)	500	500	500	500	500
Ordinary Dividends	(2%) 400	(4%) 800	(5½%) 1,100	(13%) 2,600	(7½%) 1,500

There are two main types of preference share, these being Non-cumulative Preference Shares and Cumulative Preference Shares. A non-cumulative preference share is one which is entitled to a yearly percentage rate of dividend, and should the available profits be insufficient to cover the percentage dividend then the deficiency cannot be made good out of future years' profits. On the other hand, any deficiency on the part of cumulative preference shares can be carried forward as arrears, and such arrears are payable before the ordinary shares receive anything.

Illustrations of the two types of share should make this clearer:

Exhibit 28.2

A company has 5,000 £1 ordinary shares and 2,000 5 per cent non-cumulative preference shares of £1 each. The profits available for dividends are: year 1 £150, year 2 £80, year 3 £250, year 4 £60, year 5 £500.

Year	1	2	3	4	5
	£	£	£	£	£
Profits	150	80	250	60	500
Preference Dividend (limited in years 2 and 4)	100	80	100	60	100
Dividends on Ordinary Shares	50	—	150	—	400

Exhibit 28.3

Assume that the preference shares in Exhibit 28.2 had been cumulative, the dividends would have been:

Year	1	2	3	4	5
	£	£	£	£	£
Profits	150	80	250	60	500
Preference Dividend	100	80	120*	60	140*
Dividends on Ordinary Shares	50	–	130	–	360

*including arrears.

The total of the Share Capital which the company would be allowed to issue is known as the Authorized Share Capital, or alternatively as the Nominal Capital. The share capital actually issued to shareholders is known as the Issued Capital. Obviously, if the whole of the share capital which the company is allowed to issue has in fact been issued, then the authorized and the issued share capital will be the same figure.

Where only part of the amount payable on each share has been asked for, then the total amount asked for on all shares is known as the Called-up Capital. The Uncalled Capital is therefore that part of the amount payable on all the shares for which payment has not been requested. Calls in arrear relate to amounts requests (called for) but not yet received, while calls in advance relate to moneys received prior to payment being requested. Paid-up Capital will be that part of the capital which has actually been paid by shareholders.

An illustration should make this clearer. This is shown as Exhibit 28.4.

Exhibit 28.4

(i) Better Enterprises Ltd was formed with the legal right to be able to issue 100,000 shares of £1 each.

(ii) The company has actually issued 75,000 shares.

(iii) None of the shares have yet been fully paid up. So far the company has made calls of 80p (£0.80) per share.

(iv) All the calls have been paid by shareholders except for £200 owing from one shareholder.

(a) Authorised Nominal Share Capital is (i) £100,000.
(b) Issued Share Capital is (ii) £75,000.
(c) Called up Capital is (iii) 75,000 × £0.80 = £60,000.
(d) Calls in arrear amounted to (iv) £200.
(e) Paid-up Capital is (c) £60,000 less (d) £200 = £59,800.

Trading and Profit and Loss Accounts

From the viewpoint of the preparation of trading and profit and loss accounts, there are no differences as between public and private limited companies. The accounts now described are those purely for internal use by the company. Obviously, if a full copy of the trading and profit and loss accounts were given to each shareholder, the company's rivals could easily obtain a copy, and would then be in a position to learn about details of the company's trading which the company would prefer to keep secret. The Companies Act therefore states that only certain details of the trading and profit and loss account must be shown. Companies can, if they so wish, disclose more than the minimum information required by law, but it is simply a matter for the directors to decide whether or not it would be in the company's interest. Students who take Accounting in the next year of their course will undertake a study of these factors in year 2.

The trading account of a limited company for internal use is no different from that of a sole trader or of a partnership, but see notes on page 213 concerning published accounts. The profit and loss account also follows the same pattern as those of partnerships or sole traders except for some types of expense which are peculiar to limited companies. The two main expenses under this heading are:

1. Directors' remuneration. This is obvious, since only in companies are directors found.

2. Debenture interest. The term debenture is used when money is received on loan to the company and written acknowledgement is given, usually under seal. Thus a loan to a partnership is known as a loan, while usually a loan to a company is known as a debenture. The interest payable for the use of the money is an expense of the company, and is payable whether profits are made or not. This means that debenture interest is charged as an expense in the Profit and Loss Account itself. Contrast this with dividends which are dependent on profits having been made.

When a company is being formed there are expenses concerned with its incorporating such as stamp duties, legal expenses etc. Collectively these are known as preliminary expenses. Before 1981 these could be shown as an asset in the balance sheet, but they should now be written off as an expense immediately.

The Appropriation Account

Next under the profit and loss account is a section called, as it would also be in a partnership, the profit and loss appropriation account. The net profit is brought down from the profit and loss account, and in the appropriation account is shown the manner in which the profits are to be appropriated, i.e. how the profits are to be used.

First of all, if any of the profits are to be put to reserve then the transfer is shown. To transfer to a reserve means that the directors wish to indicate that that amount of profits is not to be considered as available for dividends in that year. The reserve may be specific, such as a Fixed Asset Replacement Reserve or it may be a General Reserve.

Out of the remainder of profits the dividends are proposed and the unused balance of profits is carried forward to the following year, where it goes to swell the profits then available for appropriation. It is very rare, assuming the firm has not been incurring losses, for there not to be any unappropriated balance of profits carried forward even if it is the policy of the firm to declare the greatest possible dividends, because dividends are normally proposed either as a whole percentage or to a one-half or one-quarter per cent. Arithmetically it is uncommon for the profits remaining after transfers to reserves to exactly equal such a figure.

Exhibit 28.5 shows the profit and loss appropriation account of a new business for its first three years of business.

Exhibit 28.5

I.D.O. Ltd has an Ordinary Share Capital of 40,000 ordinary shares of £1 each and 20,000 5 per cent preference shares of £1 each.

The net profits for the first three years of business ended 31 December are: 19-4 £5,967; 19-5 £7,864, and 19-6, £8,822.

Transfers to reserves are made as follows: 19-4 nil; 19-5, general reserve, £1,000, and 19-6, fixed assets replacement reserve, £2,250.

Dividends were proposed for each year on the preference shares and on the ordinary shares at: 19-4, 10 per cent; 19-5, 12½ per cent; 19-6, 15 per cent.

Profit and Loss Appropriation Accounts
(1) For the year ended 31 December 19-4

		£
Net Profit brought down		5,967
Less Proposed Dividends:		
Preference Dividend of 5%	1,000	
Ordinary Dividend of 10%	4,000	5,000
Balance carried forward to next year		967

(2) For the year ended 31 December 19-5

		£
Net Profit brought down		7,864
Add Balance brought forward from last year		967
		8,831
Less:		
Transfer to General Reserve	1,000	
Proposed Dividends:		
Preference Dividend of 5%	1,000	
Ordinary Dividend of 12½%	5,000	7,000
Balance carried forward to next year		1,831

(3) *For the year ended 31 December 19-6*

		£
Net Profit brought down		8,822
Add Balance brought forward		
from last year		1,831
		10,653
Less:		
Transfer to Fixed Assets		
Replacement Reserve	2,250	
Proposed Dividends:		
Preference Dividend of 5%	1,000	
Ordinary Dividend of 15%	6,000	9,250
		1,403

The Balance Sheet

Until the year 1981, a company could, *provided it disclosed the necessary information,* draw up its Balance Sheet and Profit and Loss Account for publication in any way that it wished. The 1985 Companies Act lays down the precise manner of display.

In this chapter the final accounts shown generally fit in with the requirements of the 1985 Companies Act without going into the detail required by the Act.

Now shown is a company balance sheet. See also the notes on the following page.

Balance Sheet as at 31 December 19-7

	Cost	Depreciation to date	Net
Fixed Assets	£	£	£
Buildings	15,000	6,000	9,000
Machinery	8,000	2,400	5,600
Motor Vehicles	4,000	1,600	2,400
	27,000	10,000	17,000
Current Assets			
Stock		6,000	
Debtors		3,000	
Bank		2,000	
		11,000	
Less Current Liabilities			
Proposed Dividend	1,000		
Creditors	3,000	4,000	
Working Capital			7,000
			24,000

Financed by:

Share Capital	£	£
Authorized 20,000 shares of £1 each		20,000
Issued 12,000 Ordinary shares of £1 each, fully paid		12,000
Reserves		
Share premium	1,200	
General reserve	3,800	
Profit and Loss Account	1,000	
		6,000
		18,000
Debentures		
Six per cent Debentures		6,000
		24,000

Notes:

1. Fixed assets should normally be shown either at cost or alternatively at some other valuation. In either case, the method chosen should be clearly stated.

2. The total depreciation from date of purchase to the date of the balance sheet should be shown.

3. The authorized share capital, where it is different from the issued share capital, is shown as a note.

4. Reserves consist either of those unused profits remaining in the appropriation account, or transferred to a reserve account appropriately titled, e.g. General Reserve, Fixed Assets Replacement Reserve, etc. At this juncture all that needs to be said is that any account labelled as a reserve has originated by being charged as a debit in the appropriation account and credited to a reserve account with an appropriate title. These reserves are shown in the balance sheet after share capital under the heading of 'Reserves'.

On reserve that is in fact not labelled with the word 'reserve' in its title is the Share Premium Account. For reasons which will be examined by those who take the module Accounting in the second year, shares can be issued for more than their face or nominal value. The excess of the price at which they are issued over the nominal value of the shares is credited to a Share Premium Account. This is then shown with the other reserves in the Balance Sheet.

5. Where shares are only partly called up, then it is the amount actually called up that appears in the balance sheet and not the full amount.

6. The share capital and reserves should be totalled so as to show the book value of all the shares in the company.

Either the terms 'Shareholders' Funds' or 'Members' Equity' are often given to the total of share Capital plus Reserves.

Assignment Exercises

28.1 A limited liability company has an authorized capital of £200,000 divided into £20,000 6 per cent preference shares of £1 each and 180,000 ordinary shares of £1 each. All the preference shares are issued and fully paid: 100,000 ordinary shares are issued with 75p per share paid on each share.

On 31 December 19-2, the company's revenue reserves were £30,000, current liabilities £7,500, current assets £62,750, fixed assets (at cost) £90,000 and provisions for depreciation on fixed assets £20,250.

Make a summarized balance sheet as at 31 December 19-2 to display this information. Set out the balance sheet in such a way as to show clearly the net value of current assets.

28.2 A Limited company has an authorized capital of £100,000 divided into 25,000 7% preference shares of £1 each and 75,000 ordinary shares of £1 each. All the preference shares were issued and fully paid and 60,000 ordinary shares were issued and fully paid.

At 1 January 19-7 there was a 'general reserve' of £25,000 and a credit balance on profit and loss account of £3,000. Creditors were £12,550, fixed assets £48,000 (cost £60,000) and current assets £86,000.

The net profit for the year ended 31 December 19-7 was £10,200. The preference dividends had been paid and the directors had recommended a transfer of £2,500 to general reserve and a dividend of 10% for the year on the ordinary shares.

You are required to prepare the profit and loss appropriation amount for the year ended 31 December 19-7 and a balance sheet as at that date.

28.3A The T.A.P. Company Ltd is registered with 100,000 shares of £1 each made up of 40,000 6% Preference Shares and 60,000 Ordinary Shares.

During the year ended 31 December 19-8 20,000 6% Preference Shares and 40,000 Ordinary Shares were issued to the public for subscription. All the shares were taken up and fully paid for by the public.

At the end of the year the sum of £9,000 was realized as the net profit and the Directors decided to deal with the net profits as follows:
(a) Pay the Preference Shareholders' dividends;
(b) Pay a dividend of 5% to the ordinary shareholders;
(c) Write off preliminary expenses of £500;
(d) Carry the balance forward.

You are required to prepare the Profit & Loss Appropriation Account for the year ended 31 December 19-8, and to show how the items should appear in the Balance Sheet as at the end of that year.

Note: You are not required to complete the Balance Sheet.

28.4 The following is the trial balance of B.C. Ltd. as on 31 December 19-3:

	Dr. £	Cr. £
Share Capital Issued: Ordinary Shares £1		75,000
Debtors and Creditors	28,560	22,472
Stock 31 December 19-2	41,415	
Bank	16,255	
Machinery at cost	45,000	
Motor Vehicles at cost	28,000	
Depreciation Provisions at 31.12.19-2:		
Machinery		18,000
Motor Vehicles		12,000
Sales		97,500
Purchases	51,380	
Motor Expenses	8,144	
Repairs to Machinery	2,308	
Sundry Expenses	1,076	
Wages and Salaries	11,372	
Directors' Remuneration	6,200	
Profit and Loss Account as at 31.12.19-2		6.138
General Reserve		8,600
	239,710	239,710

Given the following information you are to draw up a Trading and Profit and Loss Account for the year ended 31 December 19-3, and a Balance Sheet as at that date:

(i)   Authorised Share Capital: £100,000 in ordinary shares £1.
(ii) Stock at 31 December 19-3 £54,300.
(iii) Motor Expenses owing £445.
(iv) Ordinary Dividend proposed of 20 per cent.
(v)   Transfer £2,000 to General Reserve.
(vi) Provide for Depreciation of all fixed assets at 20 per cent reducing balance method.
(vii) Ignore Taxation.

28.5A You are to draw up a Trading and Profit and Loss Account for the year ended 31 December 19-4, and a Balance Sheet as at that date from the following trial balance and details of B.T. Ltd:

	Dr.	Cr.
	£	£
Bank	6,723	
Debtors	18,910	
Creditors		12,304
Stock 31 December 19-3	40,360	
Buildings at cost	100,000	
Equipment at cost	45,000	
Profit and Loss Account as at 31.12.19-3		15,286
General Reserve		8,000
Foreign Exchange Reserve		4,380
Authorised and Issued Share Capital		100,000
Purchases	72,360	
Sales		135,486
Carriage Inwards	1,570	
Carriage Outwards	1,390	
Salaries	18,310	
Rates and Occupancy Expenses	4,325	
Office Expenses	3,022	
Sundry Expenses	1,986	
Provisions for Depreciation at 31.12.19-3:		
Buildings		32,000
Equipment		16,000
Directors' Remuneration	9,500	
	323,456	323,456

Notes at 31 December 19-4:

(i)   Stock at 31 December 19-4 £52,360.
(ii) Rates owing £280; Office Expenses owing £190.
(iii) Ordinary Dividend of 10 per cent proposed.
(iv) Transfers to Reserves: General £1,000; Foreign Exhange £800.
(v)   Depreciation on cost: Building 5 per cent: Equipment 20 per cent.
(vi) Ignore Taxation.

29 The Calculation of Wages and Salaries Payable to Employees

In the U.K. wages are generally taken to be the earnings paid on a weekly basis to employees, whilst salaries are those paid on a monthly basis.

The earnings of employees, whether paid monthly or weekly, are subject to various deductions. These can consist of the following items.

(1) Income Tax. In the U.K. the wages and salaries of all employees are liable to have income tax deducted from them. This does not mean that everyone will pay Income Tax, but that if Income Tax is found to be payable then the employer will deduct the tax from the employee's wages or salary.

Each person in the U.K. is allowed to set various personal reliefs against the amount earned to see if he/she is liable to pay Income Tax. The reliefs given for each person depend upon his or her personal circumstances. Extra relief is given to a man who is married, as compared to a single man; further extra relief will be given for factors such as having dependent relatives, and so on. The reliefs given are changed from time to time by Parliament. Most students will know of the 'Budget' which is presented to Parliament by the Chancellor of the Exchequer, in which such changes are announced. After discussion by Parliament, and subject to possible changes there, the changes will be incorporated into a Finance Act. This means that, for instance, a single man earning a given amount might pay Income Tax, whereas a married man who is eligible for extra reliefs might earn the same amount and pay no Income Tax at all.

Once the reliefs have been deducted from the earnings, any excess of the earnings above that figure will have to suffer Income Tax being levied on it. As the rates of Income Tax change regularly, all that can be given here are the basic principles; the rates given are for purposes of illustration only. A further complication arises because the rate of tax increases in steps when the excess of the earnings exceeds certain figures.

For instance, assume that the rates of Income Tax are (on the amount actually exceeding the reliefs for each person):

On the first £1,000   Income Tax at 20 per cent
On the next £5,000   Income Tax at 30 per cent
On the remainder   Income Tax at 50 per cent

The Income Tax payable by each of four persons can now be looked at.

Miss Jones earns £1,500 per annum. Her personal reliefs amount to £1,700. Income Tax payable = Nil.

Mr Bland earns £4,000 per annum. His personal reliefs are £3,400. He therefore has £600 of his earnings on which he will have to pay Income Tax. As the rate on the first £1,000 taxable is 20 per cent, then he will pay £600 × 20 per cent = £120.

Mrs Hugo earns £6,500 per annum. She has personal reliefs amounting to £2,700. She will therefore pay Income Tax on the excess of £3,800. This will amount to:

On the first £1,000 tax at 20 per cent	=	200
On the remaining £2,800 tax at 30 per cent	=	840
Total Income Tax		£1,040

Mr Pleasance has a salary of £10,000 per annum. His personal reliefs amount to £3,560. He will therefore pay Income Tax on the excess of £6,440. This will amount to:

On the first £1,000 tax at 20 per cent	=	200
On the next £5,000 tax at 30 per cent	=	1,500
On the next £440 tax at 50 per cent	=	220
Total Income Tax		£1,920

The actual deduction of the Income Tax from the earnings of the employee is made by the employer. The tax is commonly called P.A.Y.E. tax, which represents the initial letters for Pay As You Earn. The amount of reliefs to which each employee is entitled is communicated to the employer in the form of a Notice of Coding, on which a code number is stated. The code number is then used in conjunction with special tax tables to show the amount of the tax deductible from the employee's earnings.

So far the amount of tax payable by anyone has been looked at on an annual basis. However, P.A.Y.E. means precisely that: it involves paying the tax as the earnings are calculated on each pay date, weekly or monthly, and not waiting until after the end of the year to pay the bill. The code numbers and the tax tables supplied to the employer by the Inland Revenue are so worked out that this is possible. It is outside the scope of this book to examine in detail how this is done. However, in the case of the three people already listed who will have to pay Income Tax, if we assume that Mrs Hugo is paid weekly, then from each week's wage she will have to pay one week's tax, in her case £1,040 ÷ 52 = £20. If Mr Bland and Mr Pleasance are paid on a monthly basis, then Mr Bland will have to pay £120 ÷ = £10 per month, and Mr Pleasance £1,920 ÷ 12 = £160 per month.

It may well have crossed the reader's mind that, for many people, the year's earnings are not known in advance, and that the total amount payable, divided neatly into weekly or monthly figures, would not be known until the year was finished. The operation of the P.A.Y.E. system automatically allows for this problem. A book on Income Tax should be studied if the reader would like to investigate further how this is carried out.

(2) In the U.K. employees are also liable to pay National Insurance contributions. The deduction of these is carried out by the employer at the same time as the P.A.Y.E. Income Tax deductions are effected. The payment of such National Insurance contributions is to ensure that the payer will be able to claim benefits from the State, if and when he is in a position to claim, such as unemployment benefit, sickness benefits, retirement pension and so on.

There is a lower limit for each employee below which no National Insurance is payable at all, and there is also a top limit, earnings above this amount being disregarded for National Insurance. These limits are changed by Parliament, usually annually. Any figures given in this book are by way of illustration only.

If it is assumed that the lower limit of earnings eligible for National Insurance contributions is £1,000, and that the top limit is £10,000, and that the rate of National Insurance payable by the employee is 5 per cent, then the following contributions would be made:

Mrs Jones: part-time cleaner, earns £900 per annum. National Insurance contribution nil.

Miss Hardcastle, earnings £3,000 per annum. National Insurance contribution £3,000 × 5 per cent = £150. The fact that there is a lower limit of £1,000 does not mean that the first £1,000 of the earnings are free of National Insurance contributions, but simply that anyone earning less than £1,000 will not pay any. Someone earning £1,100 would pay National Insurance of £1,100 × 5 per cent = £55.

Mr Evergreen earns £12,000 per annum. He would pay at the rate of 5 per cent on £10,000 only = £500.

As with the P.A.Y.E. Income Tax, the National Insurance contribution is payable per week or per month.

It should be noted that in the U.K. part of the National Insurance contributions are in respect of a supplement to the retirement pension. This supplement to the pension is based on the amount actually earned by the person during the years he was paying towards this supplement, and on the number of years he actually paid contributions. The more he earned, the more he would pay in contributions, and he would therefore get a bigger supplement than someone earning less and contributing less.

However, it was recognized when the scheme was started that some firms had special superannuation funds (dealt with later in this chapter), so that the employees in those firms would not necessarily wish to have an extra supplement from the State on top of their State retirement pension. At the same time they would therefore not want to pay as much in National Insurance as the man who wanted such a supplement. These firms were therefore given the right to 'opt out', and employees in these firms pay a lower percentage of their earnings in National Insurance contributions.

(3) Superannuation contributions. Many firms have superannuation schemes. These are schemes whereby the employee will receive a pension on retiring from the firm, plus, very often, a lump sum payment in cash. They also usually include benefits which will be paid to an employee's spouse if the employee dies before reaching retirement age.

Some of these schemes are non-contributory. This means that the firm pays for these benefits for its employees without deducting anything from the employee's earnings. The other schemes are contributory schemes whereby the employee will pay a part of the cost of the scheme by an agreed deduction from his earnings. The actual percentages paid by employees will vary from firm to firm. In addition the firm will pay part of the cost of the scheme without any cost to the employee. With the advent of the State scheme for a supplement to the retirement pension some firms opted out of the State supplement scheme, so that their employees rely on the firm's superannuation scheme instead. They still qualify for the basic State retirement pension, it will only be the supplement that they will not receive. Other firms carry on their own superannuation scheme and are also in the State and the benefits from their firm's superannuation scheme on top as well.

Normally the contributions of employees to the superannuation schemes of their firms are tax deductible. This means that the part of their earnings taken as their contribution to the firm's scheme will escape Income Tax. This is not so with the contribution to any part of the State National Insurance scheme at the time that this book is being written.

Calculation of Net Wages/Salary Payable

Two illustrations of the calculation of the net pay to be made to various employees can now be looked at.

			£
(A) G. Jarvis:	Gross Earning for the week ended 8 May 19-4		100
	Income Tax: found by consulting tax tables and employee's code number		12
	National Insurance 5%		

G. Jarvis: Payslip week ended 8 May 19-4

	£	£
Gross pay for the week		100
Less Income Tax	12	
,, National Insurance	5	17
Net Pay		83

			£
(B) H. Reddish:	Gross earnings for the month of May 19-4		800
	Income Tax (from tax tables)		150
	Superannuation: 6% of gross pay		
	National Insurance 5% of gross pay		

H. Reddish: Payslip Month ended 31 May 19-4

	£	£
Gross pay for the month		800
Less Income tax	150	
,, Superannuation	150	
,, National Insurance	40	238
Net Pay		562

National Insurance: Employer's Contribution

Besides the amount of the National Insurance which has to be suffered by the employee, the employer also has to pay a percentage based on the employee's pay as the firm's own contribution. This expense is suffered by the firm; it has no recourse against its employee. The percentage which the firm will have to pay varies as Parliament amend it to deal with the changing economic climate of the country. In this book it will be treated as though it is 10 per cent, but this figure is simply to illustration purposes. If does, however, at the time that this book is being written, equate to the approximate proportion which the employer pays as compared with that paid by the employee, the latter being about one-half of that suffered by the employer.

The entry of salaries and wages in the books of a firm can now be seen. A firm owned by H. Offerton has one employee, whose name is F. Edgeley. For the month of June 19-3 the payslip made out for Edgeley has appeared as:

F. Edgeley: Payslip month ended 30 June 19-3

		£
Gross Pay for the month		600
Less Income Tax	90	
,, National Insurance 5%	30	120
Net Pay		480

Additional to this, the firm will also have to pay its own share of the National Insurance contribution for Edgeley. This will be 10 per cent of £600 = £60. Therefore to employ Edgeley in the firm for this month has cost the firm the amount of his gross pay £600, plus £60 National Insurance, a total of £660. This means that when the firm draws up its Profit and Loss Account, the charge for the employment of this person for the month should be £660.

The firm has however acted as a collecter of taxes and Natioanl Insurance on behalf of the government, and it will have to pay over to the government's agent, which is the Inland Revenue, the amount collected on its behalf. If it is assumed that the £90 deducted from pay for Income Tax, and the £30 deducted for National Insurance, are paid to the Inland Revenue on 30 June 19-3, then the cash book will appear as:

Cash Book (bank columns)

	Dr			Cr	
			19-3		£
			Jun 30 Wages (cheque to Edgeley)		480
			,, ,, Inland Revenue (see below)*		180
*Made up of: Income Tax P.A.Y.E.	90				
National Insurance (employee's part)	30				
National Insurance (employer's part)	60				
	180				

In a firm as small as the one illustrated, both the figure of £480 and the £180 could be posted to a 'Wages and National Insurance Account', to give a total for the monthy of £660. In a larger firm such payments would be best posted to separate accounts for National Insurance and for P.A.Y.E. Income Tax, transfers then being made when the final accounts are drawn up.

224

Assignment Exercises

29.1 H. Smith is employed by a firm of carpenters at a rate of £1.50 per hour. During the week to 18 May 19-5 he worked his basic week of 40 hours. The Income Tax due on his wages was £8, and he is also liable to pay National Insurance contributions of 5 per cent. Calculate his net wages.

29.2 B. Charles is employed as an undertaker's assistant. His basic working week consists of 40 hours, paid at the rate of £2 per hour. For hours worked in excess of this he is paid at the rate of 1½ times his basic earnings. In the week ended 12 March 19-6 he worked 60 hours. Up to £40 a week he pays no Income Tax, but he pays it at the rate of 30 per cent for all earnings above that figure. He is liable to pay National Insurance at the rate of 5 per cent. Calculate his net wages.

29.3 B. Croft has a job as a car salesman. He is paid a basic salary of £200 per month, with a commission extra of 2 per cent on the value of his car sales. During the month of April 19-6 he sells £30,000 worth of cars. He pays Income Tax at the rate of 30 per cent on all earnings above £100 per month. He also pays National Insurance at the rate of 5 per cent on the first £500 of his monthly earnings, paying nothing on earnings above that figure. Calculate his net pay for the month.

29.4A T. Penketh is an accountant with a firm of bookmakers. He has a salary of £500 per month, but he also has a bonus dependent on the firm's profits. The bonus for the month was £200. He pays National Insurance at the rate of 5 per cent on his gross earnings up to a maximum of £600 per month, there being no contribution for earnings above that figure. He pays Income Tax at the rate of thirty per cent on his earnings between £100 and £300 per month, and at the rate of 50 per cent on all earnings above that figure. However, before calculating earnings on which he has to pay Income Tax, he is allowed to deduct the amount of superannuation payable by him which is at the rate of 10 per cent on gross earnings. Calculate his net pay for the month.

29.5A R. Kennedy is a security van driver. He has a wage of £100 per week, and danger money of £1 per hour in addition for every hour he spends in transporting gold bullion. During the week ended 16 June 19-3 he spends 20 hours taking gold bullion to London Airport. He pays Income Tax at the rate of 25 per cent on all his earnings aboe £80 per week. He pays National Insurance at the rate of 5 per cent on gross earnings. Calculate his net wage for the week.

29.6A V. Mevagissey is a director of a company. She has a salary of £500 per month. She pays superannuation at the rate of 5 per cent. She also pays National Insurance at the rate of 5 per cent of gross earnings. He Income Tax, due on gross salary less superannuation, is at the rate of 30 per cent after her personal reliefs for the month, other than superannuation, of £300 have been deducted. Calculate her net pay for the month.

30   Financial Performance: Differing Points of View

Later in the course you will be introduced to the interpretation of the financial performance of organisations. When that stage is reached it is very easy to be so hypnotised by the sheer amount or variety of statistics and facts given you, that you cannot easily see the whole picture in proper perspective. This chapter is concerned with giving you a general outline, against which the details of the financial performance can be set, and a more balanced judgement obtained.

How does anyone know whether a particular financial result is good or bad? Can a financial performance be judged as good by all parties concerned? Is it possible to have an organisation where a low profit can be judged as being good? These are some of the factors which are going to be considered in this chapter.

You will often have heard on the news, or read it in the newspapers, that the profits of (say) XYZ plc were £25 million for the past year. Such a figure, when stated on its own, and without being shown as a percentage of anything else, is said to be an *absolute* measure. When stated like this, such a figure is fairly meaningless. We will now look at a few instances where such a profit result may be either good or bad, depending on circumstances.

1.   Suppose that the company is in a market which has recently been enjoying a generally high level of prosperity, and that capital employed is £1,000 million.
This means that it has only made a return of 2.5% on capital employed. Surely this would count as a terrible result.
2.   Instead, imagine an industry going through very bad times, with all of its competitors incurring huge losses. A return of 2.5% in this case may be extremely good, indicating management of a very high calibre.
3.   Consider an organisation whose aim is to help its members in some way, and for whom profit-making is not an objective, but rather it sets out simply to break even. In this case £25 million might well mean that it has been overcharging its members for the services rendered to them.
4.   Take instead a company that has enjoyed a technological breakthrough in its industry. With only £10 million capital employed it has managed to make £25 million profits by pushing up its prices to gain benefits in the short-term, but it has not been ploughing anything back into the company to lay down a foundation for the future, and

other companies are now catching up on the technological front. Can you simply judge the company from profits alone?

The lessons to be learned from these cases, and from many more which could be put forward, is that a single absolute figure of profit is meaningless by itself. It has to be considered against what the rest of that industry is doing, and also against many other factors. When the financial performance of one organisation is compared against other performances, then the measures are said to be *relative* measures.

Some relative measures are within the same organisation, for instance how our current profits compare with our profits from the last five years. Simply listing the profit figures for the past years alongside the current year's profits invites people to consider how this year has fared *relative* to the past. Other relative measures will be with the profits of other organisations.

With relative measures one tries to compare like with like. There is not much point in comparing the results of an oil company against those of an hotel, and from such an analysis expect to get much of a clue as to how to bring about a better financial performance from either organisation. Similarly, if our company has completely changed its products over the past year then a comparison with previous years will have to bear this in mind.

Trends and Performance

Whilst we can learn something from studying what has gone on in the past, what we are really interested in is what is going to happen in the future. The past is gone, we cannot now influence it, the future has yet to come and this is, hopefully, something we can influence by putting past experience into helping us bring about better financial performance.

We can help ourselves in trying to predict what might happen in the future, assuming our organisation does not alter its ways, by plotting past results as trends. It can be done on graph paper by linking together financial ratios over the past few years, or it may be possible to do it simply by looking at the past few years' figures without even graphing them if the trend is an obvious one. For instance, suppose that the amount of gross profit per £100 sales for the last five years has been falling as follows: 15%: 14%: 13%: 12%: 11%, then the trend is an obvious one. The big question is whether the trend can somehow be reversed. It does at least highlight the fact that it needs serious investigation to figure out what has been happening, and whether it has to continue like this.

Objectives and Performance

It may seem that all that the authors are doing in this chapter is to ask you, the reader, a lot of questions, rather than simply tell you how to judge performance. This is because one has to ask quite a lot of questions before performance can be judged properly. Something you should have learned so far is that we cannot simply judge our performance by itself, we have to place it against other factors. Certainly we must do this, but we must also, and this is of extreme importance, judge the results of an organisation against the objective which it has set itself.

In the case of a company the board of directors will set out the objectives of the company. In some large companies they actually publish what the objectives of the company are, but this is not usually the case. In the vast majority of organisations, and this would be most usual in smaller ones, the objectives are never written down at all.

To some it may seem that the only objective of a profit-making concern is to make as much money as possible. Even if that was the case, it would still beg the question as to whether the long-term or the short-term was being considered. A company might cut out all expenditure other than that considered vital for the immediate future. This could push up current profits by quite a lot in many cases. However, this could be very short-sighted as it may seriously damage the long-term prospects for the company. Suppose that all staff facilities were cut to the barest minimum, also staff bonuses abolished. This might possibly have the effect that the members of staff who could get jobs elsewhere would leave, so losing many of the company's best workers and leading to the company being unable to compete effectively in the future.

Another company may set itself fairly low profit targets in the short-term, because it is trying to keep its prices low and thereby get a much larger share of the market for its particular type of goods.

Imagine instead a company whose task it is to supply goods for use by the British government. It may have to keep its profits relatively low, as to make excessive profits might arouse the wrath of the government, leading to the company not getting any contracts in future. So short-term lower profits may lead, in such a case, to the company being able to get more profits in the long-term.

You should now be able to see that the setting of financial targets is only one aspect of the objectives of an organisation. There are all sorts of other factors which will affect decisions on financial objectives.

One factor which has come out clearly so far is the effect of our financial objectives on the particular kind of market in which we are situated. But this is not the whole of the story. Suppose that we are a company quoted on the stock exchange and that our share price is low because we have consistently set ourselves low profit targets. This might attract a takeover bid from another company who could possibly set higher profit targets, and therefore such a takeover might be very attractive to them. Our board of directors may then have to change the financial targets in an attempt to repel a takeover which they consider not to be in the best interests of our shareholders.

The degree of risk is also very much a factor which affects financial targets and performance. In a high-risk business, such as in the fashion industry, the profit targets may be very high compared to a company making some long-established but mundane type of clothing. The first company will probably be far more likely to make serious misjudgements which could easily lead to it having to cease trading, whereas the second one may come across such conditions very rarely. Therefore high-risk industries will look for higher profits, compared with safer industries. If you as an investor were asked to put your money into two businesses, one in which you may easily lose all of that investment, and the other in which your investment was considered very safe indeed, then you would expect a much higher dividend from the high-risk investment. Otherwise you would always put your money into safe investments if you got the same percentage return.

In non-profit making organisations the financial objectives may be imposed on them by outside bodies. An instance of this would be public bodies, such as the National Health Service, where it is the Government which tells it how much money it has to spend within each financial year. That therefore has to be the financial objective of that organisation. How it sets out to achieve that objective may be completely at its own discretion, but the objective has to be achieved somehow. Other public bodies may be carried on with the intention of making a profit, and the government may well fix the profit target for it. As governments change, then so do the methods of setting financial targets for public bodies.

In a private club, such as a golf club, the financial objectives may be to provide simply the best conditions for its members to play golf, and may simply fix a subscription for its members so that the club either makes a very small profit or may break-even, i.e. it makes neither a profit nor a loss. On the other hand, suppose that a golf club wants some extra land next to its course, it may possibly fix higher subscriptions so that it makes profits out of which the land can be paid for over the next few years.

Different Intepretation by Interested Parties

There is certainly nothing unusual about different interested parties putting a different interpretation on to a particular set of results. If Manchester United beat Liverpool 1-0 in a football match it would hardly be likely that both United's supporters and Liverpool's supporters were to have the same thoughts about the result. The same sort of diversity of opinion applies to the views of the financial performances of organisations.

It might be thought that all shareholders will want to see good profits so that they will get good dividends. However, different types of shareholders may see the results quite differently. A preference shareholder receiving a fixed dividend may well get upset if long-term performance is given second place to higher profits now, which may benefit only the ordinary shareholder, and may even jeopardise the long-term prospects of the preference shareholder if such activities lead to the closure of the company. Even shareholders of the same type, e.g. ordinary shareholders may view events quite differently. This could be the case with a company making good profits but not ploughing enough back into the company to ensure that it has a long-term future, e.g. renewing machinery. The shareholder who wants high dividends now with no thought for the future would see it quite differently from the shareholder who wants a steady and relatively safe income from his dividends for many years to come.

A trade union may see high profits in a company as being the result of not paying workers high enough wages. This may encourage the union to press its wage claims against the company to a much greater extent. If low profits are made then the union may change its stance, seeing the poor performance not as the company paying too much in wages, but rather as the result of bad management of the company. On the other hand, a different trade union may see high profits as providing steady employment for its members working in the company, and low profits as a threat to their future employment, and be happy in such a case to moderate wage claims. It is therefore impossible to be too rigid about the way that trade unions in general would view financial performances.

A prospective employee may well look at financial performances with the thought that he wants employment with an organisation that seems to have a long-term future. No one can usually deduce that much from sets of final accounts, but at least a company that is profitable and has healthy reserves would be better than one that is losing money and is insolvent.

A bank manager will have as his first priority that any organisation to which he lends money will be able to service the debt. This means that it can afford to pay the interest on the debt and will also be able to repay the debt by the agreed date. He will then monitor the results of the organisation during the period of debt to ensure that the ability to service the debt still applies. The balance sheet values of the assets will not be the values in which he is interested. Instead he will want to know how much the assets would fetch if the organisation suddenly had to cease normal activities and be shut down completely. It would be cynical to say that this was the only view of a bank, but it must certainly be at the front of any banker's mind.

The view of an income tax inspector is simply one of ensuring that the taxable profits have all been declared, and that they have been properly calculated in accordance with the taxation laws. He is not interested in any income which is not taxable, and he will not be concerned if the payment of the tax places the organisation in a very difficult position.

31 An Introduction to the Analysis and Interpretation of Accounting Statements

Throughout the book there have been quite a few references to such items as the use of Accounting Ratios, or to the fact that accounts do not disclose all the information about a business. For students who will not carry their study of Accounting beyond the coverage of this book, this chapter will give the basic essentials.

Fixed and Variable Expenses

Some expenses will remain constant whether activity increases or falls, at least within a given range of change of activity., These expenses are called 'fixed expenses'. An example of this would be the rent of a shop which would remain at the same figure, whether sales increased 10 per cent or fell 10 per cent. The same would remain true of such things as rates, fire insurance and so on.

Wages of shop assistants could also remain constant in such a case. If, for instance, the shop employed two assistants then it would probably keep the same two assistants, on the same wages, whether sales increased or fell by 10 per cent.

Of course, such 'fixed expenses' can only be viewed as fixed in the short term. If sales doubled then the business might well need a larger shop or more assistants. A larger shop would almost certainly mean higher rates, higher fire insurance and so on, and with more assistants the total wage bill would be larger.

'Variable' expenses on the other hand will change with swings in activity. Suppose that wrapping materials are used in the shop, then it could well be that an increase in sales of 10 per cent may see 10 per cent more wrapping materials used. Similary an increase of 10 per cent of sales, if all sales are despatched by parcel post, could well see delivery charges increase by 10 per cent.

Some expenses could be part fixed and part variable. Suppose that because of an increase in sales of 10 per cent, that telephone calls made increased by 10 per cent. With telephone bills the cost falls into two parts, one for the rent of the phone and the second part corresponding to the actual number of calls made. The rent would not change in such a case, and therefore this part of telephone expense would be 'fixed' whereas the calls cost could increase by 10 per cent.

This means that the effect of a percentage change in activity could have a more/or less percentage change in net profit, because the fixed expenses (within that range of activity) may not alter.

Exhibit 31.1 shows the change in net profit in business (A) which has a low proportion of its expenses as 'fixed' expenses, whereas in business (B) the 'fixed' expenses are a relatively high proportion of its expenses.

Exhibit 31.1

Business (A)			(i) If sales fell 10%		(ii) If sales rose 10%	
			£		£	
Sales		50,000		45,000		55,000
Less Cost of Goods Sold		30,000		27,000		33,000
Gross Profit		20,000		18,000		22,000
Less Expenses:						
Fixed	3,000		3,000		3,000	
Variable	13,000	16,000	11,700	14,700	14,300	17,300
Net Profit		4,000		3,300		4,700

Business (B)			(i) If sales fell 10%		(ii) If sales rose 10%	
			£		£	
Sales		50,000		45,000		55,000
Less Cost of Goods Sold		30,000		27,000		33,000
Gross Profit		20,000		18,000		22,000
Less Expenses:						
Fixed	12,000		12,000		12,000	
Variable	4,000	16,000	3,600	15,600	4,400	16,400
Net Profit		4,000		2,400		5,600

The comparison of percentage changes in net profit therefore works out as follows:

	(A)	(B)

Decrease of 10% in sales

$$\frac{\text{Reduction in profit}}{\text{Original profit}} \times \frac{100}{1} \quad \frac{700}{4,000} \times \frac{100}{1} = 17.5\% \quad \frac{1,600}{4,000} \times \frac{100}{1} = 40\%$$

Increase of 10% in sales

$$\frac{\text{Increase in profit}}{\text{Original profit}} \times \frac{100}{1} \quad \frac{700}{4,000} \times \frac{100}{1} = 17.5\% \quad \frac{1,600}{4,000} \times \frac{100}{1} = 40\%$$

It can be seen that a change in activity in business (B) which has a higher fixed expense content, will result in greater percentage changes in profit, 40% in (B) compared with 17.5% in (A).

An Introduction to Accounting Ratios

(a) Mark-up and Margin

The purchase and sale of a good may be shown as

Cost Price + Profit = Selling Price.

The profit when expressed as a fraction, or percentage, of the cost price is known as the mark-up.

The profit when expressed as a fraction, or percentage, of the selling price is known as the margin.

$$\text{Cost Price} + \text{Profit} = \text{Selling Price.}$$
$$\text{£4} \quad + \quad \text{£1} = \quad \text{£5.}$$

Mark-up $= \dfrac{\text{Profit}}{\text{Cost Price}}$ as a fraction, or if required as a percentage

multiply by $\dfrac{100}{1}$

$$= \frac{£1}{£4} = \frac{1}{4}, \text{ or } \frac{1}{4} \times \frac{100}{1} = 25 \text{ per cent.}$$

Margin $= \dfrac{\text{Profit}}{\text{Selling Price}}$ as a fraction, or if required as a

percentage multiply by $\dfrac{100}{1}$

$$= \frac{£1}{£5} = \frac{1}{5}, \text{ or } \frac{1}{5} \times \frac{100}{1} = 20 \text{ per cent.}$$

The following illustrations[1] of the deduction of missing information assume that the rate of mark-ups and margins are constant, in other words the goods dealt in by the firm have uniform margins and mark-ups and they do not vary between one good and another. It also ignores wastages and pilferages of goods, also the fact that the market value of some goods may be below cost and therefore need to be taken into stock at the lower figure. These items will need to be the subject of separate adjustments.

1. The following figures are for the year 19-5:

	£
Stock 1.1.19-5	400
Stock 31.12.19-5	600
Purchases	5,200

A uniform rate of mark-up of 20 per cent is applied.
Find the gross profit and the sales figure.

---

1. The horizontal style of accounts will be used in this chapter, simply because it is less confusing when showing illustrations of missing figures.

Trading Account

	£		£
Stock 1.1.19-5	400	Sales	?
Add Purchases	5,200		
	5,600		
Less Stock 31.12.19-5	600		
Cost of goods sold	5,000		
Gross profit	?		

Answer:

It is known that: Cost of goods sold + Profit = Sales

and also that: Cost of goods sold + Percentage Mark-up = Sales

The following figures are also known: £5,000 + 20 per cent = Sales

After doing the arithmetic: £5,000 + £1,000   = £6,000

    The trading account can be completed by inserting the gross profit £1,000 and £6,000 for Sales.

2.   Another firm has the following figures for 19-6:

	£
Stock 1.1.19-6	500
Stock 31.12.19-6	800
Sales	6,400

A uniform rate of margin of 25 per cent is in use.

Find the gross profit and the figure of purchases.

Trading Account

	£		£
Stock 1.1.19-6	500	Sales	6,400
Add Purchases	?		
Less Stock 31.12.19-6	800		
Cost of goods sold	?		
Gross Profit	?		
	6,400		6,400

Answer: Cost of goods sold + Gross Profit = Sales

Therefore	Sales	− Gross Profit	= Cost of Goods Sold
	Sales	− 25 per cent	
		Margin	= Cost of Goods Sold
	£6,400	−£1,600	= £4,800

Now the following figures are known:

	£
Stock 1.1.19-6	500
Add Purchases (1)	?
(2)	?
Less Stock 31.12.19-6	800
Cost of goods sold	4,800

The two missing figures are found by normal arithmetical deduction:

No. (2) less £800 = £4,800
Therefore No. (2) = £5,600
So that: £500 opening stock + No. (1) = £5,600
Therefore No. (1) = £5,100

The completed trading account can now be shown:

Trading Account

	£		£
Stock 1.1.19-6	500	Sales	6,400
Add Purchases	5,100		
	5,600		
Less Stock 31.12.19-6	800		
Cost of goods sold	4,800		
Gross Profit	1,600		
	6,400		6,400

This technique is found very useful by retail stores when estimating the amount to be bought if a certain sales target is to be achieved. Alternatively, stock levels or sales figures can be estimated given information as to purchases and opening stock figures.

The Relationship Between Mark-Up and Margin

As both of these figures refer to the same profit, but expressed as a fraction or a percentage of different figures, there is bound to be a relationship. If one is known as a fraction, the other can soon be found.

If the mark-up is known, to find margin take the same numerator to be numerator of the margin, then for the denominator of the margin take the total of the mark-up's denominator plus the numerator. An example can now be shown:

Mark-up	Margin
$\dfrac{1}{4}$	$\dfrac{1}{4+1} = \dfrac{1}{5}$
$\dfrac{2}{11}$	$\dfrac{2}{11+2} = \dfrac{2}{13}$

If the margin is known, to find the mark-up take the same numerator to be the numerator of the mark-up, then for the denominator of the mark-up take the figure of the margin's denominator less the numerator:

Margin	Mark-up
$\dfrac{1}{6}$	$\dfrac{1}{6-1} = \dfrac{1}{5}$
$\dfrac{3}{13}$	$\dfrac{3}{13-3} = \dfrac{3}{10}$

There are some ratios that are in common use for the purpose of comparing one period's results against those of a previous period. Two of the ones most in use are the ratio of gross profit to sales, and the rate of turnover or stockturn.

(b) Gross Profit as Percentage of Sales

The basic formula is:

$$\frac{\text{Gross profit}}{\text{Sales}} \times \frac{100}{1} = \text{Gross profit as percentage of sales.}$$

Put another way, this represents the amount of gross profit for every £100 of sales. If the answer turned out to be 15 per cent, this would mean that for every £100 of sales £15 gross profit was made before any expenses were paid.

This ratio is used as a test of the profitability of the sales. Just because the sales are increased does not of itself mean that the gross profit will increase. The trading accounts in Exhibit 31.2 illustrates this.

Exhibit 31.2

Trading Accounts for the year ended 31 December

	19-6 £	19-7 £		19-6 £	19-7 £
Stock	500	900	Sales	7,000	8,000
Purchases	6,000	7,200			
	6,500	8,100			
Less Stock	900	1,100			
Cost of goods sold	5,600	7,000			
Gross Profit	1,400	1,000			
	7,000	8,000		7,000	8,000

In the year 19-6 the gross profit as a percentage of sales was:

$$\frac{1,400}{7,000} \times \frac{100}{1} = 20 \text{ per cent.}$$

In the year 19-7 it became:

$$\frac{1,000}{8,000} \times \frac{100}{1} = 12\frac{1}{2} \text{ per cent.}$$

Thus sales had increased, but as the gross profit percentage had fallen by a relatively greater amount the actual gross profit has fallen.

There can be many reasons for such a fall in the gross profit percentage. Perhaps the goods being sold have cost more but the selling price of the goods has not risen to the same extent. Maybe, in order to boost sales, reductions have been made in the selling price of goods. There could be a difference in the composition of types of goods sold, called the sales-mix, between this year and last, with different product lines carrying different rates of gross profit per £100 of sales. Alternatively there may have been a greater wastage or pilferage of goods. These are only some of the possible reasons for the decrease. The idea of calculating the ratio is to highlight the fact that the profitability per £100 of sales has changed, and so promote an inquiry as to why and how such a change is taking place.

As the figure of sales less returns inwards is also known as turnover, the ratio is also known as the gross profit percentage on turnover.

(c) Stockturn or Rate of Turnover

This is another commonly used ratio, and is expressed in the formula:

$$\frac{\text{Cost of goods sold}}{\text{Average stock}} = \text{Number of times stock is turned over within the period}$$

Ideally, the average stock held should be calculated by taking a large number of readings of stock over the accounting year, then dividing the totals of the figures obtained by the number of readings. For instance, monthly stock figures added up then divided by twelve. It is a well-known statistical law that the greater the sample of figures taken the smaller will be the error contained in the answer.

However, it is quite common, especially in examinations or in cases where no other information is available, to calculate the average stock as the opening stock plus the closing stock and the answer divided by two. The statistical limitations of taking only two figures when calculating an average must be clearly borne in mind.

Using the figures in Exhibit 31.2:

$$19\text{-}6 \quad \frac{5,600}{(500+900) \div 2} = \frac{5,600}{700} = 8 \text{ times per annum.}$$

$$19\text{-}7 \quad \frac{7,000}{(900+1,100) \div 2} = \frac{7,000}{1,000} = 7 \text{ times per annum.}$$

In terms of periods of time, in the year 19-6 a rate of 8 times per annum means that goods on average are held 12 months $\div$ 8 = 1.5 months before they are sold.

For 19-7 goods are held on average for 12 months $\div$ 7 = 1.7 months approximately before they are sold.

When the rate of stockturn is falling it can be due to such causes as a slowing down of sales activity, or to keeping a higher figure of stock than is really necessary. The ratio does not prove anything by itself, it merely prompts inquiries as to why it should be changing.

(d) Rate of Return of Net Profit on Capital Employed

In chapter 22 it was stated that the term 'Capital Employed' had not been standardised. In this chapter the average of the capital account will be used, i.e. (Opening Balance + Closing Balance) $\div$ 2.

In businesses (C) and (D) in Exhibit 31.3 the same amount of net profits have been made, but capitals employed are different.

Exhibit 31.3

Balance Sheets	(C)	(D)
	£	£
Fixed + Current Assets − Current Liabilities	10,000	16,000
Capital Accounts:		
Opening Balance	8,000	14,000
Add Net Profits	3,600	3,600
	11,600	17,600
Less Drawings	1,600	1,600
	10,000	16,000

Return on Capital Employed is:

(C) $\dfrac{3,600}{(8,000+10,000) \div 2} \times \dfrac{100}{1} = 40\%$

(D) $\dfrac{3,600}{(14,000+16,000) \div 2} \times \dfrac{100}{1} = 24\%$

The ratio illustrates that what is important is not simply how much profit has been made but how well the capital has been employed. Business (C) has made far better use of its capital, achieving a return of £40 net profit for every £100 invested, whereas (D) has received only a net profit of £24 per £100.

(e) Profitability and Liquidity

The return of profit on capital employed gives an overall picture of profitability. It cannot always be assumed, however, that profitability is everything that is desirable. Page 5 of this volume stresses that accounting is needed, not just to calculate profitability, but also to know whether or not the business will be able to meet its commitments as they fall due.

The two main measures of liquidity are the Current Ratio and the Acid Test Ratio.

$$\text{Current Ratio} = \frac{\text{Current Assets}}{\text{Current Liabilities}}$$

This compares assets which will become liquid in approximately 12 months with liabilities which will be due for payment in the same period.

$$\text{Acid Test Ratio} = \frac{\text{Current Assets} - \text{Stock}}{\text{Current Liabilities}}$$

This shows that provided creditors and debtors are paid at approximately the same time, a view might be made as to whether the business has sufficient liquid resources to meet its current liabilities.

Exhibit 31.4 shows how two businesses may have a similar profitability, yet their liquidity positions may be quite different.

Exhibit 31.4

	(E)		(F)	
Fixed Assets		40,000		70,000
Current Assets				
Stock	30,000		50,000	
Debtors	45,000		9,000	
Bank	15,000		1,000	
	90,000		60,000	
Less Current Liabilities	30,000	60,000	30,000	30,000
		100,000		100,000
Capital				
Opening Capital		80,000		80,000
Add Net Profit		36,000		36,000
		116,000		116,000
Less Drawings		16,000		16,000
		100,000		100,000

(Note: Sales for both E and F amounted to 144,000)

Profitability: This is the same for both businesses.

Net Profit as a percentage of sales $= \dfrac{36,000}{144,000} \times \dfrac{100}{1} = 25\%$

Net Profit as a percentage of capital employed

$= \dfrac{36,000}{(80,000 + 100,000) \div 2} \times \dfrac{100}{1} = 40\%$

However, there is a vast difference in the liquidity of the two businesses.

Working Capital ratios (E) $= \dfrac{90,000}{30,000} = 3 : (F) = \dfrac{60,000}{30,000} = 2$

this looks adequate on the face of it, but the acid test ratio reveals that (F) is in distress, as it will probably find it difficult to pay its current liabilities on time.

Acid Test ratio (E) $= \dfrac{60,000}{30,000} = 2 : (F) = \dfrac{10,000}{30,000} = 0.33$

Therefore, for a business to be profitable is not enough, it should also be adequately liquid as well.

Trend Figures

In examinations a student is often given just one year's accounting figures and asked to comment on them. Obviously, lack of space on an examination paper may preclude several year's figures being given, also the student lacks the time to prepare a comprehensive survey of several year's accounts.

In real life, however, it would be extremely stupid for anyone to base decisions on just one year's accounts, if more information was available. What is important for a business is not just what, say, accounting ratios are for one year, but what the trend has been.

Given two similar types of businesses G and H, both having existed for 5 years, if both of them had exactly the same ratios in year 5, are they both exactly desirable as investments? Given one year's accounts it may appear so, but if one had all the 5 year's figures it may not give the same picture, as Exhibit 31.5 illustrates.

Exhibit 31.5

		Years				
		1	2	3	4	5 (current)
Gross Profit as % of Sales	G	40	38	36	35	34
	H	30	32	33	34	34
Net Profit as % of Sales	G	15	13	12	12	11
	H	10	10	10	11	11
Net Profit as % Capital Employed	G	13	12	11	11	10
	H	8	8	9	9	10
Liquidity Ratio	G	3	2.8	2.6	2.3	2.0
	H	1.5	1.7	1.8	1.9	2.0

From these figures G appears to be the worst investment for the future, as the trend appears to be downwards. If the trend for G is continued it could be in a very dangerous financial situation in a year or two. Business H, on the other hand, is strengthening its position all the time.

Of course, it would be ridiculous to assert that H *will* continue on an upward trend. One would have to know much more about the business to be able to judge whether or not that could be true. However, given all other desirable information, trend figures would be an extra important indicator.

Limitations of Accounting Statements

Final accounts are only partial information. They show the reader of them, in financial terms, what has happened *in the past*. This is better than having no information at all, but one needs to know much more.

First, it is impossible to sensibly compare two businesses which are completely unlike one another. To compare a supermarket's figures with those of a chemical factory would be rather pointless. It would be like comparing a lion with a lizard.

Second, there are a whole lot of factors that the past accounts do not disclose. The desire to keep to the money measurement concept, and the desire to be objective, both dealt with in chapter 10, exclude a great deal of desirable information. Some typical desirable information can be listed, *beware,* the list is *indicative* rather than exhaustive.

(*a*) What are the future plans of the business? Without this an investment in a busines would be sheer guesswork.

(*b*) Has the firm got good quality staff?

(*c*) Is the business situated in a location desirable for such a business? A ship-building business situated a long way up a river which was becoming unnavigable, to use an extreme example, could soon be in trouble.

(*d*) What is its position as compared with its competitors? A business manufacturing a single product, which has a foreign competitor which has just invented a much improved product which will capture the whole market, is obviously in for a bad time.

(*e*) Will future government regulations affect it? Suppose that a business which is an importer of goods from Country X, which is outside the E.E.C., finds that the E.E.C. is to ban all imports from Country X?

(*f*) Is its plant and machinery obsolete? If so, the business may not have sufficient funds to be able to replace it.

(*g*) Is the business of a high-risk type or in a relatively stable industry?

(*h*) Has the business got good customers? A business selling largely to Country Y, which is getting into trouble because of shortage of foreign exchange, could soon lose most of its trade. Also if one customer was responsible for, say, 60 per cent of sales, then the loss of that one customer would be calamitous.

(*i*) Has the business got good suppliers of its needs? A business in wholesaling could, for example, be forced to close down if manufacturers decided to sell direct to the general public.

(*j*) Problems concerned with the effects of distortion of accounting figures caused by inflation (or deflation).

The reader can now see that the list would have to be an extremely long one if it was intended to cover all possibilities.

Assignment Exercises

31.1 R. Stubbs is a trader who sells all of his goods at 25 per cent above cost. His books give the following information at 31 December 19-5:

	£
Stock 1 January 19-5	9,872
Stock 31 January 19-5	12,620
Sales for year	60,000

You are required to:

(*a*) Ascertain cost of goods sold.

(*b*) Show the value of purchases during the year.

(*c*) Calculate the profit made by Stubbs.

Show your answer in the form of a trading account.

31.2A C. White gives you the following information as at 30 June 19-7:

	£
Stock 1 July 19-6	6,000
Purchases	54,000

White's mark-up is 50 per cent on 'cost of goods sold'. His average stock during the year was £12,000.

Draw up a trading and profit and loss account for the year ended 30 June 19-7.

(*a*) Calculate the closing stock as at 30 June 19-7.

(*b*) State the total amount of profit and loss expenditure White must not exceed if he is to maintain a *net* profit on sales of 10 per cent.

31.3 J. Green's business has a rate of turnover of 7 times. Average stock is £12,600. Trade discount allowed is 33⅓ per cent off all selling prices. Expenses are 66⅔ per cent of gross profit.

You are to calculate:

(*a*) Cost of goods sold. (*b*) Gross Profit. (*c*) Turnover. (*d*) Total Expenses. (*e*) Net Profit.

31.4A The following figures relate to the retail business of J. Clarke for the month of May 19-8. Goods which are on sale fall into two categories, A and B.

	Category A	Category B
Sales to the public at manufacturer's recommended list price	£6,000	£14,000
Trade discount allowed to retailers	20%	25%
Total expenses as a percentage of sales	10%	10%
Annual rate of stock turnover	12	20

Calculate for each category:

(*a*) Cost of goods sold. (*b*) Gross profit. (*c*) Total expenses. (*d*) Net profit.

(*e*) Average stock at cost, assuming that sales are distributed evenly over the year, and that there are twelve equal months in the year.

31.5A The following information was available on Discs Ltd.

	19-6	19-7	19-8
	£	£	£
Opening Stock			
Purchases	17,000		
Closing Stock	10,000		
Sales		280,000	
Gross Profit	50,000		
Variable expenses			37,800
Fixed expenses	11,000	10,000	
Net profit			18,200

For 19-6:
1. Gross profit was 20% of sales.
2. Variable expenses were 10% of sales.
3. All purchases cost £2 per unit and stocks were valued at £2 per unit.

For 19-7:
1. The purchase price of units increased by 10%, but the volume bought increased by 20% compared with 19-6.
2. The closing stock of 8,000 units were bought in 19-7.
3. Variable expenses amount to 13% of sales.

For 19-8:
1. The net profit/sales ratio was 1% greater than the 19-7 figure.
2. Fixed expenses increased by £2,000 on the 19-7 figure.
3. The number of units purchased was 90,000 at the 19-7 purchase price.

Required:
Draw a table the same as the one above. Use the information given to make the necessary calculations and complete the table.

31.6A Trading Account for the year ended 31 December 19-1.

	£		£
Stock 1 January 19-1	9,000	Sales	180,000
Purchases	141,000		
	150,000		
Stock 31 December 19-1	13,500		
Cost of sales	136,500		
Gross profit	43,500		
	180,000		180,000

  E. Ironside presents you with the trading account set out above. He always calculates his selling price by adding 33⅓% of cost on to the cost price.
(a) If he has adhered strictly to the statement above, what should be the percentage of gross profit to sales?
(b) Calculate his actual percentage of gross profit to sales.
(c) Give two reasons for the difference between the figures you have calculated above.
(d) His suppliers are proposing to increase their prices by 5%, but Ironside considers that he would be unwise to increase his selling price. To obtain some impression of the effect on gross profit if his costs should be increased by 5% he asks you to reconstruct his trading account to show the gross profit if the increase had applied from 1 January 19-1.
(e) Using the figures given in the trading account at the beginning of the question, calculate Ironside's rate of stock turnover.
(f) Ironside's expenses amount to 10% of his sales. Calculate his net profit for the year ended 31 December 19-1.
(g) If all expenses remained unchanged, but suppliers of stock increased their prices by 5% as in (d) above, calculate the percentage reduction in the amount of net profit which Ironside's accounts would have shown.

32 Computers

For accounting work computers followed on logically from punched cards. Computers were first used for business purposes around the year 1952. The first computers were quite large machines. As a rough illustration of the comparison with today, a machine that would fill up the whole of the space in a room could today have its work performed quicker and more efficiently by a machine that would easily fit on to the top of your desk.

A computer has five basic component parts:
  (i)   An input unit.
  (ii) A store or memory unit.
  (iii) An arithmetic unit.
  (iv) An output unit.
  (v)   A control unit.

Whatever was written about the use of computers in business would be out-of-date by the time that this book is printed and on sale. It is therefore pointless in a general textbook to be too specific about particular makes of computers. This book will therefore apply itself to a consideration of the general principles involved.

The larger computers, used by bigger firms, have very substantial memories and are called 'main-frame computers'. A 'mini-computer' has all the characteristics of a mainframe computer, but it is on a much smaller scale and will cost less than a main-frame computer. A 'micro-computer' is the smallest in the range of computers, and is based on micro-chips which are small electronic devices which enable the computer to be small in size. There is no clear dividing line between main-line and mini-computers. In addition there is very little practical difference between the smaller of the mini-computers and the larger of the micro-computers.

Main-frame computers cost a lot of money and take up a fair amount of space. This is not true of micro-computers which are relatively cheap and take up very little space. The time has now come when the production of micro-computers means that any business, except the very smallest, can afford to have and to use a computer *if it wants to do so.*

As the micro-computer is almost certainly the type of computer which most students will meet, whether at college or at home, then it is this type of computer with which this book will be concerned. At one time whenever discussion of a computer took place, then there used to be quite a fair amount of technical detail given as to how a computer worked. This stage in the development of computers has now passed, what people need to know is not so much exactly how it works, but instead they will want to know what the computer can do for them. Whilst it may be desirable to have a very general idea as to how a computer works, much more than that will not be needed by most users. After all, when you have a remote controlled television set you are not very much bothered how it functions, what you want is that when you press the button to put the TV set on BBC 1 then the TV set responds correctly.

This brings us to the view expressed by some students that if computers can perform book-keeping extremely well, then why should they bother to learn book-keeping. After all, if they can be taught to press a few buttons then that is all that is needed. Using the instance in the last paragraph, when you pressed the button for BBC 1 you would know if instead you got Channel 4. On BBC 1 you were going to watch a pop music programme, instead if it went wrong you might see a political programme. Using a computer for book-keeping needs the ability to be able to see if the transactions being entered have been done properly. Normally if you feed the correct data into the computer in the prescribed manner then you will get the correct answers. However, if something has gone wrong and you do not know book-keeping properly then you are going to believe the book-keeping records produced on the computer. We all know the student who multiplies 25 by 14 on a pocket calculator and gets an answer of 13,360 and believes it. Basic knowledge of arithmetic should have told the student that the answer cannot be more than a few hundred. Similar considerations apply when using computers.

Hardware

For small firms the typical micro-computer system will consist of four main types of equipment, or 'hardware' as it is called.

(i) The micro-computer itself. It will resemble a small typewriter with a keyboard, on which you can type instructions and data. Besides this it will have a 'memory' on which it can store the information, and it will also have a processing unit in which the calculations are performed.

(ii) A visual display unit, or VDU as it is usually referred to. This is rather like a television set. In fact most readers will know that personal computers often use your own ordinary television set to keep costs down. Any information which is inside the computer can be displayed on the VDU.

(iii) A printer. This will produce printed copies of the ledger accounts, journals, trial balance etc.

(iv) A disk drive. Only a limited amount of information can be held in a computer's memory. Also most micro-computers have this information wiped out when the machine is switched off. For business use a computer must keep a copy of everything that it is told. In micro-computers this information is usually kept stored on magnetic disks, called 'floppy disks' which will be described later.

The machine which enables us to record information on to the floppy disks is known as the disk drive. Anyone having a personal computer will probably use audio-cassettes with ordinary cassette recorders. These will not normally be very suitable for much in the way of business use.

Software

The computer has to be given instructions as to exactly what the user wants it to do. These instructions are called 'programs'. Notice the spelling of the word 'program' in computer language as compared with the word 'programme' in normal English usage. The collective name given to computer programs is 'software'.

The programs will vary, depending on exactly what it is that you want the computer to do, and they will also vary with different makes of computers. If you were sufficiently expert, and had enough time, you could write a set of programs for your computer. However, most software is written by computer experts, and for it to be a good program it should have been exhaustively tested before being put on to the market for sale.

The software is normally supplied on 'floppy disks'. These are plastic disks, which are flexible, thus the use of the word 'floppy'. They work in a similar manner as an audio-cassette, but they contain much more information and they can also record it much faster. Exactly how much information can be supplied on a floppy disk will depend on the type of disk drive in use.

Book-keeping Programs

There are in fact a large number of book-keeping programs available on the market. Each make of micro-computer will need a different program, or alterations made to it, as at present it is often impossible to use programs written for one make on another make without some form of alteration.

Even if you have the same make of micro-computer as the firm down the road you may well use a different program for the same book-keeping function. A firm with several branches would probably want a different program from that of a firm without branches. A firm which only had cash sales would want a different program from a firm which only had credit sales. A firm which supplied services only would want a different program from a firm which supplied goods only.

To start off, the program is 'loaded' into the computer. This is effected differently in different computers, but when the stage is complete the computer will have copied the program from the disk into its own memory. This will be done very quickly. Once that this is done, either the programme starts running automatically, or else the key marked 'run' on the computer keyboard has to be pressed. The title of the programme will be displayed on the VDU. The program shown on the screen will tell you when and how to feed in the data which is to be processed, e.g. entering credit sales. If would be impossible here to state how this should be done, for every program is different.

In an ordinary manual system of book-keeping the entering of credit sales would be in the Sales Journal and in the Sales Ledger accounts. Similarly credit purchases would be entered in the Purchases Journal and the Purchases Ledger. That would completely finish the book-keeping entries. With most book-keeping programs run on a computer it is possible to get automatic by-products of the data fed in for other reasons. If sales are known in detail, exactly which items have been sold, and how many of each item, and purchases are known, and how many of each item has been bought, then it is possible for the computer automatically to produce stock records, for every single item of stock.

In a firm dealing in quite a few types of goods a simple book-keeping system would not have shown how many of a particular item should be in stock at any time. The only way this could have been found out would have been for someone to actually go and count the items. In a computerised system the entering of items sold will not only be entered in the figures in the Sales Journal, but will also be automatically entered in the stock records as well. Similarly with items bought. Given the opening stock of every individual item, if the sales and purchases of each item is put into the stock records then the closing stock of each item on a particular day can be automatically produced by the computer. There will be actual physical stock checks from time to time to ensure that the computer system is working properly.

Wages Programs

Imagine the wages clerks of some decades ago manually calculating the wages of employees. They would first of all multiply the hours worked by the amount paid per hour, if work was done on a time basis, and make allowances for any overtime. This would give them the gross wages figure. From this they would need to deduct P.A.Y.E. income tax, by consulting a set of tax tables. Then they would deduct national insurance by consulting another set of tables. Any superannuation would then have to be worked out, also any further deductions. Once these had been deducted from the gross wages the net wages figure would be shown.

All of this would take a lot of time, and the room for errors was quite considerable. Now all that would be needed would be to enter the employee's works number into the computer and the number of hours worked. As the tax tables, national insurance tables, superannuation arrangements and other deduction details will already be in the computer, the computer will print out a pay slip giving full details of all the above items. Assuming that workers are paid in cash then it will also work out for the entire workforce how many £10 notes, £5 notes and coins are needed to make up the wage packets. This would all be done in a mere fraction of the time taken to do it manually.

Collection of Data

With manual accounting systems the information required is written into the system from original documents, such as orders received from customers or from issue tickets for stock records. The basic entry into the accounts may then be transferred or 'posted' to the other accounts involved which requires further written entries. This system may be improved as has been mentioned earlier by 'three in one' systems – which cut down on the amount of 'posting' and thus reduce both time and errors in the recording process.

Modern manual accounting systems attempt wherever possible to cut down on repetitive copying of entries into journals and use instead files of the original documents. Careful design of the stationery used for invoices and other documents also helps to reduce the time needed to maintain the records.

Computer Inputs

Where computers are used in the accounting process, the basic information instead of being hand written into the system needs to be entered into the processing by a means that the computer can accept. This can be through a number of methods which are briefly described.

Keyboard Systems

For most accounting transactions the information will be entered through a keyboard like a typewriter. The keyboard often has a screen (Visual Display Unit or VDU) attached which shows what has been entered on the keyboard. The operator thus enters the information onto the keyboard, and can check visually that the entry is correct.

The keyboard can be connected to equipment which will record the information entered. The method of recording will vary from system to system. The most common method of recording now is on to magnetic disks, or the smaller diskettes (floppy disks). Very large amounts of information can be recorded onto a single disk. Disks and diskettes are very convenient in size and cost and provide a fast, quiet and reliable means of recording data for transmission to the computer. Magnetic tape cassettes (standard audio cassettes) can also be used in much the same way as disks – but are not as widely used in practice except in small home computers.

For some purposes it may be desirable to record the data on to punched cards rather than magnetic disk. Some keyboards therefore produce a card – which can be read manually because of a printed interpretation on it. Cards can be sorted in different ways away from the computer and can act if necessary as a source document or record card.

Magnetic Ink Character Recognition (MICR)

It is possible for equipment to read information directly from a document, if that information is recorded in magnetised ink. The best known use of this method of collecting information for the computer is the standard bank cheque which contains magnetised ink characters on the front which allow the cheques to be sorted automatically between all the clearing banks.

Optical Recognition

Equipment can be obtained which will 'read' either marks on preprinted forms, or specially printed writing. Thus instead of feeding information through a keyboard it can be read directly thus saving time and cost. Perhaps the most widely seen use of this approach is in supermarket checkouts where a bar code (see Exhibit 32.1) on each product can be read by a special reader. The bar code contains full details of the product being sold. These types of system tend to be expensive and have problems with some input material.

Exhibit 32.1

A Bar Code.

Problems of Data Collection

Whatever method of data collection is used its accuracy and completeness is vital if a computer system is to work properly. There is a standard saying for computers – Garbage In Garbage Out (GIGO) which means that if you do not put the correct data into the computer you cannot possibly get the correct output when required. Great care has therefore to be taken to check the accuracy of the input. This may for example involve having two independent operators prepare input tapes from the original data. These will be compared automatically and only used if they agree. This is only one of a whole range of checks to make sure a system is accurate.

Mistakes are just as important in a manual system, but they can usually be traced more easily since a written record can be looked at directly. Once information is recorded onto magnetic disk it is much less visible and errors become harder to spot.

Coding Information

One special requirement when entering data into a computer system is to describe the input in a way that enables the computer to work efficiently. In a manual system words as well as numbers are used to describe the data being entered. A customer will be entered by name and the products he is ordering will be described in words, in addition to the quantities involved.

A computer system works much better if the information is transformed into numerical terms. Thus, instead of describing the customer as Mr. Jones, the computer will require a code number for Mr. Jones, say customer number 3562. Similarly it is necessary to have code numbers for the products rather than simply to use a name. To help people using information from the computer, usually the printout shows the customer name in addition to the number, but for working purposes the computer is only interested in the number.

Thus when information is being fed into the system it is necessary for the code numbers to be included. When a customer's order is received somebody will have to check that the goods ordered are correctly coded – not simply described in words. The accuracy of the coding is vital.

The simplest type of coding is to give a single consecutive number to each transaction. For example Sales Invoices might be numbered in consecutive order 1, 2, 3, 4, and so on. Each new customer could be allocated a number at the end of the list which is unique to him. This type of numbering is called a Sequence Code as it simply classifies things according to the sequence in which they arise. Sequence codes are commonly used and may be applied not only to customers, but also to suppliers and employees who are described by employee number as well as name and products which have a number code.

Sequence codes do not give much information other than a specific and unique number in the sequence. For accounting purposes it is usually important to classify the information in more detail. A logical coding system can be drawn up which allocates numbers in blocks which fit the accounting structure. If we want to code the account number then a Chart of Accounts should be drawn up and code numbers allocated to each part of the chart as shown: –

DESCRIPTION OF ACCOUNT	CODE NUMBER
ASSETS	100 – 299
LIABILITIES	300 – 499
CAPITAL	500 – 599
SALES REVENUES	600 – 699
EXPENSES	700 – 899
OTHER ITEMS	900 – 999

One block of numbers 100 – 299 is allocated to assets. Within this block individual asset accounts will be given a specific number e.g.

100 – 199	Fixed Assets
101	Land
102	Buildings
103	Plant and Machinery
	and so on
200 – 299	Current Assets
201	Bank Account
202	Trade Debtors
203	Stock in Trade
	and so on

Block Coding uses sequences to put items in order but by grouping things into a logical structure of blocks makes them easier to understand for someone working with the system.

A single block code usually does not contain enough information about a transaction. It is therefore common to find a series of codes grouped together. This Group Code will consist of fields or groups of numbers each describing separate aspects of the transaction. For example if a business buys a tyre to repair a car from the XYZ garage it will want to code –

Field 1   The suppliers code number
Field 2   The expense account involved

If the XYZ Garage were supplier number 4362 and the motor repair expense account number 852 then the invoice would be coded 4362852. The computer will then ensure that the invoice for the tyre is recorded as a credit to XYZ Garage personal account in the purchase ledger and a debit to the Motor Repair Account in the nominal ledger.

The number of fields is not limited and can be extended to contain as much information as is necessary for later analysis by the computer. If the information is not coded the computer cannot use it. However if the code gets very long there are more likely to be mistakes in the original coding process – which could outweigh the benefits.

To help make the code numbers easier for people to understand they are developed to have more meaning than a simple sequence code. This is often done for assigning numbers to products in the inventory. For example: In the sports shop at a ski-resort hotel:
The first digit describes the nature of the product:

1. Hats
2. Socks
3. Gloves
4. Trousers

The second digit describes the material from which the item is made:

1. Wool
2. Cotton
3. Nylon
4. Felt

The third digit may describe the colour of the product: –

1. Blue
2. Grey
3. Black
4. White

Thus a product with number 142 would be a grey felt hat.

This is called Faceted Coding and is designed to be more informative than sequential coding. It will generally be used as part of a Group Code. The crucial problem with coding is to try to eliminate errors. This can only be done by training people well in the first place and by using a well thought out coding system which is as simple as possible. Checks will have to be included in the system – both specific double checking the person doing the coding, and also getting the system to check itself by including check digits in the codes themselves.

It is beyond the scope of this book to describe exactly how checks are built into the system, but a couple of examples will give the reader a general idea of how they work. Suppose that a payroll is put on to the computer, and in error one employee is shown as working 250 hours in a week, obviously quite impossible. Included in the automatic check which will be thrown up by the computer is that no one can work more than (say) 100 hours per week. Also if a sales invoice works out as minus £280 then that will be shown up automatically by the check, as minus figures are impossible for sales.

When feeding numeric data into a computer, the following types of error can be made:

Error	Example
Transcription	12345 becomes 12545
Transposition	12345 becomes 12435
Double Transposition	12345 becomes 12543
Omission	12345 becomes 1345
Addition	12345 becomes 123745
Random	A combination of two or more of the above, or any other error.

Since people remember words more easily than numbers it is sometimes useful to combine words or letters with the numbers. A good example is the coding of flights from airports which include an abbreviated description of the airline with a specific flight number e.g. BA 192 British Airways flight number 192. People find this easier to remember and check than just five numbers.

Data Processing

Since there is an enormous difference between firms, both in terms of the work that they do and their size and organisation, there are correspondingly a very wide variety of methods of data processing for accounting purposes. Each organisation must decide which is the way it wants to keep its information, both with regard to cost and effectiveness. A very small firm will normally find that a simple manual recording system is adequate, whereas a large firm will need to handle a much higher volume of data and therefore require a computerised system. Because computers have become so much cheaper, and have become so versatile, they have effectively taken over from accounting machines and punched card equipment. The issue today therefore is whether the expense of a computer is justified or not to take over the manual accounting system.

Benefits of Computerisation

The benefits which can be gained from the computer, if it is properly used are:

1. Speed.   Once the information has been fed into the machine it is handled very fast.

2. Good Service.   Because it is so fast all queries should be answered faster, and goods sent out sooner.

3. Better Information.   Since it can handle huge amounts of data and process it in a short time – managers can be given better information at the right time.

4. Volume.   Where there are large volumes of data to handle – the computer is much cheaper than other methods and indeed may be the only possible way of doing the work.

5. Accuracy.   Once correct data has been fed in, the computer is very accurate.

6. Versatile.   Computers can be used over a very wide area of the organisation for many purposes – not only accounting. In addition they can deal with peak workloads with more flexibility than people – since the machine does not object to working overtime.

Problems with Computers

Computers can cause many problems to an organisation including:

1. Cost.   Setting up an effective system – both for hardware and software is very expensive. This cost needs to be carefully justified by the benefits.

2. Introductory Problems.   When a computer is brought in it will require new ways of doing things which if not carefully managed can disrupt the whole business.

3. Dependence.   Once the computer takes over the whole system depends on it. If it breaks down or is damaged or sabotaged – the firm can lose all its records very easily. Care must be taken to keep copies.

4. People Problems.   People can respond badly to the introduction of computers – resenting their impact on the work they have always done. They do not want to work in a dehumanised environment.

5. Systems Errors.   The development of software can be difficult and involve error until properly sorted out. Because it is a very skilled job – this may cause many problems if properly trained people are not employed.

6. Inflexible.   Once a system is introduced it must be followed. Computers will not generally allow people to change minor procedures in a way as they can with manual procedures.

Introducing a Computer

When thinking about introducing a computer therefore, a business needs to conduct a feasibility study. This study is to assess the benefits and problems associated with whether or not to introduce a computer to take over from a manual procedure. Computers are not an automatic choice since they will only provide a benefit if they are introduced with great care. This will be expensive and may not be justified in some small businesses. However the availability of good ready designed software packages to do standard accounting work on ledgers, analysis, wages and stock records – is continually increasing. This together with the reducing cost of the hardware means that the benefits of computers are extending to more and more organisations.

Non-Computerised Book-keeping Methods: Advantages and Disadvantages

It has already been stated that only a feasibility study can determine whether or not it is advantageous for a computerised system to be introduced or not. It is a matter for each organisation, with its own unique set-up to determine this, only someone with an inside knowledge of the organisation can manage to carry out such a study.

However, it is possible to say that a great deal of the original mechanical means of carrying out book-keeping has been rendered obsolete, and the more recent advances in micro-computer technology have made obsolescence the case with most firms. Where mechanical means, bought largely before computers on their present scale had arrived, are still in use then one advantage is that the money was spent several or more years ago and that nothing else needs to be spent, which would not be true if a computerised system was to be bought. The old system may possibly give all the information that could be used by the firm, but with some other firms a computer system could be used to give extra *cost-effective* information.

Manual methods have the great advantage of flexibility, and there can be no bother about the machinery or computer developing faults. Whether it would be cheaper or not, only a feasibility study could decide. One can hardly imagine that a small fish and chip shop for instance could make really profitable use of a computer. On the other hand it would be difficult to imagine a firm with, say, 200 people, not being able to make good use of a computer. These are generalisations only, the author has no doubt that individual cases could give a different answer when all the facts were properly known. The three-in-one system also has the benefit of three different entries being made with one writing action.

Assignment Exercises

32.1 The sports shop of the Ski Hotel also sells sports shoes for squash or tennis which are made by ABC Ltd. The manufacturer produces shoes in half-sizes as follows:

Size Ranges

Mens	6½ to 9½
Boys	2 to 6
Ladies	3 to 8
Girls	1 to 6

An eight-digit code is used to identify shoes. Reading from left to right, it is made up as follows:

Digit one shows whether the shoes are mens, boys, ladies or girls. The numbers in use are mens 1, boys 2, ladies 3, girls 4.

Digit two shows the situation concerning laces. No laces is given number 0, short black laces 1, long black laces, 2 short brown laces 3, long brown laces 4, short white laces 5, long white laces 6.

Digit three shows the colour. Black 1, Dark Brown 2, Tan 3, White 4, Blue 5, Green 6, Yellow 7.

Digit four shows the material of the upper part of the shoes. Leather 1, Synthetic 2, Canvas 3, Suede 4.

Digit five shows the material of the sole. Leather 1, Rubber 2, Synthetic 3.

Digit six shows whether any guarantee is given to purchaser as to period of use during which shoes can be returned if worn out. No guarantee 0, three months 1, six months 2, one year 3.

Digits seven and eight show size. Size one is shown as 10, size one and a half as 15, size two as 20, size two and a half as 25, and so on.

Examples of codes are:
Code 10433085 is a pair of mens shoes, no laces, white canvas, synthetic sole, no guarantee given, size 8½.
Code 43211240 is a pair of girls shoes, short brown laces, dark brown leather uppers with leather soles, six months guarantee, size four.

(a) You are required to give the code numbers which would apply to:
  (i) Boys shoes, with long black laces, black in colour, synthetic uppers, leather soles, six months guarantee, size 5.
  (ii) Ladies shoes, no laces, yellow, leather uppers and soles, no guarantee, size 6½.
  (iii) Mens tan shoes, leather sole, synthetic uppers, short brown laces, three months guarantee, size 9½.
  (iv) Girls blue shoes, size 3½, no laces, suede uppers and leather soles, no guarantee.

(b) State exactly what kind of shoes are denoted by the following code numbers:
  (i) 31123045
  (ii) 26432060
  (iii) 10223085
  (iv) 40612320

(c) If red shoes were added to the product range, what do you think would happen to the code?

(d) What would you suggest should happen to the code numbers if the range of footwear was extended to boots for men and for boys?

(e) What other information do you think would be desirable for ladies shoes not already given in the code?

(f) If the exact system of coding was adhered to, and the company extended its men's shoe range up to size 12, what problems would result?

32.2 What kinds of errors are these:
(i) 56789 shown in error as 5679
(ii) 56789 shown in error as 56987
(iii) 56789 shown in error as 56879
(iv) 56789 shown in error as 567899
(v) 56789 shown in error as 56779
(vi) 56789 shown in error as 658976

33 The Public Sector

Introduction

In providing its services to the nation, the government makes use of what are called public corporations. Indeed, its own central departments – the Home Office, Ministry of Defence, etc – taken together as a whole form a public corporation called 'The Crown'. Besides the services provided by the central departments the State has, over a period of many years, become responsible for other functions such as local government, personal health, transport, coal-mining, broadcasting, and electricity supply which are allocated to a number of public corporations. These bear a confusing range of titles – Board, Authority, Council, as well as Corporation, of course. (At the time of writing, the government is busy returning services to private hands and, in view of the present uncertainty as to the fate of certain services, these are not referred to specifically in the text).

The internal arrangements of each public corporation are unique because each is designed for its own particular task. The powers and duties appropriate to a commercial or industrial undertaking differ from those needed by a social service. A trading organisation tends to be more streamlined than a social welfare body which is more concerned with matters not connected with finance, and which may also require the power to make a compulsory levy to meet its needs. There are differences in scale, as some services are national in scope, while others operate in a locality. There is also the government's attitude as to the degree of control it needs where a corporation is important to national security or has been given monopoly powers.

In spite of these differences between corporations, it is possible to see a number of shared characteristics:

1. Each is a legal person, but the doctrine of ultra vires applies to it, so that it (or, rather, its managers who act for it) can only do what the law gives it the power to do.

2. Each is supervised on important matters by a departmental Minister who can make the managers conform with national policy as regards the level of charges, capital spending, external financing limits, forward planning, and (in suitable cases) the rate of return on capital employed. Corporations do, however, have a measure of discretion as to how they carry out their duties, so they are not mere government agents. In cases of dispute, the Minister can dismiss appointed members or they can resign on principle.

3. Public bodies have a duty to meet all reasonable demands for their servics at the lowest cost at which an efficient service can be run, but welfare or other considerations can over-ride economics, if the law or the Minister requires it.
4. An independent person audits the accounts, the year end usually being 31 March. The body's annual report, accounts and auditor's report go to Parliament via the Minister who may have to answer questions put by the MPs.
5. There is provision for public participation. The members of the managing boards are either appointed by the government or elected by the public. Users' and consumers' councils, ombudsmen, external auditors, the press, MPs and trades union representatives are all channels of complaints or suggestions.

The Need for Financial Control

Managers of a public sector body need effective financial control for various reasons:
1. They must be confident that the plans they make are soundly based and properly carried out.
2. They must fulfil their duty of stewardship of the large sums of public money entrusted to them by Parliament, calling for a higher level of conduct than in ordinary business matters.
3. Where there is a power of monopoly, it lays a duty on the managers to resist the temptation to exploit the public and to avoid inefficiency. They must persist in trying to give the cheapest and most efficient service as required by law.
4. The managers must also avoid the temptation that, because they are safe from the dangers of liquidation facing private businesses, they can rely upon the public purse to recoup continuous losses.
5. Managements of public organisations have difficulty in assessing the success of their operations, as they must have regard to the social aspects of their work. While trading undertakings can calculate a profit or loss, this is only an estimate of their performance, as it ignores non-measurable factors, such as the quality of the service, or the forgoing of profit or the incurring of expense on social grounds. (Though the government does give grants to some corporations in specific cases).

   Non-trading services, by their very nature, make losses, but a social service run at the lowest cost is not necessarily the most successful in its aims. This is because its action may disrupt people's lives to an unnecessary extent, and while some forms of inconvenience may be evaluated in money terms, it is almost impossible to put a price on the loss of happiness. The cheapest method of rehousing an area might not be the best, because it might cause the most upset to those removed. On a cost basis, it is a success, but socially it might well be a disaster. Attempts are made to evaluate the overall effects of specific schemes by cost benefit analysis, but with varying degrees of success.

These reasons make it essential for the managers to apply internal controls and the government to apply external controls to the activities of public sector organisations.

Internal Control

The managers have a duty to draw up a system of internal control which should contain the following features to be effective:

1. A committee of members controls all the organisation's financial arrangements.

2. A chief accountant or treasurer carries out the decisions of the finance committee, acts as a member of the management team of officers, gives financial advice to the committee and team, helps in the control of budgets, and heads a finance staff which keeps the accounts, collects all income, checks and pays all bills and salaries and wages, and sees to loans, insurances and financial negotiations. He may also control the computer installation.

3. A set of financial regulations or standing orders lays down the approved way of doing all financial work. All staff must be aware of the need to comply with the regulations. Duties must be allocated on internal check principles. Cash and other assets must be protected from theft and wastage. Reliable records must be kept so as to lead the managers to take correct decisions, and those decisions must be carried out promptly and properly.

4. A system of budgetary control includes, at least, four main types of budget:

   (a) The revenue budget contains detailed estimates of running costs and current income for the coming year. As expenditure is incurred and income is received during the year, they are compared with the budget items. There are procedures for overspending to be met by supplementary estimates or by transfers (i.e. virements) from underspent estimates.

   It may be possible to explain, in a very simplified way, a basic difference in approach to budgeting between trading and non-trading services. A trading undertaking first of all estimates its income from sales, etc, then it calculates the expenditure needed to meet that volume of demand. A non-trading authority, however, decides on the cost of the service it intends to supply and then works out the amount of income (usually a compulsory levy) which it needs to meet the expenditure envisaged.

   (b) The capital budget gives estimates of the cost of the programme of capital schemes for the next, say, five years. It gives an overall view which makes changes in priority and timing easy. It deals with the forms of finance needed – loans, capital receipts, revenue contributions, etc – and indicates the effect of the costs upon the revenue budget.

(c) The manpower budget shows the authorised number of employees, the amount of pay they should receive for the year, and the allocation of manpower to the various services and schemes. This controls the number of staff and links up with the financial figures for staffing costs.

(d) The cash budget forecasts the flow of receipts inwards and payments outwards. This enables arrangements to be made in advance to borrow if money is to be short or lend if there is to be surplus cash in hand. The careful use of funds is particularly important in times of high interest rates.

5. A staff of internal auditors is employed to keep a continuous check upon the efficiency of the financial controls, and, where it is shown to be necessary, make sure that they are improved. The internal auditors also assist the external auditor when called upon.

External Control

Managers of public sector bodies, by the very nature of their work, are subjected to various kinds of influences from outside their organisations in the decisions they make and the action they take. These controls and pressures upon their freedom of action may be classified as legal, financial, social and political, though the dividing lines are often not clear.

The legal controls are the laws passed by Parliament and the decisions of the law courts on such matters as ultra vires. These combine to form a frame within which the managers must operate for their actions to be legal. Two important factors are the power of direction given to Ministers and the duty to appoint an external auditor.

The financial controls (for which there must be a legal basis) are designed to make managers conform with the government's wishes by affecting their finances. The methods used include giving or withholding grants, rate-capping in local authorities, limiting borrowing and capital expenditure. Pressure from elsewhere would be the action of users of a service in cutting demand, after an increase in prices or charges.

The social pressures come from the public or users who have grievances about a poor level of service or an instance of bad administration. Criticisms, complaints and suggestions for improvements can be made by individuals or pressure groups, the press, MPs and political parties, users' councils, ombudsmen, external auditors, trade union representatives, etc. Trade unions also influence actions related to (among other things) conditions of service of their members – whose attitude at work is an element in making internal control effective!

Political pressure can come from questions put by opposition (and government) MPs in the House of Commons. Managers who represent other organisations in their membership of boards may also put those organisations' points of view. There is also the power of the ballot box, whereby the voters can change the ruling party and thus cause changes in government policy regarding public sector activities.

Sources of Income

Income is divided for accountancy purposes into two main classes – revenue and capital. Each class receives a different treatment in the accounts.

Revenue income arises from three main sources:

1. Sales of goods and charges for services or work done comprise the major source of income of trading corporations, but are relatively minor in non-trading authorities. Trading bodies usually charge on an economic basis, whereas in non-trading services, charges are often either nominal or related to the income of the recipient, so as not to frighten away those who need the service most – the poor.

2. A form of taxation is a large component of the income of most non-trading organisations. Local and some related authorities have the power to charge a rate upon the occupiers of property in their areas. The central departments and the NHS are supported by the proceeds of national taxes, and the BBC from TV licence fees.

3. Government grants are receivable in support of running costs of services by any corporation which is eligible under the relevant regulations. Grants form a larger part of the income of non-trading bodies than of trading undertakings. The giving of grants (and the threat of withholding them) enables the government to encourage the development of new services, favour one service against another, enforce a national minimum standard of service, retain a hold over services of national importance, enforce compliance with national economic plans, and help those authorities whose income is below an acceptable level or which have special problems.

    Grants can support one service or a range of services and can be paid as a percentage of net expenditure, a sum per unit of service, or as a block sum calculated by a formula.

Revenue income mainly finances revenue expenditure, though it can also be used to meet capital expenditure in the form of revenue contributions to capital outlay. In addition, items of a capital nature but of small value, such as typewriters, are often bought out of revenue and their cost debited to the revenue or profit and loss account. The only permanent record of such items is, therefore, on an inventory of equipment.

Capital income also comes from three main sources:

1. Loans can be received from individuals or institutions, such as firms or banks, in the form of stock, bonds, mortgages and short-term (or temporary) loans, etc, or from government sources in the shape of loans out of central funds, including Public Works Loan Board advances. (It must be mentioned that short-term loans may be borrowed as revenue money when funds run short pending current income, e.g. a rate levy, coming in.) All these borrowings usually pass through a separate loans fund or account and are repaid over a period of years by charging the revenue account with an annual sum as an instalment of loan repaid or sinking fund contribution, as it is sometimes called.

2. The government pays grants towards the cost of specific capital schemes in respect of services which it is official policy to support. These consist of single lump-sum payments which reduce the capital cost and, consequently, the amount that the authority needs to borrow or provide in other ways.

3. Sums of money are received from the sale of capital assets, i.e. capital receipts.

Capital income must be used to finance capital expenditure, unless unusual circumstances lead a supervising department to make an exception and permit it to be used to meet revenue costs. Corporations also build up reserve funds out of current income and capital receipts and then use them to pay for capital schemes. In this way, the authorities avoid having to pay interest on loans, even out costs over the years, create a buffer against hard times, and reduce governmental involvement in the particular schemes financed in this way. (Again, it must be mentioned that reserve funds also exist for revenue purposes, e.g. the renewal and repair of buildings or vehicles.)

Revenue and Capital Expenditure

In the same way as they accept the accounting conventions, accountants in both public and private sectors are fully in agreement as to the nature of revenue and capital expenditure. Differences do occur in practice, however, but these are related mainly to the treatment of capital (i.e. fixed) assets. The failure to capitalise items of minor value which have been charged to revenue has already been mentioned. Also, in a case such as where a scheme of accumulated repairs is paid for out of a loan, it is treated as a capital asset as a matter of convenience, although repair is a running cost. Some authorities also avoid accruing liabilities at year end in relation to capital schemes, so that, in effect, their capital expenditure comprises their capital payments — again, this is a matter of convenience.

The problem of depreciation has been treated by each class of corporation in its own way to meet its particular circumstances. With reservations, it might be said that public trading organisations follow the commercial approach. Non-trading services, however, tend to retain assets of continuing value at cost in the balance sheet and treat the amount provided each year for repaying debt as a form of depreciation which accumulates as a capital provision entitled 'capital discharged' or 'loans repaid'. Assets which have no realisable value are often written down by non-trading bodies so as to equal the debt still owed on them, until they finally vanish from the balance sheet.

The position in the central departments as regards accounting arrangements is interesting, if not astonishing, to an accountant. Although they insist upon public corporations keeping their accounts upon income and expenditure principles, they themselves, with very few exceptions, operate on a cash basis, i.e. receipts and payments, and also make no distinction between capital and revenue.

Accounting Conventions

Accountants in both the business world and the public sector are in complete agreement as to the validity of the basic accounting conventions and concepts, of which the major examples are money measurement, going concern, matching, accrual, consistency and prudence.

In order to ensure that there is consistency in applying the conventions in the preparation of financial statements, the professional accountancy bodies in the private sector have drawn up a set of standard practices which must be observed by their members. Although there are differences between the legal and financial codes governing the two sectors, public authority accountants also apply these standards to their accounts, so far as they are able. Indeed, non-observance of a relevant standard practice can be a matter on which an external auditor to a public sector body may make a report to the management.

The Form of the Accountancy Records

The basic books of account kept by a public sector body are, as in commerce, the cash account, ledger and journal. These are supported by the customary prime records. It must be realised, however, that as modern corporations have computerised systems, the above records may be stored in the memory and produced by visual display or printed out.

The entries in the cash book and the bank account are linked, because the financial regulations of the body require all receipts and payments to be channelled via the bank. Bank reconciliation takes place at the least every month end. Much use is made of petty cash accounts which must be on the imprest system in accordance with the regulations.

The ledger is analysed so as to agree with the budget headings. A non-trading service has a revenue account (or income and expenditure account) which gives a surplus or deficiency for the year. A trading undertaking prepares a manufacturing account (if appropriate), and a trading and profit and loss account with an appropriation section. The form of the balance sheet also is affected by the nature of the organisation − those of trading bodies conforming with commercial practice and those of non-trading authorities follow standard formats such as those recommended by the Chartered Institute of Public Finance and Accountancy. The government is at present considering whether to bring in compulsory standard forms for these accounts.

Frequent use is made of total, control or holding accounts for various purposes. There are the sundry debtors and creditors accounts in which each entry is a total of the individual items in the cash book, payments schedules, invoices rendered file or day book, etc. There are also expenditure and income control accounts which collect and hold sums for later allocation to other accounts − one example is the administration costs of a department which are to be charged out to others on a services rendered basis. The use of total accounts makes the extraction of the trial balance and error finding much easier, as one figure replaces a myriad of individual balances in the trial balance. Where the trial balance fails to balance, each section can be checked separately (i.e. sectional balancing is carried out) but at the same time by different members of staff. Thus time is saved.

The journal is now used less than it was formerly. Ledger transfers are often preferred − the debit and credit entries being cross-referenced to one another and the narration being included in the entries. Year end transfers between departments and funds are mostly done by scheduling and ledger and cash account entries as needed.

Stock records may be kept on a continuous basis where a full costing system is in operation, or a stock-taking at the date of the balance sheet may be regarded as adequate where the value involved is small. Costing records of staff costs, materials consumed, etc. depend for their existence and content upon the need for costing in any particular service. The cost figures are usually reconciled with those in the financial accounts so as to check the accuracy of both. The costing methods used in the public sector are the same as those encountered in commerce. They include job costing (repair of a water boiler at a hospital), batch costing (making pavement-crossings for cars at a number of houses on one street in one operation), contract costing (electrification of a railway line), output costing (cost per ton of refuse collected and disposed of), operating or operation costing (cost per passenger-mile), and process costing (production of smokeless fuel). Marginal costing, whereby the allocation of fixed overheads is avoided, is often convenient, and some use of standard costing is made, though this is restricted by the non-measurable aspects (i.e. the standard of care) of public services in the laying down of targets.

Current Trends in Public Sector Accounting

The managers of public sector organisations are constantly searching for ways of providing services more economically and efficiently. Progress is being made in a number of directions.

Unit costs are being used more and performance indicators are being researched for the measuring of quality of service, e.g. the percentage of out-patients who return for further treatment. The aim is to use these, together with the intended standardisation of published accounts, to improve the comparison of service costs.

The degree of computerisation is constantly on the increase. This is designed to help in improving management and operations in many ways. The use of visual display units for rapid decision-making is one instance, besides the ability to store much more data with access via a large number of terminals.

Budgeting systems are under development in attempts to ensure resources are used optimally. Examples are PPBS (planning, programming, budgeting systems) where the effects of a scheme are evaluated throughout all departments of an organisation, and zero-based budgeting, whereby all the expenditure on a service has to be justified.

Management techniques are receiving greater acceptance in the improvement of management methods by organisation and methods, work study, network analysis, etc, or the best use of resources by operational research, discounting methods, etc. Management services sections are usually staffed with experts from a number of disciplines – accountants, economists, mathematicians, scientists, etc.

New accounting procedures are in the offing – to deal with new financing methods, such as deferred purchase and leasing of fixed assets, and new income sources, such as the possible replacement of the local rate and the introduction of advertising which is being mooted on the BBC programmes.

Public Sector Organisations

This section of the book contains brief descriptions of the duties, structure and financial arrangements of a number of the organisations which operate in the public sector.

1. Local Authorities

The principal forms of local authority are the county councils and (more locally) the district or borough councils. Each authority has its area and a range of services which varies according to its status. The local services provided include education, housing, roads, planning, police, firefighting, and environmental health. A council of elected councillors (who form themselves into committees) and a number of chief officers and their staffs manage the authority. The financial work is controlled by a finance sub-committee. The major central department involved with local government is the Department of the Environment. The external auditor is appointed by the Audit Commission and is either a District Auditor (a government official) or a private-sector auditor.

The revenue income of local authorities comes from charges for services, (e.g. housing rents), government grants and the general rate. The districts levy the rate and pay over a share to the county. The rate is paid by occupiers of property in the area, as a number of pence in the £ of the property's rateable value.

Local authorities must publish summaries or abstracts of their annual accounts which are called statements of accounts and are prepared on the historical cost basis. They contain a report on the accounts by the authority, a statement of the accounting policies observed, and the auditor's report. Then there is a consolidated balance sheet for all funds, and the revenue accounts, capital and other statements of the various funds. These include the general rate fund services (districts or boroughs) or county fund services (counties), rating (districts or boroughs), housing revenue account (districts or boroughs), loans fund, trading undertakings (e.g. markets), capital, renewal and repair, and insurance funds, trust funds (e.g. employees' pensions, if a county, though district staffs are included). Finally, corresponding figures for the previous year are required by law.

Example of Local Authority Accounts

Housing Revenue Account
Year ended 31 March 19-7

	£000	£000
Expenditure		
Loan Charges		8,435
Repairs		5,798
Management		2,934
		17,167
Income		
Gross Rents	13,206	
LESS Housing Benefits	6,387	6,819
Exchequer Grants		8,611
Other Income		1,854
Rate Fund Rebates		670
		17,954
Surplus for Year		787
Accumulated Surplus		2,608

2. Health Authorities

The National Health Service (NHS) makes personal health care available to the whole of the population. It operates via regional health authorities (RHA), district health authorities (DHA) within the regions, and units within the districts. As the NHS is part of the Department of Health and Social Security (DHSS) (or of the Welsh Office for Wales), it is part of the Crown. This integration means that the Health Minister can be questioned on matters of detail regarding the running of the NHS, unlike the position with other public sector bodies. The members of the RHAs and DHAs are appointed by the Minister or nominated by local authorities, and there is a requirement for trade unions to be represented.

A relatively small amount of income comes from prescription charges, private beds, etc, but the bulk of the cost of the service, capital and revenue, is met out of taxation. The annual budget procedure is a two-way operation. The DHAs compile estimates of the needs of their administration and units for the coming year in line with guidelines laid down by the DHSS. These are passed to the RHAs who adjust them for their own needs. The RHAs pass the figures to the DHSS where they are totalled for the country and made to fit in with the money made available by Parliament in the national budget. The DHSS then divides the revised amounts among the RHAs who inform the DHAs of their entitlements.

Management teams of officers operate at the three levels of the NHS, the leaders being general managers. The finance officer's role in the team is to offer financial advice and to carry out the financial work entailed.

Community health councils made up of local representatives look after the interests of the public and patients and help the HAs in matters such as health education.

The NHS provides four main categories of service:

1. The community health service — the care of mothers and young children, home nursing, health visiting, prevention of illness, vaccination, etc.
2. The hospital and specialist services — treatment of in- and out-patients in hospitals.
3. The family practitioner services — provide general medical, pharmaceutical, dental and ophthalmic services via family practitioner committees.
4. The miscellaneous services — ambulances, blood transfusion and banks, mass radiography for the detection of disease, etc.

The form in which the annual accounts are prepared is prescribed in detail and reflects the integrated nature of the NHS. Each DHA produces a revenue account for each of its services but revenue income, capital expenditure and income are each shown in a single multi-service account. A statement of source and application of funds and a subjective analysis of expenditure (e.g. salaries and wages, transport, etc) are given. Details of all trust and endowment funds (which are distinct from NHS funds) are given in an income and expenditure account, capital account, accumulated income (i.e. 'other funds') account, and balance sheet. As the DHSS is a central department, it keeps its accounts on a cash basis, but it requires the HAs to use an income and expenditure system. The two systems are reconciled by statements of balances, viz. debtors, creditors, stocks held, cash in hand or overdrawn, and monies due from or overpaid by the DHSS. No balance sheet is produced and all values are on historical cost basis. The RHA prepares similar statements for its own services, e.g. regional planning, etc, and incorporates summary figures for its DHAs to give an overall view of the Region's services. Corresponding figures for the previous year are given throughout the accounts.

Two sets of auditors are involved in the system. The audit of the accounts is usually carried out by the staff of the Audit Directorate of the DHSS but there is provision for private-sector auditors to be appointed. In addition, because the NHS is within the DHSS, the central government auditors — the National Audit Office headed by the Comptroller and Auditor General — also audit the accounts.

Example of Health Authority Account

Income Account Year ended 31 March 19-7

Health Services Income (excluding Capital and Family Practitioner Services)

		£
From Patients	repairs to patient's appliances, etc	10,479
	prescriptions dispensed by hospitals	21,411
	accommodation	1,456
	private in-patients	52,670
	private non-resident patients	24,098
	overseas visitors	2,108
Road Traffic Act		82,364
Miscellaneous	rents	20,369
	sale of equipment	1,273
	other income	727
Total income		216,955

Family Practitioner Services Income	
Prescription charges	110,412
Dental and optical charges	8,107
Other income	1,457
Total FPS income	119,976
Total revenue income	336,931

3. The Electricity Supply Industry

The electricity supply industry consists of the Electricity Council which is responsible for general policy-making, the Central Electricity Generating Board which runs the power stations and the grid, and the Area Electricity Boards which buy the electricity from the CEGB and supply it to the public together with the hire, sale and repair of appliances and equipment. The Secretary of State for Energy who is responsible for overseeing the industry, appoints the members of all these bodies.

The interests of the consumers are looked after by Electricity Consultative Councils in each Area and the Electricity Consumers' Council at national level. The members of these bodies are also appointed by the Minister after consulting local and other organisations.

The Electricity Council produces its own income and expenditure account and balance sheet. Its working expenses are met from contributions levied on the CEGB and the Area Boards. It also publishes a consolidated profit and loss account, balance sheet and statement of source and application of funds on current cost basis for the whole industry, together with performance indicators, e.g. total cost of kWh sold, net return on average net assets, etc.

The annual accounts of the CEGB are on a current cost basis − a profit and loss account, balance sheet and statement of source and application of funds. Details are given of electricity sold, analyses of costs and fixed assets, etc. There are also performance indicators, e.g. turnover/units sold, trading profit/average net assets.

Each Area Board prepares current cost accounts also — a profit and loss account, balance sheet and statement of source and application of funds. The accounts are supported by analyses of items, e.g. sales and purchases of electricity, fixed and current assets, and performance indicators, e.g. employees per thousand customers, average period without supply.

All these accounts contain statements of the accounting policies adopted and give comparative figures for the previous year. The Minister appoints the external auditors who must be private-sector auditors. He places the annual report, final accounts and auditor's report for each body before the House of Commons.

Example of Account

Electricity Supply Account for the Year ended 31 March 19-7

	£000	£000
Turnover		
Sales of Electricity	945,000	
Other Income	12,000	
		957,000
Operating Costs		
Purchases of Electricity	770,000	
Distribution	95,000	
Consumer Service	20,000	
Meter Reading, Billing and Collection	23,000	
Administration and General Expenses	22,000	
Training and Welfare	7,000	
		937,000
Operating Profit		20,000

Assignment Exercises

33.1A What elements are needed in an internal control system of a public corporation to make it effective?

33.2A Outline some of the influences which affect the decisions of managers of public sector bodies.

33.3A In what ways may a public authority receive capital income and on what purposes may it be spent?

33.4A Outline the duties of the treasurer of a public sector organisation.

33.5A Indicate some of the ways in which the nature of a public organisation can affect its accounting arrangements.

33.6A For what reasons are government grants paid to public bodies and on what bases may their amounts be calculated?

33.7A Outline the major sources of income of a district council.

33.8A What are the main services of the NHS, how is it financed and in what way does it differ in status from other public organisations?

33.9A What organisations form the electricity supply industry and what are their functions?

33.10A Draw up a form of Education Revenue Account suitable for inclusion in the annual statement of account of a metropolitan borough council for the year ended 31 March 19-7, using the following figures.

	£000
Expenditure	
Nursery Education	600
Primary Education	18,000
Secondary Education	30,000
Special Education	3,800
Further Education	25,000
Administration and Support	8,000
Income	
Nursery Education	100
Primary Education	200
Secondary Education	1,500
Special Education	200
Further Education	12,000
Administration and Support	2,000

33.11A Draw up a tabulation for inclusion in the final accounts which shows the sums spent on the various health services in a region in 19-7/8 and (in brackets) in 19-6/7. Show the spending in £ thousands and as a percentage of total spent in respect of each year. Use the following figures which are in £ thousands:

Hospitals	670,500	(621,320)	Administration and Support		
Community Health	91,460	(82,200)	Services	36,780	(33,507)
Ambulance	23,564	(22,103)	Other	20,345	(17,643)
Blood Transfusion	6,119	(5,986)	Family Practitioner Service		
			(after a sub-total)	273,247	(256,985)

33.12A Prepare an Appliance Marketing Account for the year ended 31 March 19-7 in respect of sales of electrical appliances, and, using the following figures, calculate the operating profit for the year.

	Dr. £000	Cr. £000
Turnover		
Sales		66,000
Credit Charges and Other Income		12,000
Cost of Sales	50,000	
Other Operating Costs		
Salaries and Related Costs	5,300	
Transport, Travelling and Subsistence	300	
Delivery, Assembly and Connection of Appliances	5,000	
Work under Guarantee and Sundry Expenses	4,000	
Bad and Doubtful Debts	700	
Publicity and Exhibitions	1,800	
Training and Welfare	900	
Administration and General Expenses	3,000	
Rent and Rates	800	
Depreciation	200	

34   Cost Behaviour and Control

In Chapter 31 the fact that costs behave in different ways as volumes of activity change was introduced. It is important to know how different costs will behave under changing circumstances both for planning purposes as well as cost control. For planning it is necessary to look forward to predict the costs of different projected levels of sales, so that likely profits or losses can be seen in the budgeted accounts. For control of costs the analysis usually looks back at actual costs that have been incurred — in order to see if they are too high — and if savings could be made. This is a way of attempting to ensure that employees are held responsible for not wasting the organisation's resources.

In order to work out how a cost will behave it will be necessary to examine as much historic data as possible to see how actual costs have corresponded to different levels of output. At the same time it is important to find out the facts which determine how the cost is actually incurred, so that all the reasons for any fluctuations are understood.

Variable Costs

A variable cost is one that changes in proportion to changes in output. The following data illustrates how material cost has behaved for the Jupiter Company in the past six periods.

Period	Output £	Units	Material Price	Cost (£)
1	1000	100	£1	100
2	1500	150	£1	150
3	1200	120	£1	120
4	1300	130	£1	130
5	1600	160	£1	160
6	1400	140	£1	140

Shown on a graph the information would be as shown in Exhibit 34.1

Exhibit 34.1

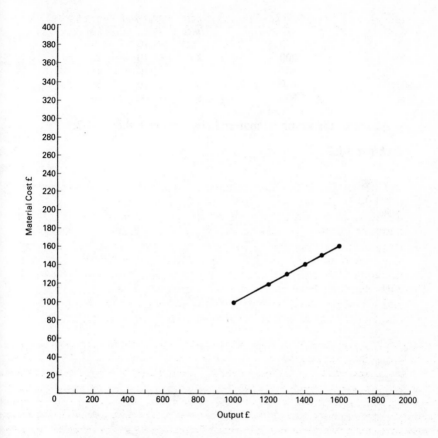

The graph shows that for the information plotted the costs are variable directly with sales — all the points joined together form a straight line. The range of outputs plotted is between £1000 in period 1 and £1600 in period 6. Between these two output figures we can be fairly confident of what the material costs should be. If however we were trying to predict the material cost for an output of say £600 — great care would be needed. The facts determining material prices would have to be known. If the current cost of material of £1 per unit is based on buying at least 80 units per period — then the cost may increase to £1.10 per unit if only 60 units are bought. In other words the cost line changes at lower volumes, since the variable cost per unit increases.

The information for the lower volumes would be:

Output £	Units	Material Price	Cost
0	0	£1.10	0
200	20	£1.10	22
400	40	£1.10	44
600	60	£1.10	66
800	80	£1.00	80

Added to the graph of material cost we get Exhibit 34.2.

Exhibit 34.2

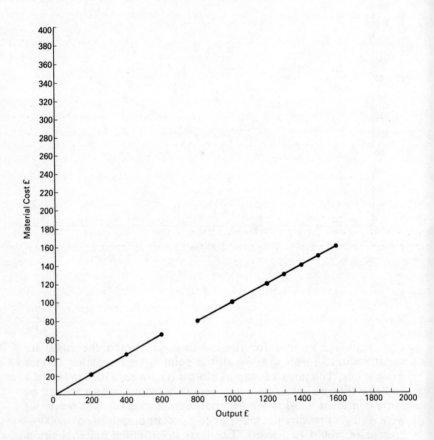

Similarly at higher volumes extra discount may be obtained which will reduce the unit costs. What this implies is that the analysis of costs is useful but must be examined very carefully before forecasts outside current output levels are made.

Many costs will have a random element which means that when the costs are plotted against volume they do not fall exactly on a straight line. For example for Jupiter Company the costs in the last six periods of power were as follows:

Period	Output £	Power Cost £
1	1000	200
2	1500	330
3	1200	210
4	1300	260
5	1600	320
6	1400	270

This information is shown on the graph Exhibit 34.3.

Exhibit 34.3

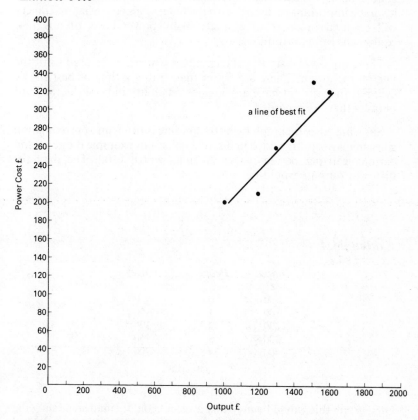

In Exhibit 34.3 the information has been recorded and the points plotted are scattered. This type of graph is often called a scatter diagram. One straight line will not joint all the points. It is possible however to insert a line of 'best fit' which seeks to approximate a line fitting the information by reducing the distances between the points plotted and the line to a minimum. Where the information plotted is consistently linked together it will be quite easy to fit a line to the data, from which a cost can be predicted. If the points plotted are all random say in a circular pattern it may not be possible to develop a good fitting line. The important thing is to understand the underlying behaviour of the cost. In the example of power — the reason that the cost does not vary directly with output in each case is due to the fact that because of machine breakdown the production process has to use standby equipment which is less power efficient. When this equipment is used the power consumed per unit of output goes up. Since breakdowns happen on a random basis there is never a standard pattern in any one period of the power used per unit. However the variations are not very large and for planning the 'best fit' provides a good estimate. If the business intends to increase output in the future it will be important to discuss with the plant engineers what machinery will be used in order to estimate likely power costs of any new equipment to be introduced.

There are several statistical techniques which can be used to fit the line on the graph. These are better than fitting a 'line of best fit' by eye, but they do not have any greater reliability outside the range of outputs that are recorded.

Showing costs on graph by a straight line is often an approximation since many costs are added in discrete units. For example if one person earning £50 per period makes 20 units worth £100. The data for different outputs would be:

Exhibit 34.4

Output £	People	Wages
0	0	0
100	1	50
200	2	100
300	3	150
400	4	200

On a graph this would be in reality a succession of small steps showing that each person employed could produce from 0 to 20 units each, and that once taken on we should have to pay the full wage. The line joining the plotted points would normally be good enough for planning purposes.

Exhibit 34.5

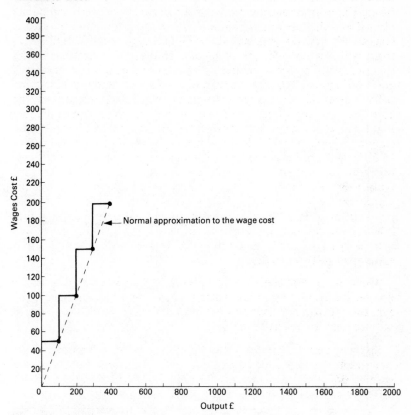

Normal approximation to the wage cost

Fixed Expenses

Fixed expenses are those that do not change in sympathy with levels of output. If a company pays rent of £2000 per period for premises, this cost does not increase or reduce with changes in output. For example using the Jupiter Company the costs for the last six periods would be:

Period	Output £	Rent £
1	1000	2000
2	1500	2000
3	1200	2000
4	1300	2000
5	1600	2000
6	1400	2000

On the graph in Exhibit 34.6 the line for fixed cost is a straight line. However as with variable cost it is not safe to assume that fixed cost will remain constant over all ranges of output. For example if output

Exhibit 34.6

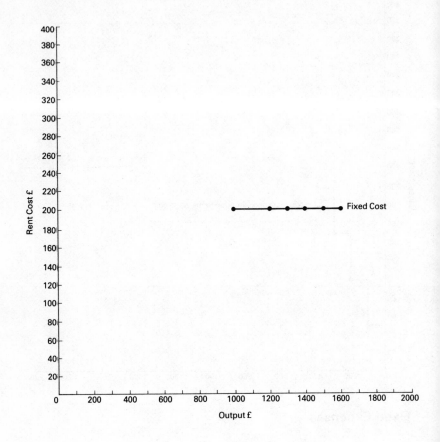

were to increase to 2000 units per period it may be necessary to rent further space for any extra production. This would mean that the rent cost would increase in one step up to a new higher level. Similarly if the business declined significantly at some stage the management will probably move into smaller premises thus reducing the rent. The real graph of rent cost would therefore be as in Exhibit 34.7. However the changes which are shown in this case are well outside the current output range and are likely to happen only in other periods. It is quite common therefore to simplify a cost graph for the current period of

Exhibit 34.7

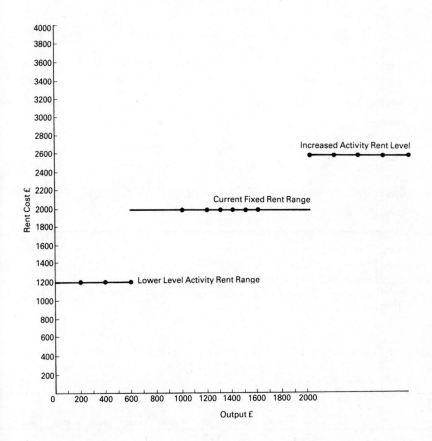

time as in Exhibit 34.8. This appears to show that there is one level of fixed cost covering the range of output from zero to beyond the current output levels. This simplification is acceptable only if it is remembered that the graph is valid for a limited range of outputs and the current time period.

Exhibit 34.8

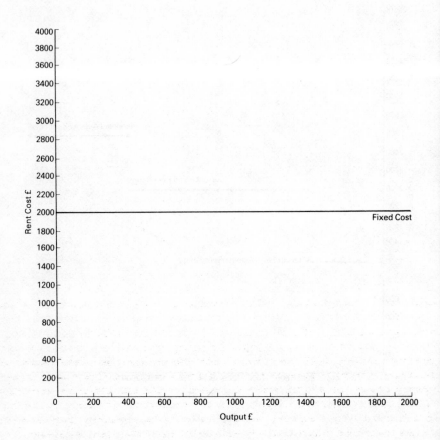

A similar simplification is often used with variable costs. For example the information in Exhibit 34.1 would be shown as though the cost line extended from zero output onwards, as shown in Exhibit 34.9.

Exhibit 34.9

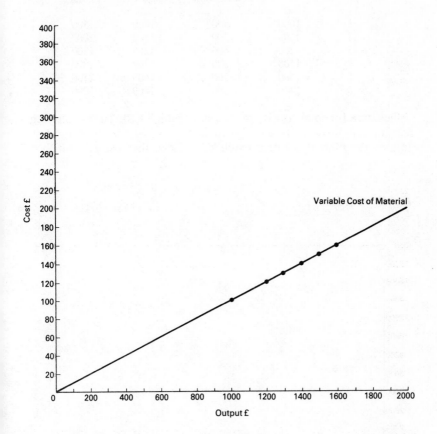

As is the case for fixed cost this extension is purely a simplification; the only valid part of the graph being in the area of current output and in the current period. A more correct analysis would be as in Exhibit 34.2 but this is not necessary for decisions which are only involved with the current levels of cost and output rather than for longer term planning.

Semi Variable Costs

Many types of cost include both variable and fixed elements. For example, equipment is often hired on the basis of a fixed rental per period plus an additional charge for the number of units consumed. Using data based on a machine hired by Jupiter Company on this basis the data would be as follows:

Period	Output	Machine Cost		
		Fixed Rent	Usage Cost	Total
	£	£	£	£
1	1000	500	1000	1500
2	1500	500	1500	2000
3	1200	500	1200	1700
4	1300	500	1300	1800
5	1600	500	1600	2100
6	1400	500	1400	1900

The data for total cost is graphed in Exhibit 34.10. The simplifying assumption fitted to this is shown in Exhibit 34.11 where the line joining the plotted points is extended back to the cost axis which it

Exhibit 34.10

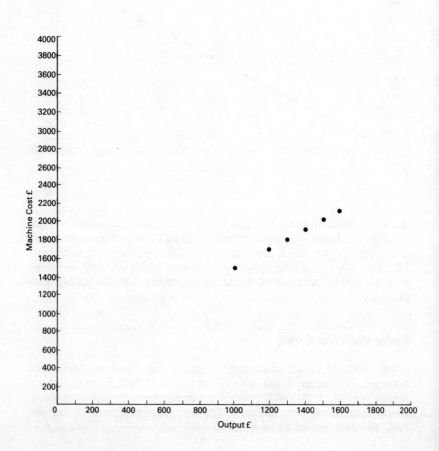

Exhibit 34.11

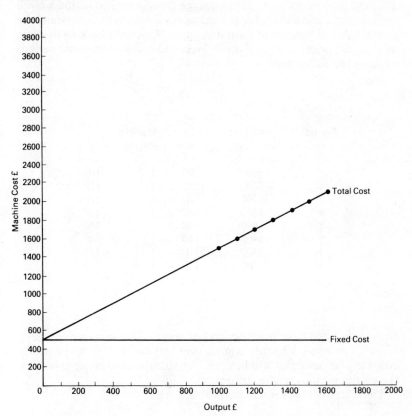

meets at the point of fixed cost £500. What the graph does is to give a visual image to the numbers. The numbers reflect a fixed cost of £500 throughout the output range plus a variable cost of £1 for every £10 of output. Whilst in this case the terms for renting a machine are easily available in other cases it may not be known exactly how the cost pattern is built up. It is in this type of case that fitting a graph to the data is particularly useful. Then the difference between the fixed and variable elements can only be seen from the graph. The graph Exhibit 34.11 showing a cost pattern of both fixed and variable cost is very similar to that which would represent the total costs of the whole business. This type of analysis is shown in the next chapter on Break Even Analysis.

Problems of Cost Analysis

One major problem that has not been mentioned so far is the effect on our analysis of changing prices for the items being compared. We have been attempting to analyse the relationship between cost and output in different time periods. As prices change from period to period we will need to make allowances for price changes if we are to understand the changes due to volume of output changes. Referring back to the data on material prices used in Exhibit 34.1, and adding two more periods we have the following:

Period	Output		Material	
		Units	Price	Cost
	£		£	£
1	1000	100	1	100
2	1500	150	1	150
3	1200	120	1	120
4	1300	130	1	130
5	1600	160	1	160
6	1400	140	1	140
7	1100	110	1.50	165
8	1200	120	1.50	180

In periods 7 and 8 the price per unit of material has increased by 50%. In order to make a proper comparison between output and material cost for past periods it will be necessary to adjust the material cost for the earlier periods to the current prices.

The adjusted figures will be as follows:

Period	Output		Material	
		Units	Adjusted Price	Adjusted Cost
	£		£	£
1	1000	100	1.50	150
2	1500	150	1.50	225
3	1200	120	1.50	180
4	1300	130	1.50	195
5	1600	160	1.50	240
6	1400	140	1.50	210
7	1100	110	1.50	165
8	1200	120	1.50	180

This information is plotted on Exhibit 34.12.

Exhibit 34.12

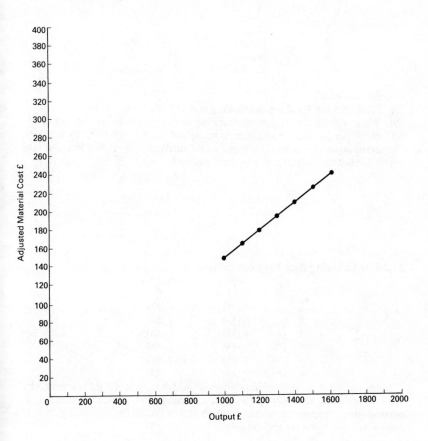

This adjusted graph now represents the current cost relationships and is therefore helpful for current analysis. A similar adjustment will be needed to the ouput values if current selling prices change: then the sales value of past outputs will need to be adjusted to current prices. If we are forecasting into the future then estimates of inflation will need to be added to current prices.

Assignment Exercises

34.1 Plot the following data on a graph:

Period	Production £	Total Manufacturing Cost £
1	10,000	1,600
2	12,000	1,800
3	14,000	2,000
4	15,000	2,100
5	13,000	1,900

Using the graph
(a) What are the fixed manufacturing costs?
(b) What should the total manufacturing cost be at an output of £11,000?
(c) Next period the production is expected to be £16,000. In addition manufacturing costs are expected to increase by 10%. What is the expected manufacturing cost next period?

34.2 The following data has been collected for the past six periods:

	Output £	Repair Cost £
1	5,000	1,000
2	6,000	1,200
3	4,000	900
4	7,000	1,400
5	8,000	1,500
6	3,000	700

In the current period the selling prices on which output is based increased by 10%. Plot the adjusted data on a graph and using a line of best fit estimate the current cost of repairs at an output of £9,000 in new prices, assuming current cost prices will apply in this range.

34.3 Identify which graph from Exhibit 34.13 shows the cost behaviour you would expect in the following cases:
1. Raw material cost where two units of material are used in each unit of output.
2. The hire charge for a photocopier where there is a fixed rental plus a charge for each copy made.
3. The cost of power, where £10,000 fixed charge is made for power used from 0 to 1000 units. Over 1000 units an extra charge of £1 per unit is made with a maximum charge for the period of £20,000.

34.4 Describe the nature of costs that you might expect to conform to the pattern shown in graph (j) in Exhibit 34.13.

Exhibit 34.13

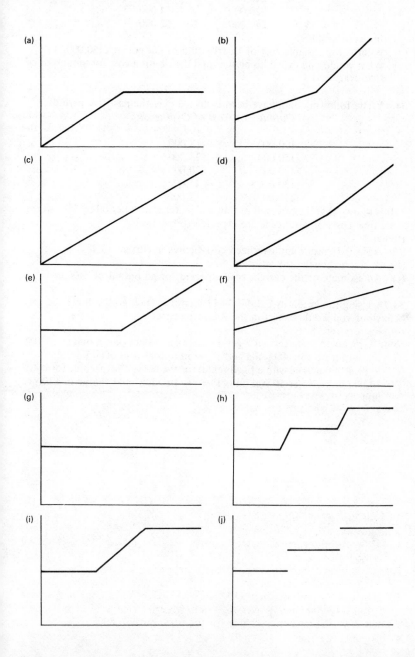

(a)

(b)

(c)

(d)

(e)

(f)

(g)

(h)

(i)

(j)

34.5A Plot the following data on a graph and estimate the line of best fit.

Period	Output £	Distribution Cost £
1	200,000	50,000
2	250,000	60,000
3	240,000	58,000
4	220,000	54,000
5	260,000	62,000

Using your graph:
(a) What is the variable cost of Distribution of Output of £250,000.
(b) What would you expect to be the total distribution cost for an output of £270,000.

34.6A The following data have been collected over the past five periods:

Output £	Cost of Overheads £
100,000	18,000
150,000	23,000
120,000	20,000
130,000	21,000
110,000	19,000

It is known that the prices of output will increase next period by 5%. At the same time costs of overheads are expected to rise by 10%.
Prepare:
(a) Adjusted output and overhead cost figures in current values.
(b) A graph showing the adjusted data.
(c) An estimate of the current cost expected for an output of £100,000.

34.7A Using the graph in Exhibit 34.13 identify which graph shows the cost behaviour you would expect in the following cases:
(a) Factory rent.
(b) Payments to managers who get a basic fixed salary plus a bonus of 10% on output up to 5000 units and 15% on output over 5000 units.
(c) Renting a machine with a fixed rental for the use of the machine for up to 10,000 units. Over 10,000 units there is an additional charge of £10 per unit.

35 Break-Even Analysis: Part I

The level of activity achieved by a firm is of paramount importance in determining whether the firm is making a profit or loss, and the size of such profits or losses. Let us take an example to which the answer is obvious. If a firm has fixed costs of £10,000 and its total revenue is £8,000, then, no matter how much the variable costs are, the firm is bound to make a loss. A firm has to cover both its fixed costs + its variable costs before it can make a profit. With very low revenue, as in the case already stated, a loss would be bound to be incurred.

There is, therefore, a great deal of interest in exactly how much revenue (i.e. sales) has to be earned before a profit can be made. If revenue is below fixed costs then a loss will be incurred: if revenue is below fixed costs + variable costs then a loss will still be incurred. Where revenue is greater than fixed costs + variable costs then a profit will have been made. The question then arises — at what point does the firm stop incurring a loss and with the next unit of revenue it will make a profit, i.e. at what point does the firm break-even or make neither a profit nor a loss?

Fixed costs stay unchanged over stated ranges in the volume of production, but variable costs are those that change with volumes in production. As revenue increases so do variable costs, so that the only item that remains unchanged is that of fixed costs. Let us look at an example of a firm showing the changing costs and revenue over differing volumes of production.

Apollo Ltd. has fixed costs of £5,000. The variable costs are £2 per unit. The revenue (selling price) is £3 per unit. Looking at production in stages of 1,000 units we can see that the figures emerge as in Exhibit 35.1.

Exhibit 35.1

No. of Units	Fixed Cost £	Variable Cost £	Total Cost: Variable + Fixed £	Revenue (Sales) £	Profit £	Loss £
0	5,000	Nil	5,000	Nil		5,000
1,000	5,000	2,000	7,000	3,000		4,000
2,000	5,000	4,000	9,000	6,000		3,000
3,000	5,000	6,000	11,000	9,000		2,000
4,000	5,000	8,000	13,000	12,000		1,000
5,000	5,000	10,000	15,000	15,000	Nil	Nil
6,000	5,000	12,000	17,000	18,000	1,000	
7,000	5,000	14,000	19,000	21,000	2,000	
8,000	5,000	16,000	21,000	24,000	3,000	
9,000	5,000	18,000	23,000	27,000	4,000	

With activity of 5,000 units the firm will break-even, it will make neither a profit not a loss. Above that the firm moves into profit, below that the firm would never make a profit.

We could have calculated the break-even point without drawing up a schedule of costs etc as in Exhibit 35.1. Instead we could have said that for one unit the revenue is £3 and the variable cost is £2, so that the remainder of £1 is the amount out of which the fixed costs have to come and anything left over would be profit. The £1 is thus the 'contribution' towards fixed costs and profit. Now if the contribution was only just enough to cover fixed costs then there would be no profit, but neither would there be any loss. There are £5,000 fixed costs, so that with a contribution of £1 per unit there would have to be 5,000 units to provide a contribution of £5,000 to cover fixed costs. It could be stated as:

$$\text{Break-even Point} = \frac{\text{Fixed Costs}}{\text{Selling price per unit} - \text{Variable Costs per unit}}$$

i.e. in the case of Apollo Ltd. $\dfrac{£5,000}{£3 - £2} = \dfrac{5,000}{1} = 5,000$ units.

The Break-Even Chart

The information given in Exhibit 35.1 can also be shown in the form of a chart. Many people seem to grasp the idea of break-even analysis rather more easily when they see it in chart form. This is particularly true of people who are not used to dealing with accounting information. We will, therefore, plot the figures from Exhibit 35.1 on a chart which is shown as Exhibit 35.2.

The use of the chart can now be looked at. It would be extremely useful if you could draw the chart as shown in Exhibit 35.2 on a piece of graph paper. The larger the scale that you use the easier it will be to take accurate readings. Plot the lines from the figures as shown in Exhibit 35.1.

To find the break-even point in terms of units of product, draw a line straight down from the break-even point so that it meets the base line at right-angles. This is shown in Exhibit 35.3 as line A, which when read off on the base line gives units of products and Sales as 5,000 units. Now draw a line direct to the vertical £'s line so that it meets that at a right-angle. This is line B and shows £15,000. This means that according to the chart the break-even point is shown at 5,000 units where both costs and revenue are equal at £15,000. This is naturally the same answer as given by ordinary means in Exhibit 35.1.

As production and sales goes above 5,000 units then the firm makes profits. When production and sales is above 5,000 units then the difference represents the "safety margin" as this is the number of units in excess of the break-even point, below which the firm would incur losses.

Look at the chart again, and without consulting the book attempt to answer the following; answer by taking readings off your chart:

(i) What would the total costs of the firm be at (a) 2,000 units, (b) 7,000 units, (c) 8,500 units.

Exhibit 35.2

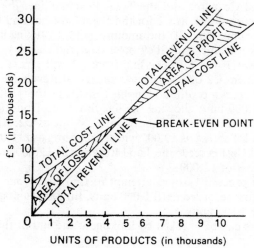

Exhibit 35.3

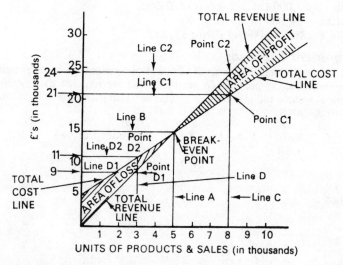

(Remember: take a line up from the product line for the figure needed, then from where the cost line is bisected draw a line to the £'s line to meet it at right angles.)

(ii) What is the revenue for (a) 3,000 units, (b) 6,000 units, (c) 7,500 units.

Before proceeding further now look at the answers which are shown at the end of this chapter.

Now we will try to find the amount of profit or loss at various levels by looking at the chart in Exhibit 35.3. First let us calculate the profit made if 8,000 units are going to be made and sold. Draw a line up from the product line at right angles (shown as line C) until it bisects both the Total Cost line and the Total Revenue line, the points of intersection being shown as C1 for the Total Cost line and C2 for the Total Revenue line. Read off the amounts in £'s by taking lines across to the £'s vertical line until they meet it at right angles. These are shown as lines C1 and C2. The line from C1 will give a reading of £21,000 and from C2 of £24,000. As the Total Revenue exceeds the Total Costs there is a profit, and in this case the profit is £3,000. If we now try for 3,000 units showing the line drawn up from the product line will be at point D1 and of the Total Cost line as D2. Reading off to the £'s line D1 shows as £9,000 whilst D2 shows as £11,000. In this case the Total Cost exceeds the Total Revenue by £2,000 and there is, therefore, a loss of £2,000.

Before you proceed further, attempt to find from your own chart the profit or loss recorded at (i) 1,000 units, (ii) 4,000 units, (iii) 6,500 units and (iv) 8,500 units.

The answers can be checked by looking at the end of this chapter.

Answers
  (i) (a) £9,000 (b) £19,000 (c) £22,000
  (ii) (a) £9,000 (b) £18,000 (c) £22,500
  (i) Loss £4,000 (ii) Loss £1,000
  (iii) Profit £1,500 (iv) Profit £3,500

Assignment Exercises
35.1A Hedges Ltd has fixed costs of £8,000. The variable costs are £4 per unit. The revenue (selling price) is £6 per unit. You are required (i) to draft a schedule as follows filling in the columns (a) to (f) for each stage of 1,000 units up to 10,000 units.

No. of units	(a) Fixed Cost £	(b) Variable Cost £	(c) Total Cost £	(d) Revenue £	(e) Profit -£	(f) Loss £
0						
1,000						
2,000						
3,000						
4,000						
5,000						
6,000						
7,000						
8,000						
9,000						
10,000						

(ii) You are also required to draw a break-even chart from the data in this schedule. Draw it carefully to scale on a piece of graph paper. Retain your answer, you will need it for some questions which follow later.

35.2A Cover up the schedule you constructed as your answer to 35.1(i) and look instead at the break-even chart constructed as the answer to 35.1(ii). Answer the following:

(a) What are the total costs at production levels of (i) 4,000 units, (ii) 7,000 units, (iii) 9,000 units, (iv) 5,500 units.

(b) What is the total revenue at (i) 3,000 units, (ii) 8,000 units, (iii) 5,500 units.

35.3A Look at your schedule in answer to 35.1(i) and answer the following:

(i) What are the total costs at production levels of (i) 4,000 units, (ii) 7,000 units, (iii) 9,000 units, (iv) 5,500 units — you will have to deduce this amount as it is not shown as a figure on the schedule.

(ii) What is the total revenue at (i) 3,000 units, (ii) 8,000 units, (iii) 5,500 units.

35.4A From your break-even chart per 35.1(ii) calculate the profit or loss that will be made at levels of (i) 3,000 units, (ii) 10,000 units, (iii) 4,000 units, (iv) 7,000 units, (v) 8,500 units.

35.5A From the schedule in 35.1(i) calculate the profit or loss that would be made at levels of (i) 3,000 units, (ii) 10,000 units, (iii) 4,000 units, (iv) 7,000 units, (v) 8,500 units (this last figure will have to be deduced as it is not a figure on the schedule).

35.6A Carlos Ltd. has fixed costs of £6,000 and variable costs of £6 per unit. Revenue is £7 per unit. (i) You are required to draw up a schedule as follows, filling in the columns (a) to (f) for each stage of 1,000 units of production up to 10,000 units.

No. of units	(a) Fixed Cost £	(b) Variable Cost £	(c) Total Cost £	(d) Revenue £	(e) Profit £	(f) Loss £
0						
1,000						
2,000						
3,000						
4,000						
5,000						
6,000						
7,000						
8,000						
9,000						
10,000						

(ii) You are required to draw a break-even chart from the data in this schedule. Draw it carefully on a piece of graph paper. Retain your answer, you will need it for some questions which follow later.

35.7A Cover up the schedule you constructed as your answer to 35.6(i) and look instead at the answer to 35.6(ii). Answer the following:

(i) What are the total costs at production levels of (i) 3,000 units, (ii) 5,000 units, (iii) 8,000 units, (iv) 9,500 units.

(ii) What is the total revenue at (i) 2,000 units, (ii) 7,000 units, (iii) 8,500 units.

35.8A Look at your schedule in answer to 35.6(i) and answer the following:

(i) What are the total costs at levels of (i) 3,000 units, (ii) 5,000 units, (iii) 8,000 units, (iv) 9,500 units.

(ii) What is the total revenue at (i) 2,000 units, (ii) 7,000 units, (iii) 8,5000 units — you will have to deduce this amount as it is not shown as a figure on the schedule.

35.9A From your break-even chart per 35.6(ii) calculate the profit or loss that will be made at levels of (i) 4,000 units, (ii) 6,000 units, (iii) 7,500 units, (iv) 9,000 units.

35.10A From the schedule in 35.6(i) calculate the profit or loss that would be made at levels of (i) 4,000 units, (ii) 6,000 units, (iii) 7,500 units, (iv) 8,000 units.

35.11 Carol Ltd. has fixed costs of £20,000. Variable costs are £8 per unit, and Revenue £12 per unit.

(i) What are the total costs at production levels of:
(i) 3,000 units, (ii) 5,000 units, (iii) 7,000 units.

(ii) Calculate the profit or loss that would be made at levels of
(i) 4,000 units, (ii) 6,000 units, (iii) 9,000 units, (iv) 7,500 units.

(iii) At what level would the firm break even?

35.12 Wilkes Ltd. has fixed costs of £150,000. Variable costs are £20 per unit, and revenue £26 per unit.

(i) What are the total costs at production levels of:
(i) 15,000 units, (ii) 22,000 units, (iii) 44,000 units.

(ii) Calculate the profit or loss that would be made at levels of:
(i) 20,000 units, (ii) 29,000 units, (iii) 38,000 units, (iv) 48,000 units.

(iii) At what level would the firm break even?

36 Break-Even Analysis: Part II

Changes and Break-Even Charts

The effect of changes on profits can easily be shown by means of drawing fresh lines on the chart to show the changes, or intended changes, in the circumstances of the firm. Let us first of all consider what factors can bring about a change in the profits of a firm. These are:

(*a*) The selling price per unit could be increased (or decreased).

(*b*) A possible decrease (or increase) in fixed costs.

(*c*) A possible decrease (or increase) in variable costs per unit.

(*d*) Increase the volume of production and sales.

We will investigate these by starting with the same basic information for a firm and then seeing what would happen if each of the changes (*a*) to (*d*) were to happen.

The basic information, before suggested changes, is as follows:

No. of Units	Fixed Cost £	Variable Cost £	Total Costs: Variable + Fixed £	Revenue (Sales) £	Profit £	Loss £
100	2,000	400	2,400	900		1,500
200	2,000	800	2,800	1,800		1,000
300	2,000	1,200	3,200	2,700		500
400	2,000	1,600	3,600	3,600	Nil	Nil
500	2,000	2,000	4,000	4,500	500	
600	2,000	2,400	4,400	5,400	1,000	
700	2,000	2,800	4,800	6,300	1,500	
800	2,000	3,200	5,200	7,200	2,000	
900	2,000	3,600	5,600	8,100	2,500	

The above information shows that variable costs are £4 per unit and selling price £9 per unit. We can draw a chart to incorporate this information before considering the changes being contemplated. This is shown as Exhibit 36.1 on the next page.

(a) Increase Selling Price

Taking a copy of the old chart as a base we can now draw an extra line on it to represent an increase in selling price. Let us suppose that the selling price could be increased by £2 per unit. This can now be shown on a Break-Even chart, see Exhibit 36.2. The line shown as 'New Total Revenue' could then be added. This would mean that the break-even point would change as the increased revenue would mean that costs were covered sooner. The dotted area shows the reduction in the loss area that would be incurred at the same volume of sales, whilst the shaded area shows the increase in profit at the various volumes of sales.

Exhibit 36.1

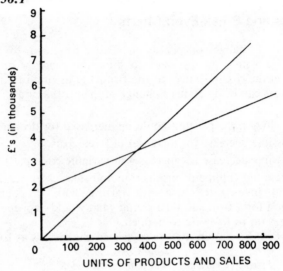

Exhibit 36.2

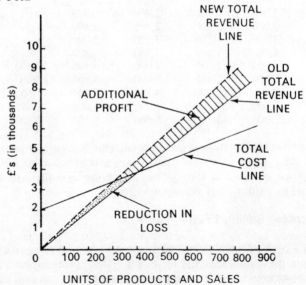

(b) Reduce Fixed Costs

Again taking a copy of the old chart we can now draw extra lines etc. on it, see Exhibit 36.3. The reduction of £800 in fixed costs results in a new line being drawn for New Total Costs. The reduction in loss if sales were at a low volume is represented by the dotted area whilst the shaded area shows the additional profit at various volumes of activity. The change in profit or loss will be constant at £800 over these volumes.

Exhibit 36.3

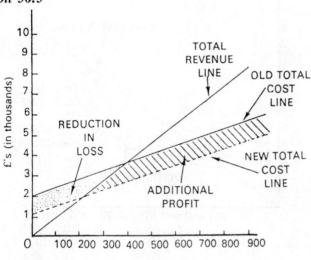

UNITS OF PRODUCTS & SALES

(c) Reduce Variable Costs

Here Exhibit 36.4 shows the position when variable costs per unit are reduced, the particular example being a reduction of £2 per unit. The dotted area shows the reduction in loss compared with the facts if the costs had not changed, whilst the shaded area shows the additional profit at different levels of activity. A reduction in fixed costs in Exhibit 36.3 showed a constant difference of £800 compared with previously over the whole range of activity, whereas a reduction in variable costs as in Exhibit 36.4 brings about different increases of profit, or reduction of loss, over the whole range of activity. The greater the activity the greater the gain with variable cost savings, whereas the gain remains constant with fixed cost savings.

(d) Increased Production and Sales

In this case it is merely a matter of extending the lines for Total Revenue and of Total Costs. Exhibit 36.5 shows this for an increase of 300 units. The new profit indicated will be greater than the old profit because all extra units are being sold at a profit.

The Limitations of Break-Even Charts

In each of the cases looked at it has been assumed that only one of the factors of variable cost, fixed cost, selling price, or volume of sales has in fact altered. Usually this is not the case. An increase in price may well reduce the number sold. There may well be an increase in fixed cost which has an effect which brings down variable costs. The changes in the various factors should, therefore, be studied simultaneously rather than separately.

Exhibit 36.4

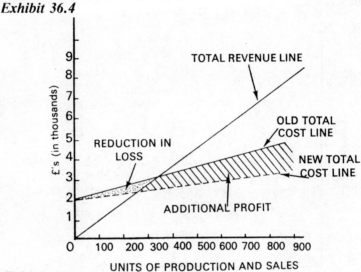

Exhibit 36.5

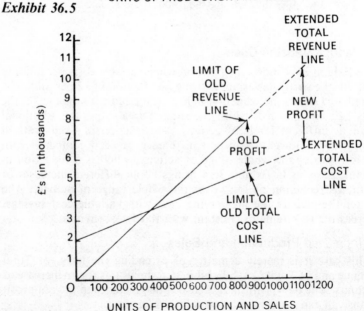

In addition where there is more than one product, the proportions in which the products are sold, i.e. the product mix, can have a very important bearing on costs. Suppose that there are two products, one has a large amount of fixed costs but hardly any variable costs, and the other has a large amount of variable costs but little fixed costs. Therefore if the proportions in which each are sold change very much this could mean that the costs and profit could vary tremendously, even though the total figures of sales stayed constant. An illustration of this can be seen in Exhibit 36.6.

Exhibit 36.6

In considering the break-even analysis we may expect that the following will occur.

Fixed Costs £1,000, Variable Costs: Product A £5 per unit, B £20 per unit.

Selling prices: A £10 per unit, B £30 per unit.

Expected Sales: A 150, B 50. Actual Sales: A 30, B90.

The expected sales are A 150 × £10 + B 50 × £30 = £3,000.

The actual sales are A 30 × £10 + B 90 × £30 = £3,000.

The actual and expected sales are the same, but the costs and profit are quite different.

			£
Expected:	Sales		3,000
Less Variable Costs: A 150 × £5 =		750	
B 50 × £20 =		1,000	1,750
	Contribution		1,250
	Less Fixed Costs		1,000
	Net Profit		£250

			£
Actual:	Sales		3,000
Less Variable Costs: A 30 × £5 =		150	
B 90 × £20 =		1,800	1,950
	Contribution		1,050
	Less Fixed Costs		1,000
	Net Profit		£50

Variable costs are usually taken to be in direct proportion to volume, so that 1,000 units means (say) £5,000 variable costs and therefore 2,000 units would mean £10,000 variable cost, 3,000 units equal £15,000 variable cost and so on. This is often a reasonable estimation of the situation, but may well hold true only within fairly tight limits. For instance 3,100 units could mean £16,000 costs instead of the £15,500 that it would be if a linear relationship existed. This is also true of sales, because to increase sales beyond certain points some may be sold cheaply. Thus 1,000 units might be sold for £9,000; 2,000 units sold for £18,000; but to sell 2,200 units the revenue might be only £19,100 instead of the £19,800 (2,200 × £9) that might be expected if a linear relationship existed over all ranges.

It is assumed that everything produced is sold, and that stocks-in-trade remain constant. It would be difficult to do otherwise as both sales revenue and costs relate to one and the same measure of volume.

Assignment Exercises

Table A. This table consists of data on which questions 36.1 to 36.6 inclusive are based.

No. of units	Fixed Costs £	Variable Costs £	Total Costs £	Revenue £	Profit £	Loss £
0	800	nil	800	nil		800
100	800	300	1,100	500		600
200	800	600	1,400	1,000		400
300	800	900	1,700	1,500		200
400	800	1,200	2,000	2,000	nil	nil
500	800	1,500	2,300	2,500	200	
600	800	1,800	2,600	3,000	400	
700	800	2,100	2,900	3,500	600	
800	800	2,400	3,200	4,000	800	
900	800	2,700	3,500	4,500	1,000	

36.1A (*a*) What was the break-even point from the data in Table A?

(*b*) It is suggested that selling price be increased by 10 per cent. What would the new break-even point be if this was adopted and the other data remained constant?

(*c*) Draw a break-even chart on graph paper showing: (i) The original data in Table A, (ii) A line superimposed on it to show the selling price increase by 10 per cent per unit, (iii) Put a dotted area on the chart to represent the reduction of the loss area, (iv) Put a shaded area on the chart to represent the increase in profit at the various volumes of sales.

36.2A (This question does NOT link up with 36.1.)
Fixed costs can possibly be reduced to £500.

(*a*) Assuming the other data in Table A remains constant, what would the new break-even point be?

(*b*) Draw a break-even chart on graph paper showing: (i) The original data in Table A, (ii) The new data re-fixed costs superimposed on it, (iii) Put a shaded area to represent the additional profits that would be made, (iv) Put a dotted area to represent the reduction in the loss area.

36.3A (This question does NOT link up with 36.1 or 36.2)
Variable costs may be reduced to £2 per unit.

(*a*) Assuming that the other data in Table A remains constant what would the new break-even point be?

(*b*) Draw a break-even chart on graph paper showing: (i) The original data from Table A, (ii) The new data re variable costs superimposed on it, (iii) Put a shaded area to represent the additional profits that would be made, (iv) Put a dotted area to represent the reduction in the loss area.

36.4A (This is not linked up with 36.1, 36.2 or 36.3.)

Production and Sales may be increased to 1,100 units without any increase in Fixed Costs. Assuming that the increase in variable costs and revenue per Table A is extended in the same ratio as shown throughout the table, then:

(*a*) What would the profit be at the volume of 1,100 units?

(*b*) Draw a break-even chart showing the original data from Table A with the new data extended on it.

36.5A (This is not linked up with 36.1; 36.2; 36.3 or 36.4.)

If variable costs are increased to £4 per unit, but all the other items in Table A remain constant then:

(*a*) What would the new break-even point be?

(*b*) Draw a break-even chart showing (i) The original data from Table A, (ii) The new data re variable costs superimposed on it, (iii) Put a shaded area showing the reduction in profit, (iv) Put a dotted area showing the increase in loss.

36.6A (This is not linked up with 36.1; 36.2; 36.3; 36.4 or 36.5.)

If revenue is reduced to £4.5 per unit, but all the other items in Table A remain constant, then:

(*a*) What would the new break-even point be?

(*b*) Draw a break-even chart showing (i) The original data from Table A, (ii) The new data about revenue superimposed on it, (iii) Put a shaded area showing the reduction in profit, (iv) Put a dotted area showing the increase in loss.

Table B. This table consists of data on which questions 36.7 to 36.10 are based.

No. of units	Fixed Costs £	Variable Costs £	Total Costs £	Revenue £	Profit £	Loss £
0	16,000	—	16,000	—		16,000
1,000	16,000	7,000	23,000	9,000		14,000
2,000	16,000	14,000	30,000	18,000		12,000
3,000	16,000	21,000	37,000	27,000		10,000
4,000	16,000	28,000	44,000	36,000		8,000
5,000	16,000	35,000	51,000	45,000		¡6,000
6,000	16,000	42,000	58,000	54,000		4,000
7,000	16,000	49,000	65,000	63,000		2,000
8,000	16,000	56,000	72,000	72,000	nil	nil
9,000	16,000	63,000	79,000	81,000	2,000	
10,000	16,000	70,000	86,000	90,000	4,000	

36.7A

(*a*) What was the break-even point from the data in Table B?

(*b*) It is suggested that selling price be increased by £2 per unit. What would the new break-even point be if this was adopted and the other data remained constant?

(*c*) Draw a break-even chart on graph paper showing (i) The original data in Table B, (ii) A line superimposed on it to show the selling price increased by £2 per unit, (ii) Put a dotted area on the chart to represent the reduction of the loss area, (iii) Put a shaded area on the chart to represent the increase in profit at the various volumes.

36.8 (This question does NOT link up with 36.7.)

Variable costs may be reduced to £6.5 per unit. Assuming that the other data in Table B remained constant what would the new break-even point be?

36.9 (This question does not link up with 36.7 or 36.8.)

Fixed costs can be reduced to £13,000. Assuming the other data in Table B remains constant, what would the new break-even point be?

36.10 (This question does not link up with 36.7; 36.8 or 36.9.)

Production and Sales may be increased to 12,000 units. This can be accomplished without any increase in fixed costs. Other costs and revenue will move in the same ratio as previously. What would the profit be at a volume of 12,000 units.

36.11

No. of units	Fixed Costs £	Variable Costs £	Total Costs £	Revenue £	Profit £	Loss £
0						
100						
200						
300						
400						
500						
600						
700						
800						
900						

(a) Complete the above table if Fixed Costs are £1,400, Variable Costs £6 per unit, and Revenue £10 per unit.

(b) What was the break even point.

(c) What would be the new break even point in each of the following situations assuming in each case that the other data remained constant:

  (i) Selling price increased by 10 per cent.

  (ii) Selling price reduced by 20 per cent.

  (iii) Fixed costs rose to £2,000.

  (iv) Fixed costs fell to £1,200.

  (v) Variable costs rose to £8 per unit.

  (vi) Variable costs fell to £5 per unit.

37 Marginal Costs

The chapter which was concerned with cost behaviour was involved with analysing different types of cost into fixed and variable elements. Once we know for example that the product cost for any period is £1000 fixed cost and £1 per unit of output for variable cost then it is possible to develop plans and take decisions which involve that cost. If output is expected to be 500 units then the expected cost of the product for that period is:

Product Cost	£
Fixed Cost	1000
Variable Cost 500 units	
× £1 per unit	500
	1500

The total cost of the product for the output of 500 units is thus £1500, which means that the average cost per unit of output will be $\frac{\text{Total Cost}}{\text{Number of Units}} = \frac{1500}{500} = £3$ per unit. This average cost per unit will change if the output changes because the £1000 fixed cost element of the total cost does not change as the output goes up or down. For example if we look out the average cost for outputs of 100 units and 1000 units:

Product Cost	100 Units £	1000 Units £
Fixed Cost	1000	1000
Variable Cost at £1 per unit	100	1000
Total Cost	1100	2000
Average Cost = $\frac{\text{Total Cost}}{\text{Number of Units}}$ =	$\frac{1100}{100}$	$\frac{2000}{1000}$
	= £11 per unit	£2 per unit

Clearly the higher the output the lower the average cost, since the fixed cost element is divided over a much greater number of units.

Notice particularly that the average cost cannot be used to work out the likely costs at different levels of output. If we had worked out from a current level of output of 100 units that the product cost was £11 per unit, then we might expect the cost of the product for 1000 units to be £11,000, whereas we know it should be £2,000, which represents a very large difference!

Marginal Costs

Because average cost can be so misleading it is often necessary when decisions which use costs are taken to look at the cost of producing one additional unit of output. The cost of an additional unit is called the 'Marginal Cost'. For example if the current output is 500 units then we have already worked out the product costs to be £1500 which is an average cost of £3 per unit. If we decide to make one more unit then the cost will be:

Product Cost	£
Fixed Cost	1000
Variable Cost 501 units × £1	501
	1501

The additional cost of an extra unit is £1 which is the same as the variable cost of product per unit since this is the only cost that changes as output goes up. Thus marginal cost is normally the same as the variable cost.

Whilst marginal cost is normally the same as variable cost — there may be circumstances when the marginal cost is not the same. For example if the maximum output of the factory machinery is at 1000 units, then if more than 1000 units are needed, the business must spend £5000 on new equipment to expand the capacity of the factory which will be depreciated at £500 per period, then the marginal cost will be different:

Product Cost	1000 units	1001 units
Fixed Cost	1000	1000
Cost of equipment	–	500
Variable cost at £1 per unit	1000	1001
	2000	2501

Thus the marginal cost of 1 extra unit above the capacity of 1000 units is seen to be £501 rather than simply the variable cost of £1.

Using Marginal Costs

Managers are often required to take decisions where the cost of a unit of output is important. For example if a manager is asked to supply 10 extra units of the product above the level of 500 units he currently produces, he needs access to all the cost information we have discussed. He should know that at 500 units the total cost is £1500 with an average cost of £3 per unit. He should also know that the marginal cost per unit for the product is £1.

If therefore he can supply the extra 10 units at a selling price of £2.50, should he accept or not? The £2.50 is clearly below his average costs. However, since the £2.50 is higher than the marginal cost of £1 he would be better off with the extra ten units than without. This is shown below:

	Cost of Product		
	500 units	*510 units*	*Marginal Cost*
	£	£	£
Fixed Cost	1000	1000	–
Variable Cost	500	510	10
	1500	1510	10

Extra revenue would be 10 units × £2.50 = £25 the business would be better off by £15 which is the revenue of £25 less the marginal cost of £10.

Problems Using Marginal Costs

Whilst we have just shown that the business would be better off with the extra revenue, this does not mean that the manager should automatically accept the order. This is because a manager will often be faced with a whole range of opportunities for using the output of his business. Normally there is a limit on the capacity of his factory or office and therefore accepting an additional order may involve a wider range of 'opportunities' than the marginal cost of producing the extra units recognises. For example the manager may be close to negotiating a deal to supply an extra 500 units to another customer. If this goes through it will bring the output up to 1000 units which is capacity — without extra capital expenditure. As was shown earlier the marginal cost over 1000 units may be £501!

Another factor may be that if he supplies the product, in this case at £2.50 per unit, all his other customers may come back demanding price cuts. This could be very costly to him and far outway the benefits of the extra 10 units!

The costs associated with decisions can be very complicated. A manager needs to consider all the ramifications of a decision. 'Opportunity cost' is a term used to cover all the costs and benefits which would arise from taking a decision. Marginal cost will only be a good guide to opportunity cost if the decision taken does not lead to significant changes in other business opportunities.

Assignment Exercises

37.1 The costs of producing Warmo Washing Powder are estimated to be £50 per ton of variable cost and £10,000 fixed cost, in the next operating period. These costs are valid for outputs between 100 tons and 500 tons per period.
  Calculate:
(a) Total Cost of producing 300 tons and 400 tons of powder
(b) The average costs of the two outputs in (a)
(c) The marginal cost of 1 ton at the two outputs in (a)
(d) Explain the difference between the figures you have calculated in parts (b) and (c) for average and marginal cost.

37.2 The management of Bluebell Doors have worked out the following information:

Cost of Door No. 834 for 1000 doors

	£
Variable Cost	5000
Fixed Cost	3000
Total Cost	8000

  Although they currently product 1000 doors in a period which sell for £12 they have been offered a special order for 500 doors at a price of £7 per door.
(a) Assuming that they have the manufacturing capacity to produce the extra 500 doors, prepare the information in a way that would help the management take a decision.
(b) What other factors should influence the decision as to whether or not to accept the order.

37.3A You have been told that the average cost of producing Glofax is £15 per foot for an output of 10,000 feet. The variable cost per foot is £5. To produce more than 10,000 feet and up to 15,000 feet will require the purchase of a new machine which when depreciated will cost £2000 per period. Variable cost will remain the same.
  Calculate:
(a) The fixed cost at output of 10,000 feet
(b) The average cost at an output of 15,000 feet
(c) The marginal cost of an additional foot when currently at the capacity of 10,000 feet production.

37.4A The average cost of Maxoil is £6 per tin. Its fixed cost is £10,000 per period and variable cost is £4.
(a) How many tins are currently produced?
(b) The marginal cost of £4 per tin will remain constant up to a production level of 6000 tins. Explain the importance of marginal cost for management as distinct from average cost.
(c) Explain the idea of opportunity cost. Are opportunity cost and marginal cost the same?
(d) If the company could buy in tins of Maxoil at a price of £3 and could therefore cease manufacture explain the implication of this for your answer in (c).

38 Budgeting and Budgetary Control

Part One: An Introduction

It can be stated that management control is needed to try to ensure that the organisation achieves its objectives. Once the objectives have been agreed, plans should be drawn up so that the progress of the firm can be directed towards the ends specified in the objectives. Now it must not be thought that plans can be expressed only in accounting terms, for example quality of the product might be best shown in engineering terms, or social objectives shown in a plan concerned with employee welfare. But some of the objectives, such as the attainment of a desired profit, or of the attainment of a desired growth in assets can be expressed in accounting terms. When a plan is expressed quantitively it is known as a 'budget' and the process of converting plans into budgets is known as 'budgeting'. In this book we are concerned primarily with budgets shown in monetary terms, i.e. financial budgets.

The budgeting process may be quite formal in a large organisation with committees set up to perform the task. On the other hand in a very small firm the owner may jot down his budget on a piece of scrap paper or even on the back of a used envelope. Some even manage without writing anything down at all, they have done the budgets in their heads and can easily remember them. This book is concerned with budgeting in a formal manner.

Budgets and People

Probably in no other part of accounting is there a greater need for understanding other people than in the processes of budgeting. Budgets are prepared to try to guide the firm towards its objectives. There is no doubt that some budgets that are drawn up are even more harmful to a firm than if none were drawn up at all.

Budgets are drawn up for control purposes, that is an attempt to control the direction that the firm is taking. Many people, however, look upon them, not as a guide, but as a straightjacket. We can look at a few undesirable actions that can result from people regarding budgets as a straightjacket rather than as a guide.

(a) The sales manager refuses to let a salesman go to Sweden in response to an urgent and unexpected request from a Swedish firm. The reason — the overseas sales expenses budget has already been spent. The result — the most profitable order that the firm would have received for many years is taken up instead by another firm.

(b) The works manager turns down requests for overtime work, because the budgeted overtime has already been exceeded. The result — the job is not completed on time, and the firm has to pay a large sum under a penalty clause in the contract for the job which stated that if the job was not finished by a certain date then a penalty of £20,000 would become payable.

(c) Towards the end of the accounting year a manager realises that he has not spent all of his budget for a particular item. He then launches on a spending spree, completely unnecessary items being bought, on the basis that "If I don't spend this amount this year they will cut down next year when I will really need the money." The result: a lot of unusable and unnecessary equipment.

(d) The education budget has been spent, therefore the education manager will not let anyone go on courses for the rest of the year. The result: the firm starts to fall behind in an industry which is highly technical, the staff concerned become fed up, and the better ones start to look for jobs in other firms which are more responsive to the need to allow personnel to keep in touch with changing technology.

Studies have shown that the more that managers are brought into the budgeting process, then the more successful budgetary control is likely to be. A manager on whom a budget is imposed, rather than a manager who had an active part in the drafting of his budget, is more likely to pay less attention to the budget and use it unwisely in the control process.

Having sounded the warning that needs to be borne in mind constantly when budgeting, we can now look at the positive end of budgeting — to see the advantages of a good budgetary control system.

Budgets and Profit Planning

The methodology of budgetary control is probably accountancy's major contribution to management. Before we get down to the mechanics of constructing budgets we should first of all look at the main outlines of drafting budgets.

When the budgets are being drawn up the two main objectives must be uppermost in the mind of top management, that is that the budgets are for:

(a) Planning. This means a properly co-ordinated and comprehensive plan for the whole business. Each part must interlock with the other parts.

(b) Control. Just because a plan is set down on paper does not mean that the plan will carry itself out. Control is exercised via the budgets, thus the name budgetary control. To do this means that the responsibility of managers and budgets must be so linked that the responsible manager is given a guide to help him to produce certain desired results, and the actual achieved results can be compared against the expected, i.e. actual compared with budget.

Preparation of Estimates

The first thing to establish is what the limiting factors are in a firm. It may well be the fact that sales cannot be pushed above a certain amount, otherwise it might be the fact that the firm could sell as much as it can produce, but the productive capacity of the firm sets a limit. Whatever the limiting factor is, there is no doubt that this aspect of the firm will need more attention than probably any other. There would not, for instance, be much point in budgeting for the sale of 1,000 units a year if production could not manufacture more than 700, or to manufacture 2,000 a year if only 1,300 of them could be sold.

There is no doubt that usually the most difficult estimate to make is that of sales revenue. This can be done by using one of two methods:

(i) Make a statistical forecast on the basis of the economic situation, conditions applying reference to the goods sold by the company, and what is known about the actions of competitors.

(ii) The opposite is to make an internal forecast. This is usually done by asking each salesman, or group of salesmen, to estimate the sales in their own areas, and then total the estimates. Sometimes the salesmen are not asked at all.

Now we should remember that much of the subject matter that you have read about, or are currently reading in Economics, is very relevant here. A knowledge of elasticity of demand, whether the product is a complementary product, e.g. the price of egg-cups is linked to the demand for eggs, whether it is a substitute, e.g. that a rise in the price of butter may induce housewives to turn to other commodities instead, is very relevant in this area. Factors such as whether the firm has a monopoly, whether the firm has many small customers, a few large customers, or even one large customer, are of crucial importance. Estimating sales revenue is very much a matter of taking all the economic factors into account allied to other factors.

The sales budget is, however, more than just a sales forecast. Budgets should show the actions that management is taking to influence future events. If an increase in sales is desired the sales budget may show extra sales, which may well be an indication of the action that management is going to take by means of extra television advertising, making a better product, or to give retailers better profit margins and push up sales in that way.

The Production Budget

The production budget stems from the sales budget, but the first question that has to be settled is that of the level of the stock of finished goods which will be held by the firm.

If sales are even over the year, then production can also be in keeping with the sales figure, and the stock figure can remain constant. Suppose that the firm sells 50 units every month, then the firm can produce 50 units per month. In almost every firm, a stock level will have to be maintained, the amount of stock will be dependent on factors such as amount of storage space, the estimated amount needed to cater for breakdowns in production or for delays in receiving raw materials etc. Nonetheless, if the stock level was to be a minimum of 70 units it would still mean that production was at the rate of 50 units per month.

On the other hand sales may not be constant. Sales may average 50 units per month, but the figures may well be as follows:

| January | 20 units | February | 30 units | March | 60 units |
| April | 80 units | May | 70 units | June | 40 units |

This would mean that if production levels were kept at 50 units per month the stock levels would usually have to be more than 100 units, whilst if the stock levels were to be kept at 100 units minimum the production figures each month would equal the sales figures. We can now compare the two levels of production.

(a) Even Production Flow

The problem here is to find the stock level that the firm would need on 1st January if (i) sales are as shown, (ii) the stock must not fall below 100 units, (iii) production is to be 50 per units per month. It can be found by trial and error. For instance, if you decided to see that would happen if the firm started off with 100 units in stock at 1st January you would find that, after adding production and deducting sales each month, the stock level would fall to 90 units in May. As 100 units of stock is the minimum needed you would need to start off on 1st January with 110 units. The method is that if you start off your calculation with an estimated figure of stock, which must at least be the minimum figure required, then if you find that the lowest figure of stock shown during the period is 10 units less than the minimum stock required, go back and add 10 units to the stock to be held on 1st January. If the lowest figure is 30 units less than required add 30 units to the 1st January stock, and so on. We can now look at the figures in Exhibit 38.1.

Exhibit 38.1

UNITS	January	February	March	April	May	June
Opening Stock	110	140	160	150	120	100
Add Units Produced	50	50	50	50	50	50
	160	190	210	200	170	150
Less Sales	20	30	60	80	70	40
Closing Stock	140	160	150	120	100	110

Before we look at the implications of maintaining an even production flow we can look at another example. Try and work it out for yourself before looking at the answer in Exhibit 38.2. The Sales are expected to be January 70, February 40, March 50, April 120, May 140 and June 70. The stock level must not fall below 120 units and an even production flow of 80 units is required. What stock level would there have to be on 1st January?

Exhibits 38.2

UNITS	January	February	March	April	May	June
Opening Stock	140	150	190	220	180	120
Add Units Produced	80	80	80	80	80	80
	220	230	270	300	260	200
Less Sales	70	40	50	120	140	70
Closing Stock	150	190	220	180	120	130

It is more important in many firms to ensure a smooth production flow than to bother unduly about stock levels, assuming that the minimum stock level is always attained. If the work is skilled then that type of labour force may take several years to become trained, and skilled labour in many industries does not take kindly to being sacked and re-employed as the demand for the goods fluctuates. This is not always true with skilled labour, for instance in the building industry such craftsmen as bricklayers may go to a builder until he has completed a contract such as building a college, a hospital, or a housing estate, and then leave and go to another employer on the completion of the job.

On the other hand, a skilled engineer concerned with the manufacturer of say, diesel engines, would not expect to be fired and re-employed continuously. The bricklayer has a skill that is easily transferable to many other building employers in an area, whereas the diesel engineer may have only one firm within fifty miles of his home where he can perform his skills properly. A man employed as labourer might work on a building site in one part of a year and then transfer as a labourer to an engineering factory as a labourer in another part of the year. Whether a firm could carry on production with widely uneven production levels depends so much on the type of firm and the type of labour involved. A firm would only sack skilled labour which it needed again shortly if it could persuade the men or women to come back when required. If the people who had been sacked were likely to find other employment, and not return to the firm when required, then this would mean that the firm would probably keep them on its payroll and production would continue and stocks of finished goods would begin to pile up. Many firms do in fact realise their social obligations by only laying off workers when no other alternative is at all reasonable. In many organisations there are probably more workers from time to time than the firm actually needs — this is known as "organisational slack", so that there is a leeway between the increasing of production and having to take on extra workers.

(b) Uneven Production Levels

Some firms by their very nature will have uneven production levels, and this will be accepted by their labour force. An ice-cream firm would find sales at the highest levels in summer, tailing off in winter. It is not really possible to build up stocks of ice-cream very much in the winter for summer sales! Even if it could be done technically, the costs of refrigerating large quantities of ice-cream for several months could hardly be economic. The large labour force used in the summer months will probably include quite a few students occupying their vacation periods profitably, and not able anyway to work at the job all the year round even if they wanted to. Such a kind of firm will normally have a far greater relationship between current stock levels and current sales than a firm which has even production levels.

The calculation of the quantity to be produced is then:

Opening Stock + Units Produced − Sales = Closing Stock

This means that if the opening stock will be 80 units, the sales are expected to be 100 units and the desired closing is 50 units it becomes:

	units
Opening Stock	80
Add Production	?
Less Sales	100
Closing Stock	50

Production will, therefore, be the missing figure, i.e. 70 units (80 + Production 70 = 150 for sale less actually sold 100 = closing stock 50).

Exhibit 38.3 shows the units to be produced if the following information is known — Stock required 1st January 40, at end of each month, January 60, February 110, March 170, April 100, May 60, June 20. Sales are expected to be January 100, February 150, March 110, April 190, May 70, June 50.

Exhibit 38.3

UNITS	January	February	March	April	May	June
Opening Stock	40	60	110	170	100	60
Production required(?)	120	200	170	120	30	10
	160	260	280	290	130	70
Less Sales	100	150	110	190	70	50
Closing Stock	60	110	170	100	60	20

Linked with the production budget will be a materials purchase budget. It may well be that an order will have to be placed in January, received in March and issued to production in April. The purchase of materials will have to be planned as scientifically as possible.

Assignment Exercises

38.1 What would the production levels have to be for each month if the following data was available:

Units 19-5	Jan.	Feb.	March	April	May	June
(i) Stock levels wanted at the end of each month	690	780	1,100	1,400	1,160	940
(ii) Expected sales each month	800	920	1,090	1,320	1,480	1,020

(iii) The stock level at 1 January, 19-5 will be 740 units.

38.2 For the year ended 31 December, 19-9 the sales of units are expected to be:

January	110	July	70
February	180	August	30
March	170	September	170
April	150	October	110
May	120	November	150
June	100	December	190

The opening stock at 1 January 19-9 will be 140 units. The closing stock desired at 31 December, 19-9 is 150 units.

(*a*) What will production be per month if an even production flow is required and stock levels during the year could be allowed to fall to zero?

(*b*) Given the same information plus the constraint that stock levels must never fall below 80 units, and that extra production will be undertaken in January 19-9 to ensure this, what will be the January production figure?

38.3 What stock should be held by a firm on 1 January 19-7 if the following data is available:

Units 19-7	Jan.	Feb.	Mar.	April	May	June
(i) Sales expected to be	160	190	300	180	110	290
(ii) Production expected to be	200	220	240	260	280	300

(iii) Desired stock level at 30 June, 19-7 is 430 units.

38.4A For the year ended 31 December, 19-6 the sales of units are expected to be:

January	70	July	20
February	90	August	30
March	60	September	60
April	40	October	70
May	30	November	90
June	20	December	50

The opening stock at 1 January, 19-6 will be 120 units. The closing stock desired at 31 December, 19-6 is 150 units.

(*a*) What will production be per month if an even production flow is required and stock levels during the year could be allowed to fall to zero?

(*b*) Given the same information plus the constraint that stock levels must never fall below 110 units, and that extra production will be undertaken in January 19-6 to ensure this, what will the January production figure be?

38.5A A firm wants to maintain an even production flow for the first six months of 19-4 followed by an even production flow of 20 units per month greater for the last six months of 19-4.

Opening stock of units at 1 January, 19-4 are	50
Closing stock of units wanted at 31 December, 19-4	120
Sales of units during the year	650

How many units should be manufactured per month (*a*) January to June 19-4, (*b*) July to December 19-4?

38.6A What stock should be held by a firm on 1 July, 19-7 if the following data is available:

Units 19-7		July	Aug.	Sept.	Oct.	Nov.	Dec.
(i)	Sales expected to be	100	140	180	270	190	130
(ii)	Production expected to be	160	200	220	250	210	180
(iii)	Desired stock level at 31 December, 19-7 is 320 units.						

Part Two: Cash Budgets

It is no use budgeting for production and for sales if sometime during the budget period the firm runs out of cash funds. When talking about cash in budgets we are also usually including bank funds, and therefore in this book we will not be differentiating between cash and cheque payments or between cash and cheques received. Cash is, therefore, also budgeted for, so that any shortage of cash can be known in advance and action taken to obtain permission for a loan or a bank overdraft to be available then, rather than wait until the shortage or deficiency occurs. Bank managers, or anyone concerned with the lending of money, certainly resent most strongly one of their customers needing a bank overdraft without prior warning, when in fact the customer could have known if he had drawn up a cash budget in advance which revealed the need for cash funds on a particular date.

The finance needed may not just be by way of borrowing from a bank or finance house, it may well be a long-term need that can only be satisfied by an issue of shares or debentures. Such issues need planning well in advance, and a cash budget can reveal (*a*) that they will be needed (*b*) how much is needed and (*c*) when it will be needed.

We can now look at a very simple case. Without being concerned in this first exhibit with exactly what the receipts and payments are for, just to keep matters simple at this stage, we can see the dangers that are inherent in not budgeting for cash.

Exhibit 38.4

Mr. Muddlem had a meeting with his accountant on 1st July, 19-3. He was feeling very pleased with himself. He had managed to get some very good orders from customers, mainly because he was now allowing them extra time in which to pay their accounts. Sprite, the accountant, said, 'Can you afford to do all that you are hoping to do?'

Muddlem laughed, 'Why, I'll be making so much money I won't know how to spend it.'

'But have you got the cash to finance everything?' asked Sprite.

'If I'm making a good profit then of course I'll have the cash,' said Muddlem. 'I know the bank manager says that any bank overdraft could not be more than £1,000, but I doubt if I need it.'

'Don't let us rely on guesses,' says Sprite. 'Let's work it out.'

After an hour's work the following facts emerge.
(*a*) Present cash balance (including bank balance) £800.
(*b*) Receipts from debtors will be: July £2,000, August £2,600, September £5,000, October £7,000, November £8,000, December £15,000.
(*c*) Payments will be: July £2,500, August £2,700, September £6,900, October £7,800, November £9,900, December £10,300.

This is then summarised:

	July £	August £	Sept. £	Oct. £	Nov. £	Dec. £
Balance at start of the month:	+ 800	+ 300	+ 200			
Deficit at the start of the month:				− 1,700	− 2,500	− 4,400
Receipts	2,000	2,600	5,000	7,000	8,000	15,000
	2,800	2,900	5,200	5,300	5,500	10,600
Payments	2,500	2,700	6,900	7,800	9,900	10,300
Balance at end of the month:	+ 300	+ 200				+ 300
Deficit at the end of the month:			− 1,700	− 2,500	− 4,400	

'I'm in an awkward position now,' says Muddlem. 'I just cannot borrow £4,400 nor can I cut down on my sales, and anyway I don't really want to as these new sales are very profitable indeed. If only I'd known this, I could have borrowed the money from my brother only last week but he's invested it elsewhere now.'

'Come and see me tomorrow,' says Sprite. 'There may well be something we can do.'

Fortunately for Muddlem his luck was in. He arrived to see his accountant the following morning waving a cheque. 'My wife won £5,000 on a jackpot bingo last night,' he said.

'Thank goodness for that, at least in future you'll learn to budget ahead for cash requirements. You can't be lucky all the time,' says Sprite.

Timing of Cash Receipts and Payments

In drawing up a cash budget it must be borne in mind that all the payments for units produced would very rarely be at the same time as production itself. For instance the raw materials might be bought in March, incorporated in the goods being produced in April, and paid for in May. On the other hand the raw materials may have been in hand for some time, so that the goods are bought in January, paid for in February, and used in production the following August. Contrary to this, the direct labour part of the product is usually paid for almost at the same time as the unit being produced. Even here a unit may be produced in one week and the wages paid one week later, so that a unit might be produced on say 27th June and the wages for the direct labour involved paid for on 3rd July.

Similarly the date of sales and the date of receipt of cash will not usually be at the same time, except in many retail stores. The goods might be sold in May and the money received in August, or even paid for in advance so that the goods might be paid for in February but the goods not shipped to the buyer until May. This is especially true, at least for part of the goods when a cash deposit is left for specially made goods which will take some time to manufacture. A simple example of this would be a made-to-measure suit on which a deposit would be paid at the time of order, the final payment being made when the completed suit is collected by the buyer.

Exhibit 38.5

A cash budget for the six months ended 30th June, 19-3 is to be drafted from the following information.

(*a*) Opening cash balance at 1st January, 19-3 £3,200.

(*b*) Sales; at £12 per unit: cash received three months after sale.

Units: 19-2			19-3								
Oct.	*Nov.*	*Dec.*	*Jan.*	*Feb.*	*Mar.*	*April*	*May*	*June*	*July*	*Aug.*	*Sept.*
80	90	70	100	60	120	150	140	130	110	100	160

(*c*) Production: in units.

19-2			19-3								
Oct.	*Nov.*	*Dec.*	*Jan.*	*Feb.*	*Mar.*	*April*	*May*	*June*	*July*	*Aug.*	*Sept.*
70	80	90	100	110	130	140	150	120	160	170	180

(*d*) Raw Materials used in production costs £4 per unit of production. They are paid for two months before being used in production.

(*e*) Direct Labour. £3 per unit paid for in the same month as the unit produced.

(*f*) Other variable expenses, £2 per unit, ¾ of the cost being paid for in the same month as production, the other ¼ paid in the month after production.

(*g*) Fixed Expenses of £100 per month are paid monthly.

(*h*) A Motor Van is to be bought and paid for in April for £800.

Schedules of payments and receipts are as follows:

PAYMENTS: (The month shown in brackets is the month in which the units are produced)

January	£	February	£
Raw Materials: 130 (March) × £4	520	140 (April) × £4	560
Direct Labour: 100 (January) × £3	300	110 (February) × £3	330
Variable: 100 (January) × ¾ × £2	150	110 (February) × ¾ × £2	165
90 (December) × ¼ × £2	45	100 (January) × ¼ × £2	50
Fixed:	100		100
	£1,115		£1,205

March	£	April	£
Raw Materials: 150 (May) × £4	600	120 (June) × £4	480
Direct Labour: 130 (March) × £3	390	140 (April) × £3	420
Variable: 130 (March) × ¾ × £2	195	140 (April) × ¾ × £2	210
110 (February) × ¼ × £2	55	130 (March) × ¼ × £2	65
Fixed:	100		100
Motor Van			800
	£1,340		£2,075

May	£	June	£
Raw Materials: 160 (July) × £4	640	170 (August) × £4	680
Direct Labour: 150 (May) × £3	450	120 (June) × £3	360
Variable: 150 (May) × ¾ × £2	225	120 (June) × ¾ × £2	180
140 (April) × ¼ × £2	70	150 (May) × ¼ × £2	75
Fixed:	100		100
	£1,485		£1,395

RECEIPTS: (The month shown in brackets is the month in which the sale was made)

			£
January	80 (October)	× £12	960
February	90 (November)	× £12	1,080
March	70 (December)	× £12	840
April	100 (January)	× £12	1,200
May	60 (February)	× £12	720
June	120 (March)	× £12	1,440

CASH BUDGET

	Jan. £	Feb. £	Mar. £	April £	May £	June £
Balance from previous month	3,200	3,045	2,920	2,420	1,545	780
Add Receipts (per schedule)	960	1,080	840	1,200	720	1,440
	4,160	4,125	3,760	3,620	2,265	2,220
Less Payments (per schedule)	1,115	1,205	1,340	2,075	1,485	1,395
Balance carried to next month	3,045	2,920	2,420	1,545	780	825

Assignment Exercises

38.7 R. Jeeves seeks your advice. He has exactly £1,000 cash with which to start a business. He has also received permission from a bank manager to have an overdraft of up to £10,000 during his first six months of business starting 1 January 19-8.

His plans for his first six months trading are:

(a) Payments for goods and supplies: January £5,500, February £7,200, March £9,700, April £10,500, May £9,600, June £6,900.

(b) Receipts from debtors will be: January £3,900, February £5,900, March £6,000, April £7,100, May £8,400, June £9,500.

(c) Loan receivable on 1 March £700 to be repaid in full plus £100 interest on 1 June 19-8.

(d) Drawings £300 per calendar month.

You are required to draw up a cash budget, showing the balances each month for the six months to 30 June 19-8. Also make any suitable comments.

38.8 Draw up a cash budget for N. Morris showing the balance at the end of each month, from the following information for the six months ended 31 December 19-2:

(a) Opening Cash (including bank) balance £1,200

(b) Production in units:

19-2									19-3	
April	May	June	July	Aug.	Sept.	Oct.	Nov.	Dec.	Jan.	Feb.
240	270	300	320	350	370	380	340	310	260	250

(c) Raw Materials used in production cost £5 per unit. Of this 80 per cent is paid in the month of production and 20 per cent in the month after production.

(d) Direct Labour costs of £8 per unit are payable in the month of production.

(e) Variable expenses are £2 per unit, payable one-half in the same month as production and one-half in the month following production.

(f) Sales at £20 per unit:

19-2								19-3	
Mar.	April	May	June	July	Aug.	Sept.	Oct.	Nov.	Dec.
260	200	320	290	400	300	350	400	390	400

Debtors to pay their accounts three months after that in which sales are made.

(g) Fixed expenses of £400 per month payable each month.

(h) Machinery costing £2,000 to be paid for in October 19-2.

(i) Will receive a legacy £2,500 in December 19-2.

(j) Drawings to be £300 per month.

38.9A B. Ukridge comes to see you in April 19-3. He is full of enthusiasm for a new product that he is about to launch on to the market. Unfortunately his financial recklessness in the past has led him into being bankrupted twice, and he has only just got discharged by the court from his second bankruptcy.

'Look here laddie,' he says, 'with my new idea I'll be a wealthy man before Christmas.'

'Calm down,' you say, 'and tell me all about it.'

Ukridge's plans as far as cash is concerned for the next six months are:

(a) Present cash balance (including bank) £5.

(b) Timely legacy under a will — being received on 1 May, 19-3, £5,000. This will be paid into the business bank account by Ukridge.

(c) Receipts from debtors will be: May £400, June £4,000, July £8,000, August £12,000, September £9,000, October £5,000.

(d) Payments will be: May £100, June £5,000, July £11,000, August £20,000, September £12,000, October £7,000.

You are required: (i) To draw up a cash budget, showing the balances each month, for the six months to 31 October, 19-3.

(ii) The only person Ukridge could borrow money from would charge interest at the rate of 100 per cent per annum. This is not excessive considering Ukridge's past record. Advise Ukridge.

38.10A Draw up a cash budget for J. Clarke from the following information for the six months 1 July, 19-9 to 31 December, 19-9.

(a) Opening cash (includes bank) balance 1 July 19-9 £1,500.

(b) Sales at £20 per unit:

	April	May	June	July	Aug.	Sept.	Oct.	Nov.	Dec.
Units	110	120	140	160	180	190	130	80	70

Debtors will pay two months after they have bought the goods.

(c) Production in units:

	April	May	June	July	Aug.	Sept.	Oct.	Nov.	Dec.	Jan.
Units	150	170	180	200	130	110	100	90	70	60

(d) Raw materials cost £6 per unit and are paid for 3 months after the goods are used in production.

(e) Direct labour of £5 per unit is payable in the same month as production.

(f) Other variable expenses are £3 per unit. Two-thirds of this cost is paid for in the same month as production and one-third in the month following production.

(g) Fixed expenses of £150 per month are paid one month in arrears — these expenses have been at this rate for the past two years.

(h) A machine is to be bought and paid for in September for £6,000.

(i) Clarke will borrow £3,000 from a relative in December 19-9. This will be put into the business bank account immediately.

Part Three: Co-ordination of Budgets

The various budgets have to be linked together and a 'Master Budget', which is really a budgeted set of Final Accounts drawn up. We have in fact looked at the Sales, Production and Cash Budgets. There are, however, many more budgets for parts of the organization, for instance there may be:

(i)   A selling expense budget,

(ii) An administration expense budget,

(iii) A manufacturing overhead budget,

(iv) A direct labour budget,

(v)   A purchases budget,

and so on. In this book we do not wish to get entangled in too many details, but in a real firm with a proper set of budgeting techniques there will be a great deal of detailed backing for the figures that are incorporated in the more important budgets.

Now it may be that when all the budgets have been co-ordinated, or slotted together, the Master Budget shows a smaller profit than the directors are prepared to accept. This will mean recasting budgets to see whether a greater profit can be earned, and if at all possible the budgets will be altered. Eventually there will be a Master Budget that the directors can agree to. This then gives the target for the results that the firm hopes to achieve in financial terms. Remember that there are other targets such as employee welfare, quality product etc. that cannot be so expressed.

The rest of this chapter is concerned with the drawing up of budgets for an imaginary firm, Walsh Ltd, culminating in the drawing up of a Master Budget.

To start with we can look at the last Balance Sheet of Walsh Ltd as at 31st December, 19-4. This will give us our opening figures of stocks of raw materials, stock of finished goods, cash (including bank) balance, creditors, debtors etc.

Walsh Ltd.
Balance Sheet as at 31 December 19-4

Fixed Assets	Cost	Depreciation to date	Net
	£	£	£
Machinery	4,000	1,600	2,400
Motor Vehicles	2,000	800	1,200
	6,000	2,400	3,600

Current Assets

Stocks: Finished Goods (75 units)		900	
Raw Materials		500	
Debtors (19-4 October £540 + November £360 + December £450)		1,350	
Cash and Bank Balances		650	
		3,400	

Less Current Liabilities

Creditors for Raw Materials (November £120 + December £180)	300		
Creditors for Fixed Expenses (December)	100	400	
Working Capital			3,000
			6,600

Financed by:

Share Capital: 4,000 shares £1 each	4,000
Profit & Loss Account	2,600
	6,600

The plans for the six months ended 30th June, 19-5 are as follows:

(i) Production will be 60 units per month for the first four months, followed by 70 units per month for May and June.

(ii) Production costs will be (per unit):

	£
Direct Materials	5
Direct Labour	4
Variable Overhead	3
	£12

(iii) Fixed overhead is £100 per month, payable always one month in arrears.

(iv) Sales, at a price of £18 per unit, are expected to be:

	January	February	March	April	May	June
No. of units	40	50	60	90	90	70

(v) Purchases of direct materials (raw materials) will be:

January	February	March	April	May	June
£	£	£	£	£	£
150	200	250	300	400	320

(vi) The creditors for raw materials bought are paid two months after purchase.

(vii) Debtors are expected to pay their accounts three months after they have bought the goods.

(viii) Direct Labour and variable overhead are paid in the same month as the units are produced.

(ix) A machine costing £2,000 will be bought and paid for in March.

(x) 3,000 shares of £1 each are to be issued at par in May.

(xi) Depreciation for the six months: Machinery £450, Motor Vehicles £200.

We must first of all draw up the various budgets and then incorporate them into the Master Budget. Some of the more detailed budgets which can be dispensed with in this illustration will be omitted.

Materials Budget

	Jan.	Feb.	March	April	May	June
Opening Stock £	500	350	250	200	200	250
Add Purchases £	150	200	250	300	400	320
	650	550	500	500	600	570
Less Used in Production:						
Jan.—April 60×£5	300	300	300	300		
May and June 70×£5					350	350
Closing Stock £	350	250	200	200	250	220

Production Budget (in units)

	Jan.	Feb.	March	April	May	June
Opening Stock (units)	75	95	105	105	75	55
Add Produced	60	60	60	60	70	70
	135	155	165	165	145	125
Less Sales	40	50	60	90	90	70
Closing Stock	95	105	105	75	55	55

Production Cost Budget (in £'s)

	Jan.	Feb.	March	April	May	June	Total
Materials Cost £	300	300	300	300	350	350	1,900
Labour Cost £	240	240	240	240	280	280	1,520
Variable Overhead £	180	180	180	180	210	210	1,140
	720	720	720	720	840	840	4,560

Creditors Budget

	Jan.	Feb.	March	April	May	June
Opening Balance £	300	330	350	450	550	700
Add Purchases £	150	200	250	300	400	320
	450	530	600	750	950	1,020
Less Payments £	120	180	150	200	250	300
Closing Balance £	330	350	450	550	700	720

Debtors Budget

	Jan.	Feb.	March	April	May	June
Opening Balances	1,350	1,530	2,070	2,700	3,600	4,320
Add Sales £	720	900	1,080	1,620	1,620	1,260
	2,070	2,430	3,150	4,320	5,220	5,580
Less Received £	540	360	450	720	900	1,080
Closing Balances £	1,530	2,070	2,700	3,600	4,320	4,500

Cash Budget

	Jan.	Feb.	March	April	May	June
Opening Balance £	+ 650	+ 550	+ 210			+ 1,050
Opening Overdraft £				− 2,010	− 2,010	
Received (see schedule) £	540	360	450	720	3,900	1,080
	1,190	910	660	1,290	1,890	2,130
Payments (see schedule) £	640	700	2,670	720	840	890
Closing Balance £	+ 550	+ 210			+ 1,050	+ 1,240
Closing Overdraft £			− 2,010	− 2,010		

Cash Payments Schedule

	Jan.	Feb.	March	April	May	June
Creditors for goods bought two						
months previously £	120	180	150	200	250	300
Fixed Overhead £	100	100	100	100	100	100
Direct Labour £	240	240	240	240	280	280
Variable Overhead £	180	180	180	180	210	210
Machinery £			2,000			
£	640	700	2,670	720	840	890

Cash Receipts Schedule

	Jan.	Feb.	March	April	May	June
Debtors for goods sold three						
months previousl £	540	360	450	720	900	1,080
Shares Issued £					3,000	
					3,900	

Master Budget

Forecast Operating Statement for the Six months ended 30 June 19-5

		£
Sales		7,200
Less Cost of Goods Sold:		
Opening Stock of Finished Goods	900	
Add Cost of Goods Completed	4,560	
	5,460	
Less Closing Stock of Finished Goods	660	4,800
Gross Profit		2,400
Less:		
Fixed Overhead	600	
Depreciation: Machinery	450	
Motors	200	650	1,250
Net Profit		1,150

Forecast Balance Sheet as at 30 June 19-5

Fixed Assets	Cost £	Depreciation to date £	Net £
Machinery	6,000	2,050	3,950
Motor Vehicles	2,000	1,000	1,000
	8,000	3,050	4,950

Current Assets			
Stocks: Finished Goods		660	
Raw Materials		220	
Debtors		4,500	
Cash and Bank Balances		1,240	
		6,620	

Less Current Liabilities:			
Creditors for Goods	720		
Creditors for Overheads	100	820	
Working Capital			5,800
			10,750

Financed By:	
Share Capital	7,000
Profit and Loss Account (2,600 + 1,150)	3,750
	10,750

Capital Budgeting

The plan for the acquisition of fixed assets such as machinery, buildings etc. is usually known as a Capital Budget. Management will evaluate the various possibilities open to it, and will compare the alternatives. This is a very important part of budgeting, and is dealt with in Chapter 42.

Assignment Exercises

38.11 D. Smith is to open a retail shop on 1 January, 19-4. He will put in £25,000 cash as Capital. His plans are as follows:
(i) On 1 January 19-4 to buy and pay for Premises £20,000, Shop Fixtures £3,000, Motor Van £1,000.
(ii) To employ two assistants, each to get a salary of £130 per month, to be paid at the end of each month. (P.A.Y.E. tax, National Insurance contributions etc. are to be ignored.)
(iii) To buy the following goods (shown in units):

	Jan.	Feb.	March	April	May	June
Units	200	220	280	350	400	330

(iv) To sell the following number of units:

	Jan.	Feb.	March	April	May	June
Units	120	180	240	300	390	420

(v) Units will be sold for £10 each. One-third of the sales are for cash, the other two-thirds being on credit. These latter customers are expected to pay their accounts in the second month following that in which they received the goods.

(vi) The units will cost £6 each for January to April inclusive, and £7 each thereafter. Creditors will be paid in the month following purchase. (Value stock-in-trade on F.I.F.O. basis.)

(vii) The other expenses of the shop will be £150 per month payable in the month following that in which they were incurred.

(viii) Part of the premises will be sub-let as an office at a rent of £600 per annum. This is paid in equal instalments in March, June, September and December.

(ix) Smith's cash drawings will amount to £250 per month.

(x) Depreciation is to be provided on Shop Fixtures at 10 per cent per annum and on the Motor Van at 20 per cent per annum.
You are required to:

(a) Draw up a Cash Budget for the six months ended 30 June, 19-4, showing the balance of cash at the end of each month.

(b) Draw up a forecast Trading and Profit and Loss Account for the six months ended 30 June 19-4 and a Balance Sheet as at that date.

38.12 Newman and Harris are to form a private limited company in the name of Craft Limited. They tell you that their plans for their first six months of trading for the period 1 January 19-4 to 30 June 19-4 are:

(a) Harris will put £20,000 into the business bank account on 1 January 19-4. He will be issued with 20,000 ordinary shares of £1 each at par.

(b) Newman will put £40,000 into the business bank account on 1 January 19-4. He will then be issued with 32,000 ordinary shares of £1 each at par, and a 7 per cent debenture of £8,000.

(c) Sales, all on credit, will be; January £12,000; February £16,000; March £28,000; April £22,000; May £24,000; June £26,000. All debtors will pay their accounts three months after that in which they buy the goods.

(d) Purchases, all on credit, will be: January £48,000; February £16,000; March £18,000; April £20,000; May £14,000; June £10,000. Creditors will be paid in the month following that in which the goods are bought.

(e) Wages and salaries will be £800 per month, payable on the last day of each month.

(f) Newman and Harris are to be the only directors. They are to be paid directors' remuneration totalling £1,200 per month, payable on the last day of each month.

(g) The first debenture interest will be paid on 31 December 19-4.

(h) Premises costing £30,000 will be occupied on 1 January 19-4 and will be paid for in February 19-4.

(i) All other expenses of £600 per month for the first five months and £840 for June are to be paid in the month following that in which they are incurred.

(j) Equipment will be bought on 1 January 19-4 for £12,000, payment being made of £6,000 in March 19-4 and £6,000 in June 19-4.

(k) Stock-in-Trade at 30 June 19-4 will be £21,800.

(*l*) Depreciation is to be written off the equipment at the rate of 20 per cent per annum.

You are required to:

(i) Draft a cash budget, showing clearly the bank balance at the end of each month.

(ii) Draft the budgeted Trading and Profit and Loss Account for the six months ended 30 June 19-4 and a Balance Sheet as at that date.

Ignore Taxation.

38.13A B. Cooper is going to set up a new business on 1 January, 19-8. He estimates that his first six months in business will be as follows:

(i) He will put £10,000 into a bank account for the firm on 1 January, 19-8.

(ii) On 1 January, 19-8 he will buy Machinery £2,000, Motor Vehicles £1,600 and Premises £5,000, paying for them immediately out of the business bank account.

(iii) All purchases will be effected on credit. He will buy £2,000 goods on 1 January and he will pay for these in February. Other purchases will be rest of January £3,200, February, March, April, May and June £4,000 each month. Other than the £2,000 worth bought in January all other purchases will be paid for two months after purchase.

(iv) Sales (all on credit) will be £4,000 for January and £5,000 for each month after that. Debtors will pay for the goods in the third month after purchase by them.

(v) Stock-in-trade on 30 June, 19-8 will be £2,000.

(vi) Wages and Salaries will be £150 per month and will be paid on the last day of each month.

(vii) General Expenses will be £50 per month, payable in the month following that in which they were incurred.

(viii)He will receive a legacy of £5,500 on 21 April, 19-8. This will be paid into the business bank account immediately.

(ix) Insurance covering the 12 months of 19-8 will be paid for by cheque on 30 June, 19-8, £140.

(x) Rates will be paid as follows: for the three months to 31 March, 19-8 by cheque on 28 February, 19-8: for the 12 months ended 31 March, 19-9 by cheque on 31 July 19-8. Rates are £360 per annum.

(xi) He will make drawings of £80 per month by cheque.

(xii) He has substantial investments in public companies. His bank manager will give him any overdraft that he may require.

(xiii)Depreciate Motors 20 per cent per annum, Machinery 10 per cent per annum.

You are required to:

(*a*) Draft a cash budget (includes bank) month by month showing clearly the amount of bank balance or overdraft at the end of each month.

(*b*) Draft the projected Trading and Profit and Loss Account for the first six month's trading, and a Balance Sheet as at 30 June, 19-8.

38.14A The balance sheet of Gregg Ltd at 30 June, 19-6 was expected to be as follows:

Balance Sheet 30 June, 19-6

Fixed Assets	Cost	Depreciation to date	Net
Land and Buildings	40,000	—	40,000
Plant and Machinery	10,000	6,000	4,000
Motor Vehicles	6,000	2,800	3,200
Office Fixtures	500	220	280
	56,500	9,020	47,480

Current Assets		
Stock-in-Trade: Finished Goods	1,800	
Raw Materials	300	
Debtors (19-6 May £990 + June £900)	1,890	
Cash and Bank Balances	7,100	11,090
		£58,570

Financed By:		
Share Capital		50,000
Profit and Loss Account		7,820
		57,820

Current Liabilities		
Creditors for Raw Materials (April £240 + May £140 + June £160)	540	
Creditors for variable overhead	210	750
		£58,570

The plans for the six months to 31 December 19-6 can be summarised as:

(i) Production costs per unit will be:

	£
Direct Materials	2
Direct Labour	5
Variable overhead	3
	£10

(ii) Sales will be at a price of £18 per unit for the three months to 30 September and at £18.5 subsequently. The number of units sold would be:

	July	Aug.	Sept.	Oct.	Nov.	Dec.
Units	60	80	100	100	90	70

All sales will be on credit, and debtors will pay their accounts two months after they have bought the goods.

(iii) Production will be even at 90 units per month.

(iv) Purchases of direct materials — all on credit — will be:

July	Aug.	Sept.	Oct.	Nov.	Dec.
£	£	£	£	£	£
220	200	160	140	140	180

Creditors for direct materials will be paid three months after purchase.

(v) Direct labour is paid in the same month as production occurs.

(vi) Variable overhead is paid in the month following that in which the units are produced.

(vii) Fixed overhead of £90 per month is paid each month and is never in arrears.

(viii) A machine costing £500 will be bought and paid for in July. A motor vehicle costing £2,000 will be bought and paid for in September.

(ix) A debenture of £5,000 will be issued and the cash received in November. Interest will not start to run until 19-7.

(x) Provide for depreciation for the six months: Motor Vehicles £600, Office Fixtures £30, Machinery £700.

You are required to draw up as a minimum:

(a) Cash Budget, showing figures each month.

(b) Debtors Budget, showing figures each month.

(c) Creditors Budget, showing figures each month.

(d) Raw Materials Budget, showing figures each month.

(e) Forecast Operating Statement for the six months.

(f) Forecast Balance Sheet as at 31 December, 19-6.

In addition you may draw up any further budgets you may wish to show the workings behind the above budgets.

Part Four: Further Thoughts on Budgets

The process of budgeting with the necessary participation throughout management, finally producing a profit plan, is now a regular feature in all but the smallest firms. Very often budgeting is the one time when the various parts of management can really get together and work as a team rather than just as separate parts of an organisation. When budgeting is conducted under favourable conditions, there is no doubt that a firm which budgets will tend to perform rather better than a similar firm that does not budget. Budgeting means that managers can no longer give general answers affecting the running of the firm, they have to put figures to their ideas, and they know that in the end their estimated figures are going to be compared with what the actual figures turn out to be.

It has often been said that the act of budgeting is possibly of more benefit than the budgets which are produced. However, the following benefits can be claimed for good budgeting:

(a) The strategic planning carried on by the board of directors or owners can be more easily linked to the decisions by managers as to how the resources of the business will be used to try to achieve the objectives of the business. The strategic planning has to be converted into action, and budgeting provides the ideal place where such planning can be changed into financial terms.

(b) Standards of performance can be agreed to for the various parts of the business. If sales and production targets are set as part of a co-ordinated plan, then the sales department cannot really complain that production is insufficient if they had agreed previously to a production level and this is being achieved, nor can production complain if its production exceeds the amount budgeted for and it remains unsold.

(c) The expression of plans in comparable financial terms. Some managers think mainly in terms of say units of production, or of tons of inputs or outputs, or of lorry mileage etc. The effect that each of them has upon financial results must be brought home to them. For instance a transport manager might be unconcerned about the number of miles that his haulage fleet of lorries covers until the cost of doing such a large mileage is brought home to him, often during budgeting, and it may be then and only than that he starts to search for possible economies. It is possible in many cases to use mathematics to find the best ways of loading vehicles, or of the routes taken by vehicles so that fewer miles are covered and yet the same delivery service is maintained. This is just one instance of many when the expression of the plans of a section of a business in financial terms sparks off a search for economies, when otherwise such a search may never be started at all.

(d) Managers can see how their work slots into the total activities of the firm. It can help to get rid of the feeling of 'I'm only a number not a person', because he can identify his position within the firm and can see that his job really is essential to the proper functioning of the firm.

(e) The budgets for a firm cannot be set in isolation. This means that the situation of the business, the nature of its products and its work force etc., must be seen against the economic background of the country. For instance it is no use budgeting for extra labour when labour is in extremely short supply, without realising the implications, possibly that of paying higher than normal wage rates. Increasing the sales target during a 'credit squeeze' needs a full investigation of the effect of the shortage of money upon the demand for the firms' goods and so on.

The charges made against budgeting are mainly that budgets bring about inflexibility, and that managers will not depart from budget even though the departure would bring about a more desirable result. Too many budgets are set at one level of sales or production when in fact flexible budgets (discussed later in this chapter) ought to be used. It is very often the case that budgeting is forced upon managers against their will, instead the firm should really set out first of all to do a 'selling job' to convince managers that budgets are not the monsters so often thought. A trial run for part of a business is far superior than starting off by having a fully detailed budget set up right away for the whole of the business. Learning to use budgets is rather like learning to swim. Let a child get used to the water first and remove its fear of the water, then it will learn to swim fairly easily. For most children (but not all), if the first visit to the baths meant being pushed into the deep end immediately, then reaction against swimming would probably set in. Let a manager become used to the idea of budgeting, without the fear of being dealt with severely during a trial period, and most managers will then become used to the idea and participate properly.

Flexible Budgets

So far in this book budgets have been drawn up on the basis of one set of expectations, based on just one level of sales and production. Later, when the actual results are compared with the budgeted results expected in a fixed budget, they will have deviated for two reasons:

(1) Whilst the actual and budgeted volumes of production and sales may be the same there may be a difference in actual and budgeted costs.

(2) The volumes of actual and budgeted units of sales and production may vary, so that the costs will be different because of different volumes.

The variations, or variances as they are more commonly known, are usually under the control of different managers in the organisation. Variances coming under (1) will probably be under the control of the individual department. On the other hand variances under (2) are caused because of variations in plans brought about by top management because of changing sales, or at least the expectation of changing sales.

Budgets are used for control purposes, therefore a manager does not take kindly to being held responsible for a variance in his spending if the variance is caused by a type (2) occurrence if he is working on a fixed budget. The answer to this is to construct budgets at several levels of volume, and to show what costs etc. they should incur at different levels. For instance, if a budget had been fixed at a volume of 500 units and the actual volume was 550, then the manager would undoubtedly feel aggrieved if his costs for producing 550 units are compared with the costs he should have incurred for 500 units. Budgets which do allow for changing levels are called 'Flexible Budgets'.

To draft a full set of flexible budgets is outside the scope of this book, but an instance of one department's flexible budget for manufacturing overhead can be shown in Exhibit 38.6.

Exhibit 38.6   Data Ltd
Budget of Manufacturing Overhead, Department S
(This would in fact be in greater detail)

Units	400	450	500	550	600
	£	£	£	£	£
Variable overhead	510	550	600	680	770
Fixed overhead	400	400	400	400	400
Total overhead (A)	£910	£950	£1,000	£1,080	£1,170
Direct Labour hours (B)	200	225	250	275	300
Overhead rates (A) divided by (B)	£4.55	£4.22	£4.0	£3.92	£3.9

Notice that the variable costs in this case do not vary in direct proportion to production. In this case once 500 units production have been exceeded they start to climb rapidly. The flexible budget makes far greater sense than a fixed budget. For instance if a fixed budget had been agreed at 400 units, with variable overhead £510, then if production rose to 600 units the manager would think the whole system unfair if he was expected to incur only £510 variable overhead (the figure for 400 units). On the contrary, if the comparison was on a flexible budget then costs at 600 units production would instead be compared with £770 (the figure at 600 units).

39 Sources of Finance

In the earlier chapters which were dealing with the financial accounts of business you were introduced to sources of funds into different types of business organisation — whether sole trader, partnership or limited company. The Balance Sheet distinguishes between Capital — a source which is the obligation to the proprietors, and Liabilities — sources which are obligations to third parties. The liabilities are usually split into current liabilities, which will require to be repaid in the short-term and other forms of liability which will be repaid in the medium or the long-term.

This chapter will be concerned with explaining some of the factors involved when a business needs to raise more funds. When this happens there will be a choice between different sources each of which will have some advantages and disadvantages.

In considering what form of finance to raise there are a number of key issues to be resolved. Of primary concern is the requirement that the kind of financial funding matches the application to which it is being put. For example if a company wants to buy a building for its own use, the funds used to buy that building will be tied up until that building is sold, which is likely to be a long time into the future. It would not therefore be sensible to borrow the money for a short period — say six months — at the end of which time a new loan would be needed. It is not sensible because it is quite possible that the availability of short-term loans could become very limited in the future and the company would have great difficulty in providing funds for the loan repayment. Remember that if a loan is not repaid when it is due, the lender can apply to the courts for repayment and the creditor company will be wound up, or the individual concerned declared bankrupt.

Short-term borrowing has a useful role to play in financing current assets, since it can be adjusted up or down at short notice, to match the asset requirements. However holding excessive liquid funds if they are not put to use is expensive and wasteful. We can repeat that short-term borrowing is not suitable to finance long-term investment.

Another major part of the decision about how to finance an organisation relates to the risks which are associated with lending. From a lender's point of view the risk is based on the likelihood or not of being repaid an amount owing when it is due. The lender looks at his security in terms of the organisation's valuable assets and the total amount of other borrowing outstanding. The risk is clearly lowest when the asset value is high and total borrowing low. Some lenders take steps to reduce risk to them by securing their loan by a legal mortgage charged on assets of the organisation. Whilst helping the secured lender this increases the risk to any unsecured lenders who will rank after the secured creditors if the organisation is wound up.

There is a balance to be found between borrowing and the equity capital of the proprietor. The higher the proportion of borrowing (called high gearing) the higher the risk to the lender of not recovering his money. In a low geared situation the lender will expect to be covered by the equity capital funded assets which could be used to repay creditors first.

Why does an organisation borrow money and not fund all its activities from equity capital (ordinary shares)? The answer is that borrowing money allows a good organisation to expand even when its proprietors have no immediate extra funds available. For example an organisation has Equity Capital of £100,000, it can borrow £20,000 at 10% interest and thus have total funds of £120,000. This would be worthwhile for the proprietors if the assets when acquired guaranteed profits returning more than 10%. This can be shown if we assume the return on all assets of say 15%:

	Equity Only £	Equity plus loan £
Funds employed: Capital	100,000	100,000
Loan	–	20,000
	100,000	120,000
Profits at return of 15%	15,000	18,000
less interest of 10% on loan	–	2,000
	15,000	16,000

The profit remaining for the owners of capital has increased by £1000 on the same investment of £100,000 since they retain the excess of profit over the cost of interest. This extra profit is not however earned without an increase in risk — since the organisation now has to ensure the lender is repaid his interest and capital when due — otherwise winding up will ensue! The owner can thus increase his return but only by increasing his level of risk.

Some types of organisation such as Public and Local Authorities or Government Agencies cannot raise Equity Capital, since ownership is in public hands. They can and do, however, raise funds by borrowing. Usually the security of lending to a public authority is considered to be impeccable — the risk is therefore low. Loans in low risk situations are made at lower interest rates than for high risks. Thus public authorities and good low risk business organisations borrow at lower rates of interest than high geared and risky looking businesses. The decision on an organisation as to how much can be lent without undue risk and punitive interest rates will be based on general commercial judgements of the nature of business and all surrounding facts. There will always be a range of judgement — no absolute hard and fast rules.

Specific Sources of Funds
Short and Medium-Term Borrowing

The main source of short-term funds for business comes from the banks and a range of finance houses. For limited amounts of borrowing the most popular form is the bank overdraft which allows the business to 'overdraw' its current account up to an amount agreed with the bank. The advantage of this system is that interest is only charged on the actual amount overdrawn. In most businesses this loan will fluctuate at different times. For example before Christmas most retail businesses will have bought in a large inventory of goods for sale, and will have to borrow to finance it. If successful in the Christmas period and through the January sales cash will come flowing in allowing the overdraft to be paid back. This is exactly how the banks like to see overdrafts used; for short terms (bank overdrafts are in fact repayable on demand). They do not want overdrafts used to form permanent finance. Banks do not like to accept high levels of risk when they lend to a business. They therefore examine the accounts carefully to ensure that the proprietors have an adequate 'equity' capital stake in the business themselves. They will often require to secure their lending by taking a mortgage charge on business assets. For small proprietor owned business they also usually require the owners to give personal guarantees and security even though the business may be a limited company.

In addition to security the banks and indeed all other lending agencies are very concerned to know about the future plans of any business. This is because they do not want to lend to people who are likely to fail in business, even though they are secured. One of the best indicators of likely success is a good business plan or budget for the future. Thus the discussion of budgets which was covered earlier in the book is not only important for management itself, but essential nowadays when negotiating to raise finance.

It should be clear by now that for a new business setting up for the first time it may be very hard to raise borrowed funds unless the proprietor has a lot of wealth to start off with. Because the Government is trying to promote the development of new business it started a new scheme for providing guarantees on bank loans in 1981. This 'Loan Guarantee Scheme' aims to reduce the risk to the lending bank by providing some insurance cover in the event of failure, even though proper lending criteria still apply. Thus it is hoped a business which would be considered risky for normal bank lending can obtain a loan up to a maximum amount of £75,000. The scheme is financed by charging a 'premium' of 2.5% over the current overdraft rates on 70% of the loan (this equals 1.75% on the total loan). The premiums are used to form an insurance fund from which any bank that finds a loan is not recoverable may get back 70% of the amount due. Again with this scheme all available business assets are pledged as security. A business plan must be produced and financial accounts on a quarterly basis provided to the bank.

Medium-Term Loans

The banks provide a range of medium-term loans for periods up to ten years or even longer to finance business which is not suitable for overdraft type funding. A term loan is usually fixed in amount, interest payable and repayment dates. The business pays interest on the full amount of borrowing agreed and is required to make the repayments agreed over the time period (term) of the loan. This type of loan has the advantage of a positive time commitment unlike an overdraft which can be recalled at any time by the bank. However if a fluctuating amount of borrowing is required the borrower will continue to have to pay interest on the full amount of the agreed loan, which may make this type of borrowing more expensive than an overdraft.

Other short-term sources of funds

Apart from borrowing from banks and similar financial institutions there are a number of other common ways of raising capital. Many organisations obtain assets by leasing them or taking out hire purchase from specialised providers of this type of finance. In this type of deal the main feature is that the person providing the finance retains the legal ownership of the asset concerned, at least for a long enough period for him to recoup his outlay. Often the person using the asset may buy it for a nominal sum at the end of an agreed period after making regular rent payments. This type of finance is popular in certain types of business, for example, to acquire lorries, coaches and cars, where the fund provider has the security of an asset which can fairly readily be sold off, if the customer defaults.

Another method of raising funds is to 'factor' an organisation's debtors, as explained in chapter 17. The factoring company takes over the debt immediately after the sale is made in exchange for cash. Needless to say the cash payment is 'discounted' to allow the factor a return on his funds and to cover other services provided. Sometimes the service may include operating all the invoicing and sales ledger activity. Another aspect is who covers bad debts? Quite clearly there has to be a precise understanding in this issue. If the factor carries the risk of bad debt he will usually have to evaluate the credit risk on all the business customers.

This type of fund raising, whether leasing or factoring, has the same result as obtaining a loan from a bank. Very often the real cost measured in APR is higher than general bank lending. (The meaning of APR which means Annual Percentage Rate of Interest is defined in the next chapter.) In some circumstances the tax relief on rent payments may make the deal attractive but it is usually because this type of finance is associated with riskier business, which the specific security from the asset makes it possible for the lender to provide.

Debtors and Creditors

The management of debtors is in itself a very important contribution to cash resources. How long a credit period is given to customers, whether to offer discounts to encourage early payment, and the efficient collection of debt money is vital. In a badly managed firm debtors may take, for example, two months to pay even though they are only allowed one months credit officially. If annual sales are £1,200,000 then one months sales could be $1/12 \times 1,200,000 =$ £100,000. Thus if debtors can be persuaded to pay on time the organisation will immediately have an extra sum of £100,000 in its bank account.

A similar process should be looked at when buying goods. Buying goods on credit is similar to obtaining a short-term loan. If goods can be bought from supplier A for £50,000 for immediate cash or supplier B for £50,000 on one months credit, then the goods should be bought from B. Trade Credit offered by suppliers is an important aspect of buying goods and can provide useful short-term funds. Negotiations with suppliers are the key, rather than simply failing to pay on time!

Internally Generated Funds

It would be wrong not to mention the vital role of profits in providing funds in a business. Making profits and retaining them in the business is the largest source of growth funds most organisations have. The amount retained is clearly at the discretion of the owners who have to decide how much of available profit to withdraw each year for themselves.

Internally generated funds can provide a long-term source of finance. However in a rapidly growing business which is seeking to acquire long-term assets, it may be necessary to find other sources of long-term funds.

Long-Term Funds: Equity

Equity Capital, or in other words the funds provided by the ordinary shareholders in a limited company, and the proprietors stake in sole traders or partnerships, has a vital role to play in financing a business.

It not only provides the risk capital, but also has the power to control the way the business is run, provided a majority of votes are controlled. To keep control of a business may be a very important element influencing the way the equity capital is expanded. Companies often appeal directly to existing shareholders for new funds. Very often when new funds are needed the existing majority owners of capital do not themselves have sufficient additional cash to put into the business. Borrowing money does not of course give voting rights to the lender and may be preferred, but there is a limit to the proportion of funds which can safely be borrowed.

If any young expanding business decides on an equity issue it will need to produce evidence of its prospects. Normally three years of satisfactory past results are needed to encourage suitable financial institutions such as merchant banks to take an interest. Such professional investors are generally looking for businesses that will ultimately be large and successful enough to float on the Stock Exchange, which would normally require a minimum annual profit of at least £500,000. In recent years the development of markets for smaller business called the Unlisted Securities Market and the Over the Counter Market have encouraged the provision of equity funds to businesses at the stage before they are successful enough for a full Stock Exchange Listing. The main point about the Stock Market is that it is a secondary market. This means that it comprises sales of shares by existing shareholders who wish to dispose of their holdings to other investors. Primary markets provide funds directly to a company. The Stock Market does however act, to a more limited extent, as a primary market, where a company itself sells new shares directly to investors, but normally only for larger companies. However the presence of the secondary market is very important to investors since it enables them to sell any shares they hold at a proper market price, when they want to. The prospect of being able to do this encourages investment of funds.

Long-Term Funds other than Equity

Apart from equity capital there is the possibility of issuing Preference Shares. These offer an attractive position to existing equity holders since they do not normally give a vote. In addition preference shareholders are entitled to a predetermined level of dividend only if there are adequate profits. However from the point of view of an investor a preference share is normally not very attractive since the security if offers, behind all the creditors of the business, is not adequate for the limited return.

Usually, therefore, a business will issue Loan Stock, often called Debentures. In many ways the investor in loan stock takes a similar view to the banker lending funds. Having viewed the prospects of the company the risk will be assessed. A lower risk and interest rate will attach to a secured loan with a mortgage charge, than to an unsecured loan. In addition to the risk of a business failing, the lender is also likely to lose through inflation, since repayment of the debt and the interest paid is usually in fixed money terms. The interest rate demanded by lenders will have to cover inflation as well as an adequate risk return. The date of repayment for debentures is normally fixed in advanced. In highly inflationary periods lenders become less prepared to give long-term loans and may restrict them to from five to ten years.

Other Issues Relating to Raising Funds

This chapter has only covered the very broad issues concerned with major forms of fund raising for private business. There has not been any extensive discussion of grants made available by the government, which cover a wide range of schemes. Apart from specific grants to industries to encourage employment and investment in new technology, there are some fiscal advantages offered through the Business Expansion Scheme to encourage wealthy individuals to provide equity funds for small business.

In addition to the Government, many local authorities can offer funds to help encourage inner city development. There are special agencies encouraging industry in rural areas, and many agencies involved with developing suitable premises to accommodate small business. Despite all these various incentives, however, most organisations still require to obtain the majority of their funding from the sources described. Balancing the funds with the asset investment remains vital to the success of any business, large or small.

Assignment Exercises

39.1A The following abbreviated Balance Sheet is for ABC Ltd a private company who have asked you for a loan.

ABC Ltd
Balance Sheet 31 December 19-1

			£
Fixed Assets			
Cost		150,000	
less depreciation		60,000	90,000
Current Assets			
Inventory of cost		80,000	
Trade Debtors and repayments		40,000	
		120,000	
less Current Liabilities			
Trade Creditors	50,000		
Bank Overdraft	40,000	90,000	30,000
			120,000
Share Capital			
Ordinary Shares		50,000	
Reserves			
Profit and Loss Account		20,000	
		70,000	
Loans			
15% Debentures (secured)		50,000	120,000

(*a*) Assess the balance sheet in terms of likely risk to a lender.
(*b*) What questions about the business would you put to the directors?

39.2A A small manufacturing business wants to raise more finance to fund additional fixed assets which will have a life of 20 years. Draft a short report for the directors suggesting alternative ways of raising the funds.

39.3A Explain the importance of short-term finance for any organisation. How should this form of finance be raised and managed?

40 Simple and Compound Interest Calculations

Most financial transactions involve interest calculations since interest is the charge for using money over time. If a business wishes to borrow money it will have to pay interest on the amount it borrows. The rate of interest will depend on the going market rates and the lender's assessment of the risk associated with lending to a particular type of customer. The higher the risk the higher the rate of interest.

Simple Interest

Simple interest applies where the period involved is not greater than a year. The amount of interest due is calculated from the formula:

Amount of interest (A) = Principal amount loaned (P) ×
Rate of Interest (r) × Unit of time (t)

Example: Interest has to be calculated on a loan from a Bank of £198,000 at a rate of 12% per annum for 59 days.

Rates of interest for loans will usually be expressed on an annual basis. The unit of time will therefore be the proportion of a year (365 days) for which the loan was obtained.

Thus

$$A = P r t$$

$$A = £198,00 \times .12 \times \frac{59}{365}$$

$$A = £3,840.66$$

Note in the formula it is convenient to express r as a decimal rather than as a percentage, i.e. .12 rather than 12%.

Another illustration where simple interest is common is where a business discounts a bill of exchange with a bank. The bill of exchange represents a promise to pay (by a third party usually a customer of the business) a specified sum of money at a fixed future date.

Example: A business holds a bill of exchange which promises to pay £20,000 in 90 days time. The business wants the cash now not in 90 days and the bank quotes a discount rate of interest of 15% on this type of transaction.

$$A = P r t$$

$$A = £20,000 \times .15 \times \frac{90}{365}$$

$$A = £739.73$$

The bank will thus pay to the business the Principal sum of £20,000 less the Amount of interest £739.73 which amounts to an immediate cash advance of £19,260.27.

Note that the interest rate which the business has really paid on this transaction is more than 15%. The business has in effect borrowed £19,260.27 for 90 days and paid interest of £739.73. This is equivalent to interest of 15.6% on the amount borrowed of £19,260.27. You can check this by using the interest formula:

$$A = P r t$$

$$r = \frac{A}{P t}$$

$$r = \frac{739.73}{19,260.27 \times \dfrac{90}{365}} = 15.58\%$$

This represents the true rate of interest on the transaction as compared to the nominal rate of 15% used to work out the amount advanced on the bill of exchange. This rate is often called the annual percentage rate (APR).

In many borrowing situations it is important to note the difference between the nominal rate quoted by lender and the real rate of interest being paid. Where a loan has to be repaid by installments the real rate can be considerably higher than the nominal rate.

Example: John wants to borrow £1,000 for one year. The finance company quote interest of 10% but require £500 to be repaid after six months and the balance at the end of the year.

The interest to be paid is 10% of £1,000 =	£100

The amount borrowed will be 1,000 × ½ year =	500
500 × ½ year =	250
The equivalent amount borrowed for one year is	750

$$r = \frac{A}{P t} = \frac{100}{750 \times 1}$$

$$r = 13.33\%$$

The real rate of interest (APR) is thus 13.33% not 10%.

Compound Interest

Where a period of time greater than one year is involved the process of interest calculation becomes compound. This simply means that interest will become payable on the interest of the earlier period as well as the principal sum. If £100 is deposited in a bank for two years at 10% interest per annum, the interest earned is not twice the simple interest for one year which would be £20 (2 × £10). At the end of year one amount of simple interest of £10 would be added to the Principal and the total of £110 then reinvested for the second year at 10% which would earn £11 interest. The total interest earned over two years is thus £21.

If you compare the effect of compounding interest over a period of time with simple interest for example where the interest earned is withdrawn at the end of each year the difference is quite dramatic.

Example: Mr A invests £1,000 at 10% and allows the interest to be reinvested each year.

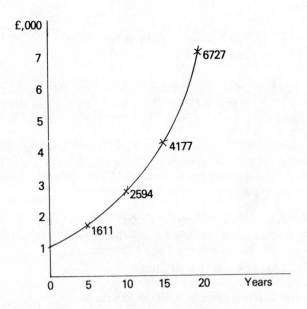

The graph shows the £1,000 increasing over 20 years to a sum of £6,727.

Compound Interest is calculated from the formula

Amount (A) = Principal (P) × (1 + rate of interest for the period (r)) × number of periods (n)

$$A = P (1 + r)^n$$

Example: What will £1,000 invested at 10% per annum compound accumulate to in 10 years?

$$A = P (1 + r)^n$$
$$= 1,000 (1 + .10)^{10}$$
$$= 2,593.74$$

The computations involved are not much problem if you have a calculator. It is also common to use tables which have been calculated for commonly used rates of interest. The tables are based on £1 invested at the rate of interest as shown in Exhibit 40.1.

Period of Compounding	*£1 at compound interest at the end of the period* Rate of interest per period			
	1%	*2%*	*5%*	*10%*
1	1.010	1.020	1.050	1.100
2	1.020	1.040	1.103	1.210
3	1.030	1.061	1.158	1.331
4	1.041	1.082	1.216	1.464
5	1.051	1.104	1.276	1.611
10	1.105	1.219	1.629	2.594
50	1.645	2.692	11.462	117.391

Example of a compound interest table

Exhibit 40.1

Example: You want to know what £500 will accumulate to over three years at 5% per annum interest.

The table shows that £1 invested for 3 periods at 5% will amount to £1.158. thus £500 will amount to £1.158 × 500 = £579.

If the compounding process is to take place more often than annually – the rate of interest must be changed to the rate for the compounding period rather than for a year.

Example: What will £500 accumulate to over three years at 5% per annum interest compounded on a quarterly basis?

The periods are now three months and therefore in total there are 12 periods in all. The rate of interest per period will be .05 ÷ 4 = .0125.

$$A = P (1 + r)^n = 500 (1.0125)^{12}$$

$$A = 580.38$$

Notice that compounding quarterly as compared to annually, as in the previous example, makes a small difference of just over £1 to the accumulated amount. Because for most purposes the difference between annual and more frequent compounding is not material this text will normally use annual compounding.

It is sometimes useful to calculate the rate of return which an increase on an investment represents over a period of time.

Example: Jones bought a house for £10,000 on 1 January 19-1 and sold it for £12,100 on 31 December 19-2. What rate of return does this represent?

Using the tables requires the figures to be expressed in terms of £1. In this case 10,000:12,100 is equivalent to 1:1.210 for a two year period.

Looking across the table on the row for 2 periods compounding it can be seen that the return is equivalent to 10%.

Or Using the formula

$$A = P (1 + r)^n$$

$$r = \sqrt[n]{\frac{A}{P}} - 1 = \sqrt[2]{\frac{12,100}{10,000}} - 1$$

$$= .1 \text{ or } 10\%.$$

Assignment Exercises

40.1
(a) What interest will be paid on a loan of £5,300 for 62 days at 17%?
(b) A bank offers to discount a bill of exchange for £9,000 with an outstanding period of 70 days at 19% interest. What will the bank pay for the bill of exchange.

40.2A What is the real rate of interest involved in discounting the bill of exchange in 40.1?

40.3 Smith borrows £1,000 on 1 January 19-1 from a moneylender at an interest charge of £200. The repayment terms are £250 at the end of March, June, September and December 19-1. What real rate of interest is he paying?

40.4 How much interest is earned if £4,000 is held for 10 years at 10% p.a. interest compound?

40.5A How much interest would have been earned if the compounding had been applied half-yearly?

40.6A Jones bought some shares on 1 January 19-1 for £8,000 and sold them 4 years later on 31 December 19-4 for £9,728. What compound rate of interest does this increase represent?

41 Present Value

In the previous chapter we calculated that if £1,000 were invested at compound interest of 10% for 10 years it would accumulate to £2,594.

If we posed this question the other way round and asked what would be the value today of £2,594 if received 10 years into the future assuming interest at 10% the answer is a present value of £1,000.

Present value is simply the reciprocal of compound interest and is a useful approach to solving a number of investment problems.

The formula for compound interest is:

$$A = P(1 + r)^n$$

For the present value calculation we know the Amount (A) and wish to calculate the Principal (P). Divide both sides by $(1 + r)^n$ gives

$$P = \frac{A}{(1+r)^n}$$

Example: You are promised a cash gift of £10,000 in two years time. The current rates of interest which you could obtain for this sum is 15%. What is its present value

$$P = \frac{A}{(1 + r)^n} = \frac{10,000}{(1.15)^2}$$

$$\text{Present Value } P = £7,561.4$$

As with compound interest the use of tables of present values is quite common. For example the values are shown here for the present value of £1 at a rate of interest of 10%. A full table is included in the appendix.

Periods	10%
1	.909
2	.826
3	.751
4	.683
5	.621

Example: If you are offered £1,000 at the end of each of the next five years in settlement of a debt of £4,000 should you accept? Assume interest at 10%.

			£
Year 1	£1,000 × .909 =		909
2	£1,000 × .826 =		826
3	£1,000 × .751 =		751
4	£1,000 × .683 =		683
5	£1,000 × .621 =		621
Present Value			3,790

The Present value of the five payments is £3,790 which is worth a little less than the debt of £4,000.

Sometimes in investment situations we happen to know in advance the Principal sum and the Amount and want to work out the rate of interest which completes the equation. This rate of interest is often called the internal rate of return.

Example: A friend offers to sell you the lease on some property which will entitle you to equal rent payments at the end of each of the next three years of £1,000.

He wants £2,550 for the lease and you want to calculate what interest rate is included in the deal.

This can be done by trial and error using the present value tables in the appendix. Firstly select a rate of interest as a guess − say 5%.

Year	£		Factor at 5%		£
1	1,000	×	.952	=	952
2	1,000	×	.907	=	907
3	1,000	×	.864	=	864
					2,723

At five per cent interest the present value exceeds the amount asked for the lease of £2,550. A higher rate of interest will be required to reduce the amount closer to target. Try 8% and 9%:

Year	£		Factor at 8%		£		9%		£
1	1,000	×	.926	=	926	×	.917	=	917
2	1,000	×	.857	=	857	×	.842	=	842
3	1,000	×	.794	=	794	×	.772	=	772
					2,577				2,531

The rate of interest which will produce a present value of £2,550 lies between 8% and 9%. If we want to be more exact we can interpolate on an approximate basis as follows:

$$8\% \text{ gives} \qquad 2,577$$
$$-2,550$$
$$9\% \qquad\qquad \underline{2,531} \qquad\qquad 19$$
$$\underline{46}$$

2,550 is thus $\dfrac{19}{46}$ of 1% below 9%

i.e. $9 - .41 = 8.59\%$

Annuities

An annuity is a series, or one of a series, of equal payments at fixed intervals. For example, rent payable every month, quarter or year, is one form of annuity. The term annuity originated in the field of insurance where in exchange for a lump sum payment or a series of premiums a regular payment would be made to the annuitant during his life. Regular payments such as rents or purchase by instalments occur frequently in business and it is, therefore, useful to know something about the calculation of annuities.

In practice there are a number of different kinds of annuity varying mainly in the details of when the regular payments are made, for example at the beginning or end of the period. In this chapter attention is centred entirely on the Ordinary Annuity in which the equal periodic payments occur at the end of the period. In practice, with a little thought it will be possible to handle most situations with a knowledge of how to calculate an Ordinary Annuity.

Formula for the Amount of an Ordinary Annuity

The amount of an annuity of £1 per period for three periods at 5 per cent interest might be determined as follows:

The first rent payment of £1 accumulates at 5 per cent interest for two periods and grows to:

$$£1 (1+0.05)^2 = £1.1025$$

The second rent payment of £1 accumulates at 5 per cent interest for one period and grows to: £1.05

The third rent is due at the end of the annuity period £1.00

These added up to £3.1525

To develop the formula for the annuity we need to examine the relationship between compound interest, and an annuity of the amount of interest. If £1 is invested for two periods at 5 per cent interest we have shown above that it will accumulate to £1.1025. Deducting the original investment from this amount we are left with the compound interest on £1 for two periods as £0.1025. This amount is simply the amount of an annuity of 5 per cent of £1 for two periods at 5 per cent.

This can be set down as:

$$0.05 \times \text{Annuity} = 1\,(1 + 0.05)^2 - 1$$

or

$$\text{Annuity} = 1\,\frac{(1 + 0.05)^2 - 1}{0.05} = \frac{(1.05)^2 - 1}{0.05}$$

Substituting generalized letters into the formula

$$\text{Annuity} = R\,\frac{(1 + r)^n - 1}{r}$$

Where R = the annuity per period.

As in previous examples tables are available calculated on the basis of £1 to assist calculations; see the Appendix.

Example: A company plans to invest £1,000 at the end of the year for each of the next five years at an interest rate of 5 per cent per annum. How much will have accumulated at the end of the fifth year?

$$£1,000\frac{(1 + 0.05)^5 - 1}{.05} = £5,525.631$$

or using tables

$$£1,000 \times 5.526 = £5,526$$

It will frequently be useful to know the amount required by way of periodic rents to accumulate to a known future sum, for example when establishing a sinking fund.

It has already been established that where the amount of an annuity = A

$$A = R\,\frac{(1 + r)^n - 1}{r}$$

$$R = \frac{Ar}{(1 + r)^n - 1}$$

Example: A company wishes to set aside equal annual amounts at the end of each year of the next four years, to accumulate to a fund of £5,000 for the replacement of assets. The amounts set aside will be invested at 6 per cent per annum interest. What amounts should be set aside?

$$R = \frac{Ar}{(1 + r)^n - 1} = \frac{5,000(0.06)}{(1.06)^4 - 1} = £1,142.9578$$

This figure can be proved correct by the table below worked (as would be normal) to the nearest £1.

	Deposit £	Interest £	Increase in fund £	Balance of fund £
End of year 1	1,143	–	1,143	1,143
End of year 2	1,143	69	1,212	2,355
End of year 3	1,143	141	1,284	3,639
End of year 4	1,143	218	1,361	5,000

Example: What amount invested annually at 5 per cent per annum will provide £1 in five years time?

$$R = \frac{Ar}{(1+r)^n - 1} = \frac{1 (0.05)}{(1.05)^5 - 1} = £0.180975$$

The Present Value of Annuities

It will often be necessary to calculate the present value of an annuity to evaluate a business problem. The present value of an annuity is the amount which if it were invested now at compound interest would be just sufficient to allow for the withdrawal of equal amounts (rents) at the end of a fixed number of periods. For example, we may wish to know whether to pay £135 cash now for a television or five instalments of £30 over the next two-and-a-half years instead. By converting the five instalments to a present cash value we can make direct comparison with the £135 cash price. If the present value of the annuity is more than £135 we should choose to pay cash. If, however, it comes to less than £135 the instalment method is cheaper. The result obtained will depend on the rate of interest used in the calculation.

The present value of an annuity will be equal to the sum of the present values of every individual rent payment. This can be illustrated in the above example, assuming an 8 per cent rate of interest. The calculation shows it better at this rate of interest to pay by instalment.

Period	£		Present Value Multiplier from Tables		£
1	30	×	0.962	=	28.86
2	30	×	0.925	=	27.75
3	30	×	0.889	=	26.67
4	30	×	0.855	=	25.65
5	30	×	0.822	=	24.66
					133.59

(*Note:* when taking a half-yearly period the annual rate of interest is halved. The multiplier is therefore from the 4 per cent column of the Present Value tables.)

The formula for finding the present value of an ordinary annuity is developed as follows:

Compound discount (equivalent to compound interest) is the amount by which the total investment at compound interest will exceed the original capital. On the basis of £1:

$$\text{Discount} = 1 - \frac{1}{(1+r)^n}$$

By the same process of argument that was used when developing the formula for an ordinary annuity, it can be shown that the compound discount on £1 at 5 per cent is equal to 5 per cent of the present value of an annuity of £1. Thus

$$r \times \text{Present Value} = 1 - \frac{1}{(1+r)^n}$$

$$\text{Present Value} = \left[\frac{1 - \dfrac{1}{(1+r)^n}}{r} \right]$$

Tables are given in the Appendix to show the present values of an annuity of £1.

Example: (details per previous example). The present value of five half-yearly payments of £30 at 8 per cent per annum would be:

$$R = \left[\frac{1 - \dfrac{1}{(1+r)^n}}{r} \right] = 30 \left[\frac{1 - \dfrac{1}{(1+0.04)^5}}{0.04} \right] = £133.57$$

or using the tables $30 \times 4.452 = £133.56$.

Finally, to prove that the present value of an annuity is the amount which if it were invested now at compound interest would be just sufficient to allow for the withdrawal of equal amounts at the end of a fixed number of periods, we can show that the present value of £133.57 just calculated would fulfil this condition for withdrawals of £30 over five half-yearly periods with interest at 8 per cent per annum.

		£	
Start		133.57	
Period 1	Interest	5.34	(133.57 at 8 per cent for 6 months)
	Payment	(30.00)	
Balance		108.91	
Period 2	Interest	4.35	
	Payment	(30.00)	
Balance		83.26	
Period 3	Interest	3.33	
	Payment	(30.00)	
Balance		56.59	
Period 4	Interest	2.26	
	Payment	(30.00)	
Balance		28.85	
Period 5	Interest	1.15	
	Payment	(30.00)	
Balance		00.00	

Assignment Exercises

41.1 A property developer offers to buy your rights under a lease to rents amounting to £5,000 p.a. for the next seven years. He offers you an immediate cash sum of £20,000. You can invest the money at 12% p.a. interest. Should the offer be accepted?

41.2A Using the information in question 41.1 what interest rate would exactly equate the developers' offer to the rental income?

41.3 A company obtains a loan of £100,000 for five years. One of the conditions of the loan is that the company will each year pay an equal amount into a sinking fund to accumulate over the five years to the amount of the loan repayable. The sinking fund will earn interest at 10% p.a. How much must be paid into the sinking fund each year?

41.4A Using the data in 41.3 how much would the amount paid into the sinking fund by if the interest rate was changed to 15% p.a.?

42 Capital Budgeting

In the budgeting chapters earlier in the book attention was given to the application of budgets in the context of management control of operations. Operating budgets of this kind concentrate mainly on the control of activity within the next twelve months. Thus in this context it is not usual to include the specific interest cost of these activities since it could make the calculations over detailed and complex and would not make a significant difference to the decisions made.

When however the business is planning investment in fixed assets or things which involve a long term committment of the organisations resources then the budgeting process should include interest as on important cost element in the decision about whether to invest or not. This process is what is termed Capital Budgeting.

The process of evaluating investments taking into account interest requires that cash budgets are dealt with rather than the figures used in profit calculations. In profit calculation for example depreciation of fixed assets is included in the expenses. However since depreciation does not involve cash − it is not relevant for capital budgeting. Interest is only relevant to cash flows and it is these that Capital Budgeting concentrates on. The two aspects of cash flows on an investment are the cash outflows on the acqustion and setting up of the project and the cash inflows which are expected to be generated. It is the balance between outflow and inflow which determines whether the investment is worthwhile.

Investment Outlays

The cash outlay involved in an investment will include a variety of different items. If for example the investment is in plant and machinery the outlay will include not only the invoice cost of the equipment bought − but also the cost of installation, commissioning which means the costs of a period of adjustment until it operates at full efficiency, and possibly training of new personnel. In addition the introduction of new plant and machinery might involve extra funds for working capital tied up in the operation.

Example: Progress Ltd is planning to introduce new machines. The outlays anticipated on the acquisition are as follows:

	Cash Flow – Outlay
	£
Invoice Cost of Machines	50,000
Carriage Inward	2,000
Installation – cost of wages of own employees	1,000
	53,000
Cost of materials and wages in commissioning machines	5,000
Training Cost – Wages of operatives	2,000
	60,000
Additional Working Capital	14,000
Cash Outlay	74,000

If the outlays in the Example for Progress Ltd had been on machinery designed to replace existing equipment – perhaps justified by claims of greater efficiency for the new machines – then the decision would be taken based on the incremental outlays compared to the incremental inflows – i.e. the net additional cash required to be invested on the new scheme compared to the additional cash earned or saved.

Thus in the example the additional outlay comparing with existing machines would not include working capital (assuming outputs are the same) since this is already required in the existing set-up. Also the buying of new equipment – implies that the old can be sold – thus the cash from sale should be deducted from the outlay

		£
i.e.	Cost of Machines and installations etc.	60,000
	less Sale of old machines	10,000
	Net Cash Outlay	50,000

The net outlay of £50,000 will then be compared with the cash saved by using the new process.

This incremental approach is important for assessing improvements and where the equipment is for example part of a large factory where it will be impossible to identify all the cash flow implications of one small part of the total unit.

The Cash outflows on an investment in a large project may be spread over a number of periods. The development can spread over several years from its first inception. It may therefore be necessary to discount back the outlays to a present value at the start of the project.

Example: The cash outlays on a new factory development were estimated as follows:

		£
Year 1	Development and Buildings	100,000
2	Installation of Equipment	50,000
3	Commissioning	30,000
		180,000

The Present Value of these outflows if interest is assumed to be 10% would be:

Period	£			£
1	100,000 ×	.909	=	90,900
2	50,000 ×	.826	=	41,300
3	30,000 ×	.751	=	22,530
	Present Value			£154,730

The Present Value of outlays at the start of the project – often called period 0 – is £154,730. This figure would be compared with the Present Value of Inflows.

An important aspect of investment cash flows is that they will give rise to tax implications. The purchase of Plant and Machinery for example will give rise to allowances which can be deducted from taxable income. Thus for a company which buys a new machine for £100,000 and pays Corporation Tax[1] at 52% on its profits the cash flows will be firstly an outlay on purchase of £100,000 secondly its tax bill when due for payment will be reduced by 52% of £100,000 i.e. £52,000. The machine this costs a net amount of £48,000 although since tax payments lag behind actual events the £52,000 saving of tax may be spread over the remaining life of the asset.

The actual calculation of tax payments can be complex and requires a detailed knowledge of the tax laws, which are beyond the scope of this book. However in principle all that needs to be taken into account are the cash outflows or inflows for tax which will arise from the investment decision. These may have to be calculated by a person competent in tax matters.

Cash Inflows

The other aspect of the Capital Budgeting process is to estimate the cash which will be generated by the new investment.

If the investment is in something new – then the estimates will be cash budgets of the sales and expenses expected to be generated by the new investment. The approach will be exactly the same as for the operating cash budgets prepared for management in planning its cash requirements – except that the requirement here is usually for the annual figures over the anticipated life of the investment, rather than on a month by month basis.

---

1. Corporation Tax rates are subject to change in the Finance Act every year.

If the investment is an improvement or replacement of an existing process then the cash inflow will be the savings expected as compared to the existing situation.

As with the cash outflows the net inflows expected from an investment will be subject to tax. The tax consequences of the new business must be worked out and the cash payments for tax included in the calculation of net cash inflows.

Example: The expected results from buying a new machine for £6,000 have been estimated to produce sales of £6,000 per annum for four years and the production costs would be £2,500 for materials, labour and other cash outlays. Working Capital required will be £2,000 which will be recoverable at the end of the fourth year. Depreciation per annum would be £1,500 and the company pays Corporation tax nine months after its accounting year end at 52%.

The profit expected each year is thus:

		£
Sales		6,000
Material, Labour and other costs	2,500	
Depreciation	1,500	4,000
		2,000
Corporation Tax		1,040
Net Profit		960

But for Capital Budgeting the cash flow analysis would be:

Investment Outlay	Year 1	2	3	4	5
Cost of Machine	(6,000)				
Working Capital	(2,000)			2,000	
Taxation Allowance on Capital Expenditure		3,220			
	(8,000)	3,220	–	2,000	–
Cash Flows					
Sales	6,000	6,000	6,000	6,000	
Costs of Material and Labour etc	(2,500)	(2,500)	(2,500)	(2,500)	
Tax (52% × 3,500)		(1,820)	(1,820)	(1,820)	(1,820)
	3,500	1,680	1,680	1,680	(1,820)

Exhibit 42.1

The evaluation of the budgeted cash flows will be dealt with in the next chapter.

Assignment Exercises (all tax rates given for illustration only).

42.1 The Raynor Company's project engineers have made the following estimates of costs on a new project:
19-1

1 January	Rent paid for one year to 31 December 19-1 on premises for the plant	£5,000
31 January	Machinery purchased	£50,000
31 March	Installation costs paid for machinery	£10,000
31 December	Cost of Wages and material in commissioning plant	£15,000

19-2

1 January	Rent paid for year to 31 December 19-2	£5,000
31 March	Further commissioning costs	£8,000
30 June	Training costs for labour	£2,000
30 September	Working Capital provided for inventories and debtors (extra to that required in existing plant)	£10,000
31 December	Cash received from scrap value of old plant replaced by the project	£8,000

Ignoring taxation prepare a statement of the cash outlay on the project in 19-1 and 19-2. The plant is estimated to be in full use on 1 October 19-2.

42.2 Using the data in question 42.1 and assuming that the company is taxed at a rate of 50%, nine months after the end of its financial year on the 31 December, show the impact of tax on the cash flows. For tax purposes the company can obtain 100% allowance on the cost of machinery in its assessment based on 19-1. The scrap value cash in 19-2 will be fully taxable in that year.

42.3 Using the net of tax cash flows produced in question 42.2 and assuming an interest rate of 15%, what is the present value of the cash flows at the start of the project?

42.4A The annual profit expected from a new project is calculated as follows:

		£
Sales		50,000
Materials, Labour and Overheads	20,000	
Depreciation	5,000	
		25,000
Net Profit before tax		25,000
Corporation Tax at 50%		12,500
Net Profit after tax		12,500

The investment in machinery will take place on 1 July 19-1 amounting to £25,000 it will last five years with no residual value. Working Capital will also be required from 1 July 19-1 amounting to £10,000 and will be recovered at the end of the project. Tax allowances of 100% of the cost of machinery can be claimed in the first year. Tax at the rate of 50% of profits is payable 9 months after the accounting year end which is 30 June. Profits on the project will start immediately the machinery is installed.

Prepare a budget of the cash flows arising from the project.

42.5A What is the Present Value of the Net Cash flows in question 42.4A if the interest rate is 10% p.a.?

42.6A The installed and commissioned cost of a new machine is estimated to be £100,000. Corporation Tax payable will be reduced by 52% of the cost of machinery in the year following its purchase. The new machinery is estimated to have a five year life with nil residual value and will be depreciated straight line. The new machine replaces an old piece of equipment which would be depreciated over the next five years at £3,000 per year, if not replaced, and would then have a nil book value. The new equipment is estimated to save material costs each years of £30,000. The old equipment could be sold (in the first year) for £6,000, but tax at 52% would be payable next year. All profits are taxed at 52% payable a year after the accounting date.

Prepare the cash flow statement necessary to evaluate the project.

How will the reported profits change in the financial accounts?

43 Capital Expenditure Evaluation I

There are several ways of working out whether or not a capital expenditure is worthwhile. The simplest systems do not include interest in the evaluation and are therefore deficient in this important respect. They are however frequently used and may be a worthwhile addition to the more complete evaluations which include interest.

Payback

This measures the time taken to recover the cash outlay on the project. If we use the data on cash flows from Exhibit 42.1 the cash figures are as follows:

Year	Investment Outlay £	Cash Inflow £	Net Cash Flow £	Cumulative Cash Flow £
1	(8,000)	3,500	(4,500)	(4,500)
2	3,220	1,680	4,900	400
3	–	1,680	1,680	2,080
4	2,000	1,680	3,680	5,760
5	–	(1,820)	(1,820)	3,940

The net cash flow is negative in the first year but becomes positive in the second year. To work out the time when the cash outlay is recovered assuming the cash flows evenly during ther year we calculate

$$\frac{4,500}{4,900} \times 365 \text{ days} = 335 \text{ days}.$$

Thus the payback on this project occurs after 1 year 335 days or approximately 1.92 years.

Firms using payback as a method of evaluation would normally have a period fixed as a cut off point. For example if the cut off time were 3 years then all projects which had a payback of more than 3 years would be rejected.

The advantage of the payback method is that it emphasises the early return of cash which may be of utmost importance to a firm with liquidity problems. The disadvantage it has is that it ignores the results after payback has been achieved. For example if we had a project which showed a cumulative cash flow of: year 1 £(4,500) and year 2 £400 and no further cash flows then the payback would still be 1.92

years and no regard is given to subsequent years. It would therefore be given the same evaluation as the previous example where cash flows continued into the future. Whilst in this case the difference between the two would be clear – in a more complicated case it may not be easy to discriminate between alternatives.

Accounting Rate of Return

This is defined as: $\dfrac{\text{Average annual net profit after tax}}{\text{Average investment}}$

If again we use the information from Exhibit 42.1 in the previous chapter we know that the expected profit after tax in each of the four years is expected to be £960. The investment in machinery is £6,000 at the start and nil at the end assuming it is being depreciated straight line. The average investment would normally be calculated at $\frac{1}{2}$ the opening value + closing value i.e. $\frac{1}{2}$ (6,000 + 0) = £3,000. The working capital remains constant at £2,000 – the calculation for working capital is the same $\frac{1}{2}$ (2,000 + 2,000) = £2,000. Thus the total average investment would be £3,000 + £2,000 = £5,000. The tax relief on the capital expenditure is included with the corporation tax assessed on profits.

The return is therefore $\dfrac{960}{5,000}$ = 19.2%.

This accounting rate of return relates to the results shown in the annual accounts. However as an average it should not be forgotten that there will be significant differences between the start and end of the projects life. In the example given the figures each year would be:

Net Profit	Year 1	Year 2	Year 3	Year 4
Net Book Value of Machine + Working Capital at mid-year	$\dfrac{960}{7,250} = 13.2\%$	$\dfrac{960}{5,720} = 16.7\%$	$\dfrac{960}{4,250} = 22.6\%$	$\dfrac{960}{2,750} = 34.9\%$

With a depreciating asset the rate of return appears to increase as the net book value declines, even though profits are constant.

Present Value and Internal Rate of Return

So far the methods employed to evaluate capital expenditure have ignored interest which means that only in certain circumstances would these methods approximate to the correct evaluation employing compound interest. Taking the facts again from the previous example in Exhibit 42.1 we can calculate the return assuming a required rate of interest of 15%.

	Investment Outlay	Cash Inflow	Net Cash Flow
1	(8,000)	3,500	(4,500)
2	3,220	1,680	4,900
3		1,680	1,680
4	2,000	1,680	3,680
5		(1,820)	1,820

	Investment Outlay			Cash Inflow			Net Cash Flow	
1	(8,000) × .870 =	(6,960)	3,500 × .870 =	3,045		(4,500) × .870 =	(3,915)
2	3,220 × .756 =	2,434	1,680 × .756 =	1,270		4,900 × .756 =	3,704
3	–	–	1,680 × .658 =	1,105		1,680 × .658 =	1,105
4	2,000 × .572 =	1,144	1,680 × .572 =	961		3,680 × .572 =	2,105
5	–	–	(1,820) × .497 =	(904)		(1,820) × .497 =	(904)
		(3,382)		5,477			2,095

The Net Present Value of this project using an interest rate of 15% is £2,095, which indicates that the discounted value of the inflows exceeds the discounted value of the investment outlay by this net amount. The project is therefore worthwhile provided the funds of the business do not cost more than 15%.

The Internal Rate of Return is the rate of interest which will when applied to the cash flows equate Investment Outlay and Cash Inflow or in other words discount the Net Cash Flow to zero.

As was previously illustrated this is done by trial and error. Using the rates from the tables at 50% and 60% we get

Year	Net Cash Flow	r = 50% factor		r = 60% factor	
1	(4,500)	.667	(3,001)	.625	(2,812)
2	4,900	.444	2,176	.391	1,916
3	1,680	.296	497	.244	410
4	3,680	.198	729	.153	563
5	(1,820)	.132	(240)	.095	(173)
Net Present Value			161		(96)

Interpolating between the two one can estimate that the rate producing a Net Present Value of zero will fall $\frac{96}{257} \times$ 10% i.e. 4% below 60% i.e. at approximately 56% which is the Internal Rate of Return on the Project. The actual return in this project is therefore well above the cost of capital to the company – assuming that this is 15%.

Assignment Exercises

43.1 A project to install new equipment has the following estimated cash flows:

Year	Investment Outlay	Cash Inflow	Net Cash Flor
1	20,000	(11,000)	9,000
2	–	(6,000)	(6,000)
3	–	(3,000)	(3,000)
4	(2,000)	–	(2,000)
	18,000	(20,000)	(2,000)

(figures in brackets represent cash inflows)

What is the payback period for the project?

43.2 Using the data in 43.1 calculate the Net Present Value of the project with a discount rate of 10%.

43.3 Using the data in 43.1 calculate the Internal Rate of Return generated by the project.

43.4A Project Delta involves the outlay of £400,000 at the start of the project with net cash inflow of £200,000 at the end of year 1 and £100,000 at the end of year 2 and £300,000 at the end of year 3.

Calculate — payback period, internal rate of return and net present value with interest at 15%.

43.5A The Rathbone Company buys a machine for £100,000 which will be depreciated straight line over five years to a residual value of £5,000. The Profits estimated on the project will be as follows (for each of the five years)

		£
Sales		60,000
Operating Costs	30,000	
Depreciation	19,000	
		49,000
Net Profit		11,000

Ignoring taxation — what is the accounting rate of return?

43.6A Using the data in 43.5A calculate the internal rate of return. Assume cash arises in the same year as sales — and no working capital is required.

44 Capital Expenditure Evaluation II

In the majority of cases both the Present Value method and the Internal Rate of Return method will give the same result. In certain circumstances there can be conflict and it is necessary therefore to know which method is yielding the right result.

The circumstances in which the conflict arises is where projects are mutually exclusive − that is where only one can be chosen − and where there are differences in the timing of cash flows or in the size of cash flows on the projects.

Example: The Cash Investment in each of two projects is £10,000 Project A has a cash inflow in year 2 of £13,000 whilst Project B for a cash inflow in year 5 of £17,620.

Assuming that the rate of interest used by the company is 10% then the Present Value of the projects is

	Cash Outlay Year 0	Cash Inflow Year 2	Year 5	Present Value Factor at 10%	P.V. of Inflow	Net Present Value
Project A	10,000	13,000		.826	10,739	738
Project B	10,000		17,620	.621	10,942	942

Exhibit 44.1

i.e. Project B would be selected.

The Internal Rate of Return on these cash flows is:
Project A approximately 14% (13,000 × .769 = 9,997)
and Project B approximately 12% (17,620 × .567 = 9,991)
i.e. Project A would be selected.

The conflict in the two measures arises because of the difference in the timing of cash flows between the two alternative investments. Project A produces its cash inflow in year 2 whereas Project B is delayed until year 5. To determine which method is the best selector − the opportunity value of the cash funds generated has to be considered, i.e. what rate of return can be earned on the funds elsewhere. It Project A's inflow can be reinvested at 14% then it is the best choice. However if only 10% can be generated then B is better.

This problem could be looked at rather like a bank deposit problem. Up until the end of year 2 both A & B are overdrawn by £10,000. At the end of year 2 project A receives £13,000 and thus goes into credit for year 3, 4 and 5. if interest is less than 14%, whereas project B stays overdrawn until the end of year 5. Numerically the accounts would be as follows if 10% and 14% interest were charged and earned in the account.

	Project A		Project B	
	using 10%	using 14%	using 10%	using 14%
Year 0	(10,000)	(10,000)	(10,000)	(10,000)
Year 1 interest	(1,000)	(1,400)	(1,000)	(1,400)
	(11,000)	(11,400)	(11,000)	(11,400)
Year 2 interest	(1,100)	(1,596)	(1,100)	(1,596)
cash	13,000	13,000	(12,100)	(12,990)
	900	Say 0		
Year 3 interest	90		(1,210)	(1,819)
	990		(13,310)	(14,815)
Year 4 interest	99		(1,331)	(2,074)
	1,089		(14,641)	(16,889)
Year 5 interest	109		(1,464)	(2,365)
cash	–		17,620	17,620
	1,198	0	1,515	(1,634)

As we showed using the present value approach project B has accumulated a bigger value at the end of the project using 10%. Notice that these end values in year 5 can be discounted back to the Net Present Value at the start, i.e. $1,198 \times .621 = 744$ and $1,515 \times .621 = 941$ (small differences are due to rounding errors). Using 14% interest Project A just breaks even whilst Project B loses – remaining in overdraft!

Thus the assumption about what the finds generated will earn elsewhere can be crucial in this type of choice where it is a question of deciding between alternatives which are mutually exclusive. As a rule of thumb many firms chose the Net Present Value since the assumption about the rate of interest earned is likely to be realistic – but this is by no means always so.

The problem just considered also raises the difficulty in general of comparing projects which have different life cycles. For example one project may involve buying equipment which requires replacement every two years whilst another requires replacement every five years. In comparing the alternatives it may be helpful to work out the annualised cost of each based on a period of time which is the lowest common multiple of the two or more choices. For example a 10 year cycle would be taken for projects with 2 and 5 year lives.

The way to calculate the annualised figure of cash flow is to firstly calculate the net present value of the alternatives. If for example using data in Exhibit 44.1 the N.P.V. of a project with a two year life were £738 and assuming that a 10% rate of interest were appropriate then the annualised figure is the amount of the annuity for two years with a present value of £738. Referring to the tables we can see that the present value of £1 per period for two years at 10% is £1.736. It x is the annualised amount then

$$1.736x = 738$$
$$\therefore x = 425$$

Diagrammatically what we have done is current cash flows as follows: –

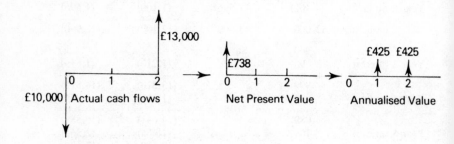

Exhibit 44.2

Using the data from Exhibit 44.1 for Machine B which has a five year life the accumulated net cash flow figure would be calculated using the N.P.V. of £942 and the figure from the tables for the present value of an annuity for five years at 10% which equals 3.791 then

$$3.791\ x = 942$$
$$x = 248$$

We can then compare annualised net cash flow for machine B of £248 with that for machine A of £425. Selecting the alternative with the highest net cash flow on an annualised basis would give project A.

This technique can be used to compare projects on the basis of costs rather than net cash flows − when the alternative with the lowest annualised cost would be selected.

Assignment Exercises

44.1 A company is considering a project which has two possible alternative solutions A or B. The estimated data is shown below — calculate Internal Rate of Return and N.P.V. using 12% interest. Which should be selective?

	Net Cash Outlay Year 0 £	Net Cash Benefit Year 4 £
Project		
A	16,000	(28,984)
B	44,000	(74,324)

44.2A A company is considering two mutually exclusive projects C and Y. Calculate the internal rate of return and N.P.V. at a 10% discount rate. Which alternative should be chosen?

Project	Net Cash Outlay Year 0 £	Net Cash Benefits Year 2 £	Year 6 £
X	30,000	(39,012)	–
Y	30,000	–	(59,172)

44.3 A machine is estimated to generate the following cash flows:

Year	Net Cash Flows
0	8,000
1	(4,000)
2	(2,000)
3	(6,000)

(Cash inflow shown in brackets)
(1)   Calculate the N.P.V. using 12% interest.
(2)   What is the annualised amount of the net benefits from this project?

44.4 An atlernative to the machine in question 44.3 is equipment with an expected life of 6 years. The N.P.V. of the unequal net cash flows from this equipment amounts to £2,264 using 12% interest rate. What is the annualised equivalent of the £2,624 N.P.V.? Would you choose the machine from 30.3 or this equipment — based on annualised benefits?

44.5A The Repair Co. is considering alternative investments in machines. Machine X costing £2,000 will last for 3 years only and cost £1,000 p.a. to operate Machine Y costs £5,000 but will last for 6 years. It will cost £100 p.a. for the first three years and £600 p.a. for the last three years of its life to operate. Calculate the annualised cost of Machine X and Y over a six year period, assuming that the replacement cost for Machine X at the end of year 3 is £1,800 and interest rate of 10%. Which machine would you choose based on this data?

45 Leasing

Leasing is an important method for many organisations to acquire assets. Things as diverse as motor vehicles, televisions, computers, machinery and buildings are commonly leased rather than bought. In a lease the lessor owns the object and leases it to the user, the lessee. The agreement which is legally binding and non-cancellable usually covers the major part of the economic life of the asset. The lessee in exchange for the use of the asset usually agrees to pay a rental, keep the item in good condition, insure it and properly service it. The rental payments and other costs are fully chargeable against the taxable profits of the lessee. The lessor as owner of the assets can claim all Capital Allowances for tax purposes against his taxable profits.

Leasing is possible because of the different costs of capital and tax situations between lessors and lessees. For example a company wishing to obtain a computer costing £100,000 may find it attractive to lease because the financial institution funding the operating can borrow at much lower rates than the company and its marginal tax rates against which the capital allowances on the computer can be set are significantly higher for the financial institution than the company.

The problem facing an organisation therefore is to compare the relative attractiveness of obtaining the use of an asset by buying it outright funding from normal sources of capital or whether to lease it.

The Interest Rate Implied in a Lease

In the type of decision which has to be made the purchase price of an asset is known, as are the rental terms. From this an interest rate can be derived:

A computer costing £100,000 has an expected life of 5 years with no scrap value. It can be leased for £27,740 per annum. The interest rate is that at which:

The Cost of the Item = Present Value of the annual rental payments.

$100,000 = 27,740 \times x$ (where x is the factor for the present value of an annuity of £1 for 5 years)

$$\therefore x = \frac{100,000}{27,740} = 3.605$$

By looking across the tables for the present value of an annuity on the five year period it will be seen that 3.605 corresponds to a rate of interest of 12%.

If scrap values are involved the calculation would have to be made as in the trial and error method of calculating internal rate of return.

This calculation has ignored the impact of taxation which may be crucial in the ultimate choice between leasing or buying. In the example we have just examined the rental payments would be deducted from taxable income and the net of tax cost would therefore be reduced by the tax borne by the company on its profits. If the tax rate were 42% of profits then the net of tax cost of the lease could be 58% of £27,740 = £16,089 and the corresponding interest rate would be 58% × 12% = 6.96%. (This ignores possible time lags in obtaining tax relief).

This net of tax rate of interest can be compared with the organisations net of tax cost of capital.

Using annualised cost

In the previous chapter the method of converting cash flows into annualised amounts is one method of comparing the buying decision with the alternative of leasing. The cost of buying the computer we know is £100,000. Capital Allowances for tax purposes of 100% of costs would be obtained in year 1 at the tax rate of 42%. There is a nil residual value at the end of 5 years. The Company's net of tax cost of capital is 10%.

Cash Flows

Year 0   (100,000)
      1   42,000   (assuming tax bill reduced by 42% × 100,000)
      2   −
      3   −
      4   −
      5   −

N.P.V. = (100,000) − (42,000 × .909) = (61,822)

The annualised figure is thus:

$$61,822 = 3.791 \times x$$
$$x = 16,307$$

The annualised cost of buying the asset is £16,307 and should be compared with the net of tax cost of leasing which amounted to £16,089. Since these figures are so close − the organisation would consider all the other factors surrounding the decision before making its choice.

It would also have been possible to compare the N.P.V. of the lease payments with the N.P.V. for buying.

For leasing the N.P.V. net of tax =
Rental × Present Value of an annuity of £1 for 5 years at 10% =
$$16,089 \times 3.791 = £60,993.$$

The N.P.V. of leasing is an outlay of £60,993 compared to buying of £61,822. Notice that the organisations costs of capital of 10% has been used to discount the rental payments to a N.P.V. rather than the interest rate implied in the lease of 6.96%. It is normal to use the average cost of capital rather than the marginal rate implicit in the particular transaction.

Notice that the benefits of the investment in the equipment have not be considered. We have simply compared alternative costs of buying or leasing the same equipment. The overall investment decision could be taken by comparing these costs with the benefits accruing from the investment.

The Financial Implications of Leasing

Signing a lease creates a legal obligation to continue paying the rental. The amount of the obligation to the lessor and the benefits obtainable by the organisation under the lease may not normally appear on the face of the organisation's Balance Sheet in conventional accounting. In considering the organisations financial structure however − a lease represents the equivalent of a loan (as a clear alternative to a direct loan to acquire an asset).

The equivalent loan would be the N.P.V. of the outstanding lease payments discounted by the rate of interest for borrowing. For example the N.P.V. of a five year lease with rental of £27,740 and a rate of interest of 14% (before tax) would be $27,740 \times 3.605 =$ £100,000.

Assignment Exercises

45.1 Some Plant can be leased for five years at a rent of £13,190 per annum. The cash price is £50,000. What is the implied interest rate?

45.2A A company is considering buying or leasing a computer which has a four year life. The rental would be £8,000 per annum and the cash price £23,000. The company pays corporation tax one year after its accounting year end at a rate of 52%. 100% of the cost of the computer would be allowed against taxable profit reducing tax paid in year 2. If a net of tax cost of capital is 10%, calculate the net present value of the lease and of the purchase after tax.

45.3A The net of tax annual cost of renting the computer if timing of tax relief is ignored would be $8,000 (1 - \cdot 52) = £3,840$ p.a. Using the data in question 45.2A what is the real annualised cost of the leasing transaction using 10% interest?

45.4 A company which could buy an asset for £80,000 with a four year life and nil residual value is offered a lease with rental of £26,338 p.a for four years. The tax rate is 40% − assuming tax relief is obtained in the same eyar as payments − what is the implicit interest in the lease?

45.5 A company enters into a lease which requires rental payments of £5,000 per annum over 10 years. The rate of interest payable on borrowing for this type of funding is 14%. What is the capital value of the lease?

46 The Accounting Profession

The Accounting Profession in its modern form and context started about 100 years ago. At this time business and government were being influenced by the industrial, scientific, and financial development called 'The Industrial Revolution'. Business units started to become larger and more complex. The financial institutions such as the banks and stock exchange were developing to meet the needs of the new business. Accountants started to find new roles and opportunities.

Whilst for centuries individuals had studied bookkeeping and accounting which they used to record business activities, these individuals had not organised themselves into a 'professional' body which would regulate their affairs. The thing that brought this about was the problem caused by bankruptcy and business failures. For whilst the Industrial Revolution produced many successful organisations it also saw many failures, which led to financial ruin for those concerned. Accountants began to find a specialised and lucrative role in managing the winding up of the affairs of bankrupts and insolvent businesses.

Then as now there were many unscrupulous 'sharks' around who were ready to defraud the creditors — whilst masquerading as accountants working in the creditors interest. Following a number of scandals surrounding such cases — the reputable accountants banded together to form a professional body which would establish a reputation in the public mind as having the highest integrity and competence.

Thus started the Institutes of Chartered Accountants first in Scotland, then in England and Wales. Their members are subject to strict ethical rules controlling their conduct of business affairs. Their technical knowledge is tested by examinations which are a prerequisite of membership, as is evidence of satisfactory practical experience. The professional bodies investigate all complaints against members — expelling those found to be in breach of acceptable standards. In addition the professional bodies have increasingly become involved in the continuing education of their members and in setting technical standards of accounting practice. The early accounting profession thus created consisted of individuals or firms of several partners who offered their expertise in accounting and financial matters to the public, in return for a fee. The professional bodies insist that their members trade as individuals or partnerships: they are not allowed to limit their liability for giving wrong advice, by trading as limited companies.

In the last hundred years the range of work done by accountants in public practice has expanded considerably. Many are very large organizations, with hundreds of offices in different parts of the world. These firms employ qualified accountants as staff in addition to the partners.

Although insolvency work still figures as an important element it ranks behind Audit, Taxation and Management Consultancy as specialisms. This brief description however, covers a very wide range of work covering many of the financial aspects of business management to personal finance.

The early creation of the Institute of Chartered Accountants did not satisfy everybody who was interested in offering their services as an accountant. Ever since its creation up to the present day there have been new professional groupings created which those who join them feel can offer some specific advantage to their members and the public. Some of these bodies have low standards and entry appears to be based mainly on an ability to pay a subscription. However there are now quite apart from this less reputable element a number of major bodies which are highly respected for their professional competence.

It is important to realise that there is no legal requirement for somebody who wants to work as an accountant to belong to a professional body. However most employers and members of the public wanting accounting advice would usually have the sense to look at a person's qualifications for doing a particular job. Membership of a recognised body gives some evidence of technical knowledge and the ethical support of a large responsible body which will take proper action to put this right if one of their members defrauds a member of the public.

Apart from the Institutes of Chartered Accountants in Scotland in England and Wales and in Ireland the next largest major body is the Association of Certified and Corporate Accountants. The majority of the Associations members are employed by organisations both in the public and private sectors as accountants. There are, however, some members who are in practice, offering their services to the public as do the Chartered Accountants.

The third largest body, the Institute of Cost and Management Accountants, has all its members employed by organisations and does not have members in public practice. As its title suggests its main aim is to promote professional standards for accountants in the areas of cost and management accounting.

The smallest of the major bodies is the Chartered Institute of Public Finance and Accounting, whose members work mainly in local and national government and in other public authorities and industries. They are the most specialised of the major accounting professional bodies.

Approximately half the members of the Institutes of Chartered Accountants as well as the great majority of the Certified and Cost and Management Accountants work in industrial and commercial organisations. The work that they do within these organisations varies quite extensively but in terms of its importance would be as follows:

Financial Management
General Management
Management and Financial Accounting
Corporate Finance
Internal Audit
Company Secretarial
Taxation
Management Consultancy

Although these headings give some idea of the work that is done there are in addition a great many other roles fulfilled by accountants.

The total number of members of the major accounting bodies mentioned here is currently a little over 150,000. Of these about 62% are Chartered Accountants, 17% Certified Accountants, 15% Cost and Management Accountants and 6% belong to the Chartered Institute of Public Finance and Accountancy. This number is growing fast at the moment, since the demand for Accountants has been growing very considerably in recent years.

47 Management in its Environment

When talking about any organisation, in particular what it is doing or planning at the moment, it is important to remember that what we mean by 'organisation' in this respect is the top management. Organisations such as limited companies are inanimate — they do not think and act themselves. It is either a powerful individual or more usually a group of individuals who control the top decisions that really form what we mean by the organisation. Often the organisation is represented by an employee who is not a senior manager — such as a salesman or a police constable. Our contacts with individuals like these, good or bad, will certainly influence our view of the organisation as a whole. However, people at these lower levels of management have only got authority to act for the organisation within guidelines or limits set by top management. If they act outside these guidelines you can complain and usually obtain some redress if they are at fault. Top management sets these guidelines — which are generally called objectives — in order that those working in the organisation know what is expected of them. When we are talking about 'top management' it is something like talking about the 'Government'. Whilst in business organisations there are no general elections, nonetheless the composition of the 'cabinet' of senior managers changes regularly, and from time to time there may be a complete change — if the business is taken over by another organisation. Thus whatever the type of organisation the top management will always change from time to time, which means that their objectives and therefore those of the organisation will also change.

Although top management set the objectives of the firm they cannot do this in isolation from the world outside. They are dependent for their continuing existence on their ability to survive. Survival as a top manager will depend on satisfying a wide range of competing interests in the affairs of the organisation. Whilst it is unlikely that every outside interest will always be happy with how things are being run, if too powerful an opposition is created, management will be replaced.

If we are thinking about an industrial or commercial organisation then the interested groups can be conveniently divided into seven sets. For non-commercial organisations many of these groups will also apply. The seven groups which will be discussed in turn are

1. The equity investor group
2. The loan creditor group

3. The employee group
4. The analyst adviser group
5. The business contact group
6. The government
7. The public

The Equity Investor Group

By 'equity' is meant the ordinary shareholders who own the right to profits after all prior claims are met, but are also likely to lose most of the business fails. The ordinary shares carry a vote — a majority of which will control the company. A top management group has thus got to maintain the support of a majority of voting shareholders. In some organisations the top management may individually own a majority of the shares in which case this equity investor group is of much less concern to them, but in many large organisations the holdings of shares are widely spread — a majority often in the hands of pension funds and other financial institutions. In these circumstances a fairly small holding by top managers may allow them to run the business, since the financial institutions may not interfere if they are happy with the way management is running the business. If however, this major group become convinced that a new management could do better, they then have considerable power to vote for a change. In public authorities the 'equity' belongs to the government of the day who will act in much the same way as the shareholders group in a limited company.

The Loan Creditor Group

This group includes a wide range of banks, business organisations and individuals who have provided loans and credit to the organisation. Part of this group will be secured, which means that they have obtained some specific legal rights to recover the money owing to them if the organisation gets itself into financial difficulty. Others will be unsecured; if the business fails they will only get their money repaid to them if there are sufficient assets after preferential and secured creditors have had first claim. Whilst all types of creditor rank before shareholders for repayment this is small comfort if the organisation ends up with a major deficit leaving them unpaid. Thus all this creditor group have a major interest in the success of the group and in particular in financial policies which minimise the risk of loss to creditors. Clearly lenders committed to long-term lending to an organisation may have a longer term perspective than short-term loan creditors, but fundamentally they have a business interest. Their rights to act against management policies may be included in the lending agreement particularly for long-term lenders. Short-term lenders will be more likely to act by demanding immediate repayment and refusing to extend further credit where they are unhappy with the management.

The Employee Group

The employee group has a very direct and clear interest in any organisation. Security of employment is one major factor which will interest employees. The other factor of major concern will be an organisation's ability to offer continuing development of career opportunity as well as prospects of pay progression. For an organisation to be successful the authority of top management should be based on respect for their ability to provide proper leadership of the organisation. This respect will clearly be based on competence rather than inherited power.

The employee is often represented in his dealings with organisations by a trade union. The unions now represent a very articulate contribution to the consideration of top management objectives in any area that is likely to impinge on employment.

The Analyst Adviser Group

Whilst this particular group are in fact normally no more than representatives of the other parties, nonetheless because of their particular expertise and influence they are usually considered as a separate group. Perhaps the most influential part are the financial journalists who may be seeking to uncover any policies or results which may be considered morally, or politically unacceptable. These matters then make good reports in the press. Investigative journalism of this type can have a considerable influence on top management.

Other analysts often working for stockbrokers or banks examining the results of organisations have particular importance for investors, since they recommend people to purchase shares, or to make loans. As distinct from the general public they are experts in techniques of analysis and examine the economic environment of the organisations they are concerned with. Specialised analysts also work for other interested parties such as Trade Unions and Public Consumer Groups to help them take effective action in criticising management.

The Business Contact Group

The suppliers, trade creditors and customers of a business all have an interest in its management. Many of these groups will have some close personal interest since dealings with another organisation can have a major impact on continuing success. Failure to continue with supply of materials which are not readily obtained elsewhere is one example. Failure to pay debts owing is another. Thus the business contact group is vitally interested in the ability of management to successfully ensure reliable supply or demand — uninterrupted by strikes or breakdowns, and in their ability to remain solvent as a good credit risk.

It is worth mentioning here the position of competitors, since they will also be examining the performance of an organisation. They will be looking for opportunities to take business away, and their actions will often be influenced by their assessment of the ability of top management of a competitor to thwart them. In the extreme case a takeover may be launched for a badly managed competitor.

The Government

The Government's involvement with management, either nationally or locally, is considerable. In public authorities and utilities, the government itself usually lays down the organisation's objectives and appoints managers to carry them out. Even, however, in the private sector the impact of legislation covers almost every aspect of business. In addition the Government is itself a major customer for many businesses and will therefore take a particular interest, especially where strategic issues, e.g. defence, are involved. The Government is involved with organisations both to tax their profits for revenue, and also to control them as far as possible to act in the wider social interest of the country, whether in terms of employment, environmental issues or strategic national defence.

The Public

The interest of the public in management's control of organisations, may be perhaps felt to be already covered by a democratically elected government. However, the process of government is now very complex and issues of local concern may not be adequately covered. Similarly minority groups may feel that they need to bring things of particular interest to them into a proper focus for government.

Thus there have developed a range of organisations who act as pressure groups to bring special attention to bear on matters of concern to them. The Consumers Association acts on behalf of consumers to draw attention to faults in products and legal procedures and is particularly concerned with matters affecting health and safety, as well as 'good value for money'. Other special interest groups look after environmental issues and conservation. Indeed most aspects of any organisation's activity are likely to be covered by a pressure group for the public interest. Any management which crosses swords with such groups is likely to be met with both legal action as well as physical demonstrations of the public's views.

Management and Conflicts With the Outside Group

As has already been pointed out — management has to survive by maintaining a relationship with the groups of outside interests we have mentioned. The interests of the organisation and those of the outside group may from time to time be in direct conflict. For example the organisation may want to reduce its workforce whilst the employees oppose this. The Government may refuse the organisation the right to expand its business in a particular location on the grounds that it would spoil an area of natural beauty and amenity. Examples of this kind are many.

However, a good top management will normally accept that its long-term interests are best served by maintaining objectives that are consistent with the interests of the whole set of interested parties. Organisations must be responsive to the needs not only of their immediate customers but of the wider community of social interest. The organisation does not exist in a vacuum and it will only succeed long-term if the community in which it operates also succeeds.

48 Management Objectives

In the previous chapter the fact that objectives for an organisation were set by top management was discussed in relation to outside interests. However it would be wrong to consider that the way in which objectives are set is purely conditioned by external pressures. As was emphasised management consists of individuals whose personal and collective attitudes will also contribute considerably to objective setting.

What then determines the way that managers set objectives? What is it that motivates people to manage organisations? There are no simple answers to these questions since most people are influenced by a wide range of personal psychological factors, as well as the external influences.

The early books on management written over fifty years ago tended to assume that managers were motivated almost entirely by economic factors. In other words it was assumed that the overriding objective was to maximise profits, and that all other aspects of management were an extension of this objective. Whilst industrial and commercial organisations depend for their existence on an ability to generate profit, the extent to which management maximise rather than produce 'satisfactory' profits has been closely examined. Most research in this area supports the idea that managers attempt not to maximise the single objective of profit but a wider range of objectives. A satisfactory profit is one that allows them to survive as managers as well as achieving their other objectives.

Psychologists have suggested that people have a range of basic needs, on top of which, when the basics are satisfied, come more sophisticated wants. The basic needs include hunger, love and security. At a more sophisticated level are the requirement for status, authority and respect. The economic reward from salaries and other payments satisfies the basic hunger as well as contributing to the achievement of other needs. However, cash does not of itself fulfil all the other human needs for respect, authority and security. After a certain point of cash reward people tend to be much more concerned with the other factors. Does this position command general respect? Are they acknowledged as leaders in the organisation? Are they respected by the people who work for and with them? Do people in the community think highly of their work?

Soldiers are motivated to do deeds of heroism, not for economic reward, but for the good of their country and the respect of their peer group. Managers are in this respect no different although clearly the analogy of a battlefield does not relate to the everyday situation. Indeed in the routine situation the average manager would become very much more concerned with personal security and providing himself with congenial, well-rewarded working conditions than ever his efforts or talents would justify.

The picture of a cosy bureaucracy in which managers are largely concerned with their own affairs to the exclusion of anybody else is never far away. The efficiency of management can only be ensured if the external groups, mentioned previously, are given the information and legal support necessary to bring pressure to bear. It is a picture of conflict of interest, producing an atmosphere of creative tension. This is the ideal of market capitalism in contrast to beaurocratic and static models.

Financial Objectives

When objectives for an organisation are written down the result inevitably reduces the full range of factors to a number of headings — usually those which are capable of being measured in accounting terms. Thus although an organisation may publish a final statement of its objectives never forget that the informal and more personal objectives of top management are likely to be just as important. Measurement of objectives is important because unless it is possible to measure performance the assessment of improvement or worsening of results is purely subjective and therefore tends to be arbitrary.

Whilst formal objectives will differ for every organisation they would normally cover the following areas:
1. Profitability: by measuring return in capital employed.
2. Marketing: by measuring share of markets.
3. Productivity: by measuring the use of the organisations resources.
4. Technology: by measuring existing and new product and process development.
5. Personnel: by measuring the attitudes and training/education of employees.
6. Social Responsibility: by measuring the extent to which the organisation has satisfied its responsibilities under the following headings
(a) Health & Safety
(b) Environmental Pollution and Resource Preservations
(c) Cultural and sporting contributions
(d) Charitable contributions.

In many ways it can be argued that all the headings shown for objectives are part of the essential ingredients of a successful business. Whilst short-term it may be possible to neglect some of the headings ultimately this will react unfavourably on the performance of the business. The single measure of profitability tends only to capture the current result whereas the wider range is a more realistic overall view.

Many managers would not argue with the realistic nature of measuring the first five objectives, but would find the area of social responsibility out of place because it is very difficult to measure precisely. Indeed it was said at the start of the section that these objectives should normally be measured in accounting terms. Whilst there is truth in the fact that accounting measures of social factors are difficult to make, it is nonetheless possible to do something, particularly if it is accepted that in this area more subjective measurement of performance is required than in normal matters.

Some of the areas that are involved are as follows:

Health and Safety:	Employees	avoiding accidents and health hazards
	Public	
Pollution:	Air	ensuring that emissions are cleaned and disposed of safely.
	Water	
	Waste	
Environment:	Minimising damage and restoring damaged areas	
Resources:	Minimising waste of materials and energy	
Community:	providing employment; helping set up alternatives where people are made redundant; providing other amenities	
Cultural and Sporting:	providing support for activities which would otherwise not exist	

In all of there instances there are usually minimum standards of performance set down by government laws and regulations. There are however, possibilities of performing at a standard well above the minimum. The decision about how much any organisation can afford is usually very difficult to assess since whilst the costs can be estimated the benefits to the organisation may be much harder to assess. For example, cutting smoke emission down to a legally acceptable level will be necessary since failure to do so would be visited by legal sanctions. However, for people living in the vicinity of the factory concerned it may be highly desirable to cut the smoke down even further. This will be an expensive process and the benefits, apart from gratitude from the local community may never be very tangible. The top management will have to make plans which recognise that they cannot fulfil every demand and survive. However, some allocation to what they judge most effective in the area is essential for the long-term well-being of their environment. In particular reporting on what is being done in the annual report and accounts will provide evidence of a bonafide recognition of the situation and some attempt to help solve it.

49　Personal Finance

You will now appreciate the authors' desire to leave personal finance until the end of the book. At this point we can now call on the knowledge gained from studying the finance of both private and public sector organisations, and adapt them in some way to the handling and understanding of your own finances.

Sources of Income
1. Wages and Salaries

Those students who have jobs will have read in Chapter 29 the basic mechanics underlying the calculation of wages and salaries, as well as how the deductions for P.A.Y.E. Income Tax, National Insurance and Pension and Superannuation contributions are handled.

2. Local Authority Grants

Students on full-time courses will be receiving grants towards their fees and living expenses from their local authorities. These grants may be restricted if the parents' income exceeds certains limits.

3. Covenants

A covenant is a legally binding agreement in which someone agrees to make regular payments to someone else. At the time of this book being written it is possible for tax savings to be made by using covenants for payments to students.

Parents can get tax relief on covenant payments to their children provided that
(i) The child is 18 or over, or is under 18 and married,
(ii) Neither the parent, nor spouse, benefit from the payments,
(iii) The covenant is drawn up to last for at least 6 years,
(iv) The child is a student in full-time education.
In fact covenants for students normally end when the student leaves full-time education, if this is earlier than 6 years.

Anyone else, including grandparents, can get tax relief on covenant payments, whatever the age of the student, provided that the other conditions are met.

There can be snags, some of which will be mentioned later, but first we will examine the basic structure underlying the tax saving.

Joe Wild wants to give £2,000 a year to his daughter Sally, a student.

	£
The gross amount of the payment is	2,000
But Joe can deduct tax at the standard rate* of 30%	600
Joe therefore gives Sally cheques annually for	1,400

The tax of £600 deducted by Joe does not have to be paid to the Inland Revenue if, on his own income, he pays at least £600 tax.

*The standard rate of tax may well have altered from 30%.

Sally, for her part can have a taxable income well above £2,000 without paying any tax. Her income is as follows:

	£
Non-taxable income (e.g. grant)	800
Net amount of covenant from father	1,400
As she does not have enough taxable income on which tax should be levied, Sally can claim refund from the Inland Revenue of:	600
Total income	2,800

Sally has therefore had her income increased from £800 to £2,800, a sum of £2,000. This increase in her income cost her father only £1,400.

What has been described is subject to quite a few complications. The current state of play regarding the effect of covenants upon supplementary benefits in the summer holidays, and on grants and any other income of students should be ascertained. Leaflet IR47 and a covenant form can currently be obtained from the Inland Revenue: the Consumers' Association publishes a Which? Covenant Kit: the National Union of Students also gives information on covenants in their literature.

It should also be added that, in the case shown, Sally did not have enough income to be taxed. If she has a lot of earnings from a part-time job, on which she paid tax, then the refund of tax from covenant payments could not be claimed. There will obviously be interim stages where she may be able to claim part of the tax refund but not all of it. Only a study of the up-to-date literature will give you the exact position for any particular case.

4. Part-time earnings

If you earn more than the personal relief for the tax year then you will have to suffer P.A.Y.E. income tax on it. In addition you may also have to pay national insurance contributions if your earnings are large enough.

5. *Income from Investments*

If you do not have enough income in total from all sources to be taxable, then you should compare your income allowing for tax which you may be able to get refunded.

For instance, assuming you do not receive enough money to have to pay income tax, and you have £1,000 invested in a British government stock, which pays 10 per cent less tax at 30%, and you also have £1,000 invested in the HHH Building Society, which pays you 8½% after deduction of tax at the source. In the case of a building society the tax deducted cannot be refunded to you. In the case of the government stock the tax deducted can be refunded if you submit a claim. Which is the best investment for you?

	Building Society £	Government Stock £
Received	85	70
Add tax reclaimable	nil	30
Total Income from investment	85	100

Obviously the government stock is the best investment for you in this case. If however the investment income was all liable to tax because your earnings absorbed all your personal reliefs, then the building society investment would have meant you having the largest amount of income, £85 instead of £70, as the £30 tax would not now be reclaimable from the Inland Revenue.

6. *Supplementary Benefits and Housing Benefits*

Some students may be able to claim these from the Department of Health and Social Security.

Personal Borrowing

Before we start to look at ways of borrowing money, let us consider several important points which should be considered.

(i) You have read in Chapter 40 that the rate of interest which is relevant is the 'true rate of interest'. This is not the nominal rate but the rate that takes into account the speed in which you have to pay back the amount borrowed. For most items bought on credit nowadays the law insists that the APR (annual percentage rate) charged should be clearly stated. So always compare the APR charged between one organisation and another.

(ii) Always ensure that you can afford to pay back the amount owing within the time allowed.

(iii) Be certain you understand what will happen if you fail to pay the instalments on time.

(iv) If you can get tax relief on interest paid on your borrowings, e.g. on building society interest paid by you, then take the tax into your calculations when comparing it with other methods of borrowing.

We can now look at the major forms of personal borrowing.

1. Relations or friends

Although such borrowing may be informal, it may save a lot of trouble and disagreements later on if full details of the agreement are written down and signed by both parties.

2. Banks

Banks lend money either by bank overdraft or by personal loans.

(a) *Bank Overdrafts*. The bank agrees an amount by which the customer can pay more money out of his bank account than he has put into it. Also agreed is the date by which the bank overdraft has to be paid off by the customer. Interest is charged on overdrafts, the rate of interest being expressed as x per cent over 'base' rate. The base rate is a standard rate used as a base for calculating how much interest should be charged. How much extra is charged over the base rate will depend very much on the financial standing of the customer and how much bargaining power the customer possesses. As an instance, with a base rate of 10 per cent, a very good customer might pay base rate plus 1% = total 11%, whilst someone of not such good standing might pay base rate plus 4% = total 14%.

Interest is paid on a day to day calculation only on the amount actually owing. This means that if a customer has permission to have an overdraft for £1,000, but never in fact overdraws more than £200 then the amount charged as interest will be quite low, whereas someone with permission to have a £1,000 overdraft and who is overdrawn almost up to that figure all the time until final repayment will pay much more in interest.

(b) *Personal loans*. The amount of the loan, how much per month is to be paid off the loan, and the time in which the loan is to be paid off are all agreed by the bank and its customer. The interest charged however has been worked out in a completely different manner to that on a bank overdraft. Here the interest charged is always calculated on the full opening amount of the loan, ignoring the fact that as each month goes by and repayments are made then the actual amount owing falls.

This means that although the nominal rate of interest may appear to be fairly low, the annual percentage rate (APR) is much higher than it would have been for a bank overdraft of the same amounts over the same period. Small wonder then that the banks prefer personal loans, and customers may find it difficult, if not almost impossible at times, to get bank overdrafts for personal matters.

(*c*) *Credit cards*. With credit cards such as Access, Barclaycard, Visa and the like, if the amount spent by using the card is not paid off by a certain date, then the credit card company will charge interest on the amount owing.

The rate of interest charged is quite substantial. If therefore one wishes to use the card without paying interest then the debit should be paid off before the given due date. As a few weeks are usually given before interest is charged it is possible to use the credit card to buy goods and services, then pay for them several weeks later before interest is accrued and so get the use of some of the credit card company's money 'interest-free' for that period.

The income for the credit card company does not come solely from interest from its customers, it also charges the retail shops and selling outlets for the use of its services. The retail shop cannot charge the customer anything extra by paying by credit card instead of cash.

(*d*) *Property Mortgages*. For most people the buying of a house represents the time in their lives when they will need to borrow the most money. The main source of loans are the building societies, but the banks also lend money for house purchase.

The duration of the loan and details of the interest are agreed. It would be impossible here to go into a very detailed survey of all of the different schemes available, which can involve for example, taking out endowment policies with insurance companies and linking them to the building society mortgage. As this is an important decision for most people then further advice should be sought. The Consumers' Association magazine *Which* has published various reports on comparisons of the various methods in the past.

The 'mortgage' aspect is that the lender can take possession of the property if proper repayments are not made. The property would then be sold, the lender would collect the money owing to him from the proceeds, and hand the remainder, if any, back to you.

One major advantage of buying a property by borrowing through a building society or bank is that (if the tax laws are not changed) the borrower is allowed to deduct tax relief at source, and pay only the net amount. This is all worked out for you by the building society, and the net repayment figure is given to you. This is known as MIRAS; mortgage interest relief at source. If you own two or more homes you cannot get MIRAS on interest on both of the properties, but only on your main residence.

Personal borrowing from a bank to buy something, such as a car, does not attract tax relief on interest paid. On the other hand building society interest is usually quite a lot lower then that levied on bank personal loans, plus the fact that tax relief is also given on it, so that the actual comparable rate of interest suffered by you is considerably less. This means that, for most people, a mortgage on a property is a very cheap way of borrowing, and should figure in your overall look at your finances as you get older.

Various factions have tried to bring pressure to bear on the abolition of tax relief on property mortgage interest. This certain has many moral advantages, as the poor who have to live in rented property cannot get tax relief on their occupancy costs. To the time of writing no government has been willing to change the system, as the abolition of tax relief could bring about a strong reprisal from voters at election time.

It is possible for someone buying a property through a normal building society mortgage or the like to borrow money on a second mortgage, using the resources of a finance company. As most people find it difficult enough to cope with one mortgage, let alone two, then this method is not one that would get a good response from those well versed in the financial scene. Remember that you can lose your property if you fail to pay either of the mortgages.

(e) *Money Lenders.* It is possible, if you have some form of acceptability, for you to borrow money from money-lenders. They have to observe various legal requirements, and some of these cover the amount of interest they are allowed to charge. However, you should remember that the greater the risk the greater the interest. As the risk element attaching to money-lenders' loans is much greater than with a normal bank's lending then the rate of interest which will be charged will also be greater.

(f) *Hire Purchase and Credit Sales.* If you buy goods by either method you have the use of the goods immediately, but are able to pay for them in instalments. The difference between the two methods is that with a credit sale the goods legally become your property as soon as you have paid the deposit, whereas under hire purchase you are legally 'hiring' the goods until you have paid the final instalment. Only when the final instalment is paid do the goods become your legal property. This is very important, because you are not allowed to sell goods being bought on hire purchase until that final instalment is paid. The converse is true, since if you buy something which is still under hire purchase, e.g. a car, you will have no legal title to the car. If you have any doubts when purchasing a car then you should check through a motoring organisaion or a Citizens' Advice Bureau that the goods are not subject to a hire purchase agreement.

Investments

The first thing to consider is exactly what you are investing for. Only when you have decided that can you match an investment or investments against your objectives. We can look briefly at some of the more common forms of investing, but they will be restricted mainly to what you might possibly expect younger adults to consider. In this book all that can be claimed is that this is a very brief look indeed at investments. Anyone seriously considering investing a relatively large sum of money would be well advised to read a publication such as *The Which? Book of Saving and Investing*. This would give them a far better idea as to the route they should follow in their particular case. Your local librarian could tell you about other publications that you might read.

Stocks and shares

The stock exchange is the market for the purchase and sale of shares in most public companies and for government stocks. You cannot go to the stock exchange yourself and actually buy shares. If you want to buy shares or stock you will have to do this, either directly through a stockbroker or else your bank manager will arrange it via the bank's own stockbrokers. Unless you have quite a lot of knowledge about stocks and shares then this sort of investment is best avoided. After all, if you put all your spare cash into the shares of one company then you could lose all of it if the company gets forced into liquidation.

Unit trusts

Instead of investing your money directly into particular companies, you can spread the risk by investing in a unit trust. Thus a unit trust may hold shares in, say, 50 companies, and so buying units means that you are in effect buying a bit in each of these 50 companies yourself. It is hardly likely that all of the 50 companies could fail, and so your money is relatively safer than just being invested in one or two companies only. Unit trusts very often specialise, for instance you may decide that you want to put your money into property companies, and there are unit trusts that cater especially for that, or in the leisure industry, or in financial institutions such as banks, and there will be unit trusts for these as well. In addition you will find 'general' trusts that do not cater for investing in a specialised area, but which will put the money into a wide variety of companies.

Building Society Accounts

There are now many types of account by which you can lend money to a building society and earn interest on the amount deposited. There are a few building societies which offer higher rates of interest, so you should shop around before depositing your money.

One thing you will have to decide at the onset is how long you want your money to be deposited before you withdraw it. Usually you can get a higher rate of interest if you have to give a long period of notice before you get a repayment. Only by comparing the rates, and terms, as between building societies will you find the one which will offer you the highest rate possible when your own plans are taken into consideration.

Income tax will already have been paid by the society, so, unless you have a large income and pay higher rates of tax, you will not have to suffer any further tax on the interest. On the other hand, if your income is so small that you do not have to pay tax then you will not be able to claim back a refund of the tax already suffered on your building society interest.

Endowment Policies

An endowment policy with an insurance company is basically a long-term investment incorporating life insurance. Just as with buying stocks and shares, or buying units in a unit trust, you are investing in the underlying value of companies, government stocks and the like, but you do it through the medium of the insurance company. The main sorts of endowment policies are:

(a) *Non-profit policies.* You agree to save for a specific period, which must be for 10 years or more. At the end of the 10 years or on an appropriate date, it is guaranteed that you will receive a stated amount. If you die within the term of the policy then that amount is paid into your estate, for distribution to your heirs. Such policies are very unlikely to be a good bargain for most students because of the effects of inflation.

(b) *With-profits policies.* You agree to save for a specified period, which must be for 10 years or more. The amount you are initially covered for if you die is lower than with the non-profit policy. However, as the years go by bonuses are declared by the insurance company and this increases the amount for which your life is covered, and it also increases how much you will draw from the policy if you live until the final agreed date of the policy.

(c) *Unit-linked policies.* In the case of the with-profits policies (b) you are dependent on the bonuses being declared adding to the value of your policy, and you personally cannot influence the amount of bonus in any way; it is totally the province of the insurance company to fix the rate of bonus. With the unit-linked policy matters are different. Usually the amount of immediate life cover given is very small, compared to either non-profits or with-profits policies. A stated percentage of the premiums goes to finance this life cover, and the rest of the premiums go to buy units in a unit trust. The unit trust is one that can be chosen by you from a selection offered by the insurance company. If you therefore think that unit trust (**A**) has better prospects over the term of your insurance than unit trust (**B**), then you will ask for (**A**) to be the unit trust in which your premiums are going to be invested.

Should you die during the term of the policy your estate will receive either the amount guaranteed or the value of the units at the date of your death if their value is greater. If you survive the term of insurance then you will receive the units, which you can either keep or cash in. Whatever profits will have been accumulated by the units over the years will belong to you.

Surrender Values of Endowment Policies

The 'surrender value' is the amount that the insurance company will give you back if you stop paying your premiums before the final agreed date of the policy, for any reason other than death. When an insurance company first enters into the policy contract with you, then it pays out quite a lot of charges. These include the administration costs and also commission expenses to insurance agents, brokers and the like. Such costs can be quite heavy. Therefore if you want to surrender your policy in the early years when you have paid little of the total premiums, the amount which the insurance company will return to you will be relatively low. Suppose you have paid them only £700 and they have already paid out £500 on commission, they would hardly want to pay you back the whole of the £700. On the other hand, as time goes by the proportion of premiums returned will be higher; for instance if £10,000 has been paid on the same policy then the £500 costs are but a small proportion, and therefore the insurance company will offer a much higher proportionate amount as surrender value.

You should therefore be warned against taking out endowment policies unless you are able to pay the premiums and are also convinced that you want to keep on paying the premiums. Many people take out policies, and then surrender them very early. Such people lose a lot of money, and would have been well advised to invest in some other way.

It is well worth pointing out that, when you have an endowment policy with an insurance company, it is usually possible to get a loan from the insurance company. The amount of the loan will not exceed the surrender value of the policy. Endowment policies are also accepted by banks as security against any bank loans or overdrafts that the bank may make to you. Once again the value that is put on to the policy for borrowing purposes is the amount of the surrender value.

Revenue and Capital Expenditure

You have read in Chapter 23 about the distinction between capital and revenue expenditure in a business. If one wishes to divide one's personal expenditure in a similar way then the same principles apply. Therefore the purchase of a motorcar which you expect to use for the whole of your two years at college will be capital expenditure, whilst the costs of the petrol used up from week to week is revenue expenditure. Similarly the costs of a personal typewriter for your use would also be capital expenditure, whilst the costs of paper for it would be revenue expenditure.

In personal finance, if you wish to be sensible and make the most of your money as you go through life, you will remember that businesses plan ahead for capital expenditure and so you may try to do the same. This is particularly true for major items of capital expenditure. For instance, if you plan to replace your car in two years time it would be preferable for you to arrange your cash budgets for the next two years so that you had the largest amount possible to use as immediate payment on the new car when you took delivery of it. Failure to do this might mean you having to finance the car's purchase on hire purchase, on which the rate of interest charged to you will be at a rather high rate. Failure to plan ahead and so not have the requisite funds could mean that it would cost you far more in total costs to get the car.

Likewise, failure to plan ahead, even though you are going to have to borrow the money in some way, may mean that it will still cost you more. This would be true if you had not properly assessed the best way of borrowing money, and when the time came for purchase of the car you might be forced into borrowing by a very dear method indeed. A little more thought and time in which to effect the necessary formalities could well have saved you a lot of money.

Cash Planning and Personal Cash Flow

If you use the techniques you have learned from budgeting in business, then you should gain quite a lot of benefits from carrying these out in your private life. Let us look at some of the advantages of personal budgeting.

It makes you think ahead and face some hard facts; quite a few may not be too pleasant. It is a fact of life that very few people can just spend as much money as they like, without having to ensure that they are able to pay for things when the bills fall due. Many people simply take each day as it comes, and do not take account of the fact that eventually things have to be paid for. When the bills come in they then try and rescue themselves from not being able to pay them by borrowing using credit cards and running up large amounts owed; by obtaining personal loans from the banks; by using hire purchase instead of cash.

If you do not pay at the right time you will find yourself paying out a lot of money in all sorts of charges. Interest on the credit card debts, interest on personal loans from banks, interest on hire purchase contracts, but this is very often not the whole of the story. Quite a lot of people get a bank loan or overdraft, and do not comply with the bank's terms, and eventually they may issue cheques for which they have no funds and the bank will not honour their cheques. The slang for this is that their cheques will 'bounce' but you know that it is more correctly called the cheques being 'dishonoured'. Not only will the bank issue you an extra charge for having made them dishonour the cheques but you will also be in very serious trouble with your creditors. This may well involve you in extra costs being levied on you by them as well, besides all the upheavals in your personal life.

It is always possible to find two people doing the same job for the same pay, and yet find that one person is always hard up, he can never manage to pay his bills on time, he has to catch the bus to work and never goes on a decent holiday. Alongside him in the same office may be a colleague with the same income, spends the same amount of money on food and drink and the like, yet manages also to run a car and have overseas holidays. He has got the money to do that because he has not wasted so much on paying interest to banks, credit card companies, fines for late payments, and also has been able to take advantage of having the cash available to take advantage of special bargains and so save money there as well.

If all of this sounds like the authors would like you to be 'killjoys' then think again. We are not saying that all you should do is to save a lot of money for savings sake. What we are saying is that if you plan ahead and use your money *properly* you will not waste so much of it on paying things for which you receive absolutely no tangible benefits whatsoever. £x spent on interest on overdue accounts will give you no pleasure at all, whereas if you avoid wasting your money in that way the same amount, £x will buy you quite a few theatre trips, meals out, a holiday in sunny . . . . . , and so on. A little forethought and organisation therefore brings about more pleasure, not less.

Opportunity Cost and Personal Objectives

In your other units you will have considered opportunity cost, especially with regard to organisations. The same principles apply on a personal level. The true cost, i.e. the opportunity cost, of travelling home every week to see your girlfriend/boyfriend may be the exploration trip to Iceland that you could have gone on with a group from college. You could not afford both so you had to give up the Icelandic trip. You had made up your mind to spend your money in the way that you have done, that is your prerogative.

Just as an organisation has objectives, then so will you on a personal basis. It is very rare for anyone to sit down and write out what their personal objectives are. One thing is certain, and that is that neither of the authors of this book have ever done that. On the other hand it would be true that we both have thought out what our objectives in life are. It would also be true to say that our objectives have not stayed the same throughout our lives.

Whilst it is not for anyone else to say what a particular person's objectives should be, it does at least make sense to say that a person should so arrange his personal finances in such a way that will be the best way for him to achieve his objectives. You have spent the last year studying finance and other units. Besides the benefit gained workwise you should also have gained personally, as what you have studied should help you to see your personal finances in perspective and give you greater ability in handling them.

When constructing your personal budgets you will have the best ways of achieving your objectives as the structure underlying your choices. In fact setting out such budgets for yourself should give you a far better idea of the sorts of problems facing organisations when they in turn arrange their budgets. There will undoubtedly be quite a few adjustments made in your thinking as you go through the budgeting process.

Appendix

Table 1

Compound Amount of 1

Period	1%	2%	3%	4%	5%	6%	7%	8%	9%	10%
1	1.010	1.020	1.030	1.040	1.050	1.060	1.070	1.080	1.090	1.100
2	1.020	1.040	1.061	1.082	1.102	1.124	1.145	1.166	1.188	1.210
3	1.030	1.061	1.093	1.125	1.158	1.191	1.225	1.260	1.295	1.331
4	1.041	1.082	1.126	1.170	1.216	1.262	1.311	1.360	1.412	1.464
5	1.051	1.104	1.159	1.217	1.276	1.338	1.403	1.469	1.539	1.611
6	1.062	1.126	1.194	1.265	1.340	1.419	1.501	1.587	1.677	1.772
7	1.072	1.149	1.230	1.316	1.407	1.504	1.606	1.714	1.828	1.949
8	1.083	1.172	1.267	1.369	1.477	1.594	1.718	1.851	1.993	2.144
9	1.094	1.195	1.305	1.423	1.551	1.689	1.838	1.999	2.172	2.358
10	1.105	1.219	1.344	1.480	1.629	1.791	1.967	2.159	2.367	2.594
11	1.116	1.243	1.384	1.539	1.710	1.898	2.105	2.332	2.580	2.853
12	1.127	1.268	1.426	1.601	1.796	2.012	2.252	2.518	2.813	3.138
13	1.138	1.294	1.469	1.665	1.886	2.133	2.410	2.720	3.066	3.452
14	1.149	1.319	1.513	1.732	1.980	2.261	2.579	2.937	3.342	3.797
15	1.161	1.346	1.558	1.801	2.079	2.397	2.759	3.172	3.642	4.177

Period	12%	14%	15%	16%	18%	20%	24%	28%	32%
1	1.120	1.140	1.150	1.160	1.180	1.200	1.240	1.280	1.320
2	1.254	1.300	1.322	1.346	1.392	1.440	1.538	1.638	1.742
3	1.405	1.482	1.521	1.561	1.643	1.728	1.907	2.097	2.300
4	1.574	1.689	1.749	1.811	1.939	2.074	2.364	2.684	3.036
5	1.762	1.925	2.011	2.100	2.288	2.488	2.932	3.436	4.007
6	1.974	2.195	2.313	2.436	2.700	2.986	3.635	4.398	5.290
7	2.211	2.502	2.660	2.826	3.185	3.583	4.508	5.629	6.983
8	2.476	2.853	3.059	3.278	3.759	4.300	5.590	7.206	9.217
9	2.773	3.252	3.518	3.803	4.435	5.160	6.931	9.223	12.166
10	3.106	3.707	4.046	4.411	5.234	6.192	8.594	11.806	16.060
11	3.479	4.226	4.652	5.117	6.176	7.430	10.657	15.112	21.199
12	3.896	4.818	5.350	5.936	7.288	8.916	13.215	19.343	27.983
13	4.363	5.492	6.153	6.886	8.599	10.699	16.386	24.759	36.937
14	4.887	6.261	7.076	7.988	10.147	12.839	20.319	31.691	48.757
15	5.474	7.138	8.137	9.266	11.974	15.407	25.196	40.565	64.359

Period	36%	40%	50%	60%	70%	80%	90%
1	1.360	1.400	1.500	1.600	1.700	1.800	1.900
2	1.850	1.960	2.250	2.560	2.890	3.240	3.610
3	2.515	2.744	3.375	4.096	4.913	5.832	6.859
4	3.421	3.842	5.062	6.544	8.352	10.498	13.032
5	4.653	5.378	7.594	10.486	14.199	18.896	24.761
6	6.328	7.530	11.391	16.777	24.138	34.012	47.046
7	8.605	10.541	17.086	26.844	41.034	61.222	89.387
8	11.703	14.758	25.629	42.950	69.758	110.200	169.836
9	15.917	20.661	38.443	68.720	118.588	198.359	322.688
10	21.647	28.925	57.665	109.951	201.599	357.047	613.107
11	29.439	40.496	86.498	175.922	342.719	642.684	1164.902
12	40.037	56.694	129.746	281.475	582.622	1156.831	2213.314
13	54.451	79.372	194.619	450.360	990.457	2082.295	4205.297
14	74.053	111.120	291.929	720.576	1683.777	3748.131	7990.065
15	100.712	155.568	437.894	1152.921	2862.421	6746.636	15181.122

Table 2

Present Value of 1

Period	1%	2%	3%	4%	5%	6%	7%	8%	9%	10%	12%	14%	15%
1	0.990	0.980	0.971	0.961	0.952	0.943	0.935	0.926	0.917	0.909	0.893	0.877	0.8
2	0.980	0.961	0.943	0.925	0.907	0.890	0.873	0.857	0.842	0.826	0.797	0.769	0.7
3	0.971	0.942	0.915	0.889	0.864	0.840	0.816	0.794	0.772	0.751	0.712	0.675	0.6
4	0.961	0.924	0.889	0.855	0.823	0.792	0.763	0.735	0.708	0.683	0.636	0.592	0.5
5	0.951	0.906	0.863	0.822	0.784	0.747	0.713	0.681	0.650	0.621	0.567	0.519	0.4
6	0.942	0.888	0.838	0.790	0.746	0.705	0.666	0.630	0.596	0.564	0.507	0.456	0.4
7	0.933	0.871	0.813	0.760	0.711	0.665	0.623	0.583	0.547	0.513	0.452	0.400	0.3
08	0.923	0.853	0.789	0.731	0.677	0.627	0.582	0.540	0.502	0.467	0.404	0.351	0.3
9	0.914	0.837	0.766	0.703	0.645	0.592	0.544	0.500	0.460	0.424	0.361	0.308	0.2
10	0.905	0.820	0.744	0.676	0.614	0.558	0.508	0.463	0.422	0.386	0.322	0.270	0.2
11	0.896	0.804	0.722	0.650	0.585	0.527	0.475	0.429	0.388	0.350	0.287	0.237	0.2
12	0.887	0.788	0.701	0.625	0.557	0.497	0.444	0.397	0.356	0.319	0.257	0.208	0.1
13	0.879	0.773	0.681	0.601	0.530	0.469	0.415	0.368	0.326	0.290	0.229	0.182	0.1
14	0.870	0.758	0.661	0.577	0.505	0.442	0.388	0.340	0.299	0.263	0.205	0.160	0.1
15	0.861	0.743	0.642	0.555	0.481	0.417	0.362	0.315	0.275	0.239	0.183	0.140	0.
16	0.853	0.728	0.623	0.534	0.458	0.394	0.339	0.292	0.252	0.218	0.163	0.123	0.1
17	0.844	0.714	0.605	0.513	0.436	0.371	0.317	0.270	0.231	0.198	0.146	0.108	0.0
18	0.836	0.700	0.587	0.494	0.416	0.350	0.296	0.250	0.212	0.180	0.130	0.095	0.0
19	0.828	0.686	0.570	0.475	0.396	0.331	0.276	0.232	0.194	0.164	0.116	0.083	0.0
20	0.820	0.673	0.554	0.456	0.377	0.319	0.258	0.215	0.178	0.149	0.104	0.073	0.0
25	0.780	0.610	0.478	0.375	0.295	0.233	0.184	0.146	0.116	0.092	0.059	0.038	0.0
30	0.742	0.552	0.412	0.308	0.231	0.174	0.131	0.099	0.075	0.057	0.033	0.020	0.0

Period	16%	18%	20%	24%	28%	32%	36%	40%	50%	60%	70%	80%	90
1	0.862	0.847	0.833	0.806	0.781	0.758	0.735	0.714	0.667	0.625	0.588	0.556	0.5
2	0.743	0.718	0.694	0.650	0.610	0.574	0.541	0.510	0.444	0.391	0.346	0.309	0.2
3	0.641	0.609	0.579	0.524	0.477	0.435	0.398	0.364	0.296	0.244	0.204	0.171	0.
4	0.552	0.516	0.482	0.423	0.373	0.329	0.292	0.260	0.198	0.153	0.120	0.095	0.0
5	0.476	0.437	0.402	0.341	0.291	0.250	0.215	0.186	0.132	0.095	0.070	0.053	0.0
6	0.410	0.370	0.335	0.275	0.227	0.189	0.158	0.133	0.088	0.060	0.041	0.029	0.0
7	0.354	0.314	0.279	0.222	0.178	0.143	0.116	0.095	0.059	0.037	0.024	0.016	0.0
8	0.305	0.266	0.233	0.179	0.139	0.108	0.085	0.068	0.039	0.023	0.014	0.009	0.0
9	0.263	0.226	0.194	0.144	0.108	0.082	0.063	0.048	0.026	0.015	0.008	0.005	0.0
10	0.227	0.191	0.162	0.116	0.085	0.062	0.046	0.035	0.017	0.009	0.005	0.003	0.0
11	0.195	0.162	0.135	0.094	0.066	0.047	0.034	0.025	0.012	0.006	0.003	0.002	0.0
12	0.168	0.137	0.112	0.076	0.052	0.036	0.025	0.018	0.008	0.004	0.002	0.001	0.0
13	0.145	0.116	0.093	0.061	0.040	0.027	0.018	0.013	0.005	0.002	0.001	0.001	0.0
14	0.125	0.099	0.078	0.049	0.032	0.021	0.014	0.009	0.003	0.001	0.001	0.000	0.0
15	0.108	0.084	0.065	0.040	0.025	0.016	0.010	0.006	0.002	0.001	0.000	0.000	0.0
16	0.093	0.071	0.054	0.032	0.019	0.012	0.007	0.005	0.002	0.001	0.000	0.000	
17	0.080	0.060	0.045	0.026	0.015	0.009	0.005	0.003	0.001	0.000	0.000		
18	0.069	0.051	0.038	0.021	0.012	0.007	0.004	0.002	0.001	0.000	0.000		
19	0.060	0.043	0.031	0.017	0.009	0.005	0.003	0.002	0.000	0.000			
20	0.051	0.037	0.026	0.014	0.007	0.004	0.002	0.001	0.000	0.000			
25	0.024	0.016	0.010	0.005	0.002	0.001	0.000	0.000					
30	0.012	0.007	0.004	0.002	0.001	0.000	0.000						

Table 3

Amount of Annuity of 1 per period

Period	1%	2%	3%	4%	5%	6%	7%	8%
1	1.000	1.000	1.000	1.000	1.000	1.000	1.000	1.000
2	2.010	2.020	2.030	2.040	2.050	2.060	2.070	2.080
3	3.030	3.060	3.091	3.122	3.152	3.184	3.215	3.246
4	4.060	4.122	4.184	4.246	4.310	4.375	4.440	4.506
5	5.101	5.204	5.309	5.416	5.526	5.637	5.751	5.867
6	6.152	6.308	6.468	6.633	6.802	6.975	7.153	7.336
7	7.214	7.434	7.662	7.898	8.142	8.394	8.654	8.923
8	8.286	8.583	8.892	9.214	9.549	9.897	10.260	10.637
9	9.369	9.755	10.159	10.583	11.027	11.491	11.978	12.488
10	10.462	10.950	11.464	12.006	12.578	13.181	13.816	14.487
11	11.567	12.169	12.808	13.486	14.207	14.972	15.784	16.645
12	12.683	13.412	14.192	15.026	15.917	16.870	17.888	18.977
13	13.809	14.680	15.618	16.627	17.713	18.882	20.141	21.495
14	14.947	15.974	17.086	18.292	19.599	21.051	22.550	24.215
15	16.097	17.293	18.599	20.024	21.579	23.276	25.129	27.152
16	17.258	18.639	20.157	21.825	23.657	25.673	27.888	30.324
17	18.430	20.012	21.762	23.698	25.840	28.213	30.840	33.750
18	19.615	21.412	23.414	25.645	28.132	30.906	33.999	37.450
19	20.811	22.841	25.117	27.671	30.539	33.760	37.379	41.446
20	22.019	24.297	26.870	29.778	33.066	36.786	40.995	45.762
25	28.243	32.030	36.459	41.646	47.727	54.865	63.249	73.106
30	34.785	40.568	47.575	56.085	66.439	79.058	94.461	113.283

Period	9%	10%	12%	14%	16%	18%	20%	24%
1	1.000	1.000	1.000	1.000	1.000	1.000	1.000	1.000
2	2.090	2.100	2.120	2.140	2.160	2.180	2.200	2.240
3	3.278	3.310	3.374	3.440	3.506	3.572	3.640	3.778
4	4.573	4.641	4.779	4.921	5.066	5.215	5.368	5.684
5	5.985	6.105	6.353	6.610	6.877	7.154	7.442	8.048
6	7.523	7.716	8.115	8.536	8.977	9.442	9.930	10.980
7	9.200	9.487	10.089	10.730	11.414	12.142	12.916	14.615
8	11.028	11.436	12.300	13.233	14.240	15.327	16.499	19.123
9	13.021	13.579	14.776	16.085	17.518	19.086	20.799	24.712
10	15.193	15.937	17.549	19.337	21.321	23.521	25.959	31.643
11	17.560	18.531	20.655	23.044	25.738	28.755	32.150	40.238
12	20.141	21.384	24.133	27.271	30.350	34.931	39.580	50.895
13	22.953	24.523	28.029	32.089	36.766	42.219	48.497	64.110
14	26.019	27.975	32.393	37.581	43.672	50.818	59.196	80.496
15	29.361	31.722	37.280	43.842	51.659	60.965	72.035	100.815

Period	28%	32%	36%	40%	50%	60%	70%	80%
1	1.000	1.000	1.000	1.000	1.000	1.000	1.000	1.000
2	2.280	2.320	2.360	2.400	2.500	2.600	2.700	2.800
3	3.918	4.062	4.210	4.360	4.750	5.160	5.590	6.040
4	6.016	6.326	6.725	7.104	8.125	9.256	10.503	11.872
5	8.700	9.398	10.146	10.846	13.188	15.810	18.855	22.370
6	12.136	13.406	14.799	16.324	20.781	26.295	33.054	41.265
7	16.534	18.696	21.126	23.853	32.172	43.073	57.191	75.278
8	22.163	25.678	29.732	34.395	49.258	69.916	98.225	136.500
9	29.369	34.895	41.435	49.153	74.887	112.866	167.983	246.699
10	38.592	47.062	57.352	69.814	113.330	181.585	286.570	445.058
11	50.399	63.122	78.998	98.739	170.995	291.536	488.170	802.105
12	65.510	84.320	108.437	139.235	257.493	467.458	830.888	1444.788
13	84.853	112.303	148.475	195.929	387.239	748.933	1413.510	2601.619
14	109.612	149.240	202.926	275.300	581.859	1199.293	2403.968	4683.914
15	141.303	197.997	276.979	386.420	873.788	1919.869	4087.745	8432.045

Table 4

Present Value of Annuity of 1 per period

Period	1%	2%	3%	4%	5%	6%	7%	8%	9%	10%
1	0.990	0.980	0.971	0.962	0.952	0.943	0.935	0.926	0.917	0.909
2	1.970	1.942	1.913	1.886	1.859	1.833	1.808	1.783	1.759	1.736
3	2.941	2.884	2.829	2.775	2.723	2.673	2.624	2.577	2.531	2.487
4	3.902	3.808	3.717	3.630	3.546	3.465	3.387	3.312	3.240	3.170
5	4.853	4.713	4.580	4.452	4.329	4.212	4.100	3.993	3.890	3.791
6	5.795	5.601	5.417	5.424	5.076	4.917	4.766	4.623	4.486	4.355
7	6.728	6.472	6.230	6.002	5.786	5.582	5.389	5.206	5.033	4.868
8	7.652	7.325	7.020	6.733	6.463	6.210	6.971	5.747	5.535	5.335
9	8.566	8.162	7.786	7.435	7.108	6.802	6.515	6.247	5.985	5.759
10	9.471	8.983	8.530	8.111	7.722	7.360	7.024	6.710	6.418	6.145
11	10.368	9.787	9.253	8.760	8.306	7.887	7.499	7.139	6.805	6.495
12	11.255	10.575	9.954	9.385	8.863	8.384	7.943	7.536	7.161	6.814
13	12.134	11.348	10.635	9.986	9.394	8.853	8.358	7.904	7.487	7.103
14	13.004	12.106	11.296	10.563	8.899	9.295	8.745	8.244	7.786	7.367
15	13.865	12.849	11.938	11.118	10.380	9.712	9.108	8.559	8.060	7.606
16	14.718	13.578	12.561	11.652	10.838	10.106	9.447	8.851	8.312	7.824
17	15.562	14.292	13.166	12.166	11.274	10.477	9.763	9.122	8.544	8.022
18	16.398	14.992	13.754	12.659	11.690	10.828	10.059	9.372	8.756	8.201
19	17.226	15.678	14.324	13.134	12.085	11.158	10.336	9.604	8.950	8.365
20	18.046	16.351	14.877	13.590	12.462	11.470	10.594	9.818	9.128	8.514
25	22.023	19.523	17.413	15.622	14.094	12.783	11.654	10.675	9.823	9.077
30	25.808	22.397	19.600	17.292	15.373	13.765	12.409	11.258	10.274	9.427

Period	12%	14%	16%	18%	20%	24%	28%	32%	36%
1	0.893	0.877	0.862	0.847	0.833	0.806	0.781	0.758	0.735
2	1.690	1.647	1.605	1.566	1.528	1.457	1.392	1.332	1.276
3	2.402	2.322	2.246	2.174	2.106	1.981	1.868	1.766	1.674
4	3.037	2.914	2.798	2.690	2.589	2.404	2.241	2.096	1.966
5	3.605	3.433	3.274	3.127	2.991	2.745	2.532	2.345	2.181
6	4.111	3.889	3.685	3.498	3.326	3.020	2.759	2.534	2.339
7	4.564	4.288	4.089	3.812	3.605	3.242	2.937	2.678	2.455
8	4.968	4.639	4.344	4.078	3.837	3.421	3.076	2.786	2.540
9	5.328	4.946	4.607	4.303	4.031	3.566	3.184	2.868	2.603
10	5.650	5.216	4.833	4.494	4.193	3.682	3.269	2.930	2.650
11	5.988	5.453	5.029	4.656	4.327	3.776	3.335	2.978	2.683
12	6.194	5.660	5.197	4.793	4.439	3.851	3.387	3.013	2.708
13	6.424	5.842	5.342	4.910	4.533	3.912	3.427	3.040	2.727
14	6.628	6.002	5.468	5.008	4.611	3.962	3.459	3.061	2.740
15	6.811	6.142	5.575	5.092	4.675	4.001	3.483	3.076	2.750
16	6.974	6.265	5.669	5.162	4.730	4.033	3.503	3.088	2.758
17	7.120	5.373	5.749	4.222	4.775	4.059	3.518	3.097	2.763
18	7.250	6.467	5.818	5.273	4.812	4.080	3.529	3.104	2.767
19	7.366	6.550	5.877	5.316	4.844	4.097	3.539	3.109	2.770
20	7.469	6.623	5.929	5.353	4.870	4.110	3.546	3.113	2.772
25	7.843	6.873	6.907	5.467	4.948	4.147	3.564	3.122	2.776
30	8.055	7.003	6.177	5.517	4.979	4.160	3.569	3.124	2.778

Answers to Assignment Exercises

1.1 (a) 10,700   (d) 3,150
     (b) 23,100   (e) 25,500
     (c) 4,300   (f) 51,400.

1.3 (a) Asset   (d) Asset
     (b) Liability (e) Liability
     (c) Asset   (f) Asset

1.5 Assets: Motor 2,000; Premises 5,000; Stock 1,000; Bank 700; Cash 100 = total 8,800: Liabilities: Loan from Bevan 3,000; Creditors 400 = total 3,400. Capital 8,800 − 3,400 = 5,400.

1.7 Assets: Fixtures 5,500, Motors 5,700, Stock 8,800, Debtors 4,950, Bank 1,250 = Total 26,200. Capital 23,750, Creditors 2,450.

1.9 (a) − Cash, − Creditors   (e) + Cash, + Loan
     (b) − Bank, + Fixtures   (f) + Bank, − Debtors
     (c) + Stock, + Creditors   (g) − Stock, − Creditors
     (d) + Cash, + Capital   (h) + Premises, − Bank.

2.1 (a) Dr Motor Van, Cr Cash. (b) Dr Office Machinery, Cr J. Grant & Son. (c) Dr Cash, Cr Capital. (d) Dr Bank, Cr J. Beach. (e) Dr A. Barrett, Cr Cash.

2.3 Bank Dr 2,500, Cr 150 & 600 & 750 & 280, Capital Cr 2,500, Office furniture Dr 150, Cr 60, Machinery Dr 750 & 280, Planers Dr 750, Cr 750, Motor van Dr 600, J. Walker Dr 60, Cr 60, Cash Dr 60.

2.4 Cash Dr 2,000 & 75 & 100, Cr 1,800, Bank Dr 1,800 & 500, Cr 950 & 58 & 100, Capital Cr 2,000, Office furniture Dr 120, Cr 62, Betta Built Dr 62 & 58, Cr 120, Motor van Dr 950, Evans & Sons Cr 560, Works machinery Dr 560, Cr 75, J. Smith (Loan) Cr 500.

3.1 (a) Dr Purchases, Cr Cash   (d) Dr Cash, Cr Motor van
     (b) Dr Purchases, Cr E. Flynn (e) Dr Cash, Cr Sales.
     (c) Dr C. Grant, Cr Sales

3.3 Totals − Cash Dr 1,028 Cr 955, Bank Dr 1,000 Cr 710, Purchases Dr 133, S. Holmes Dr 78 Cr 78, Capital Cr 1,000, Motor van Dr 500, Sales Cr 126, D. Moore Dr 98, Returns outwards Cr 18, Fixtures Dr 150, Kingston Equipt Co Dr 150 Cr 150, Watson (Loan) Cr 100.

3.4 Capital Cr 10,000 & 500: Bank Dr 10,000 & 250; Cr 1,070 & 2,600: Cash Dr 400 & 200 & 70 & 500; Cr 250 & 220 & 100: Purchases Dr 840 & 3,600 & 370 & 220: Sales Cr 200 & 180 & 220 & 190 & 320 & 70: Returns Inwards Dr 40 & 30: Returns Outwards Cr 140 & 110: Motor Van Dr 2,600: Office Furniture Dr 600 & 100: Cr 160: Loan from T. Cooper Cr 400: F. Jones Dr 140 & 1,070; Cr 840 & 370: S. Charles Dr 110; Cr 3,600: C. Moody Dr 180; Cr 40: J. Newman Dr 220: H. Morgan Dr 190; Cr 30: J. Peat Dr 320: Manchester Motors Dr 2,600; Cr 2,600: Faster Supplies Dr 160; Cr 600.

4.1 (a) Dr Rates, Cr Bank   (d) Dr Bank, Cr Insurance
     (b) Dr Wages, Cr Cash   (e) Dr General expenses,
     (c) Dr Bank, Cr Rent received   Cr Cash.

4.3 Totals — Bank Dr 2,005, Cr 450, Capital Cr 2,000, Purchases Dr 289, M. Mills Dr 23 Cr 175, Fixtures Dr 150, Cash Dr 175 Cr 203, S. Waites Cr 114, Rent Dr 15, Stationery Dr 27, Returns outwards Cr 23, Rent received Cr 5, U. Henry Dr 77, Sales Cr 352, Motor van Dr 300, Wages Dr 117, Drawings Dr 44.

4.4 Totals — Cash Dr 1,549 Cr 1,186, Capital Cr 1,500, Purchases Dr 421, Rent Dr 28, Bank Dr 1,000 Cr 689, Sales Cr 132, Linton Dr 54 Cr 14, Stationery Dr 15, Returns outwards Cr 17, A. Hanson Dr 296 Cr 296, S. Morgan Dr 29, Repairs Dr 18, Returns inwards Dr 14, Motor van Dr 395, Motor expenses Dr 15, Fixtures Dr 120, A. Webster Cr 120.

5.1 Balances: H. Harvey Dr 416, L. Masters Dr 621, N. Morgan —, J. Lindo —.

5.2 Balances: D. Williams Dr 58, J. Moore Dr 653, G. Grant Dr 89, F. Franklin — , A. White —, H. Samuels Cr 219, P. Owen Cr 65, O. Oliver —.

6.1 *Trial Balance* — Drs: Cash 215, Purchases 459, Rent 30, Bank 96, Hughes 129, Spencer 26, Carriage 23; Crs: Capital 250, Sales 348, Mendes 130, Booth 186, Lowe 64. Totals: 978.

6.2 *Trial balance* — Drs: Purchases 360, Bank 361, Cash 73, Wages 28, Lindo 74, Shop fixtures 50, Motor van 400, Elliot 35; Crs: King Loan 60, Braham 134, Henriques 52, Capital 800, Sales 291, Returns outwards 44. Totals: 1,381.

7.1 *Trading:* Dr Purchases 14,629 *less* Closing Stock 2,548 Cr Sales 18,462, Dr Gross Profit 6,381. *Profit and Loss:* Dr Salaries 2,150, Motor expenses 520, Rent and rates 670, Insurance 111, General 105, Net profit 2,825.

Trading: Dr Purchases 23,803, *less* Stock 4,166, Gross profits 9,157, Cr 28,794. *Profit and Loss:* Dr Salaries 3,164, Rent 854, Lighting 422, 105, Motor expenses 1,133, Trade expenses 506, Net profit

8.1 *Assets:* Premises 1,500, Motors 1,200, Stock 2,548, Debtors 1,950, Bank 1,654, Cash 40. Totals: 8,892. Capital 5,424, *add* Net profit 2,825, *less* Drawings 895, 7,354. *Liabilities:* Creditors 1,538.

8.2 *Assets:* Buildings 50,000, Fixtures 1,000, Motors 5,500, Stock 4,166, Debtors 3,166, Bank 3,847. Totals: 67,679. Capital: 65,900, *add* Net profit 2,973, Drawings 2,400, Creditors 1,206.

9.1 Dr Purchases 33,333 — Returns Out 495 + Carriage In 670 — Closing Stock 7,489 = Cost of Goods Sold 26,019, Gross Profit 11,833, Cr Sales 38,742 — Returns In 890.

9.3 Dr Opening Stock 2,368 + Purchases 11,874 — Returns Out 322 + Carriage In 310 — Closing Stock 2,946 = Cost of Goods Sold 11,284. Gross Profit 7,111: Cr Sales 18,600 — Returns In 205. P/L Dr Salares 3,862, Rent and Rates 304, Carriage Out 200, Insurance 78, Motor Expenses 664. Office Expenses 216, Lighting 166, General Expenses 314, Net Profit 1,307. Cr Gross Profit 7,111.
Balance Sheet: F.A. Premises 5,000, Fixtures 350, Motors 1,800, C.A. Stock 2,946, Debtors 3,896, Bank 482. Totals 14,474. Capital 12,636 + Net Profit 1,307 — Drawings 1,200 = 12,743 C.L. Creditors 1,731.

9.4 Dr Opening Stock 3,776 + Purchases 11,556 — Returns Out 335 + Carriage In 234 — Closing Stock 4,998, Gross Profit 7,947. Cr Sales 18,600 — Returns In 440. P/L Dr Salaries 2,447. Motor Expenses 664, Rent 576, Carriage Out 326, Sundries 1,202, Net Profit 2,732, Cr Gross Profit 7,947.
Balance Sheet F.A. Fixtures 600, Motors 2,400, C.A. Stock 4,998, Debtors 4,577, Bank 3,876, Cash 120, Totals 16,571. Capital 12,844 + Net Profit 2,732 — Drawings 2,050 = 13,526. C.L Creditors 3,045.

13.1 Totals: Cash 363, Bank 731, Balances — Cash 184, Bank 454.

13.2 Totals: Cash 380, Bank 2,700, Balances — Cash 98, Bank 2,229.

14.1 Totals: Dr Discounts 32, Cash 407, Bank 6,871, Cr Discounts 10, Cash 407, Bank 6,871, Balances c/d Cash 93, Bank 4,195.
Discounts Allowed Dr 32: Discounts Received Cr 10.

14.2 Totals: Dr Discounts 89, Cash 580, Bank 7,552, Cr Discounts 48, Cash 580, Bank 7,552. Balances c/d Cash 123, Bank 4,833.
Discounts Received Cr 48, Discounts Allowed Dr 89.

15.1 Sales Journal Total 881.

15.2 Sales Journal Total 540,(1)60 + (4) 120 + (8) 20 + (20) 180 + (31) 160.

16.1 Purchases Journal Total 2,770(1)450 + (3) 800 + (15) 600 + (20) 280 + (30) 640.

16.3 Purchases Journal Total 375, Sales Journal Total 393.

17.1 Purchases Journal Total 1,096, Returns Outwards Journal 46.

17.3 Totals: Sales Journal 1,062, Returns Inwards 54, Purchases Journal 644, Returns Outwards 48.

18.1 (i)   Invoice after Trade Discount 700 + VAT 70 = 770
(ii) Books of D. Wilson Ltd Sales G. Christie & Son Dr 770
Books of G. Christie & Son D. Wilson Ltd, Cr 770.

18.2 Sales Book totals Net 520: VAT 52.
General Ledger: Sales Cr 520; VAT Cr 52.
Sales Ledger: M. Sinclair & Co Dr 165; M. Brown & Associates Dr 286; A. Axton Ltd Dr 88; T. Christie Dr 33.

18.3 Sales Book totals Net 590; VAT 59.
Purchases Book totals Net 700; VAT 70.
Sales Ledger: Dr B. Davies & Co 165; C. Grant Ltd 242 and 154; B. Karloff 88.
Purchases Ledger: Cr G. Cooper & Son 440; J. Wayne Ltd 209; B. Lugosi 55; S. Hayward 66.
General Ledger: Sales Cr 590: Purchases Dr 700: VAT Dr 700; Cr 59; Balance c/d 11.

19.1 STRAIGHT LINE 12,500 − 1,845 = 10,655 − 1,845 = 8,810 − 1,845 = 6,965 − 1,845 = 5,120.
REDUCING BALANCE 12,500 − 2,500 = 10,000 − 2,000 = 8,000 − 1,600 = 6,400 − 1,280 = 5,120.

19.2 STRAIGHT LINE 6,400 − 1,240 = 5,160 − 1,240 = 3,920 − 1,240 = 2,680 − 1,240 = 1,440 − 1,240 = 200.
REDUCING BALANCE 6,400 − 3,200 = 3,200 − 1,600 = 1,600 − 800 = 800 − 400 = 400 − 200 = 200.

19.5 Machines (A) 19-4 Cost 3,000 − Depreciation 19-4 300, 19-5 270, 19-6 243, (B) 19-5 Cost 2,000 − Depreciation 19-5 150, 19-6 185, (C) 19-6 Cost 1,000 − Depreciation 50. Total depreciation 19-6 243 + 185 + 50 = 478.

20.1 Motors vans Dr 3,800, Provision for depreciation Cr 620.

20.2 Machinery Dr 800, 1,000, 600, 200, Provision for depreciation − 3, 80, − 4, 145, − 5, 240, − 6, 255. *Balance Sheet:* − 3,800 *less* 80, − 4, 2,400 *less* 225, − 5, 2,400 *less* 465, − 6, 2,600 *less* 720.

3 Plant Dr − 4, 900, 600, − 6, 550, Cr − 7, 900, Depreciation Dr − 7, 675, − 4, 210, − 5, 300, − 6, 355, − 7, 365. Disposals Dr Plant 900, Profit and Loss 50, Cr Depreciation 675, Cash 275. *Balance Sheet:* *less* 210, − 5, 1,500 *less* 510, − 6, 2,050 *less* 865, − 7, 1,150

21.1 (i) Bad Debts Dr H. Gordon 110; D. Bellamy Ltd 64; J. Alderton 12; Provision c/d 220; Cr Profit and Loss 406.

(ii) 406.

(iii) Debtors 6,850 *less* Provision for Bad Debts 220.

21.2 (i) Bad Debts 19-6 Dr W. Best 85; S. Avon 140; Provision c/d 550: Cr Profit and Loss 775.
Bad Debts 19-7 Dr L. J. Friend 180; N. Kelly 60; A. Oliver 250; Provision c/d 600. Cr Provision b/d 550, Profit and Loss 540.

(ii) 19-6 Bad Debts 775: 19-7 Bad Debts 540.

(iii) 19-6 Debtors 40,500 *less* Provision for Bad Debts 550: 19-7 Debtors 47,300 *less* Provision for Bad Debts 600.

22.1 Total Expenses to debit of P/L: Motor Expenses 772, Insurance 385, Stationery 2,040, Rates 880, To credit of P/L Rent Received 580.

22.3 Sales 13,475 − Returns In 242 = 13,233 − C.G.S. Purchases 11,377 − Returns Out 268 + Carriage In 47 − Closing Stock 898 = 10,258, Gross Profit 2,975 + Discounts Received 210 + Rent 104 − Expenses: Wages 652, Wages 167, Office Expenses 104, Bad Debts 184, Insurance 20, Electricity 30, Loan Interest 42, Discounts Allowed 337, Rent 393, Depreciation of Motor 99 = Net Profit 1,261.

22.5 Sales 19,740 − C.G.S. Opening Stock 2,970 + Purchases 11,280 − Closing Stock 3,510 = 10,740, Gross Profit 9,000 + Discounts Received 360, − Expenses: Wages 2,670, Rent 880, Discounts Allowed 690, Van Running Costs 510, Bad Debts 870, Depreciation Office Furniture 180, Delivery Van 480 = Net Profit 3,080.
Balance Sheet: F.A. Office Furniture 1,440 − 180, Delivery Van 2,400 − 480, C.A. Stock 3,510, Debtors 4,920 − 330, Prepaid 140, Bank 1,140, Cash 210 − C.L. Creditors 2,490, Expenses Owing 150 = Working Capital 6,950, Totals 10,130. Financed by: Capital 9,900 + 3,080 − Drawings 2,850.

23.1 Capital (a) (c) (d) (f) (j) (l): Revenue: (b) (e) (g) (h) (i) (k).

23.3 Capital (i) (ii) (v).

24.1 (i)		Motor Vehicles	Dr.	6,790	: Kingston	Cr.	6,790
(ii)		Bad Debts	Dr.	34	: H. Newman	Cr.	34
(iii)		Unique Offices	Dr.	490	: Office Furniture	Cr.	490
(iv)	(a)	Bank	Dr.	39	: W. Charles	Cr.	39
	(b)	Bad Debts	Dr.	111	: W., Charles	Cr.	111
(v)		Drawings	Dr.	45	: Purchases	Cr.	45
(vi)		Drawings	Dr.	76	: Insurance	Cr.	76
(vii)		Machinery	Dr.	980	: Systems Accelerated	Cr.	980

25.1 Receipts 100 + 78 = 178. Payments, Total 78, Motor Expenses 26, Post 17, Cleaning 11, Sundries 4, Ledger 20, Balance c/d 100.

26.1 (i) Bar trading: Dr Opening stock 730 + Purchases 3,180 − Closing stock 820 = Cost of goods sold 3,090, Gross profit 2,000. Cr Sales 5,090.

(ii) Income and Expenditure Account: Dr Salary 1,200, Wages 1,760, Postages 290, Rates 390, Sundry 280, Depreciation 200 and 40, Surplus 750. Totals 4,910. Cr Subscriptions 2,910, Gross profit on bar 2,000.

(iii) Balance sheet. Accumulated fund: Balance 7,430 + Surplus 750. Fixed assets, Premises 4,500, Equipment 1,700 − 200, Furniture 400 − 40, Current assets, Stocks 820, Subscriptions owing 30, Prepayment 20, Bank 930, Cash 20. Totals 8,180.

27.1 Net Profit 25,200 − Salaries (0) 3,000 (J) 1,000, Interest on Capitals (S) 600 (0) 400 (J) 200 = 20,000 shared (S) 8,000 (0) 8,000 (J) 4,000.

27.2 Net Profit 30,350 + Interest on Drawings (W) 240 (P) 180 (H) 130 − Interest on Capitals (W) 2,000 (P) 1,500 (H) 900; Salaries (P) 2,000 (H) 3,500 = 21,000 shared (W) 10,500 (P) 6,300 (H) 4,200.

28.1 Balance Sheet; Fixed Assets 90,000 less 20,250; Current 62,750 less Current Liabilities 7,500 to give working capital 55,250 = total 125,000; Capital: Authorised (note only), Issued, Preference 20,000, Ordinary 75,000, Revenue Reserves 30,000.

28.2 Appropriation: Cr Net Profit 10,200 + Balance c/f 3,000: Dr Prefernce Dividend 1,750, Ordinary Dividends 6,000, General Reserve 2,500, Balance to next year 2,950. Balance Sheet: Fixed Assets 60,000 − 12,000 + Current Assets 86,000 = Total 134,000. Shares 25,000 + 60,000 + General Reserve 27,500 + Profit & Loss 2,950 + Current Liabilities, Dividend 6,000, Creditors 12,550.

28.4 Trading: Cr Sales 97,500 Dr Opening Stock 41,415 + Purchases 51,380 − Closing Stock 54,300 = Cost of Goods Sold 38,495 = Gross Profit 59,005: Profit and Loss: Expenses: Wages 11,372, Motor Expenses 8,589, Repairs to Machinery 2,308, Sundries 1,076, Depreciation, Machinery 5,400, Motor 3,080, Directors Remuneration 6,200. Net Profit 20,980.

Appropriation: Cr Net Profit + Balance b/fwd 6,138, less Dividend 15,000, General Reserve 2,000, Balance carried forward 10,118.

Balance Sheet: Assets Machinery 45,000 less 23,400, Motors 28,000 less 15,680, Stock 54,300, Debtors 28,560, Bank 16,255. Share Capital, Authorised (note only) Issued 75,000, General Reserve 10,000, Profit and Loss 10,118, Creditors 22,472, Expenses Owing 445, Dividend 15,000.

29.1 Gross Pay 60; Income Tax 8; National Insurance 3; Net Pay 49.

29.2 Gross Pay 140; Income Tax 30; National Insurance 7; Net Pay 103.

29.3 Gross Pay 800; Income Tax 210; National Insurance 25; Net Pay 565.

31.1 Dr Opening Stock 9,872 + Purchases 50,748 − Closing Stock 12,620 = C.G.S. 48,000, Gross Profit 12,000. Sales 60,000.

31.3 (a) We know that $\dfrac{\text{Cost of Goods Sold}}{\text{Average Stock}}$ = Rate of Turnover

∴ substituting $\dfrac{x}{12,600}$ = 7

∴ x = Cost of Goods Sold = 88,200.

(b) If margin is 33⅓% then mark-up will be 50% Gross Profit is therefore 50% of 88,200 = 44,100.

(c) Turnover is (a) + (b) = 88,200 + 44,100 = 132,300.

(d) 66⅔% × 44,100 = 29,400.

(e) Gross Profit − Expenses = Net Profit = 14,700.

32.1 (a) (i) 22121250 (ii) 30711065 (iii) 13321195 (iv) 40541035.

(b) (i) Ladies black shoes, short black laces, synthetic uppers, synthetic soles, no guarantee, size 4½.

(ii) Boy's white shoes, long white laces, canvas uppers, rubber soles, no guarantee, size 6.

(iii) Men's dark brown shoes, no laces, synthetic uppers, synthetic soles, no guarantee, size 8½.

(iv) Girl's green shoes, no laces, leather uppers, rubber soles, one year guarantee, size 2.

(c) Digit three range will be given number 8 for red colour.

(d) Digit one range will be extended as men's boots 5, boy's boots 6, ladies' boots 7, girl's boots 8.

(e) Probably useful to know whether they are high-heel, medium heel or flat heel.

(f) Digits 7 and 8 cover size. Size 9½ is 95 and there is no room left in range of digits 7 and 8. Would either have to extend to a nine digit system or completely alter present system. Otherwise size ten (10) would be completely indistinguishable from size one (10), size 10½ could not be accommodated.

32.3 (i) Omission (ii) Double Transposition

(iii) Transposition (iv) Addition

(v) Transcription (vi) Random.

34.1 (a) £600 (b) £1700 (c) £2200 + 10% = £2,420.

34.2 Approximately £1,600.

34.3 1. (c) 2. (f) 3. (i)

34.4 Called stepped costs they are increased by discrete additions when capacity is expanded. For example the rental cost of a machine may be fixed until a second machine is needed, then a third etc.

35.11 (a) (i) £44,000, (ii) £60,000, (iii) £76,000, (b) (i) Loss £4,000, (ii) Profit £4,000, (iii) Profit £16,000, (iv) Profit £10,000, (c) 5,000 units.

35.12 (a) (i) £450,000, (ii) £590,000, (iii) £1,030,000, (b) (i) Loss £30,000, (ii) Profit £24,000, (iii) Profit £78,000, (iv) Profit £138,000, (c) 25,000 units.

36.8 $\dfrac{16,000}{9-6.5} = \dfrac{16,000}{2.5} = 6,400$ units

36.9 $\dfrac{13,000}{9-7} = \dfrac{13,000}{2} = 6,500$ units

36.10 £8,000.

36.11 (b) 350 units, (c) (i) 280, (ii) 700, (iii) 500, (iv) 300, (v) 700, (vi) 280.

37.1 (a) 300 tons = 15,000 + 10,000 = £25,000 400 tons = 20,000 + 10,000 = £30,000.

(b) $\dfrac{25,000}{300} = £83.33$ $\qquad$ $\dfrac{30,000}{400} = £75.00$

(c) £50 per ton for both.

(d) The cost of an extra ton which is the marginal cost is the same as the variable cost, provided the operation is within capacity. The Average cost includes a proportion of fixed overheads.

37.2 (a)

	1000 doors	1500 doors
	£	£
Sales	12,000	15,500
Variable cost	5,000	7,500
Contribution	7,000	8,000
Fixed Cost	3,000	3,000
Net Profit	4,000	5,000

(b) The order will increase profit as shown in (a) but could prevent accepting more profitable orders and cause existing customers to ask for lower prices.

38.1

	Jan.	Feb.	Mar.	Apl.	May	Jun.
Opening Stock	740	690	780	1,100	1,400	1,160
Add production	750	1,010	1,410	1,620	1,240	800
	1,490	1,700	2,190	2,720	2,640	1,960
Less sales	800	920	1,090	1,320	1,480	1,020
Closing stock	690	780	1,100	1,400	1,160	940

38.2 (a) Opening Stock 140, Add Production (figure to be deduced) less Sales of 1,550 = Closing Stock 150. By deduction, given the figures already known the only figure which could be inserted for production so that the equation worked out is 1,560. An even production flow of 1,560 ÷ 12 = 130 units. This has been tested to ensure that stock never becomes a negative figure.

(b) Starting with above figures the closing stock at the end of each month would be Jan 160, F 110, M 70, Apr 50, May 60, Jn 90, Jy 150, Aug 250, S 210, Oct 230, N 210, D 150. Lowest closing figure for stock is April 50, if stock is not to fall below 80 units an extra 30 units (80 − 50) will have to be produced in January making production for that month of 160 units.

38.3 Opening stock? (to be deduced) add Production 1,500, less Sales 1,230 = Closing stock 430. By arithmetical deduction the only figure that could be inserted to make the equation agree is 160 units.

38.7 Jan Capital 1,000 + Debtors 2,900 = 4,900 less Payments 5,800 = Overdraft c/f 900, Feb b/f − 900 Add Debtors 5,900, less Payments 7,500 = Overdraft c/f 2,500, March B/f − 2,500, Add Debtors 6,000, Loan 700, Less Payments 10,000, Overdraft c/f 5,800, April B/f − 5,800, Add Debtors 7,100, less Payments 10,800, Overdraft c/f 9,500, May B/f − 9,500, Add Debtors 8,400, Less Payments 9,900, Overdraft c/f 11,000, June B/f − 11,000, Debtors 9,500, Less Payments 8,000, Overdraft c/f 9,500. As permission for overdraft only 10,000 some action will have to be taken to keep overdraft below 11,000 in May.

38.8 Payments Schedules: July, Materials (320 × £4 + 300 × £1) 1,580, D Labour 320 × £8 + 2,560, Variable (300 × £1 + 320 × £1) 620, Fixed Expenses 400, Drawings 300, total 5,460. August, Materials (350 × £4 + 320 × £1) 1,720, D Labour 350 × £8 = 2,800, Variable (320 × £1 + 350 × £1) 670, Fixed 400, Drawings 300, total 5,890. September: Materials (370 × £4 + 350 × £1) £1,830, D Labour 370 × £8 = 2,960, Variable (350 × £1 + 370 × £1) 720, Fixed 400, Drawings 300, Total 6,210. October, Materials (380 × £4 + 370 × £1) 1,890, D Labour 380 × £8 = 3,040, Variable (370 × £1 + 380 × £1) 750, Fixed 400, Machinery 2,000, Drawings 300, Total,8,380. November, Materials (340 × £4 + 380 × £1) £1,740, Labour 340 × £8 = 2,720, Variable (380 × £1 + 340 × £1) 720, Fixed 400, Drawings 300, Total 5,880. December, Materials (310 × £4 + 340 × £1) 1,580, Labour 310 × £8 = 2,480, Variable (340 × £1 + 310 × £1) 690, Fixed 400, Drawings 300, Total 5,410.
Cash Budget Jul, Bal b/f 1,200 + Debtors 4,000, less Payments 5,460, O/d c/f 260, Aug O/d b/f 260, Debtors 6,400, less Payments 5,890, Bal c/f 250, Sept Bal b/f 250, Debtors 5,800, less Payments 6,210, O/d c/f 160, Oct O/d b/f 160, Debtors 8,000, less Payments 8,380, O/d c/f 540, Nov O/d b/f 540, Debtors 6,000, less Payments 5,880, O/d c/f 420, Dec O/d b/f 420, debtors 7,000, Legacy 2,500, less Payments 5,410, Bal c/f 3,670.

38.11 Payments: Totals: Jan 24,510, Feb 1,860, Mar 1,980, Apl 2,340, May 2,760, June 3,460. Receipts: Totals: Jan 400, Feb 600, Mar 1,750, Apl 2,200, May 2,900. June 3,550: Balance end each month: Jan +890, Feb −370, Mar −600, Apl −740, May −600, June −510. Trading P/L: Sales 16,500, Purchases 11,410 − Closing Stock 910 = Gross Profit 6,000 + Rent 300 − Salaries 1,560, Other Expenses 900, Depreciation Fixtures 150 & Motor Van 100 = Net Profit 3,590.
Balance Sheet Premises 20,000, Fixtures 3,000−150, Motor Van 1,000−100, Stock 910, Debtors, 5,400, − Creditors 2,310, Other 150, Bank Overdraft 510 = Totals 27,090. Capital 25,000 + Net Profit 3,590 − Drawings 1,500.

38.12 Payments Schedule: Jan, Wages 800, Directors 1,200, Total 2,000. Feb, Purchases 48,000, Wages 800, Directors 1,200, Premises 30,000, Other 600, Total 80,600. March, Purchases 16,000, Wages 800, Directors 1,200, Equipment 6,000, Other 600, Total, 24,600. April, Purchases 18,000, Wages 800, Directors 1,200, Other 600, Total 20,600. May, Purchases 20,000, Wages 800, Directors 1,200, Other 600, Total 22,600. June, Purchases 14,000, Wages 800, Directors 1,200, Equipment 6,000, Other 600, Total 22,600. Receipts Schedule: Jan, Capital 60,000, Sales: April 12,000, May 16,000, June 28,000 + and − Balances end of each month: Jan + 58,000, Feb − 22,600, March − 47,200, April − 55,800, May − 62,400, June − 57,000.

Trading A/c: Dr Purchases 126,000, less Closing stock 21,800, Gross Profit 23,800, Totals 128,000. Cr Sales 128,000. Profit & Loss: Dr Salaries 4,800, Other 3,840, Debenture Interest 280, Depreciation 1,200, Directors 7,200, Net Profit 6,480, Totals 23,800. Cr Gross Profit b/d 23,800. Balance Sheets, Fixed Assets, Premises 30,000. Equipment 12,000 less depreciation 1,200 = 10,800, Current Assets, Stock 21,800, Debtors 72,000, Current Liabilities, Bank Overdraft 57,000, Creditors 10,000, Other Expenses 840, Debenture Interest owing 280. Ordinary Shares Capital 52,000, Profit & Loss 6,480, Debenture 8,000.

40.1 (*a*)
$$5,300 \times .17 \times \frac{62}{365} = £153.05$$

(*b*)
$$9,000 \times .19 \times \frac{70}{365} = £327.95$$

The Bank will pay £9,000 − 327.95 = £8,672.05.

40.3 The amount borrowed is: −

£1,000 × ¼ =	250.0
750 × ¼ =	187.5
500 × ¼ =	125.0
250 × ¼ =	62.5
Equivalent loan for 1 year	625.0

$$r = \frac{200}{625 \times 1} = .32 \text{ or } 32\%.$$

40.4 £4,000 will accumulate to $4,000 (1 + .1)^{10}$ = £10,375.
Interest is ∴ £10,375 − 4,000 = £6,375.
(Using the tables 4,000 × 2.594 = £10,376 − note slight rounding errors).

41.1 The present value of an annuity of £5,000 p.a. for seven years at 12% = 5,000 × 4.564 = £22,820

or $$\frac{1 - \dfrac{1}{(1 + .12)^7}}{.12} \times 5,000 = £22,820$$

The offer of £20,000 would therefore appear less attractive than retaining the rental income.

41.3 $R = \dfrac{Ar}{(1+r)^n - 1} = \dfrac{100,000(0.10)}{(1+0.10)^5 - 1}$

$\quad = £16,380$ per annum.

41.4 $R = \dfrac{100,000(0.15)}{(1+0.15)^5 - 1} = £14,832$ per annum.

42.1

	Year 19-1		Year 19-2
Purchase of machine	50,000		–
Sale of old machine	–		(8,000)
Installation Cost	10,000		–
Commissioning Cost	15,000		8,000
Rent of premises to date of completion	5,000	(9 months)	3,750
Training Labour			2,000
Working Capital	10,000		
Net Cash Outlay	90,000		5,750

42.2 The net cash outlays in 19-1 and 19-2 will reduce the companys tax bill by 50%, and the cash benefit actually obtained in the next year (i.e. after 9 months). Thus the year 19-1 saving of £45,000 will be received in year 19-2 and the £2,875 from year 19-2 will be required in 19-3 as follows: –

	19-1	19-2	19-3
Net Cash Outlay	90,000	5,750	
Cash Inflow: –			
Tax saving on outlay		(45,000)	(2,875)
Net Cash flows	90,000	(39,250)	(2,875)

figures in brackets = net inflows.

42.3

Net Cash Flows	Present Value Factor for 15%	N.P.V. £
Year 19-1 90,000	.870	78,300
19-2 (39,250)	.756	(29,673)
19-3 (2,875)	.658	(1,892)
Net Present Value at start of project		£46,735

43.1 Exactly 3 years when the cumulative cash flow will be – nil – .

43.1 Exactly 3 years when the cumulative cash flow will be − nil −.

43.2

Year	Net Cash Flow	Present Value Factor for 10%	N.P.V. £
1	9,000	.909	8,181
2	(6,000)	.826	(4,956)
3	(3,000)	.751	(2,253)
4	(2,000)	.683	(1,366)

Net Present Value of Cash (inflow)   (394)

43.3

Year	Net Cash Flow	Present Value Factor for 12%	N.P.V. 12%	Present Value Factor for 14%	N.P.V. 14%
1	9,000	.893	8,037	.877	7,893
2	(6,000)	.797	(4,782)	.769	(4,614)
3	(3,000)	.712	(2,136)	.675	(2,025)
4	(2,000)	.636	(1,272)	.592	(1,184)
			(153)		70

12% Discount Rate gives N.P.V.   (153)
14% Discount Rate gives N.P.V.   70

                                              223

The IRR is $\frac{70}{223} \times 2\%$ below 14% $= 14 - .63 = 13.37\%$.

44.1

	Internal Rate of Return	N.P.V. using 12%
Project A	16%	(£2,433)
Project B	14%	(£3,270)

Using IRR the choice would be Project A but using N.P.V. with 12% interest would suggest Project B. The crucial factor is therefore the rate of interest that funds would be invested at when generated by the project, if approximating to 12% then the N.P.V. is more realistic but if closer to the I.R.R. rates then they would give better solution.

44.3

Year	Net Cash Flow £	Factor for 12%	Present Value £
0	8,000	1.000	8,000
1	(4,000)	.893	(3,572)
2	(2,000)	.797	(1,594)
3	(6,000)	.712	(4,272)
			(1,438)

(1) The N.P.V. at 12% interest is £1,438.
(2) The Present Value of an annuity of £1 for three years at 12% interest = £2.402.
∴ Present Value £1,438 = 2.402 × The annual sum
∴ The Annual sum = $\frac{1438}{2.402}$ = £598.7

44.4 The Present Value of an annuity of £1 for six years at 12% interest = £4.111

Present Value £2624 = 4.111 × The annual sum

∴ Annual sum = $\dfrac{2,624}{4.111}$ = £638.3 which is a better annual return than for machine in 44.3.

45.1 £13,190 × P.V. factor an annuity of £1 = £50,000

P.V. factor for an annuity of £1 = $\dfrac{50,000}{13,190}$ = 3.79

Referring to the tables along the 5 period row gives 10% interest for 3.79.

45.4

	£
Cost of Asset 80,000 (1 − 0.4) =	48,000
Cost of Leasing 26,338 (1 − 0.4) =	15,803

P.V. factor for four years = $\dfrac{48,000}{15,803}$ = 3.04

From P.V. of annuity tables this represents 12% interest over 4 years.

45.5 Factor for P.V. of an annuity of £1 for 10 years at 14% = 5.216

5,000 × 5.216 = £26,080 Capital Value of Lease.

Index